"This is a wide-ranging, challenging, and thought-provoking book. Anderson goes beyond the dominant Western categories of *how* the atonement works. By emphasizing the atonement as the entire mystery of reconciliation of human beings to God through the incarnation, life, death, and resurrection of Jesus Christ, Anderson calls us to be grateful and joyful participants in the Holy Spirit's ongoing work of reconciliation in our broken world."

—DORSEY MCCONNELL,
bishop emeritus, Episcopal Diocese of Pittsburgh

"There is any number of historical or constructive studies of atonement today. Fred Anderson's study is different because it is from a pastor's heart, but a book few pastors could have written. It is forged in forty-five years of learned ministry, avoiding nothing, never didactic, always hungering for the big picture. Unlike many strictly academic studies, it grew out of dialogue and is earthed in practical living. I thoroughly commend its clarity, profundity, and wisdom."

—IAIN TORRANCE,
president emeritus, Princeton Theological Seminary

"Fred Anderson is a pastor with a gift for making theological scholarship accessible to any thoughtful person who wants to understand the cross and its world changing significance. This book blessedly redeems 'the atonement' from being a divisive and exhausted debate to a compelling invitation to receive new life in Christ. It provides careful exegesis of Scripture and the theological tradition, which leads to insight on how this new life is nurtured sacramentally through Christ's ongoing ministry as our high priest."

—M. CRAIG BARNES,
president, Princeton Theological Seminary

"Fred Anderson offers readers a refreshing, wide-ranging, and highly accessible overview of atonement language from its use in Scripture to its theological development throughout the history of the church. With clarity and persuasion, he unpacks the attempts to explain this complex doctrine while demonstrating that the biblical language of sacrifice is firmly rooted in thanksgiving for divine grace rather than as an attempt to appease an angry god."

—PAUL GALBREATH,
Union Presbyterian Seminary

"In this inspiring book, Fred Anderson claims that believing in Jesus Christ is about far more than going to heaven when we die. It is also about participating in God's New Creation today. Drawing on forty-five years of pastoral ministry, Anderson punctuates his theological and historical insights with real-life questions from his congregants. After reading this, you will never look at the cross in the same way again!"

—THOMAS K. TEWELL,
founder, Macedonian Ministry Foundation

"Read this book. You may not agree with everything Anderson says about the Bible, as I did not, but you will find a magisterial and hugely instructive survey of virtually all the Christian ideas about atonement throughout the centuries. And you will end in exactly the right place: a passionate and ecumenical invitation to participation in word and sacrament as participation in Christ, in whom all the world, including all human sorrow, has been made to participate in God."

—GORDON W. LATHROP,
United Lutheran Seminary, emeritus

Why Did Jesus Die *and* What Does That Have to Do with Me?

Why Did Jesus Die *and* What Does That Have to Do with Me?

A Biblical and Sacramental Understanding of Atonement

Fred R. Anderson

WIPF & STOCK · Eugene, Oregon

WHY DID JESUS DIE AND WHAT DOES THAT HAVE TO DO WITH ME?
A Biblical and Sacramental Understanding of Atonement

Copyright © 2022 Fred R. Anderson. All rights reserved. Except for brief quotations in critical publications or reviews, no part of this book may be reproduced in any manner without prior written permission from the publisher. Write: Permissions, Wipf and Stock Publishers, 199 W. 8th Ave., Suite 3, Eugene, OR 97401.

Wipf & Stock
An Imprint of Wipf and Stock Publishers
199 W. 8th Ave., Suite 3
Eugene, OR 97401

www.wipfandstock.com

PAPERBACK ISBN: 978-1-6667-5099-7
HARDCOVER ISBN: 978-1-6667-5100-0
EBOOK ISBN: 978-1-6667-5101-7

SEPTEMBER 25, 2023 4:45 PM

All biblical citations are from the NRSV unless otherwise noted. New Revised Standard Version Bible is copyright © 1989 by the Division of Christian Education of the National Council of Churches of Christ in the United States of America. Used by permission. All rights reserved.

For Questa

Contents

Preface | ix

Abbreviations | xvii

Chapter 1
    The Question | 1

Chapter 2
    Where to Begin? | 21

Chapter 3
    Baptism and the Supper through the Eyes of the Church Then and Today | 41

Chapter 4
    Why We Need Atonement—The Problem | 67

Chapter 5
    Sacrifice in Israel's Life with God | 86

Chapter 6
    New Testament Application of Sacrifice to Jesus | 108

Chapter 7
    Atonement Theories—Post-Apostolic Church to Reformation | 133

Chapter 8
   Atonement Theories from the Enlightenment
   to the Early Twentieth Century | 153

Chapter 9
   Twentieth-Century Atonement Theologies—
   Incarnation Recovered | 174

Chapter 10
   Feminists and Liberation Theology | 192

Chapter 11
   What God Has Done in Jesus Christ | 208

Chapter 12
   God's New Creation | 230

Chapter 13
   Growing in Christ—Putting Him On | 252

Bibliography | 281

For Further Reading | 287

Subject Index | 295

Scripture Index | 319

Preface

NO ONE TODAY WRITES a book on their own, especially when one does not do so as a regular part of their professional life. Weekly sermons are one thing, with a style, art, and discipline of their own. A book that is not a collection of sermons is quite another. That is especially true when one is attempting a contemporary understanding of a major tenet of the faith. It becomes more daunting still when doing so for believers and nonbelievers alike—those who have been reared in the church all their lives and those who may be just beginning to inquire about the Christian faith. Like rearing a child: it takes a village!

I stand in absolute awe of those giants of faith and intellect—the church's first theologians—who did their work on their own. Yes, often they were in dialogue attempting to refute a heresy. But at other times they were writing out of the well of their own knowledge and conviction and gave the church a heritage it has consulted and used ever since.

I have equal admiration for those who came after, whose vocation was the monastery, giving us the first universities, whose lectures and treatises got refined by the challenge of fellow scholars' questions and debate, a dynamic still true in modern universities and seminaries. Today's academic scholars have the stimulation of their student's questions, and their work is tested and strengthened through conversations with colleagues, their writings evaluated in peer review journals and published for their respective disciplines. I especially admire those doing that before "Dr. Google"; Wikipedia's instant access to dates, times, definitions, and backgrounds; computer programs; and digital editors came into being.

I stand in great debt to all of these: not only the professors who helped shape me in seminary and the colleagues in the various professional societies to which I have been privileged to belong, but especially those leading thinkers of the last fifty years I have been in ministry, whose works I have read and learned from. In some cases, the work of those theologians has been so internalized I had forgotten their formative influence on my thought until this project. Such was certainly the case for Professors Moltmann, Jenson, Wright, and Tanner.

In other cases, I unwittingly found myself "thinking alongside" several of the last century's major thinkers, especially Donald Baillie and T. F. Torrance, particularly the latter's sacramental approach to atonement. I am grateful for his son Iain's counsel in our conversations about atonement when he was president of Princeton Seminary. And, of course, there are those whose names appear in the bibliography—many iconic giants in service to the church. Whether I agreed with them or not, they were, in their own ways, partners in this endeavor. From them I learned much, and for them I am grateful.

This venture began long before my inquiring parishioner and fellow Center of Theological Inquiry trustee asked his straightforward but complex question—"How does Jesus' death save me?" Each Good Friday for forty-three years I was thrust once again into the challenge of trying to proclaim Christ's death in a way that made sense today. The ones behind that challenge included those like me who had grown up in the church and remained active but were looking for better answers than we had been initially taught to believe. It also included those who had made it through their confirmation but then drifted away, whether in high school or college for whatever reason, but now in the complexities of adulthood wanted to give the faith a second look. In addition, at the turn of the twenty-first century, increasingly I found myself preaching to those who had never been exposed to church and the Christian gospel but because of some personal circumstance found themselves in church looking for answers about their lives and what to do with them.

My initial attempts at contemporary exploration began in adult new member classes in New York City. What does it mean to profess Jesus Christ as Lord and Savior? It is the one confessional requirement for being a member of the Presbyterian Church (U.S.A.). Those conversations with bright, well-educated, otherwise knowledgeable, successful, high-performance people across a broad spectrum of professions and disciplines led me deeper into the question. And always, it returned to Christ and his cross—what that was about and what it meant for them and for me.

The more I studied and explored the question, the more I understood it would mean challenging one of the historic confessional standards of the Presbyterian Church (U.S.A.). In my ordination I had promised to "sincerely receive and adopt the essential tenets of the Reformed faith as expressed in the confessions of our church as authentic and reliable expositions of what Scripture leads us to believe and do, and [promised to] be instructed and led by those confessions as [I] lead the people of God."[1] It is, indeed, a mouthful, and I truthfully responded, "I do, and I will!" What did it mean for me to now challenge the church's confessional answer on atonement, since I could no longer believe, much less confess it?

I knew that the confessions of our church were subordinate to Scripture and its witness, and it was those years of proclaiming those texts that had caused me to challenge the idea of penal substitutionary atonement. Thus, I began to devote my own reading and personal study, as well as part of my responsibilities for regularly teaching adult education classes in New York, to exploring the question of what God was doing in Christ on the cross. I did so for several Lenten series at Madison Avenue Presbyterian Church (MAPC), beginning to do so some twenty years ago.

I did this with a group of conversation partners, initially other pastors on staff—J. C. Austin, a very bright and gifted young associate—as well as several exceptional theological students whom I was privileged to supervise in their seminary's required fieldwork at MAPC. Before long that conversation expanded with two professional and highly respected theologians in New York City, the Rev. William G. Rusch, PhD, and the Rev. Dale T. Irvin, PhD.

Dr. Rusch, a Lutheran pastor and renowned ecumenist, had just resigned his role as director of the Faith and Order Commission of the National Council of Churches of Christ to become the executive director of the Foundation for a Conference on Faith and Order in North America. Dr. Irvin, a Baptist minister, was then professor of world Christianity at New York Theological Seminary. He would soon become its president.

Bill, Dale, and I quickly went from being associates in support of the Foundation for a Conference on Faith and Order, to colleagues and then friends. It was in a subsequent luncheon conversation with the two, exploring my own emerging thoughts on atonement theology with them, that Bill said, "Fred, you need to read Athanasius. I think you would find him helpful." To that, Dale added, "And also Irenaeus, his spiritual grandfather." Thus began a new level of exploration.

---

1. Office of the General Assembly, *Book of Order*, 104 (W–4.0404).

It was exciting to discover my questions were not simply my own or the product of modernity but were ancient—as old as the church's first theologians. And in their writings, I was finding answers far better than the ones offered by the Westminster Confession of Faith—for some three-hundred twenty years Presbyterians' sole confessional standard. Thus, an important conversational partnership began to which I owe so much. It would continue as I began to write this book. I am especially grateful for Dr. Rusch's insights and help with not only St. Athanasius but also Martin Luther's theology, in which Bill is deeply steeped and widely respected. Dr. Irvin helped me sharpen my Trinitarian theology and especially my understanding of both sides of God's incarnation in Jesus and the mystery of the hypostatic union.

I have already mentioned the Very Rev. Dr. Iain R. Torrance, then president of Princeton Theological Seminary and now "Sir Iain," enjoying retirement but continuing his scholarship and research in Scotland. The guidance to his father's work was another of those aha moments, both confirmation of my own thinking but also exposure to one of the era's most important theological minds with whom I would not have otherwise been acquainted. Iain has continued to be an encouragement and was gracious enough to read and edit the portion of chapter 8 that focuses on his father's thought on atonement.

One of the other riches of my Princeton Seminary trusteeship was forming a friendship with Professor James F. Kay, dean of the seminary faculty (now emeritus). Jim's expertise in homiletics and liturgics emerged out of his study as a systematic theologian. His former graduate school associations with Madison Avenue Presbyterian Church made for lots of stories and a strong friendship. Jim has not only been a close conversation partner, but he has also been invaluable as a source of bibliographical suggestions as well as theological guidance and critique.

It was Jim Kay who steered me to the St. Andrew's Symposium for Biblical and Early Christian Studies on atonement in the summer of 2018. And it was there I first met Professor Christian Eberhart whose work has been so important and helpful to me, especially in my initial work on sacrifice in Israel.

To that same end, I am also indebted to Fr. Robert Daly, SJ, whose seminal book, *Sacrifice Unveiled*, set a new standard for how to understand sacrifice in Israel's life and how it had come to be misunderstood in much of the church. Fr. Daly, fellow member of the Eucharistic Prayer Group at the North American Academy of Liturgy (NAAL), was the first to confirm my hunch that much of the problem in atonement theology stemmed from an inadequate understanding of sacrifice in Israel's life and how that shaped subsequent thought on atonement and then took on a life of its own in the church.

In that same vein, I am deeply grateful for the generous time and thought Professor Dennis Olson, of Princeton Theological Seminary, gave to reading the first and second drafts of my chapter "Sacrifice in Israel's Life with God." His insights and suggestions as a specialist in Hebrew Bible and observation on the status of recent Old Testament studies was especially enlightening and helpful. Dennis has been a valued colleague since the days he was part of MAPC's Sunday morning adult education series, and later when he and I served together on a presidential search committee for the seminary. I am most grateful for his scholarship, wisdom, suggestions, and continuing encouragement on the importance of this project.

The Rev. Dr. William F. Storrar, director of the Center of Theological Inquiry, has also been invaluable as a conversation partner, especially in the last five years I was immersed in writing and editing. My long association with CTI as a trustee and then chair of that board enabled me to have regular conversations with Will, probe his own theological as well as pastoral mind on the question, and receive his continuing support. It was Will who first introduced me to McLeod Campbell and the controversy that emerged in the Church of Scotland around Campbell's challenge of the Westminster Standards in Scotland in the nineteenth century.

The Rev. Drs. George E. Conway and Tomas K. Tewell, seminary classmates and friends for the last fifty years, whose weekly Zoom Bible studies were also the occasion for discussing much that is here, were great in challenging me as only close friends can do. George and Tom were gracious as I went on about Paul's understanding of sin, his use of various forms of imagery to proclaim what Christ had done, and as we first studied Romans and then the other undisputed letters of Paul together, culminating in the study of the book of Hebrews. They were patient as I explained how the sacrificial language of the Letter to the Hebrews functioned in that epistle and how sacrifice began to be misunderstood once the temple in Israel had been destroyed. They have read drafts of chapters, offered critique, and, most of all, encouraged me to see this through to the end.

Fr. Curtis Metzger, rector of All Saints Episcopal Church in Littleton, New Hampshire, is a generous colleague, thoughtful and scholarly priest, and my wife's pastor. His careful attention to text and to how laypeople would read it was especially helpful. His invitations to preach in Holy Week in the last two years gave me an opportunity to see how all of this translated into preaching in a fully eucharistic context, first on Good Friday in 2021 and then on Maundy Thursday in 2022.

The Rev. Dr. Richard Sheffield has been a theological conversation partner and friend since his days as a student intern in Pompton Plains, New Jersey, and now colleague in retirement from active pastoral ministry. Dick's keen eye, hard questions—"But what does that mean in plain English"—as well as his own pastoral experience kept calling me back to the basics both theologically and linguistically.

The Rev. Dr. Russell Sullivan, my successor once removed at Pine Street Church in Harrisburg, Pennsylvania, and who later became a gracious host, colleague, and friend, has been a stimulating conversation partner. His pastoral hospitality over the years of his ministry in Harrisburg was deeply appreciated. During the pandemic we worshipped with Pine Street digitally each Sunday, and I came to know him as a pastor who was unusually sophisticated liturgically, and one of our denominations most gifted and courageous preachers. Also an excellent theologian, Russell has kept himself current in that discipline and continually encouraged me not to dilute the theology for laypeople but translate it into understandable language for non-theologians. I am also grateful for Russell's invitation to present the heart of this work in a four-week series via Zoom, for Pine Street Presbyterian Church during the pandemic. As always, I am also grateful to the members of that class, as well as the ones I taught at MAPC, for their helpful questions and insights.

The Rev. Deborah A. McKinley was my associate in Harrisburg—the first woman to be called to pastoral ministry by a congregation in Carlisle Presbytery—thereafter associate director of the Office of Theology and Worship for the Presbyterian Church USA and then pastor to three quite different congregations before her recent retirement. Deb's keen eye and ear, her theological acumen and pastoral expertise, suggestions and encouragement were especially important as I faced the task of a rewrite after four years of work on a first draft that had clearly lost its way.

Elder Curtis Field from MAPC has known me, listened to me preach, and engaged with me in theological conversation from the days in 1991 when he was a member of the search committee that called me to MAPC. His theological insights, careful attention to text, and professional English language expertise were invaluable. His commitment to quickly turning around drafts (sorry for the split infinitive, Curtis!) replete with questions of clarification and suggestions for better sentence structure were a godsend. Curtis is among the most theologically sophisticated elders I have been privileged to work with and to know as a friend. This book owes a great deal to him.

The Rev. Denise Welsh, former deacon and elder at MAPC who then responded to a call to the ministry of word and sacrament and, after earning her MDiv, was ordained to chaplaincy ministry working with children and their parents at Mt. Sinai Hospital. Denise was one who dared to ask if sections I had written were necessary for what I was trying to accomplish. She courageously made significant and most helpful editorial cuts, while always affirming her conviction that this book was absolutely necessary. In the midst of critique, she was always generous with her enthusiasm for the book.

Elder Jane Little, also from MAPC, later moved west to care for her mother. Jane had been the producer of MAPC's recorded Sunday broadcasts on WQXR radio in her time in New York and consequently was accustomed to telling me "Do it again!" Her standards for excellence did not change when the writing went from copy for broadcasting to texts for reading. For all her support for the project, Jane never hesitated to tell me if I was going down a theological rabbit hole and needed to rework the material, sometimes reading two or three drafts of a chapter before giving her approval.

The Rev. Dr. Reford Nash, a colleague in the North American Academy of Liturgy, had been editor of some earlier writing I had done for the Association for Reformed and Liturgical Worship. Reford came fortuitously late to the project, which enabled him to be an editor as the project was nearing completion. He patiently went back to the beginning, working through the text from the standpoint of his own liturgical expertise, adding clarity, some correction, and encouragement along the way. It was Reford who constantly reminded me that I was not writing for the academy and therefore insisted on shorter paragraphs. He also reassured me, telling me how helpful this would have been in his own doctoral studies when he was sorting out atonement theology as a graduate student. In addition, it was Reford who stripped me of my Pauline propensity for run-on sentences, making the text so much more reader-friendly.

I am grateful to the people at Wipf & Stock for their encouragement and support, especially Rebecca Abbott, my copyeditor, whose keen eye, expertise, and gentle questions have greatly improved the text.

To all of these I owe an enormous debt of gratitude. And though most often I took their advice, that was not always true. And so, as always, whatever shortcomings appear here are my sole responsibility.

Finally, almost every preface I have ever read included the author's expressions of thanks to a spouse or partner for patiently enduring the isolation and aloneness the singular focus writing a book requires, depriving them of the author's presence. That has certainly been the case for my wife Questa—especially challenging for her during the broader isolation of the COVID pandemic. Questa has read every word—often more than once—made her own comments, critiques, and challenged me as only a spouse can do, while encouraging me every step of the way, even though that meant time away from one another in our retirement.

Because Questa was not reared in the church, her questions and comments have been especially important, not only for my preaching over the years but especially with this book. She is aptly named. One of the things that attracted us to one another was her "questing" after things spiritual. Not reared in any faith tradition but on a spiritual quest of her own, she was never shy with her questions about Christianity and its doctrines. Baptized a week prior to our eighteen-month-old daughter's baptism, a year later she found herself accompanying her husband to study at Princeton Seminary and working as a secretary for three years so he could do so.

It has been Questa's honest and sincere questioning of matters of faith and doctrines that has opened me to broader perspectives than those I brought with me to our marriage when I was still trying to recover from my fundamentalism. It would have been extremely easy to fall into a Reformed fundamentalism. But for her, I might have done so. In forty-two years of pastoral ministry, in three quite different congregations, it has been her continued spiritual quest and questions that have made me a better preacher, pastor, and theologian.

It is to Questa that this book is dedicated with all my love and deep gratitude for fifty-seven years of partnership and adventure into God's future for us all. And yes, she is still asking hard and important questions!

Fred R. Anderson
Narnia, Whitefield, NH

Abbreviations

TNT	Tyndale's New Testament, 1534
GEN	Geneva Bible, 1599
KJV	King James Version, 1611/1769
RSV	Revised Standard Version, 1952
NAS	New American Bible, 1977
NIB	New International Version (UK), 1978
NJB	New Jerusalem Bible, 1985
NRSV	New Revised Standard Version, 1989
NAU	New American Bible, 1995
NAB	New American Bible, 2011
CEB	Common English Bible, 2011
ESV	English Standard Version, 2016
NIV	New International Version, 2021 (US)

Chapter 1

The Question

THIS BOOK BEGAN AS a parishioner friend and I were driving to participate in a board meeting where we both serve as trustees. He turned to me and asked, "Fred, what does Jesus' death on the cross have to do with me? How does that save me?"

I responded, "Jim, the quick answer is everything! But the long answer will take some time. There have been many answers to your question, some more viable today than others—sometimes at odds with one another and sometimes not. However, the church has never given one, final, authoritative answer, as it did, for instance, on the doctrine of God as Trinity."

What does Jesus' death on the cross have to do with me? How does that save me? The Bible and theologians talk about my friend's question under the heading of atonement. Though answers are often limited simply to the cross, the Bible's answer is larger than that and encompasses all of Jesus' life: his birth, mission, ministry, passion, death, resurrection, ascension, and promised final return. It is all these together that changed things in the world between God and humanity—that "saved" us, that were part of Jesus' atonement. Indeed, the atonement is an entire story, a story about what Jesus did for us that we cannot do for ourselves—bring us into a saving relationship with God. It is why he is called Lord and Savior, among the many other titles that the Bible uses to help us understand not only who he was but who he is.

What was it that Jesus did to change things—in the narrowest sense by his self-offering and dying on the cross—but in the much fuller sense, how the whole of his life is what the church means when talking about atonement?

To answer questions like that, we will have to pose and answer others. Why did Jesus die as he did? Did he choose to do it? It has been called a sacrificial death—what does that mean? Was it the will of the One he called Father for Jesus to die, and if so, to what end? Was Jesus' work over once he died? He was raised; but what was the resurrection? Was it simply God's reward for his faithfulness, or was more going on there? And what about Jesus' post-resurrection appearances—not only immediately but also over the centuries of the church's life? These are just some of the questions this book is written to answer, and I will try to do that, first and foremost, using what the Bible says about atonement.

From the late first century CE onward, as the writing of the New Testament was ending, the leaders or bishops of faith communities began to formulate answers that later would be categorized as "theories of atonement." We will look at these theories, their strengths and weaknesses, as they sought to provide an answer to my friend's question in their own day. As I said to him, the church has never chosen one of those theories as *the* definitive answer to the question of why Jesus died. That is in part because their search for answers was utilizing the thinking and concepts of their own day, the tools they had at hand.

Since then, seven major answers or theories have emerged—some similar to one another and others seeming to be in complete opposition, as the church continued to search for language appropriate to the day. Since the mid-twentieth century, there has been an explosion in works by academic and pastoral theologians, looking at the question afresh. All of that is, in part, what this book is all about. I hope to provide you a new perspective—or, actually, retrieve a very old one—on what was taking place on the cross and what that means for us today.

However, we will not stop there, as most studies of atonement theory do. Rather, we will talk about how you and I can and do participate in the salvation Jesus accomplished in his atoning work. The atonement is, after all, about much more than simply believing it, or confessing it, or being comforted by it with a promise of eternal life beyond this life. It is about Jesus' ongoing mission of redemption in this present world—a mission that he wants to share with all those who belong to him.

The Question

What Is Atonement?

Atonement is a complex word, and we will need a brief overview of it, exploring what the word means and the different ways it has been understood over the years. Atonement is, after all, not a biblical word. Rather, it is an English construct predating the King James Bible, as an attempt to explain the meanings of the words that lie behind it in the Hebrew and Greek Scriptures.

What did those ancient Hebrew and Greek words mean when first used and did that meaning change over time, until they first appeared in the New Testament? Do the words mean the same thing now? Words have a habit of changing their meaning over time. What did it mean to "make atonement" in Old Testament times, and what was the result of doing so?

When the apostle Paul wrote to the Corinthian church to say that in Christ God was reconciling the world to Godself, Paul was also hoping to convince the Corinthians to be reconciled to himself (2 Cor 5:19). How might that help us to understand what Paul was saying? And when Paul tells the Romans that God put forward Jesus as the One in whom that atonement took place (Rom 3:25), what did he intend? This last verse has had a wide variety of renderings historically that continue to remain highly controversial to this day. We will look closely at all these texts and more, as we venture deeper into our attempts to understand atonement and the wide span of influence it has had, and continues to have, on Christians.

Atonement's Broad Net

Atonement is about much more than the cross and casts a net so wide it is safe to say that no aspect of the Christian faith is left untouched by it. Rather than focus solely on the cross, as much atonement theology does, we will reach wider; for though atonement theology lies at the center of the Christian faith, it touches every other aspect of Christian theology as well.

It begins with God's promise to Abraham—a promise that is extended through Jacob and his children, to the whole people of Israel, as God uses Moses to lead them from slavery in Egypt to the land of promise. Actually, the book of Ephesians tells us it began long before Abraham (Eph 1:4). The promise emerges within Israel again in the reign of David and is reaffirmed in the words of the early prophets as Israel looks for its messiah—David's greater son—to liberate them again, all culminating in the coming of Jesus.

Along the way, as we examine atonement's broad net, we also will ask some basic questions: What is sin? What is the difference between sin itself and an individual's sins? What about original sin? The phrase does not appear in Scripture, but that does not mean it does not exist. What is sin for us? What is evil? Where does evil come from? Who is responsible for it? What does the Bible have to say about it? Who is Satan, or more correctly "the Satan"—the member of God's angelic court whom we find in the books 1 Chronicles, Job, and Zechariah (1 Chr 21:1; Job 1:6–12; 2:1–7; Zech 3:1–2)? What is Satan's relation to the devil we find in the New Testament? These and many more are some of the questions we will need to explore as we consider the salvation Jesus' work of atonement accomplishes.

The Salvation Jesus Announced and Offered

The questions seem to never end. Did Jesus have to die to accomplish what he did? If so, why? The anonymous Letter to the Hebrews speaks of his death as a sacrifice. What did that mean in Jesus' day? Paul himself, however, never speaks of the cross as a sacrifice. How then did he see it?

How is the word sacrifice used in the later New Testament, beyond the biblical books of Hebrews and Ephesians? What did it come to mean after the destruction of the Second Temple in 70 CE—especially in the second millennium of the church's thinking, when it led to splits in the church at the Reformation?

Sacrifice was central to the making of covenants in Israel's life. What was Jesus doing in the upper room on the night he was betrayed, beyond celebrating Passover? During the meal Jesus spoke of a new covenant sealed in the shedding of his blood for the forgiveness of sin(s). We call that meal the Lord's Supper, Holy Communion, or Eucharist, depending upon our church traditions. Each name lifts up one of the dynamics of the meal that he commanded we continue as a way to remember him.

Why did Jesus charge us to do that? Is it simply a way to remember him and what he did? Or, is more going on as we commemorate it—some of us daily, some weekly, some monthly, and some quarterly? Jesus went from that meal to the garden to pray, where he was arrested and began the events that led to his crucifixion.

But why the cross? Was it a terrible miscarriage of justice? Was it all a horrible mistake? Or was it part of Jesus' plan and mission from the beginning? Today it is being described in each of those ways, and more. Yet why did Jesus submit to it, and seemingly intentionally at that? The biblical story is clear that he could have avoided it had he chosen to do so. In fact, the Gospels tell us he regularly predicted it, and Luke tells us that he intentionally "set his face to go to Jerusalem" (Luke 9:51). What did his death on the cross accomplish? Did the Word of God, which the Gospel of John tells us became flesh in him, die with Jesus?

What happened in Jesus' resurrection? What does that have to do with us? What is heaven? Is there life after death? Is that Jesus' promise of salvation? How do we receive the salvation that Jesus offers? Is it simply by believing in him, by accepting him as our Lord and Savior? Indeed, what does it mean to "believe in him" anyway?

What is baptism, and why is it important? Where does the Holy Spirit fit into all of this? What about Jesus' promised, final return? Can we, should we believe, expect, or depend upon it? If so, do we wait in hope or in fear?

Why is Jesus' final coming so important if he has already saved us? As I mentioned earlier, there is scarcely any portion of classic Christian doctrine that does not depend upon what God sent Jesus into the world to accomplish for us. How then do we receive and live out of that faithfully?

These are the questions we will be talking about together.

For Whom Is This Written?

I am writing this for working pastors, church leaders of all sorts, laypeople, seminarians and recent seminary graduates, college religion majors, and anyone in the pew who wants to know more about their faith.

I am writing for my friend whose question prompted this book, and former parishioners in the three churches I served over time. I am also writing it for those who have left the church but have not left Jesus behind—those "spiritual but not religious" people who are curious about a modern understanding of the Christian faith, one they may have considered or embraced but have now left behind.

I am writing for agnostics who are curious to know what a biblically informed contemporary theology of atonement might mean, one that challenges almost all of those that have come before now.

In my forty-five years of pastoral ministry, I regularly taught adult education classes on atonement theology and preached through the great three days from Maundy Thursday through Easter Day, each of those forty-five years. The longer I taught and preached those biblical texts, and the more deeply immersed I became in them, the more dissatisfied I became with many of the classic answers that have been provided to us as atonement theory—especially those that have emerged from the Reformation. Today I am convinced that much of that theology is not only wide of the mark but, in some cases, simply wrong. Some of it was true enough and helpful for its day, but because the worldviews that produced those notions are no longer our own, they are no longer helpful except as matters of church history.

In addition, much atonement theology in the past thousand years—starting with Anselm's brilliant but philosophically based *Cur Deus Homo (Why God Became Man)*—found itself moving further and further adrift from the biblical story. Atonement theology became beholden to philosophy and legal theories that were in practice at the time and read back into the biblical story. But as time passed, these concepts were left behind everywhere except in atonement theology.

In addition, language about sacrifice has changed dramatically from what it meant in Jesus' day. Yet, sacrifice has continued to dominate atonement language and theory, especially in church hymnody. Meanwhile, those using sacrificial language seem to fundamentally misunderstand the sacrificial system in ancient Israel and, more serious still, take little time to try to do so. The consequence is that much that has been written about Jesus' sacrifice and atonement is not only cut off from the biblical narrative but is more pagan than Jewish or Christian.

In this book, I am hoping to provide a perspective on the cross that is biblical from beginning to end, that does not escape into philosophical systems or mythological explanations, nor ultimately hide behind concepts of "divine mystery." As I have tried to do this over my years of ministry, many parishioners have asked that I turn what I have learned into a book. Pastoral responsibility kept me from doing that until retirement, when I began to take up the task.

Three years of research, reviewing the explosion of academic literature on atonement that has emerged, especially in the last seventy-five years, only further convinced me of the need for this book. It also delayed it, as I had to acquaint myself with a huge volume of new scholarly work. Then a first draft got me so caught up in the contemporary academic exchanges that I lost sight of my intended readers, as a number of my colleagues have been good enough to risk saying to me. I hope this restructuring of that first draft has not fallen into the same trap.

In this book I will attempt to get at and incorporate the broad sweep of what God was doing in Christ, putting the cross and resurrection at the center but in the larger context of God's saving acts. That is something that the laser focus of a sermon, a Lenten study, a biblical dictionary article, or academic monograph cannot do. And, as I have talked this through with many of my pastoral colleagues, they have uniformly said the same thing: "Write this! We need to get beyond the distortions and errors that have crept into atonement theology." Many acknowledge that the subject has become such a minefield that they have simply ignored atonement altogether or settled for the old answers with all the problems they bring, especially since much of the church's hymnody in the last three hundred years simply reinforces the problem.

In this book, I am setting out to describe what happened in time and space in Jesus' death and resurrection, and to do so in terms that are in sync with the rest of the biblical story, as well as with ideas and concepts credible to twenty-first-century readers and thinkers. At the same time, I am trying to put in perspective the answers about Jesus' death that, over my years of study, preaching, and teaching, I have come to understand as neither biblical, logical, nor true. I am doing so because I fervently believe there is a much more powerful and exciting story to tell than simply "Jesus died for my sins so I don't have to, and so I can go to heaven when I die, if I believe it."

A Word or Two about Language and My Use of It: Remembering the Basics

There is an axiom one learns in studying church history that says in its early years "Theology was the queen of the sciences, and philosophy was her handmaid." As the faith moved from its days of apostolic witness into the Greco-Roman world, then into the Holy Roman Empire, that relationship began to switch places, and soon philosophies were shaping the story, as we will see when we visit Anselm's work.

For our part, I am working to keep the Christian Scriptures as the touchstone—as well as some extrabiblical material that was being written in two to three hundred years before Jesus, called Second Temple literature. But even with those boundaries, we need to be reminded of several things.

First, all language about God—even that of the Bible—is figurative and often poetic. That is one of the reasons we remain on firmest ground in talking about God when we talk in terms of what Jesus reveals to us. Obviously, there is more to God than Jesus, but the church confesses that all of God that could be revealed in human form was present in Jesus. That is what the incarnation means. When we venture into talking about God "within God"—the "Holy Three within the Holy One"[1]—we need to be reminded of the figurative nature of such talk and exercise care not to literalize concepts into "facts." Again, Scripture is the touchstone, and all language about God within Godself is figurative rather than literal.

It is also important to remember that most Christians are reading the Bible through the lens of several thousand years of translation; and as any translator will tell you, "Every translation is an interpretation." Israel's Scriptures, though initially written in Hebrew, were, after the exile, either written in Aramaic or made accessible to the Aramaic-speaking Jews who returned from exile through Aramaic paraphrases, explanations, commentaries, and expansions of the original Hebrew.

When Alexander the Great brought Greek culture into the Middle East in 332 BCE, Greek soon became the people's language, and the Hebrew Scriptures were then translated into a Greek work, known as the Septuagint.[2] This was the Bible of Jesus' day, and the version from which New Testament era writers quoted. It was that same common Greek language that would be used by the writers of the New Testament and would make its way into the whole Greco-Roman world, where for the next several centuries Greek would be the working language of the church.

In the fourth through fifth centuries the Western church made the transition from Greek to Latin, and thus soon needed a new translation. That was largely accomplished by Jerome who was commissioned by the pope in 382 CE to produce a Latin version of the Bible from the Septuagint, commonly known today as the Vulgate. The Vulgate would

---

1. The Triune phrase is that of liturgical language scholar Gail Ramshaw.

2. The abbreviation for which is LXX, the Roman numeral for the number 70, reflecting the questionable tradition that it was translated from Hebrew to Greek by seventy different scholars over seventy days.

soon become the primary text for the Western church and would remain so for more than a thousand years.

It soon became the case, however—especially in England—that only priests who were scholars were adept at reading Latin. Consequently, various partial translations began to be prepared intended to help English clerics understand the Vulgate. The entire Vulgate was first translated into Old English (600–1100 CE). As Old English gave way to Middle English (1066–1500 CE), John Wycliffe produced an English Bible in 1382, which the church considered an authentic and faithful rendering of the Latin of the Vulgate.

Through all of this, Latin manuscripts were hand copied in monasteries and universities onto parchment or vellum, with varying levels of exactitude. But within a short time, ancient Hebrew and Greek biblical manuscripts began to be discovered. As scholars developed the ability to read them, an even greater diversity of meaning appeared between these newly discovered ancient texts and the Vulgate. One such scholar was a Dutch priest named Erasmus. He used the humanist commitment to return to the oldest manuscripts in Hebrew, Greek, and Latin as the most authoritative, to construct a fresh Latin and Greek New Testament.

The earlier innovation of printing with movable type both accelerated and supported the printing of biblical materials in what was becoming the prelude to the Reformation. In 1519 Erasmus published a second version of his Greek New Testament. To this edition he attached notes describing differing readings among differing older manuscripts. It came to be known as the received text (*textus receptus*), from which innumerable vernacular translations would soon emerge and appear on the scene.

In 1521, Martin Luther, hid away in Wartburg Castle with Erasmus' second edition of the Greek New Testament, translated it into German. That helped mark the beginning of the Protestant Reformation and was followed with Polish, Spanish, Czech, and French translations, as well as numerous English versions of the Bible.

William Tyndale's English New Testament appeared in 1526, as he continued work on the Old Testament; but that was cut short by his execution for doing so. Myles Coverdale finished Tyndale's work and produced the first complete Protestant English translation of the Bible. Soon thereafter came the Geneva Bible of 1560, the English Bible text that possibly had the strongest influence on the translation of the King James Version fifty-one years later. And though the Geneva Bible was the one used by Shakespeare, John Donne, John Knox, and John Bunyan, as well as the Bible taken to America on the Mayflower, it is the King James Version that became the standard in English Bibles well into the twentieth century. It was then that the culmination of nineteenth-century biblical scholarship brought forth a new explosion of Biblical translations that continues into this day.

The Bible is the most translated book in the world, which means that all the Christian world—save for biblical scholars and linguists—read their Scriptures in some form of translation or paraphrase. That is why the work of biblical scholars is so important to the church.

However, it is also critical to remember that biblical scholars do not always agree among themselves on which of the ancient textual variants is the correct one, nor even on how a faithful translation should read! In addition, scholars, whether an individual or translation team, are also affected by their own theological positions and convictions, and that too has an impact on how a translation reads. Again, every translation is also an interpretation. So, as we venture into our conversations about atonement, we will need to remember the challenge of the various translations—not only their words but, more importantly, the worldviews that once lay behind those words to give them their meaning. All of that is part of the task of those who seek to interpret Scripture faithfully.

My Use of Language

As we have seen, language changes with its cultures, and we are no exception. Today in American culture there is an emerging renewed interest in pronouns and what they convey about a person. This is no less true when the subject is God. When I was a child, the pronouns for God were He, Him, His, and Himself—all with capitalized first letters to denote it was God we were talking about. In most translations this was the case for Jesus as well. That gave way, via newer translations—first the Revised Standard Version (RSV), and then a plethora of additional translations—where God became he, him, his, and himself, with the initial pronouns uncapitalized.

In the 1970s, as new translations were emerging, and women were making themselves heard in theological conversations, the issue of gender came to the fore. All but the most conservative came to understand that *man* or *mankind* would no longer be an inclusive term for all of humanity. For several years we struggled to find language that was inclusive, and we learned that it was reasonably easy to do when talking about people, especially if you did it, as I just did, in the plural rather than the singular.

On the other hand, if a proper noun was in the singular, what was the appropriate pronoun to use as a reference? Was the doctor a he/him/his/himself or a she/her/hers/herself? That, of course, is easy if you know the doctor in question. However, when you speak of a doctor in general terms in the singular, which is the proper pronoun then? Some solved the problem by alternating between he and she regularly, while others intentionally chose the feminine alone, if only to point out how, if not specifically designated, the tendency in our male-dominant but changing culture is to default to the masculine. Today, it is becoming popular to follow a singular proper noun with a third person plural pronoun: "When one sets out to read a book like this, *they* soon find they have some new things to consider." Occasionally, you will find me resorting to that. But, more often than not, I will try to stay with plural nouns and pronouns and be as inclusive as possible.

Language for God

But what about language concerning God? I have already said that all language about God is figurative rather than literal. For some, that is sufficient, and they have chosen to maintain the traditional masculine nouns and pronouns. Just capitalize the pronouns, and you will know it refers to God. On the other hand, just as we were learning in the 1970s that *man* would not do as inclusive of women, we were also learning that male pronouns for God conveyed too much masculine freight and baggage to be appropriate—especially when speaking of God. Some found it helpful to periodically refer to God as She/Her/Hers rather than He/Him/His—often by an author trying to help the reader to realize God is beyond gender. And since that is the case, not even capitalizing the pronoun would do.

When talking about God in the Christian or Jewish sense, we have several proper names that will help with variety: God, Lord,[3] Holy One, the One Jesus called Father or Abba, though the latter two are still male dominant. But that still leaves us looking for pronouns, especially reflexive ones that maintain precision.

---

3. This is true in the United States without a royal tradition, but possibly not in countries with such a tradition.

You already have come across a word you have probably never seen or heard—*Godself*. I think I have used it once thus far. It is increasingly the word being used as a reflexive pronoun to refer to God as One who is not only above gender but also beyond the limitations of any language that does not have neutral nouns and pronouns. And it is the term I will be using in this book—not simply to be sensitive to women (or men) who would be offended by masculine language but because, at the end of the day, it is more precise; God is beyond gender and comparable only to Godself.

About Me

It is always helpful to me to know something about the person who is writing, especially in an area as important as faith. Who am I, where did I come from, how did I get here, where are the growing edges of faith for me?

I will try to keep it short! I grew up in a conservative Christian home—we were Baptists, affiliated with the Northern Baptist Convention. Dad was a deacon, and Mom was a soloist and choir member. When I came along, I joined the cradle roll of the church's nursery until I was four, when I was dedicated on Easter Day. Thereafter I was in the balcony on Sunday mornings (Dad had to work Sunday mornings, and Mom was in the choir) and between them in the pew on Sunday evening.

Church was the center of our lives, twice on Sunday, prayer meeting on Wednesday, and choir practice on Thursday. The house was always filled with music. Shortly after my baptism (by immersion) at age ten, we moved to be closer to my father's work and joined a new church development of the General Baptist Conference of America (old Swedish Baptist). There, the patterns of church life and music only deepened—Dad now chair of the board of deacons, Mom both organist and church secretary, and I the director of the youth choir. Such are the dynamics of new church developments. At age fourteen, while at summer church camp, I dedicated myself to full-time Christian service and began to think about preparation for ministry. I also continued to pursue music and my gift and love for singing.

All of that was ruptured three years later by an old-fashioned church fight over a pastor's sexual misconduct that shattered much of my naïveté about church and ended my participation in it for the next seven years.

Though my parents found another congregation, I personally dropped out, leaving any notion of pastoral ministry behind.

I never gave up on Jesus. I just did not want anything to do with church people who could be so duplicitous, hurtful—even hateful—as I had experienced them while my father was simply trying to be a faithful deacon and hold the pastor accountable. As a result, I became what today is known as a "none." I was a believer, but when asked about church preference, attendance, or membership, I had none.

It was my senior year of high school; I had excelled in music and was off to college the next year on a full scholarship for singing. That led to pursuit of a career in musical comedy, opera, concert singing, and choral music as both singer and conductor.

It was the singing that nurtured my faith in those next seven years, especially the choral music. Upon graduation with a bachelor of music degree, I took a six-year detour in the U.S. Air Force (we had a draft then, and the Vietnam War was raging). Commissioned a second lieutenant, I went off to aeronautical navigation training and became a combat crew navigator for the Strategic Air Command stationed near Springfield, Massachusetts. During that time, I met my wife and we were married and found ourselves back in church, in part thanks to a close school friend who had gone to Princeton Seminary, in part to the birth of our first daughter.

Now living in southern New England, we visited several different Protestant congregations in the area. We finally settled on an Episcopal Church in Holyoke, and were soon very active, both singing in the choir and part of a young couples' group.

Our first child having been born, we began to think about baptism. My Baptist roots and indoctrination on the subject made me skeptical. Since my wife had not been raised in a church, she too had many questions. About that time, our squadron shipped out for a six-month tour in Southeast Asia that would have a far more profound effect on me than I realized at the time. It also interrupted the conversations about baptism for our daughter but drew both of us far deeper into questions of life, faith, and purpose.

For me, it was a time to review what I believed and, more, what I no longer needed to hang onto as part of believing. Most of all, I was facing the question of what God wanted me to do about all of that. Home from the war in the spring of 1969, and preparing for discharge from the Air Force, the rector of the church and his bishop tried to recruit me for the priesthood. But I was still convinced I could serve God best and be a more effective witness to the Christian faith as a professional singer. It was the second time I said no to ministry.

Discharged, we moved to San Francisco, where our voice teacher was now on the faculty of the conservatory there. The time in Southeast Asia had taken its toll, and I needed to get back in vocal shape. I used the artist diploma program of the conservatory and the G.I. Bill to do that.

We quickly settled in and went looking for a church. We tried the nearby Episcopal church, but it was as cold as the stone it was made of, and the priest's sermon ranted on the evils of the war and all who were participating in it—not something I was ready to hear less than six months back in the States.

We tried the Methodists, but the preaching was poor, and we ended up at the Lakeside Presbyterian Church nearby. The pastor was reportedly the best preacher in the area, very personable and welcoming—himself a Naval Academy graduate—and it did not take long before we were back, full-time. Rather than rant on the evils of Vietnam, he was asking tough questions about what it meant that the nation (and the congregation!) was deeply divided over it, as well as questions of nuclear proliferation and our reliance on military rather than moral might as followers of Jesus. Those were sermons I needed to hear.

Within two months we joined, and my wife was baptized. The following Sunday, our eighteen-month-old daughter was baptized. Settled in church, we resumed our musical careers—studying, singing, and taking other work to help pay the bills. She worked as an optometrist's secretary and technician, and I as a music teacher in a Roman Catholic girls' school.

Soon we were recruited to be senior high fellowship advisors in our church. Therein began the tensions between music and ministry. The longer those struggles went on, the more I had to face what they meant. Now that I had begun singing professionally in earnest, the less it seemed as important as helping adolescent kids struggling with major life decisions. We were trying to support them in navigating the other demands of growing up, especially the drug culture of those days in San Francisco, and find meaning, purpose, and hope, helping and encouraging them to follow Jesus.

The longer we did that, the more pronounced my inner tension between music and ministry became. It was in that mix of struggles that on the following Easter Day 1970, sitting in the choir loft, as the pastor preached about the resurrection, I heard a voice in my head say, "That is what I have been calling you to do." That night I got up the courage to tell my wife, and her response was, "I've been thinking that for the last three months."

This was the third time God had knocked on the door, and it was time to open it. I applied and was accepted to Princeton Theological Seminary and was awarded the precise amount of financial aid we had calculated necessary to make seminary possible. Within one year of arriving in San Francisco from Massachusetts, we were driving back across the country to begin three years of theological study leading to a master of divinity degree and ordination as a Presbyterian minister.

Those three years were some of the most challenging, exciting, and rewarding of my life, and superb preparation for all that was to follow. Learning Greek and Hebrew were challenges, to be sure, but ultimately extremely rewarding. Digging deeply into biblical studies, church history, theology, and the practical aspects of ministry was both daunting and rewarding. The professors were asking questions I had not dared let myself ask since leaving the church. Their courses were requiring us not only to come up with academically acceptable answers but ones we internalized for more than answering questions on a test.

Church history destroyed my notion that Baptists had been so since John the Baptist, and that they had not been a part of the Reformation or the Roman Catholic Church—yes, I had been taught and believed that! Our New Testament professor kept pressing us to explain what we meant when we called the Bible "the word of God." "What about the *Word* of God it witnesses to?" he would ask. What about the Bible is "infallible," and what about it is not? Now, there was a question! After all, I had been raised a fundamentalist and had been proud of it. What is this thing called resurrection? "What are you going to say on Easter day? This is about more than the renewal of spring, flowers, bunnies, and colored eggs—Jesus coming back from the dead!"

Pastoral Care and Counseling taught me it was about much more than just giving good advice. Theology, especially the theology of worship, captured my heart and helped me understand what had drawn us to the Episcopal Church with its rich liturgy embedded in the Book of Common Prayer. Reading Calvin's *Institutes* with a recognized world-class Calvin scholar was both invigorating and liberating, especially when I learned that for Calvin, worship was not authentic unless it included both word and sacrament on the Lord's Day. I also came to understand the difference between sacrament and ordinance and why I needed the former, in which God was doing something to and within me, rather than the latter, in which I was simply professing or remembering something.

In short, I was untangling my Baptist understanding of both baptism and the Lord's Supper and found myself becoming increasingly Reformed. But three years was just the beginning of such study. We were reminded that Presbyterian ministers are never done learning, never done questioning, never done studying, never done seeking the deeper truths of the gospel. We were being trained to serve in a church whose motto is "A church reformed, always being reformed by the Word of God."

Learning the discipline of biblical exegesis—what the text meant when it was written, the factors over the years that may have had an impact on that meaning, and what that text (might) mean now in our contemporary world—was essential, as it is foundational to all theology, ministry, and preaching. It was about the living Word of God, Jesus the Christ, who by the Spirit speaks to us when we read, study, meditate upon, sing, and preach the gospel; and the risen Christ who meets us through the gifts of bread and wine, to give us himself and make us more like him. This was clearly the "singing" that God had called me to do.

I fell in love with worship and began to read liturgical theology and all I could find on worship. As I did, two major papers, one on Calvin's theology of the Lord's Supper, and the other, a comparison of Calvin's eucharistic theology and that of the Council of Trent,[4] whetted my appetite for research and more study. In response to those two major papers, I was invited to stay at Princeton Seminary and do a PhD in sacramental theology. I was thrilled with the invitation but also confused. My sense of call was to pastoral ministry, not the academic life, as my wife quickly reminded me. Yet I loved the study, research, and teaching, and, clearly, I had a gift for it.

Preparation for ministry in the Presbyterian Church required an extensive set of psychological evaluations, as well as meetings with a vocational counselor. Fortunately, these came shortly after the graduate study invitation came. The tests and evaluations all confirmed that I could do either. However, the vocational counselor pointed out that my love of working with people could be a barrier to my love for research and academic life. Academic life, he pointed out, requires extended periods of

---

4. Rome's response to the Protestant Reformation.

solitude in libraries, preparing lectures, drafting lectures, and books.[5] As he helped me think though what to do, he suggested I continue to pursue ordination, by seeking a call to serve a congregation upon graduation. I would know within three to five years if I wanted to return to PhD studies and, if so, would still be young enough to do so. It was great advice.

Ordained Ministry—A Pastor-Theologian

Upon receiving my MDiv I was called to be the pastor of a 325-member congregation that twelve years earlier had been a new church development in suburban northern New Jersey. I began in July and was ordained that September. I served there for about five and a half years. I quickly became a teaching pastor for Princeton Seminary—returning there for two days monthly, to collaborate with a cadre of other teaching pastors, not only in issues of supervising seminarians in their fieldwork but also in sharpening our own pastoral skills, pressing the edges theologically, and always continuing to learn. I collected reading lists and spent my continuing education time digging deeper into theology.

The fourth year in, I knew being pastor of a congregation was where I was called to be. But I also knew I needed to continue theological studies. I enrolled in the seminary's doctor of ministry program, knowing by now I was called to be a pastor-theologian rather than an academic one. The following year I was called to a downtown congregation of 1,200 in Harrisburg, Pennsylvania, where I would learn to love the challenges, frustrations, and rewards of ministry in a downtown, urban setting, rather than the suburbs where I had spent the last five and a half years.

The church in Harrisburg was a historic one, noted for its preaching and music, was strategically placed with the capitol of the state across the street from it, with a history of governors and senators worshipping there. As I finished my doctoral program and received my DMin (Princeton) degree, the word *street people* entered the country's lexicon, and we began to feed seventy to ninety people daily in what we named "Downtown Daily Bread."

Though Vietnam was over, there were a number of vets in the congregation for whom the war was not yet behind them. The film *Platoon*

---

5. The six years this project has taken have frequently reminded me of his counsel and confirmed its truth!

was released, and I found that as I tried to care for them, I was unpacking a good deal of my own "stuff" about the war as well.

At the same time, this historic church known for its preaching and music had been locked into "observing the Lord's Supper" only quarterly. As I preached and taught about what the sacraments brought to us, the leadership became curious and responded, allowing us to increase first to monthly observance, then to add the holy days of Easter and Christmas, and later Pentecost and All Saints Day.

At the same time, I was appointed to the denomination's task force to write a new directory for worship, the constitutional document that governs all aspects of worship for Presbyterians, and was appointed its clerk and member of its three-person writing team. It was a magical blend of the worship life of a congregation and diving more deeply into the history and theology of worship in the Reformed tradition. It was during this time that I was invited to become a member of the North American Academy of Liturgy where I found myself among some of the finest academic minds in Christian liturgical studies—an association deeply ecumenical and influenced by the work of Vatican II. I had discovered the best of both worlds—being a pastor and a working theologian.

Eight years into ministry I hit the proverbial wall—a dry patch that was the result of too much ministry and not enough self-care. It was then I remembered what a seminary professor had told us: "When ministry gets dry, and you think you have nothing more to say, return to the psalms, the font of praise and the church's first prayer book." I did, taking on the daily discipline of "metering the psalms," setting them in poetic paraphrase to be sung with well-known hymn tunes. That not only renewed my spiritual life, but it also caught the attention of people in the denomination's Office of Worship. In 1986, Westminster Press published fifty-two of those metrical settings in a book entitled *Singing Psalms of Joy and Praise*. Fifteen of those settings made their way into the new denominational hymnal that was being compiled and would be published in 1990.

By now, the new directory for worship was complete. During the time of its development, the session (the church's governing body) had decided it was time to give weekly communion a try, for at least one year. That one year came and went, and that congregation has been celebrating the sacrament weekly ever since.

With the adoption of the new directory for worship, and the subsequent publication of the *Presbyterian Hymnal* (1990), various invitations began to come my way. One of the most important was the invitation to be a trustee of Princeton Theological Seminary. As I was responding to that, another invitation came, this one to become the pastor of Madison Avenue Presbyterian Church in New York City.

I accepted both invitations, joining the seminary board in January of 1992 and moving to New York City to accept my third and final pastoral charge in March of that same year. Preaching and teaching to the members of that gifted and exceptional congregation was one of the great blessing and privileges of ministry. My predecessors' gifts and eloquence as preachers and teachers had gathered a theologically sophisticated and diverse congregation from the faculty at Union Theological Seminary, to people who had become Christians attending Billy Graham's Madison Square Garden, New York, crusade in 1957, and came to the church through that. It was quite a theological mix!

Not only was the theological bar high, but its contours were also wide. We were what would later be called a "big tent church"—folks coming from all over the spectrum of faith, from very conservative to quite liberal. In addition, many were trying to recover from bad church experiences or very narrow theological perspectives. They were trying to grow beyond that. Others still found that circumstances in their lives kept them from participation in the church of their childhood where they had been deeply nurtured by the sacraments. They were no longer welcome at the table there and had come to us. All of us found the Christ-centered preaching, the superb theology of the church's ninety-some years with just three extraordinary preachers, and a worship life supported by a history of rich and superb church music a place we could call our spiritual home.

The secret to how all this "worked" was Madison Avenue's historic commitment to an active faith built upon Scripture as it witnesses to who God is in Jesus Christ. It was a community of adults who knew the difference between preaching and teaching but wanted both. They expected both to be biblically based and relevant to the worlds they were living in, whether education, diplomacy, the arts, finance, law, medicine, or something else.

I took up the challenge. It was my privilege to serve all of them for the next twenty-three years, while also addressing the issues of homelessness, hunger, the AIDS pandemic, ministry with children in the depressed sections of the city, a ministry in partnership with a Spanish-speaking congregation in Brooklyn, and one with the Synod of Harare, in Zimbabwe, Africa. All this we did while navigating the culture wars that descended upon the church in those years over language about God, abortion, homosexuality, same-sex marriage, contemporary worship, etc., and doing so without being torn in two by them. Christ was the center of whatever it was we were doing.

In those years, I taught several courses on atonement theology, which is what I now bring as the subject of this book. And so, we ask again: What is it that God did in Christ Jesus that causes us to name him both Lord and Savior? What does Jesus' death on the cross have to do with you and me? How does that save us and the world? And, just what does this word *save* really mean?

Chapter 2

Where to Begin?

Jerusalem, Passover, the Upper Room

THE BEST PLACE TO begin our conversation about atonement is not with the various theories of it that have emerged over the years as Christians have tried to explain the cross. Rather, we must begin with what Scripture says and, more specifically still, what the Bible tells us about what it is that Jesus did on the cross. Though the Gospels are replete with Jesus' teaching and healing ministry, the story of what he does on the cross begins in earnest in Jerusalem on the Thursday night just before he was betrayed and arrested.

Passover

Jesus had come to Jerusalem with his disciples for the festival of Passover, by now an annual pilgrimage feast commemorating Israel's release from its slavery in Egypt. God had redeemed the children of Israel, ransomed them, and set them free from Egyptian bondage, doing so at the cost of everyone's firstborn, save those homes marked with the blood of the Passover lamb. The lamb's blood marked the house against the work of the angel of death, while the rest of the animal was roasted and set out to be eaten in preparation for the Israelites' rapid departure.

More than a functional meal, however, the Passover meal was to be a permanent ordinance, a commemoration of this night for Israelites and their children for generations to come. The lamb used that first Passover came to be known as a "Passover sacrifice to the LORD." The lamb was offered by the head of each household who slew the lamb, drained its blood into a basin, and then daubed that blood on the home's doorposts and lintel. It was a sign that the household was under the care of God's mercy (Exod 12:27).[1]

The sacrificial blood was a means of warding off the evil of death, what scholars today call an *apotropaic* sign of divine protection. Like most of Israel's sacrifices, it was also a meal to be eaten by the entire household, with the remaining portion of the animal that was not eaten to be consumed by fire. Indeed, the sacrificial meal was not complete until the animal had been completely consumed—eaten or burned by fire—in expectation of imminent liberation.

The angel of death did exactly what Moses had warned Pharaoh it would do if he did not let God's people go. Of course, Pharaoh had again refused. But after the angel had done its deadly work, the shock of devastation in every Egyptian household—even Pharaoh's—caused Pharaoh to relent. He finally let the Israelites go. God had ransomed and redeemed them from Egypt's bondage, and now led them though the sea to Mt. Sinai, where the Lord made covenant with them to be their God while they promised, likewise, to be God's people.

All of this is recalled in every subsequent Passover meal celebration, with the thrust of that commemoration looking back to the exodus from Egypt and its bondage, and recounting God's faithfulness to the covenant promises God first made to Abraham and then to Israel. Thus, the story of God's redemption is retold annually at a family table in a meal we know today as the Seder. It is a sacred ritual meal, reminding the people of God's covenant faithfulness and mercy throughout their history. It reminds them of God's continuing promise to raise up another but greater redeemer, one who would, like Moses, lead them into redemption and away from the bondage of their oppressors through a new exodus.

By Jesus' day the oppressor was no longer the Egyptians but the Roman Empire; many a would-be Moses had arisen as a zealot in rebellion against Rome, only to be crucified for insurrection. Passover became a time of great expectation among Jews—was this the year God would raise up the liberator? And likewise, Passover became a time when Rome was on high alert, wise enough to know that the feast was a dangerous time for insurrection. This is the tense and expectant setting we encounter

---

1. Note, the priesthood did not yet exist.

in Jerusalem as Jesus and his followers enter the city on what we now call Palm Sunday, or more recently Passion/Palm Sunday.

Jesus had told his disciples, as they were on their way to Jerusalem to celebrate Passover, that he had come "not to be served, but to give his life a ransom for many"—notice the Passover language (Mark 10:45; Matt 20:28). His entrance into Jerusalem was filled with messianic symbolism: riding on a donkey as David had done, the crowd laying their garments in the street to carpet his royal entry, shouting "Hosanna [save us]! Blessed is the one who comes in the name of the Lord!" Once within the city walls, Jesus went directly to the temple. All of this was highly suggestive that he was the One!

The more Jesus taught in the temple that week, the higher the peoples' expectation grew about him. For the religious authorities, it was clear that his teaching was directed against them, and the more they became convinced that he must die. Like every other would-be Moses, if the nation were to survive Rome's wrath at insurrection, this one must die as well. As a result, tensions were high on the first evening of the seven-day festival.

As Passover begins, Jesus gathers his disciples around him at table for the meal. He tells them that he has eagerly desired to eat this Passover with them before he suffers (Luke 22:15). In Mark and Matthew, he also tells them that soon one of them will betray him. In Luke, that word comes after the bread and wine; and there he also adds, "The Son of Man is going as it has been determined" (Luke 22:22). Jesus is about to tell them something extraordinary, something deeply tied to Passover but different. But first they must complete the Passover commemoration.

A New Passover

The crowds have often wondered about who Jesus might be, even calling Jesus a prophet (Matt 21:46; Mark 6:15; Luke 7:39; 13:33; 24:19; John 4:19; 9:17) or, more specifically still, "the prophet who is to come into the world," meaning the new Moses (John 6:14). Until now Jesus has brushed aside such expectation. But now he enacts a prophetic sign, revealing himself as what John the Baptist had named him—the Lamb of God who takes away the sin of the world (John 1:29, 36). This sacrifice will begin a new passover of liberation from sin and death. Indeed, Jesus is here inaugurating a second exodus, the one the prophet Isaiah had promised:

a servant whose suffering and death would redeem the people—not simply those of Israel—but also would be a light to "the nations" (the gentiles) by bringing God's salvation to the ends of the earth (Isa 49:1–6; 52:13—53:12). That is what is about to unfold as Jesus gives his disciples a new sacred meal of commemoration and redemption.

According to Luke

For now, let us follow the story as Luke has given it to us. Why Luke? Because of all the four portrayals of the meal, it is Luke who makes it most clear that what Jesus is about to do is not part of their Passover Seder. The annual Passover commemoration meal is over. What Jesus is about to do is something different! How do we know this? We know this because, of all four accounts, Luke's is the only report to include Jesus' blessing two cups of wine in the meal rather than one.

Of the many answers that have been suggested as to what this "double cup communion" means in Luke, the most helpful is that Luke is telling us that the Passover meal has come to an end.[2] Jesus has taken the last cup of the commemorative meal, the *hallel* cup of thanks and praise to God, has said words of thanksgiving, and given that final cup of the Passover meal to his disciples, telling them to divide it among themselves. Notice that he does not drink from it himself. Rather, he tells them he "will not drink of the fruit of the vine until the kingdom of God comes." With the Passover meal now complete, Luke picks up the narrative of Jesus' institution of what the church knows as the Lord's Supper, the Eucharist, or Holy Communion.

Let us look at each additional account of this meal closely, for although all four tell the same story, each does so a bit differently, and with each difference comes a window into deeper understanding of what this meal is and how it is related to what follows in the next two days. We will begin with the earliest account, the one the apostle Paul tells us was handed down to him long before any of the Gospels was written. Thereafter, we will fill in the pieces that each of the four Gospels adds.

---

2. Pitre, *Jesus and Last Supper*, 417–21.

According to Paul

Paul is writing to the church at Corinth. A major reason for his letter is that he knows they have been abusing the supper by permitting the wealthy of the church to disregard its poorer members and go ahead with the meal before the poorer working members can join them, thus leaving only the leftovers for the poor. Paul says that in doing so they are showing contempt for the church of God. He then writes:

> For I received from the Lord what I also handed on to you, that the Lord Jesus on the night when he was betrayed took a loaf of bread, and when he had given thanks, he broke it and said, *"This is my body that is for you. Do this in remembrance of me.* In the same way he took the cup also, after supper, saying, "This cup is the *new covenant in my blood.* Do this, as often as you drink it, in remembrance of me." *For as often as you eat this bread and drink the cup, you proclaim the Lord's death until he comes.* (1 Cor 11:23–26)[3]

Jesus is giving his body for them, giving them a cup instituting the new covenant in his own blood, and telling them to do this as a means of remembrance of him.

"Do this," in its Jewish context, evokes the notion of an action that is to be regularly repeated as part of a cultic act. And like the Passover meal, the ritual repetition is a means of bringing into the present the original saving act so that those doing the remembering are participating in the event as well. It is a memorial of the event in which remembering and participating are merged. Paul adds to this his corrective of the Corinthians' behavior at the supper: this is the church's proclamation of the Lord's death until he comes. It is this for which they are showing contempt!

According to Mark

Mark, the earliest of the four Gospels to be circulated after Paul's Letter to the Corinthians, says it this way:

> While they were eating, he took a loaf of bread, and after blessing it he broke it, gave it to them, and said, "Take; this is my

---

3. The text in italics is my way of drawing your attention to the unique emphasis in each evangelist's version of the account.

> body." Then he took a cup, and after giving thanks he gave it to them, and all of them drank from it. He said to them, *"This is my blood of the covenant, which is poured out for many. Truly I tell you, I will never again drink of the fruit of the vine until that day when I drink it new in the kingdom of God."* (Mark 14:22–25)

Mark adds to what Paul has written: *the cup of the new covenant is Jesus' blood*—the blood that seals the covenant. It is being poured out for many—not all—but "the many."

Jesus will not drink of the cup's "fruit of the vine" until that day he drinks it new in the kingdom of God. The reign of God that he had regularly proclaimed as "at hand" is somehow tied to this cup he is asking them to share. They are to drink of it even though he will not. His doing so must wait until the kingdom has come.

According to Matthew

Matthew, written to Jewish Christians, says:

> While they were eating, Jesus took a loaf of bread, and after blessing it he broke it, gave it to the disciples, and said, "Take, eat; this is my body." Then he took a cup, and after giving thanks he gave it to them, saying, *"Drink from it, all of you;* for this is my blood of the covenant, which is poured out for many *for the forgiveness of sins.* I tell you, I will never again drink of this fruit of the vine until that day when I drink it new with you in my Father's kingdom." (Matt 26:26–29)

Matthew reemphasizes that all of them are to drink it—yes, even Judas—and that Jesus' blood is being poured out for many for the forgiveness of sins.

Luke, written largely for gentile Christians writes:

> Then he took a loaf of bread, and when he had given thanks, he broke it and gave it to them, saying, "This is my body, which is *given for you*. Do this in remembrance of me." And he did the same with the cup after supper, saying, *"This cup that is poured out for you is the new covenant in my blood."* (Luke 22:19–20)[4]

Luke is more specific still: the bread over which he has given thanks and that he has broken, giving it to each of them—the way every Jewish

---

4. Notice his body is "given" for them, not "broken" for them as later crept into language of the supper.

meal begins—is something much more than an ordinary meal. This bread is his body given for them. And the cup, which is the new covenant in his blood, is poured out for them.

This meal is instituting a new covenant with the house of Israel and Judah, the one promised by the prophet Jeremiah. Unlike the covenant made at Mt. Sinai when God gave Israel the law, which Israel regularly broke, with this covenant God will make them God's people by putting the law within them, writing it on their hearts. All will know God, from the least to the greatest. And more: God "will forgive their iniquity and remember their sins no more" (Jer 31:31–34).

Like all covenants God made with Israel, especially at Mt. Sinai, this new one is sealed in sacrificial blood—the second use of sacrificial blood in the Old Testament. At Mt. Sinai, Moses had dashed the blood of the sacrificed animal on the people (Exod 24:8). In this new covenant, the people are to drink the cup of wine as Jesus' blood of the covenant that he is pouring out for the forgiveness of sins. To drink this cup is to participate in that covenant—make covenant—as surely as it was for those children of Israel at Mt. Sinai.

To drink from this cup is to receive the forgiveness of sins this new covenant brings with it. To eat this bread is to participate in the remembrance that he gave his body for them. But here, the word remembrance, as it is rendered in English, is quite inadequate for describing the Greek behind it and just what Jesus means.

Behind "remembrance of me" is the Greek word *anamnesis*. Though it can be translated "remember," the word is much richer in its meaning than "think about me" or "keep me in mind." This meal is about more than thinking about Jesus and remembering what he did. Something far more profound is taking place. The word can be rendered "remembrance," to be sure. But it also can mean "memorial," "reminder," or "recall," not so much in the cognitive sense as in the co-participant sense.

Returning to the Passover meal, Jews to this day in their Passover Seders know that they are doing more than remembering or commemorating. In keeping the ritual meal, they themselves become participants in the Israelites' coming out of Egyptian slavery. Likewise, in this new covenant meal, "memory" or "remembrance" is not reflection or recollection as much as it is participatory commemoration.

As we did with the word atonement, in search of its richer meaning, let us hyphenate remembrance: re-member, re-call, re-collect me. The French gave us the phrase *déjà vu*—the sense or feeling of having been here before or having experienced this before, as well as the word *souvenir*—memento or reminder of a place once visited. This meal is a means of being there once again or, more marvelously still, a means of participating in and experiencing Jesus in his self-giving to and for us just as he did with those first disciples on the night in which he was betrayed. Through the signs of bread and wine that Jesus identifies as his body and blood, and his command to do this as his remembrance, he is establishing a new cultic act, a new Passover sacrifice and meal, by which those who do so both recall and make present the saving effects of Jesus' death.[5] This brings us to the Gospel of John.

The Supper According to John

John's Gospel portrays the upper room in the thirteenth through sixteenth chapters of his Gospel; but the focus here is on Jesus' actions as servant, as he washes the disciples' feet and gives them a new commandment—the mandate to do likewise. As he has done with them, so they are to do with one another. Jesus then gives them a series of familiar promises and the command that they love one another as he has loved them. John's storyline then turns to Jesus' words of departure in chapter 14, his assurance that to know him is to know the One from whom he has come. Why? Because they are one. Jesus is returning to that One. But upon his departure, Jesus will send them another advocate—the Holy Spirit. Jesus is returning to the One from whom he has come. But in the midst of that, he will give them the gift of peace (John 14:15–31).

Foretelling his death in veiled language, Jesus says in a little while they will not see him, and it will give them great pain. But suddenly, that pain will be turned to joy. He warns that the hour is coming when they will be scattered—each will abandon him, leaving him alone. Yet he is not alone; "his Father" is with him. He tells them this to assure and strengthen them in peace, for in the world they will face persecution. Yet, they are to take courage. Why? Because Jesus has conquered the world (John 16:33). Notice it has already happened!

By chapter 17 the meal is ending, as John records for us what has been called Jesus' high priestly prayer, in which he intercedes for his followers (John 17:1–26). He prays for those gathered around him and for the followers who will later come to him through their witness. We will

---

5. Pitre, *Jesus and Last Supper*, 417–21.

return to this prayer in more depth when we look at the atonement Jesus accomplished that began to unfold in his conception and birth, and what he means when he says he is the way, truth, and life, and that no one can come to the Father except through him (John 14:6). But for now, look at how openly he talks about his followers and those who become followers because of them, becoming one. This at-one-ment he prays for is not only among his followers with one another, but their "at-one-ment" with him, and though him their "at-one-ment" with the One he calls Father.

> As you, Father, are in me and I am in you, may they also be in us, so that the world may believe that you have sent me. The glory that you have given me I have given them, so that they may be one as we are one, I in them and you in me, that they may become completely one, so that the world may know that you have sent me and have loved them even as you have loved me. (John 17:21–23)

What Was It John Remembered?

There is no institution of bread or cup in John's setting of the meal in chapters 13 through 16. Yet, John's is the most openly eucharistic Gospel of the four. Sacramental imagery is laced though chapter after chapter, if only we have eyes to see it. It is most explicit in chapter 6. That chapter begins with Jesus feeding the multitude on the five barley loaves and two fish. The people then recognize him as "the prophet who is to come" (John 6:14) and try to take him by force to be Israel's king. He escapes their attempt and withdraws to the mountain by himself to pray, while the disciples head out to sea, returning home to Capernaum.

Later that evening Jesus comes to the disciples, walking on the water, and they are terrified. They think they are seeing a ghost. He identifies himself, as he does so often in John, using God's ineffable name—"I AM"—telling them in words ringing with divine authority, "Fear not!"—the phrase that so often accompanies God's appearances in the Hebrew Scriptures. As Jesus steps into the boat, immediately they find themselves in Capernaum (John 6:16–21).

The following day, the crowd Jesus had fed comes to him again. Jesus chides them for seeking him simply because they ate their fill of bread. They have failed to grasp the larger vision of who he is and what he means. He begins to preach, telling them not to work for the food that perishes but for the food that endures to eternal life—food that the Son of Man will give. He is God's designated and sent One—the Son of Man (John 6:26–27).

They ask what they must to do perform the works of God; and he says simply, "Believe in him whom [God] has sent" (John 6:29). Astonishingly, as if they have forgotten the previous day's meal, they ask him to give them a sign so that they can believe in him. Moses, after all, gave their ancestors manna in the wilderness, the bread from heaven. Jesus responds that it was not Moses who gave them the manna; it is God. God is still at work in this meal—please notice the change in verb tenses—God is giving them the true bread of heaven and giving life to the world (John 6:30–32).

They ask him to give them this bread always, and he tells them, "I am the bread of life. Whoever comes to me will never be hungry, and whoever believes in me will never be thirsty" (John 6:35). Yet, having seen him, they still do not believe. He tells them that it is God's will that all who have seen the Son and believe in him may have eternal life. On the last day Jesus promises to raise them up. The crowd begins to complain about his talking this way; he is just Joseph's son. How can he claim to have come down from heaven? Jesus tells them to stop complaining; no one can come to him unless drawn by God who sent him (John 6:36–44).

The dialogue continues, and as it does, Jesus tells them ever more clearly who he is: the One sent by God to be the bread of life, a bread that gives life forever; whoever eats of this bread will live forever. To be more specific still, he tells them that the bread that he will give for the life of the world is nothing less than his flesh (John 6:48–51). This sets the people in the crowd at odds, and they begin arguing among themselves: "How can this man give us his flesh to eat?" In response, Jesus ups the game, saying that, unless they eat the flesh of the Son of Man and drink his blood, they have no life in them. Those who eat his flesh and drink his blood have eternal life, and he will raise them on the last day; for his flesh is true food and his blood is true drink.

> Those who eat my flesh and drink my blood abide in me, and I in them. Just as the living Father sent me, and I live because of the Father, so whoever eats me will live because of me. This is the bread that came down from heaven, not like that which your ancestors ate, and they died. But the one who eats this bread will live forever. (John 6:54–58)

This is why God has sent him from heaven and into the world.

New Testament scholar Raymond Brown suggests that these words were originally spoken by Jesus in the upper room, and accurately remembered by the beloved disciple who Brown believes is the original source of the Gospel. Brown believes it was the Gospel's final editor who moved these words from the upper room section in chapters 13 through 16 to be a part of the sixth chapter's emphasis on Jesus as the bread that had come down from heaven. Brown writes, "Liturgical interest seems to have been a factor in shifting eucharistic material associated with Jesus' words over the bread and wine at the Last Supper from that locale to VI 51–58."[6] Brown later writes, "It is possible that we have preserved in VI 51 the Johannine form of the words of institution," while later in the same paragraph he adds: "It may be then, that in this respect John is the closest of the Gospels to the original eucharistic language of Jesus."[7]

When many of Jesus' disciples who are in the crowd hear this, they say, "This is difficult; who can accept it?" Aware that even his disciples are objecting, Jesus raises the bar even higher, asking, "What if you were to see the Son of Man ascending to where he was before?" (John 6:60–62)—resurrection and ascension. "It is the spirit that gives life; the flesh is useless. The words that I have spoken to you are spirit and life" (John 6:63). Even among those closest to him are those who do not believe. Therefore, he has said, no one can come to him unless God grants it. At this many of his disciples turn away and leave him. Jesus turns to the twelve, asking, "Do you also wish to go away?" Peter answers, "Lord, to whom can we go? You have the words of eternal life. We have come to believe and know that you are the Holy One of God" (John 6:67–69).

At this point let me suggest you lay this book aside and reread the entire sixth chapter of John, and do so through "sacramental eyes," seeing this as John's way of introducing and understanding the supper, and as Jesus' commentary on what participating in and partaking of the supper does for those who do. To again quote Father Brown, "While the Synoptic Gospels record the institution of the Eucharist, it is John who explains what the Eucharist does for the Christian."[8]

First, notice the language of eating Jesus' body (the word in Greek quite literally means "gnaw upon") and drinking his blood, and what that

---

6. R. Brown, *Gospel According to John I–XII*, xxxvii.
7. R. Brown, *Gospel According to John I–XII*, 285.
8. R. Brown, *Gospel According to John I–XII*, 292–93.

gives those who do: it provides forgiveness of sins, satisfies hunger and thirst, gives eternal life, and offers the promise of being "raised up on the last day." Then take some time to reflect on what Jesus means when he says "Unless you eat the flesh of the Son of Man and drink his blood, you have no life in you." Think of what those words would have meant in the church for which John's Gospel was written in Ephesus near the end of the first century.

One final word: notice who is there—even the one who betrays him—Judas. We will come back to this in the last chapter.

Looking at the World through Sacramental Eyes

Why Should We Do This?

Since this is a sacramental understanding of atonement, let us begin with the word sacrament itself and what it means. Historically, *sacramentum*—the Latin word from which we get our English word sacrament—was a translation of the Greek word *mysterion*, from which we get the English word mystery. However, the word mystery in our English Bible is not used as it is in literature to describe a "whodunnit" but rather to describe God and the ways of God in the world—things that otherwise would be beyond human comprehension. As a result, sacrament is properly used to speak of the hidden things of God—things having to do with God's ways, reign, and work in the world to bring it to redemption and completion in Jesus Christ. As the Epistle to the Colossians says, things that were "hidden for the past ages and generations, but now made manifest to God's saints" (Col 1:26; see also Eph 1:9).

Today, the church uses the term *sacrament* to refer to its central ritual actions. But that is not how it first spoke of these ritual actions. In fact, it took several hundred years for the church to do so. Rather, the early church simply spoke of two major ways of responding to the gospel: first through baptism, and second through "the breaking of bread."

Baptism was and remains the act of entrance into Christ and his church. The breaking of bread that we read about in Acts 2:38, 41–42, and that the apostle Paul elsewhere calls the Lord's Supper (1 Cor 11:20), is the meal that the early church celebrated to experience the risen Christ present among them—among them to feed them as they broke bread and shared wine in an anamnestic commemoration and proclamation of his saving death and resurrection.

From Mysterion to Sacramentum

It was not until the third century that baptism and the Lord's Supper began to be spoken of as *mysterion*. But because *mysterion* was used in the Greco-Roman culture to speak of pagan initiation rites, military and otherwise, the church theologian Tertullian (155–220 CE) began to use the Latin *sacramentum* instead of *mysterion*, primarily as he wrote about baptism. This Latin term originally described an oath that Roman soldiers took to pledge allegiance both to the emperor and to the soldier's immediate commander upon entrance into the Roman army. Repeated annually at the new year, it was considered a sacred oath—from the Latin *sacer*.

Tertullian saw the connection between a soldier's entrance into a new life in the Roman army and the sacred oath associated with it and used that same term (*sacramentum*) for the beginning of a new life in Christ and his church through baptism and the Lord's Supper. Both were sacred promises—given and received—that were understood to be means of receiving the divine grace that emerges from one's union with Christ.

By Augustine's time in the fifth century, a sacrament was understood as a sign of a sacred thing that made one holy—a sign that produced what it promised—the cleansing of water in baptism and the forgiveness of sins in the supper, with its continuing nurture. However, by now the term was no longer restricted to baptism and the supper but to any religious ritual or act that was a sign of the sacred things through which God was at work in believers. And by Augustine's day there were over three hundred things that could be spoken of as sacramental!

That would cause the church to later distinguish between sacraments and sacramentals. After many centuries, *sacraments* were finally set as the classic seven: baptism, confirmation, eucharist, penance, anointing the sick and dying, marriage, and ordination of priests. *Sacramentals* were any other sign, action, or symbol that assisted people in prayer and devotion—holy water, the sign of the cross, fasting, prayer, etc.

At the Reformation, with its emphasis on the necessity of a scriptural warrant for things, the Reformers could identify only two of the seven that Jesus commanded of all his followers—baptism and the Lord's Supper. As a result, for most Protestants, the other five became *sacramental*, means of experiencing God's grace, to be sure, but not by the specific promise and command of Jesus.

Contemporary Ways to Speak of Sacraments

Today we often speak of sacraments as channels of God's grace, material means by which believers experience the presence and power of God in Christ to sanctify (make holy!), build up, nurture, and prepare them for discipleship. Roman Catholics and Orthodox Christians still maintain seven sacraments. Most Protestants affirm two: baptism and the Lord's Supper, also called Eucharist and Holy Communion. Lutherans often add confession-absolution. Meanwhile, Anglicans and Methodists teach that there are only two sacraments ordained by Christ in the Gospels—baptism and the Supper of the Lord—but also affirm the other five, commonly called sacraments but not "dominical sacraments," that is, those instituted (or "ordained") by the Lord.

Non-Sacramental Churches

In contrast, those churches that come from the Anabaptist[9] tradition do not believe in sacraments as means through which God is actively doing something in the believer but call these actions *ordinances*. Holy Communion, often called the Lord's Supper, is a means of devotional memory, and baptism is an expression of personal commitment to Christ. Since infants cannot make that personal commitment for themselves, Anabaptists insist upon rebaptism for someone who was baptized as an infant. However, there is no strict uniformity within the Baptist tradition, especially among those Baptists who adhere to the Reformed theology of John Calvin. Known as Reformed or Particular Baptists, these other Baptists do consider baptism a sacrament, baptize the infants of believers, and understand Holy Communion as more than a means of devotional memory.

Without digressing into the histories behind these distinctions, and for our purpose of trying to understand the relation between the sacraments and atonement, we will focus on the two actions or rites that Paul and the Gospels tell us Christ commanded for all his people, and that are embraced as sacraments by most of Christ's church (Matt 28:18–20; Luke 22:19; Rom 6:3–4; 1 Cor 11:24–25; 12:13; Gal 3:27). We will look at baptism and the Lord's Supper as channels through which the Holy Spirit

---

9. Those churches that require people to be baptized again if they had been baptized only as an infant or had not been fully immersed at the time of their adult baptism.

- unites us to Christ,
- clothes us in Christ,
- cleanses us in Christ,
- continues to make us holy in Christ,
- brings us into God's presence in Christ,
- and feeds and nurtures us on and with Christ,

so that we may grow ever more into Christ's fullness as God's beloved children.

Is Atonement a Verb or a Noun?

Atonement is not a biblical word; and this is where our challenges in atonement theology begin. Rather, it is a Middle English word that means "to bring concord between persons or groups." The simple teacher's trick of hyphenating a word to unlock its meaning will help us better understand it as "at-one-ment"—a condition in which two or more who have been out of relationship with one another are reunited as one.

Katallasso/Katallege

It was first used in this context by William Tyndale in his 1525 English translation of the New Testament, as he translated 2 Cor 5:18a: "Neverthelesse all things are of god which hath *reconciled* vs vnto him sylfe by Iesus Christ" (emphasis added). But at the end of that verse, when he came to the same word in its form as a noun rather than a verb, rather than translate it "reconciliation," as do virtually all modern English translations today, he rendered it "and hath geven vnto vs the office to preach the *atonement*" (emphasis added). And so, the word entered the English theological vocabulary.

The Greek word that Tyndale translated as "reconcile" and "atonement"[10] originally had to do with the act of making a financial exchange, not unlike the one American travelers to another country make at money exchange stations, translating their dollars into the local currency. They "reconcile" the value of one currency with another. The Greek word Tyndale translated "atonement" had to do with the *profit* a moneychanger

---

10. *Katallasso* and its associated noun, *katallege*.

would make for the business transaction, the product of the action if you will, not the action itself. Atonement was the result—the profit, if you will—of Christ's reconciling work, *not what he did to accomplish it!*

But as most words have both a figurative as well as literal meaning, the word atonement came to mean *the action taken* to reestablish a former relationship, reconciling people whose connection and bond had been broken. The "profit" of that action of exchange was a renewed relationship—a change from enmity to friendship—reconciliation, or at-one-ment.

Today, most modern English translations follow a stricter line than Tyndale's and use the noun that comes from the verb "to reconcile," rendering the 2 Corinthians text "All this is from God, who *reconciled* us to himself through Christ, and has given us the ministry of *reconciliation*."[11] Notice, the emphasis remains focused on the profit from what God was doing in Christ—reconciling an estranged humanity to Godself—but it also clearly points to what God did in Christ. Consequently, reconciling atonement is both an action and a condition—a verb and a noun—when it comes to what God was bringing about with us in Christ. This is especially the case when we look at this through sacramental eyes, in which baptism and communion are means of both reconciliation and union with God in Christ because of what God has done in Christ.

The Original Word in the Hebrew Scriptures

Tyndale did not live to complete his work of translating the Old Testament. His New Testament translation cost him his life just as he was about halfway through finishing his English version of the Old Testament. Consequently, the work of a full English translation fell to Miles Coverdale (1488–1569), who used Tyndale's work as well as his own to publish a full English Bible dedicated to King Henry the VIII in 1535. Twenty-five years later, when the Geneva Bible was published for the English Protestants living in exile in Geneva, the translators not only relied heavily upon the original sources as they had access to them but also upon Tyndale's translation. Consequently, the Geneva Bible regularly used "atonement" in the New Testament for the Greek verb *katallasso*, meaning "to reconcile," and the relationship that comes from that action,

---

11. KJV, RSV, NIV, NRSV; emphasis added.

its cognate noun, *katallege*, which means "reconciliation" (Rom 5:11; 2 Cor 5:18,19; Eph 2:16; Col 1:20).

The Geneva Bible also used the word atonement to translate the Hebrew verb *kaphar* and its equivalent noun *kippur*. Starting with the priestly sacrificial codes in Lev 1:4, it did so some thirty-five times.[12] When the King James Version of the Bible was published in 1611, it followed suit, revealing not only how influential the Geneva Bible was on the subsequent King James Version (KJV) but also the impact that translation would have on future atonement theology in English. It turned atonement into an action as well as a condition resulting from that action. This understanding would hold sway in much atonement theology for the next four hundred years, as the KJV became the dominant translation of the English-speaking world until the mid-twentieth century. Indeed, the King James Version remains the only translation that is acceptable to some, especially many conservative English-speaking Christians.

Kaphar/Kippur

Though subsequent English translations to this day have continued to follow the Geneva-King James practice of rendering *kaphar* and its related verb *kippur* as "atone," "cover," or "expiate," more recent scholarly work suggests the better term is "purge," for that is how *kaphar/kippur* are used in the ritual texts of the Old Testament.[13] There, *kaphar/kippur* are frequently coupled with Hebrew word for "purify" or "pronounced clean." Poetic biblical texts in Hebrew, rather than rhyme as they do in English, instead say something a second time in a slightly different way. It is this usage that suggests that *kaphar* means to smear a substance on something to cover it. From this came the notion that *kaphar/kippur* meant to cover something over. But *kaphar* also means "to wipe," or "to rub off," or "purge," and it is these latter meanings that dominate Israel's ritual texts in Leviticus and Numbers.

---

12. See esp. Lev 16:1–34, as well as the seventeen occurrences of *kaphar* in the book of Numbers.

13. Milgrom, "Atonement in Old Testament," 78.

Cultic Usage

In Israel's cultic worship life, the words *kaphar* and *kippur* are restricted in use solely to the sanctuary and its furnishings: the horns (upturned corners) of the altar within the sanctuary, the holy of holies in which the ark of the covenant lay, and the curtain that separated the holy of holies from the sanctuary. In these instances, the word always means to purge that space or cultic item of impurity. Its purpose was to rid the space or object of the contamination brought on by the peoples' sin. Otherwise, God, in God's holiness, would need to withdraw from them. There was, of course, another alternative—God could remain. However, if God did so, God's holiness would consume not only the pollution caused by the people's sin but also the things to which that contamination clung. That not only would purge those spaces and cultic items of their pollution but would also destroy them, depriving the people of any means to cleanse God's sanctuary of contamination to keep it fit for God's continuing presence among them.

Sacrifice

God gave Israel sacrifice as the means of purging their worship space and cultic items of the corruption of sin by smearing it with the blood of a proper sacrifice to preserve God's presence with them. That proper sacrifice is formally known as *hattat*, regularly translated "sin offering"—some 107 times in the Old Testament.[14] But too often that leads to the false notion that the sacrifice was a payment for sin. The primary reason for this sacrifice was to produce the blood to purge the contamination of sin, not restitution for the sin itself, and it has nothing to do with purchasing God's forgiveness.

In the *hattat* sacrifice, God is not being paid, appeased, or persuaded. Those, however, were certainly the concepts of sacrifice among ancient Israel's neighbors, where sacrifice was intended to appease or propitiate the gods, and were certainly dynamics in the later pagan sacrifices of the Greco-Roman world. But for Israel, sacrifice purged and purified God's dwelling place of the contamination of the peoples' sin. We will revisit all of this when we look more closely at sacrifice in Israel's life in chapter 5,

---

14. Three in Exodus, fifty-two in Leviticus, thirty-four in Numbers, three in 2 Chronicles, twelve in Ezra, and one in the Psalms.

and not only the *hattat* but also the other four forms of sacrifice and their purpose.

Space and Things, Not People

As important as it is to remember that *kaphar* means to purge and purify ritual spaces and objects, it is important to remember that it *is never used to speak of something done to people, as if to cleanse them, much less forgive their actions!* The one seeming exception to this could be the ritual action prescribed to restore healed lepers to the worshipping community (Lev 14:1–8).[15] However, in this rite, the cleansing *had already taken place.* The priest smearing the healed leper with the water and blood of a pigeon is a ritual declaring them clean to begin the process of reentry into the community. In Israel's ritual sacrifice for sin called *hattat*, people are always the beneficiaries of *kippur's* purging effect and not the ones being purged by it.

Kaphar as a Place Rather Than an Action

The word *kaphar* also appears in Exod 25:17–18 in the instructions for the construction of the ark of the covenant. There it appears in its derivative form, *kapporeth*, and refers to the box's gold cover and what will come to be known in English as the mercy seat. It is the place where the presence of God hovers between the outstretched arms of the cherubim.

One day each year, it was on this gold lid-seat portion of the ark that the high priest was instructed to smear the blood of a sacrificed bull to purge the contamination of that space accrued through the uncleanliness of the high priest's own sin that previous year. Then, the high priest's contamination having been dealt with, he could enter the holy of holies a second time and do likewise to purge the contamination created by the sins of the people during that same year.

It was to be an annual occurrence, when the people celebrated God forgiving their sins and purging their contamination through sacrificial blood. The sin itself had been transferred onto a goat. But even then, that goat was not slain as a sacrifice. Rather, it was dispatched into the

---

15. Note that the blood of the bird is collected in fresh water and is also applied to the additional bird, the crimson yarn, and the cedar wood, each a part of the priestly ritual to declare the former leper clean.

wilderness, thereby taking the people's sin away so they could be reconciled back into covenant fellowship with God. In Hebrew, the festival is known as Yom Kippur; in English it became the Day of Atonement (Lev 23:28; Num 15:28).

Further Development of the Word Atonement

As we earlier recalled, words have a way of taking on different meanings; and this is most certainly true and visible in what happened to the word atonement as time passed, especially after the loss of the Second Temple in 70 CE. Though biblically at-one-ment is a *condition* that results from a reconciling act of some sort, over time the word came to mean that which is done to accomplish the status of at-one-ment—the reconciling act itself. Consequently, in contemporary English, to atone means to *do something* to cover or correct whatever it is that has created the breech.

Today, making atonement can fall to either of the estranged parties. It can be as simple as offering an apology by the offender that is accepted by the one offended. It can be as complex as a series of conditions to be met to heal a complicated relationship that has been broken in order to bring the separated parties back together. All of this becomes even more intricate if the two estranged parties are not of equal stature in the first place.

Here is where things begin to get more complex theologically. Who are these parties that are broken from one another? Are they equals? Is one subservient to the other? Or are they two vastly different and very unequal entities? In these cases, who takes the initiative and action to cover what has broken the relationship? And just what action is required to effect that reconciliation and atonement? We will come back to these questions. But for now, let us look at how this bath and meal, Christian baptism and the Lord's Supper, are understood by the various churches of our day.

Chapter 3

Baptism and the Supper through the Eyes of the Church Then and Today

WHAT IS IT THE church believes and confesses about baptism and the Lord's Supper (Holy Communion, Eucharist) today? Despite Jesus' ardent prayer that his followers be one and at-one with each other, tragically, that has hardly ever been the case. Rather, the history of the church is a story of disagreement over one question after another, all too often leading to division, if not outright rejection, condemnation of one another, and schism. Church history is, in many ways, learning the issues the church argued over, why, and what was finally decided.

Those divisions included questions about who Jesus was as God's Son. Was he fully divine and just appeared human? Was Jesus just human and adopted by God as Son at Jesus' baptism or resurrection? Was he God fully incarnate in human flesh or not *fully* God but only "like God"? It took several hundred years for the church to argue out these questions.

The debate and disagreement became so severe and widespread that Constantine, the new emperor, feared that if they were not officially resolved, they would tear the empire apart and destroy his reign. Consequently, he convened a church-wide (ecumenical) council at Nicaea in 325 CE to settle the question with a confession. It was initially known as the "symbol of the faith"—symbol, in Greek and Latin, meaning token for identification. The creed/symbol is what Christians believe about God. We know it today as the Nicene Creed, named after the city in Turkey where the initial council was convened. An English translation of its original Greek reads:

The Old Nicene Creed of 354 CE

> We believe
> > in one God,
> > the Father almighty,
> > maker of heaven and earth,
> > of all things visible and invisible;
> > And in one Lord, Jesus Christ,
> > the only begotten Son of God,
> > begotten from the Father before all ages,
> > light from light,
> > true God from true God,
> > begotten not made,
> > of one substance with the Father,
> > through Whom all things came into existence,
> > Who because of us men and because of our salvation came down from the heavens,
> > and was incarnate from the Holy Spirit and the Virgin Mary and became man,
> > and was crucified for us under Pontius Pilate,
> > and suffered and was buried,
> > and rose again on the third day according to the Scriptures
> > and ascended to heaven, and sits on the right hand of the Father,
> > and will come again with glory to judge living and dead,
> > of Whose kingdom there will be no end;
> > And in the Holy Spirit, the Lord and life-giver,
> > Who proceeds from the Father,
> > Who with the Father and the Son is together worshipped and together glorified,
> > Who spoke through the prophets;
> > in one holy Catholic and apostolic Church.
> > We confess one baptism to the remission of sins;
> > we look forward to the resurrection of the dead and the life of the world to come. Amen.[1]

I have set it out in this fashion to illustrate the various points of argument the creed was written to settle. It is safe to say that virtually each line reveals one of the points of contention. What you see here is the church's official answer to those questions—what it called *orthodoxy*—which means "straight praise."

---

1. Early Church Texts, "Nicene Creed."

The Nicene Creed of 381 CE

Twenty-seven years later, in 381, tradition has it that the original was amended in the Second Ecumenical Council at Constantinople. That edition is known officially as the Niceno-Constantinopolitan Creed of 381 (hereafter simply identified as the Nicene Creed). And notice that it is now broken into three sections—sometimes called articles—one for each of the three "persons"[2] who are one "essence" or "being" in the Triune God.

I.

> We believe in One God
> the Father Almighty,
> Maker of Heaven and Earth,
> and of all things visible and invisible.

II.

> And in one Lord Jesus Christ,
> the Son of God,
> the Only-Begotten, begotten of the Father before all ages;
> Light of Light;
> True God of True God;
> begotten, not made;
> of one essence with the Father,
> by Whom all things were made;
> Who for us men and for our salvation
> came down from Heaven,
> and was incarnate of the Holy Spirit and the Virgin Mary,
> and became man.
> And He was crucified for us under Pontius Pilate,
> and suffered, and was buried.
> And the third day He arose again,
> according to the Scriptures,
> and ascended into Heaven,
> and sits at the right hand of the Father;
> and He shall come again with glory to judge the living and the dead;
> Whose Kingdom shall have no end.

---

2. Behind "persons" lies the Greek *prosopon*, meaning "face" or "aspect," and Latin *persona*, which originally was used to describe an actor's mask or a "character enacted." In the creed, "person" does not mean what it does today—a distinct self-conscious individual—but rather whatever accounts for the *unique identity* of the one being named, within the Triune God, to distinguish *him/her* from the other two within it.

III.
> And in the Holy Spirit, the Lord, the Giver of Life,
> Who proceeds from the Father;
> Who with the Father and the Son together is worshipped and glorified;
> Who spoke by the prophets.
> And in One, Holy, Catholic, and Apostolic Church.
> I acknowledge one baptism for the remission of sins.
> I look for the resurrection of the dead,
> and the life of the world to come.[3]

Notice that each of the articles in the creed is giving witness to an aspect, face, means, or way the Triune God—the Holy One—has given self-expression that distinguishes her/him/them from the other Holy Two, and is experienced as God.[4] Each of the Holy Three shares the same divine being or divine essence, and all three do their unique work but do it together with the other two—all create, redeem, and sustain, each doing their own part—to accomplish what God is doing within creation.

Within the work of the Holy One, each of the Holy Three has an identity that distinguishes him/her/them from the other Two. Christians worship one God, not three,[5] but a God made up of three unique realities who interact with One Another, rather than One who simply changes faces along the way.[6] I am intentionally avoiding the use of "person," because in our age that word conveys independent being. The Holy Three are the Holy One Triune God to which Scripture bears witness.

The creed/symbol is a summary of the orthodox faith of the Christian church about this God. It is confessed by Orthodox, Roman Catholic, Anglican, and most of the classic churches of the Reformation, generally each time they meet for worship, although there is a wide disparity of practice in the broader scope of Protestant churches. There, some use it weekly, others only when the Eucharist is celebrated, and others rarely, if ever, preferring the Apostles' Creed, believing it a better summary of

---

3. MIT, "Nicene-Constantinopolitan Creed."

4. I am intentionally avoiding the word "mode," as that was used to describe an early heresy called modalism: God appearing in various modes, first as Creator and the Holy One of Israel, then as Jesus Christ, and finally as the Holy Spirit.

5. The latter is the tritheism of Mormonism as well as the polytheism of portions of Eastern religions.

6. This latter is the heresy that was labeled *modalism*—God appeared first as Creator, then Son, and now Spirit. The Creed says that God is all three simultaneously from eternity into eternity.

Scripture than the philosophic foundation of the Nicene Creed. And some churches reject creeds altogether, insisting on "no creed but the Bible."[7]

The Apostles' Creed

The Apostles' Creed emerged in the Western portion of the church—probably fifth-century Gaul—but seems to have originated in the second century as a baptismal confession thought to embrace the faith of the apostles, based upon the Great Commission in Matt 23:19. The Apostles' Creed continued to develop in the Western church into the eighth century when it began to be used in place of the Nicene Creed. It was finally the confession mandated by Charlemagne (748–814) to be used in all the churches under his dominion. It seems to have been unknown in the churches of the East and would, two centuries later, become one of several issues that would lead to fracture and ultimate division in the church between East and West, Byzantine and Catholic, today Orthodox and Roman Catholic.

From Controversy to Schism

While the Apostles' Creed was still in development and primarily used for baptisms in the West, in the late sixth century, some of the Latin-speaking churches in the West made an addition to the Nicene Creed without any consultation with the churches of the East. The phrase "and the Son" was added to confess that the Holy Spirit "proceeds" from both the Father and the Son, rather than just the Father, as stated in the origional. Today it is known as the *filioque* clause—*filioque* being the Latin word for Son.

There had been other points of contention between Rome in the West and the Byzantine churches of the East. What was the proper language for the liturgy, Rome's Latin, or the Eastern region's vernaculars? Could priests marry, or must they remain celibate? Were icons acceptable in worship, or was the Eastern churches' veneration of them idolatrous? Must the bread of the supper be unleavened, or could it be leavened? And

---

7. This latter phrase emerged in the twentieth century in the liberal/conservative struggles within free church Protestantism, but it does not take long to realize that it fails its own test.

not surprisingly, who was the head of the whole church—the pope in Rome or the ecumenical patriarch in Constantinople?

When the Western Latin church under Pope Leo IX asserted authority over the whole church and insisted on the inclusion of the *filioque* clause in the creed, that was the last straw and brought about the great schism of 1054. It split the church doctrinally, theologically, liturgically, linguistically, politically, and geographically, with each side accusing the other of falling into heresy and causing the division.

The two churches condemned and excommunicated one another with mutual anathemas. Even the names they took for themselves were polemic; one took the name Catholic [universal] Church of the Holy Roman Empire (later the Roman Catholic Church), and the other the Orthodox [true] Churches of the Byzantium Empire, the latter identified by the regional language they used in worship. And despite occasional attempts to heal the breech, that was not to be accomplished for another 911 years.

Once the seed of division had been planted, it would continue to grow in the Western church, first through the sixteenth-century Reformation, and thereafter accelerate well into the twentieth century. It was Pope John XXIII, who, in 1962, shocked the Christian world by creating the Second Vatican Council. No one—Roman Catholic, Protestant, or Orthodox—was suspecting it would happen. One year later Pope John XXIII was dead and was followed by Pope Paul VI, who presided over the council until it concluded in 1965.

From Vatican II came movement for rapprochement and healing in the worldwide church. Not only did Rome recognize Protestants as "separated brethren," but Pope Paul VI and the ecumenical patriarch of the Eastern churches both nullified the formal excommunication of one another, beginning a new era of reconciliation between East and West.[8]

Sacramentality amid Theological Controversy

In many ways, it is astonishing that in these two thousand years of controversy and division the sacraments of baptism and communion would

---

8. Though it was common at the council's conclusion to hear theologians on all sides say, "John XXIII opened the windows of the Church so the Spirit could blow through it," it must also be said that the council's work angered the conservative side of the Roman Catholic Church, whose conservative bishops have steadily attempted to undermine the council's work ever since.

remain central in all Christian worship, though often with quite different understandings, names, and modes of practice. Let us then look at how churches understand God to be at work in these two sacraments and how they got there, beginning with baptism, and then the Holy Supper Jesus instituted as he prepared to enter his passion.

Baptism

In the ancient church, baptism was always the means of entrance to the Church, the rejection of a pagan past, and initiation by being washed in the threefold name of God in response to Jesus' command in what is called the Great Commission (Matt 28:18–20). Over the years, what changed was the way one was baptized, not what it meant, at least until the Reformation.[9]

Interestingly, though the New Testament frequently mentions baptism, it rarely defines it. The only place it is described is in Jesus' baptism by John. It appears that any source of water would do, as the Ethiopian eunuch seems to have been baptized in a pool or stream (Acts 8:36–39). How all those new believers on Pentecost were baptized is a bit of a mystery (Acts 2:38–41), and Paul talks about baptizing both individuals as well as whole households (1 Cor 1:14–16).

The Didache, the late first-century or early second-century noncanonical work whose full name is *The Teachings of the Lord to the Gentiles (or Nations) by the Twelve Apostles*, includes these instructions on baptism: "Baptize in living water in the name of the Father and of the Son and of the Holy Spirit." Living water here means running water, essentially a river or stream. It continues, "But if you do not have running water, then baptize in other water; and if you are not able in cold, then in warm. But if you have neither, then pour water on the head three times in the name of the Father and of the Son and of the Holy Spirit."[10]

From this, scholars deduce that early baptism was threefold immersion or threefold pouring (affusion) while reciting the Triune name of God. The baptismal candidate and the one baptizing were required to

---

9. The "left wing" of the Reformation, characterized by the Anabaptist movement, rejected sacraments altogether as means through which God's grace is at work in one's life.

10 F. Brown, *Didache*, 14.

fast, as well as any others who might be able to join them, with the candidate ordered to fast a day or two before the baptism.[11]

As the church became more common in the Mediterranean, baptismal pools were constructed near the entrance to the church. They were often eight-sided with steps down into them on both the western and eastern sides.[12] The baptismal candidates stood on the western side, facing east, and after renouncing evil and its ways, made promises of discipleship. Stripped of old clothing, they stepped down into the pool either to be immersed or have water poured over them in the name of the "Father, Son, and Holy Spirit." Thereafter, the newly baptized emerged up the eastern steps, were clothed in a white garment symbolic of the wedding garment for the messianic feast, and were welcomed into the church nave, where they were included in their first Eucharist. An excellent example of this is the ancient baptismal pool in Ephesus or the new Orthodox baptistry in Havana, Cuba.

As the faith moved beyond its Mediterranean roots and into colder climates, full immersion became various forms of washing, often out of health concerns for what immersion could mean in freezing weather. Consequently, there was no one way to baptize that was *the* way.

Today, in the churches of the West, there is a renewed emphasis in the church on the use of an abundance of water, whereas the churches of the East have always practiced full immersion or affusion—an abundance of water being poured over the baptismal candidates' head three times, one for each of the three names of the Triune God—Father, Son, and Holy Spirit. Even infants are fully immersed three times in a large font in Orthodox churches.

What Happens in Baptism

What is it the church understood to be taking place in such baptism? There was, of course, the precedent of the baptism of John. Behind it lay the Hebrew rites of ritual bathing for purification. Jesus had submitted to it along with all who had been coming out to John for baptism. John's baptism was an act of repentance and cleansing from sin. When John demurred at Jesus' appearance before him in the Jordan River, saying it

---

11. Roberts and Donaldson, "Didache," ch. 7.

12. The eight sides are symbolic of the day of resurrection as the "eighth day of creation," when in Christ, God took up the renewal of creation blighted by human sin.

was he who needed to be baptized by Jesus, Jesus responded, "Let it be for now; for it is proper for us in this way to fulfill all righteousness" (Matt 3:13–15).

Of the many things that verse can mean, Jesus was demonstrating his own obedience to God's righteousness and purpose in him as he prepared to take up his public ministry. Remember, the Spirit who had been active in Jesus' life from conception until now descended upon him fully at his baptism by John, revealing to Jesus and to John who Jesus was, and empowering Jesus for his subsequent ministry. Thus, baptism has always retained the notion of repentance and cleansing from the past retained from John's baptism but, more, is a new beginning in Christ, a life seeking to be obedient to God's righteousness and purpose as revealed in the Christian gospel (Rom 1:17; 3:21), a sign of that obedience as well as the gospel's promise, and the promise of empowerment for that life by the Spirit. Remember, sacraments are more than what we do or promise; God is at work through them in human lives.

Scripture is clear that adults upon their profession of faith were baptized, but Scripture also speaks of entire households being baptized (Acts 11:14; 16:15, 31, 34; 18:8; 1 Cor 1:16). For the first fifteen hundred years of the church's life, baptism was administered to adults on their conversion and to children born to believers shortly after their birth.

At the Reformation, the Anabaptist wing of the movement prohibited infant baptism, and required even those adults who had been baptized as infants to again be baptized, generally by full immersion.[13] Behind this lay the conviction that much of the trouble in the medieval church and laxity among its laity had come about because people were baptized as infants, made Christian without any commitment of their own, and, unless later entering some form of lay order or the priesthood, exhibited little Christian discipline in their personal lives.

Today, most denominations of the Anabaptist tradition do not consider baptism a sacrament—an event in which God is at work fulfilling God's promises. Rather, baptism is a rite of initiation for one old enough—having achieved the age of discretion—to make a personal profession of faith in Christ. That is often characterized as a "decision for Christ," that leads to baptism. Infants are not able to make such a decision.

The sacramental churches, on the other hand, see such baptism as both sign and *seal*—authentication, as a seal on a legal document vouches

---

13. Consequently, the term *Anabaptist*, meaning "baptize again," was shortened later to *Baptist*.

for its authenticity—of Christ's decision for the child as well as a gift given to Christian parents.[14] That fundamental distinction remains to this day. As has often been said, if the years of theological controversy over infant baptism could be resolved by resorting to texts from Scripture, that would have happened long ago.

John's Baptism and Promise

John had promised that the "coming one" would baptize with the Holy Spirit and fire (Matt 3:11; Mark 1:8; Luke 3:16; John 1:26, 33). Recall that interesting event in Paul's ministry on his third missionary journey when he arrives in Ephesus and encounters some disciples who have not yet received the Holy Spirit—they know nothing about it. When Paul asks into what they were baptized, they answer, "John's baptism." Paul responds:

> John baptized with a baptism of repentance, telling the people to believe in the one who was to come after him, that is, in Jesus. On hearing this, they were baptized in the name of the Lord Jesus. When Paul had laid his hands on them, the Holy Spirit came upon them, and they spoke in tongues and prophesied—altogether there were about twelve of them. (Acts 19:1–6; see also Acts 18:24–25)

Tongues and prophesying were two of the early signs of the Spirit's presence in a baptized believer's life. Thus, baptism in Jesus' name meant not only cleansing from sin, repentance, commitment to, and entrance into the way of Jesus but also reception and demonstration of the Holy Spirit to empower one for that life of discipleship. Herein lies one of the distinctions between the baptism of John and Christian baptism.

Christian Baptism

Because of Jesus' passion, death, resurrection, and ascension, baptism means much more still. First, it is a response to Jesus' invitation to follow him as his disciple, our promise that embraces his promise of salvation. In those waters of baptism, we not only leave the past behind but embrace

---

14. It should be noted that churches that oppose the baptism of infants offer a rite of dedication, in which the parents acknowledge their children as God's gift to them and pledge to rear them in the faith until they are old enough to decide for Christian baptism themselves.

God's future. We experience union with Christ, in the fullness of what Christ did. In that union, as believers, we do more than turn away from our pasts; we die with Christ to sin and death and are raised with him beyond sin's bondage to death; we enter the new covenant life in union with Christ.

Paul speaks of baptism as having put on Christ like a garment (Rom 6:3-11; Col 2:12; Gal 3:26-29). But that baptismal union is not only with Christ and the One Jesus called Father (John 14:20; 17:23)—at-one-ment—it is also union with all who belong to Christ, whatever tradition of the faith they embrace! In baptism we become Christ's sisters and brothers—daughters and sons of God—and members of Christ's body (Rom 12:5). All of this is captured in one of Paul's favorite phrases—"in Christ" (Rom 8:1-2; 1 Cor 1:2, 4, 30; 2 Cor 1:21-22; 5:17).

Christian baptism means not only to die with Christ to sin and death and rise with him to new life beyond sin's bondage but to become a new creature. One clothed with Christ in God is beginning a journey of discipleship as a member of God's new creation in Christ. In that journey of discipleship, one is born anew (from above!),[15] begins to mature, and is being transformed from one degree of glory to another, until reaching the very fullness of Christ himself (2 Cor 3:18; 4:17; 5:17).

All of this—union with God in Christ, putting him on like a garment, dying and rising with him, becoming one with him in his risen glory—is the work of the Holy Spirit. The Spirit comes to the faithful in the waters of Christian baptism, as the Spirit came fully upon Jesus in the Jordan. It is the gift and reality John the Baptist promised would flow from "the coming one's" baptism (Matt 3:11; Mark 1:7-9; Luke 3:16). It is a disciple's first step into the realm of God's righteousness—obedience to it and what that means for the rest of a person's life. It is a sign of entrance into the world of God's reign, spoken of in Scripture as the kingdom of God, and of one's personal commitment to living out of that reign, at one with God in Christ.

As God's promise in Christ, baptism is to be received only once and is universal (Eph 4:5). Our promises require frequent renewal; God's promise is sure, and once is enough! As divided as the church might be over so many other things, there is no division in the sacramental churches over these convictions. How then do sacramental Christians renew their own promises? This brings us to our Lord's table and the

15. The Greek is *anothen*, the same that appears in John 3:3-7, in Jesus' conversation with Nicodemus, and has the double meaning "above, again, all over, beginning."

other sacrament he commanded us to do—Holy Communion. Among the many things that take place in that meal is the renewal of our promises to God in Christ's name.

Breaking of Bread, Eucharist, Holy Communion, the Lord's Supper

The book of Acts tells us that on the day of Pentecost, those who welcomed Peter's message were baptized. Luke then tells us, "They were continually devoting themselves to the apostles' teaching and to fellowship, to the breaking of bread, and to prayers" Acts 2:41–42). Earlier in Luke's Gospel, he gives us a hint as to why.

Luke tells us about the two shattered followers of Jesus who on that Sunday afternoon after Jesus' death were returning to their home in Emmaus. They had thought Jesus to be "the one to redeem Israel" (Luke 24:21). The risen Jesus meets them in their journey, though they do not recognize him. He opens their hearts to understand the Scriptures, and as they reach their home, they urge him to spend the night. He accepts their invitation. Luke then tells us, "When he was at table with them, he took bread, blessed and broke it, and gave it to them. Then their eyes were opened, and they recognized him; and he vanished from their sight" (Luke 24:30–31).

Hence begins the history of the risen Lord revealing himself to his followers in "the breaking of bread," the meal the apostle Paul calls the the Lord's Supper (1 Cor 11:20). It is more than a commemorative meal in which believers remember Jesus and his promises. Rather, like the two of Emmaus, they come to know him to be present to them as the risen Christ as they break bread and share wine as an act of his "remembrance." From that night in Emmaus until now, this sacrament has remained Holy Communion with the risen Lord through breaking bread and sharing the cup of wine in thanksgiving for his saving presence in the world, in and to us, and all that has made that possible.

As Paul described it writing to the Corinthians, the sacrament was a full meal at the end of the Lord's Day where bread and cup were the central focus of the event and shared by the entire gathering. The meal established fellowship, communion, unity among the participants, and was an anticipation of the messianic banquet in the world that was to come. It was a proclamation of Jesus' saving death until he returned. Christians met at other times for prayer, instruction, and encouragement, but the Sunday evening eucharistic meal of thanksgiving, remembrance, and communion, with the emphasis on bread and cup, was the central act of worship in the church through the rest of the first century.

Early in the second century, the emperor Trajan became suspicious of associations in the empire that gathered in the evening for fraternal purposes. Seeing them as the breeding ground for grumbling and dissension, he banned them. Consequently, Christians began meeting early on Sunday morning in their homes, or at the site of a martyr's tomb—often at the break of day, the rising sun a witness to the risen Son. Initially the service had been one of singing hymns, renewing vows, and attending to community concerns but now grew into reading the Hebrew Scriptures and apostolic letters and offering prayers. Soon it would incorporate the eucharistic meal of receiving Christ afresh in bread and wine, celebrating and giving thanks for his risen presence in and among them.

Though the Sunday evening larger meal continued, the morning gatherings quickly became more popular and the norm. Because of the hour, and because the worshippers would soon be going to work, the meal was smaller and often included water with the traditional bread and wine. Both gatherings knew Christ present in their worship as both "host" and "food" to nurture, strengthen, and mature them as his faithful. This has been the constant confession of the sacramental churches to this day.

From Early Church Theologians to the Middle Ages

During those first years of the church, until the fall of the Roman Empire in the late fifth century, the focus of the Eucharist was upon the joy of being in the presence of the Risen Lord. It was an offering of thanksgiving and a joyful response to him for all he had done and all he continued to do, receiving him afresh through the meal and renewing baptismal promises. Iconography from this period dominantly portrays Jesus as the Good Shepherd, standing among his flock. If a cross appears at all, Jesus is either standing behind, beside, or in front of it, with his arms outstretched overhead in victory.

As time moved beyond the fall of the Roman Empire and more deeply into the Middle Ages, the emphasis began to change. It moved from the cross as Jesus' faithful self-offering as a means of defeating sin and death, to focus upon his suffering and death on a cross and what that could mean. By the tenth century, Jesus began to be portrayed suffering and dying on a cross, rather than standing beside it, hands raised in victory.

In this same period, the focus slowly shifted from Christ's dynamic presence among worshippers in the meal, to his presence to them *through* the elements of bread and wine. Thus began a shift in focus from Christ's presence as host feeding the faithful through the food of consecrated bread and wine as his body to feed us and blood to wipe out sin, to a focus on the elements themselves and how they became Christ's body and blood.

Bread and Wine: From Figurative to Literal

In the earliest centuries of the church's life, the bread and wine used in the supper were spoken of as being *changed to*, being *made into*, or *becoming* the body and blood of Christ. The first Christian text outside of the New Testament, the Didache, instructed that no one was to partake of the Eucharist unless baptized into the name of the Lord. Why? The church was not to "give that which is holy to the dogs." The consecrated bread and wine were not only "spiritual food and drink," they were also holy and for the purpose of making those who receive it holy.[16]

By the beginning of the second century, in AD 106, Ignatius of Antioch wrote, "I desire the bread of God, the heavenly bread, the bread of life, which is the flesh of Jesus Christ, the Son of God, who became afterwards of the seed of David and Abraham; and I desire to drink of God, namely His blood, which is incorruptible love and eternal life."[17]

Some fifty years later, Justin Martyr wrote that the eucharistic elements were not common bread or drink. Just as Jesus had been made flesh by the Word of God for our salvation, so the food that is blessed by "the prayer of His word, and from which our blood and flesh by transmutation are nourished, is the flesh and blood of that Jesus who was made flesh."[18]

Cyprian (200–258), to those who were substituting water for wine in the supper, said that the cup of the Lord was a representation of the

---

16. Roberts and Donaldson, "Didache," ch. 9, esp. v. 12.
17. Ign. *Rom.*
18. Martyr, "First Apology," §66.

blood of Christ.[19] At the same time, Origen (285–354) would speak of the Eucharist as a symbol of gratitude to God in bread and wine, seeming to recognize a distinction between what the elements represented and that actual reality—Jesus' risen body and blood.[20]

A Corrective to Gnosticism

It is important to remember that this was the time when the gnostic heresy was emerging in the church among Greek and Jewish Christians who doubted Jesus' true humanity.[21] Notice then, the early theologians' use of the word "flesh" rather than "body" in speaking of the elements. The Gnostics denied the incarnation. Greeks, who believed the created order corrupt, asked how the perfection of divinity could assume the corruption of humanity.

The Docetists agreed—Jesus only *appeared* to be human, when in fact he was totally spiritual.[22] All of this would drive the controversy that the new emperor, Constantine, feared would destroy his empire, and lead to his convening the council at Nicaea that produced the Nicene Creed. Go back to the original Nicene Creed on pages 42 and 43 of this chapter, and notice how much of it is an affirmation of Jesus' humanity as well as his divinity.

The theologians of the early church used their language to make the point that Jesus was truly human, with a body like those of all humans. But they also taught that once the bread and wine of the Eucharist were consecrated, they were what Jesus had identified them to be in that upper room meal—the body (flesh) and blood of Christ. But again, they were not defending a theory about how the bread and wine became Jesus' body and blood but using those familiar words from the liturgy to make the point of the truth and reality of Jesus' incarnation—he was both fully God and fully human.

Athanasius, who had been a driving force at Nicaea, insisting on the reality of the incarnation, seems almost prescient in taking a different tack, seeming to recognize the problems of considering the bread and

---

19. Cyprian, *Epistle 63*, §13.
20. Origen, *Cels.* 8.57.
21. Jesus was thought a spiritual emissary of a distant demiurge who created a corrupt world rather than the incarnation of God.
22. From the Greek *dokein*, meaning "to appear"

wine as Christ's body and blood in too literal a fashion. He wrote, "What He [Jesus] says is not fleshly but spiritual. For how many would the body suffice for eating, that it should become the food for the whole world? But for this reason, He made mention of the ascension of the Son of Man into heaven, in order that He might draw them away from the bodily notion, and that from henceforth they might learn that the aforesaid flesh was heavenly eating from above and spiritual food given by Him."[23]

Near the end of the fourth century, as the creed was in its final form, the Apostolic Constitutions instructed, "Let the bishop give the oblation,[24] saying, The body of Christ; and let him that receiveth say, Amen. And let the deacon take the cup; and when he give it say, The blood of Christ, the cup of life, and let him that drinketh say, Amen."[25]

By the fifth century, there was full affirmation that the bread and the wine were indeed what Jesus had said they were, becoming thus in the consecration by the words of Christ's institution of the meal spoken afresh in the communion prayer. Before the consecration, it was bread and wine; thereafter, it was his body and blood.

As to how the change took place, words were used like transelementation (Gregory, Bishop of Nyssa, d. 395) or transformation (John Chrysostom, d. 407). Augustine (d. 430), on the other hand, simply spoke of the consecrated bread of the Eucharist becoming the body of Christ, with no attempt to explain.[26] The question theologians have since wrestled with is, were they speaking of the bread and wine figuratively, symbolically, spiritually, or literally?

The Middle Ages—From Figurative to Literal

As time moved more deeply into the Middle Ages, the church became increasingly concerned with the metaphysics of the meal rather than its purpose, using words like transposing (Cyril of Alexandria, d. 444) or alteration (John of Damascus, d. c. 749). With the change in emphasis, a more literal or realistic understanding of Jesus' words became the

---

23. Athanasius, *Ep. fest.* 4.19. This is remarkably close to how John Calvin will resolve the issue with his eucharistic theory of "virtualism"—the Spirit lifts the faithful into Christ's risen presence, there to be fed by and on him.

24. The act of making a religious offering; here the consecrated bread of the Eucharist.

25. Donaldson, *Constitutions of Holy Apostles*, §2.13.

26. Augustine, "Sermon 272."

dominant issue, using the philosophy of the day, as always, to make the case.

Radbertus vs. Ratramnus

In the ninth century, a French abbot named Paschasius Radbertus wrote an instructional book for the monks of his abbey called *Concerning Christ's Body and Blood*. There, he argued for a "realistic" understanding, saying that the consecrated bread and wine in the Eucharist were the very same as Jesus' earthly body. Another monk from that same abbey, Ratramnus, disagreed with his abbot, arguing for a sacramental rather than a literal understanding of the bread and wine. Christ could be present in thousands of separate places at the same time because God makes him so through the sanctification of the bread and wine. However, with God having done that, the elements on the table and received were still seen and tasted as bread and wine.

Radbertus rejoined: the bread and wine were not merely symbols of Christ's body and blood but parts of the human body Christ occupied in Jesus on earth. Going one step further, the abbot added that once the priest had consecrated the bread and wine, they were nothing but Christ's body and blood.

Ratramnus disagreed, saying that the bread and wine, when consecrated, became Christ's spiritual body and blood with Christ "mystically present" in them. Thus began a debate in the Western church that would argue about real or symbolic, intrinsic or extrinsic presence, and lead to the concept of transubstantiation on one side and symbolism on the other.

Berengar of Tours

In the eleventh century, another French theologian, Berengar of Tours, who enjoyed a great reputation among bishops as a teacher, wrote a letter to the prior of an abbey in Normandy expressing regret that the prior embraced the realistic teaching of Radbertus. Berengar considered that "realistic" idea heretical. His letter opened a controversy that got Berengar excommunicated and his position on the sacrament condemned. And though under the pressure of excommunication, Berengar recanted, the controversy continued. Berengar was compelled in 1054 to a appear at a Council of Tours. There, he was forced to write a profession of faith confessing that after consecration the bread and wine were truly the body and blood of Christ. Notice that this was the same year that the great schism between East and West took place.

Though that statement satisfied the French bishops, it did not satisfy Berengar. He continued to speak out about what he viewed a wrong understanding of the consecrated bread and wine in the sacrament. As he did, he continued to gain opponents who soon became not only opponents but also, as so often happens in theology, his avowed enemies who won the day.

In 1078 Berengar was summoned to Rome, where his enemies forced upon him a formula that would later be called transubstantiation: "The bread and the wine that are placed on the altar are through the mystery of sacred prayer and the words of our Redeemer substantially changed into the true and proper life-giving flesh and blood of Jesus Christ our Lord; and that after the consecration is the true body of Christ."[27]

Transubstantiation Canonized

By now, the term *transubstantiation* was being used in the Western church to describe what was taking place with the bread and wine, but not without continuing controversy and detractors. That controversy was officially silenced in the Roman Catholic Church of the West when the Fourth Lateran Council of 1215 made transubstantiation the official dogma on the question.

The great schism between East and West had saved the East from the controversy, the Orthodox churches being content simply with the "change" (*metabole*) into Christ's body and blood as Jesus had named them, while discouraging any attempt to speculate about how this came to be. This continues to be the official stance of Orthodox churches today.

The Reformation

Martin Luther

As the Reformation unfolded, Martin Luther challenged the doctrine of transubstantiation but not his belief that the real presence of Christ took

---

27. Bradshaw and Johnson, *Eucharistic Liturgies*, 225.

place in the sacrament. Christ was present in the bread and wine because of the elements' *sacramental union* with Christ. And though it is common today for most to speak of his thinking about this as consubstantiation—the substance of the bread and wine coexisting with the body and blood of Christ—that is not an accurate description of what Luther meant.

For Luther, the body and blood of Christ are present to the communicant "in, with, and under" the elements of bread and wine because of their sacramental union with Christ. What Christ said instituting the supper had to be taken at face value. Like a person's last will and testament, they could not be changed after a person died. God's word clearly teaches that the bread and wine in the sacrament are a communion or participation in the body and blood of Christ. Yet, God's word also clearly teaches that those who misuse this sacrament, sin not against the bread and wine but against Christ's body and blood.[28] Thus, the two are united sacramentally, not physically.

Huldrych Zwingli

Luther's view of Christ's real presence via sacramental union was challenged by Swiss Reformer Huldrych Zwingli, for whom the bread and wine were only signs symbolic of Jesus body and blood, but nothing more. The meal was merely a devotional meal commemorating Jesus' death, through which Christ had an influence on the participant's soul, but not by virtue of his bodily presence in the bread and wine.

A former priest, Zwingli became a Reformed pastor and military chaplain in the north of Switzerland. He was killed in battle in 1531, keeping him from being a further participant in the Reformation dialogue about the Supper. However, his notion of symbolic presence—or more clearly, Christ's *bodily absence* in the supper—continues to dominate a portion of the church to this day, primarily, but not exclusively, the non-sacramental ones.

John Calvin

This question of Christ's presence in the supper continued to be debated between Lutheran and Reformed Christians, but now it was the second-generation reformer John Calvin who said no to Zwingli's position,

---

28. Luther, *Small Catechism*, q. 287–88.

writing that Jesus said "*ist*," not "*representare*"—"this *is* my body," not "this *represents* my body." Yet, wanting to insist on Christ's presence beside his Father in heaven—there as our advocate and pledge that the faithful would one day stand by him in God's presence—Calvin rejected any notion of Christ being physically present anywhere but in heaven, and certainly not on the altar table because of a priest's consecration.

For Calvin, in a manner akin to Athanasius in the fourth century, as the faithful gather at table and consume the consecrated elements of bread and wine, the Holy Spirit lifts them into Christ's risen presence, there to be fed by and on him. It was a theory that became known as virtualism—by virtue of the Spirit.

One wonders what would have come to be in Lutheran and Reformed circles had Zwingli lived to be able to join in the further correspondence on the subject between Luther and Calvin. At the end of the day, though, Luther and Calvin never met but only read one another's writings. Luther could acknowledge that he and Calvin were talking about the same thing but simply using different language to attempt to describe it.

Repeating Christ's Sacrifice?

Behind the Reformers' concern with the manner of Christ's presence in the elements of the supper was the question of whether the enactment of the supper was an altogether new sacrifice of Jesus' body. Was it being offered to the Father by the church in the Mass, or was it a commemoration of Jesus' once and for all self-offering on Calvary? This too was a question that divided the reformers from Rome and drove the arguments about how Christ was present in the meal. In addition, by now, for both sides, sacrifice was thought of less in terms of an offering made to God than in terms of deprivation, punishment, and payment for humanity's sin.

The English Reformation

King Henry VIII of England, by a series of parliamentary acts, finally broke away from the Church of Rome in 1534, to form the Church of England. Though officially a Protestant church, it kept much of the Catholic Church's doctrine, causing its members to this day to be known as Anglo-Catholics. This preservation included the doctrine of transubstantiation, including the provision of the death penalty for any who denied it.

Some thirty years later when Elizabeth I assumed the throne and firmly established the Church of England as Protestant, Cranmer's Thirty-Nine Articles of Faith gained influence until they were ultimately adopted. Article Twenty-Eight, "Of the Lord's Supper," in its second paragraph declares, "Transubstantiation (or the change of the substance of Bread and Wine) in the Supper of the Lord, cannot be proved by holy Writ; but is repugnant to the plain words of Scripture, overthroweth the nature of a Sacrament, and hath given occasion to many superstitions."[29]

The various national Anglican churches that subsequently emerged out of the Church of England have prided themselves on what is called a theology of *via media*, a hybrid between the Lutheranism and Calvinism of the sixteenth century, making space for a broad spectrum of positions on various questions, often using the language of transubstantiation, symbolism, and virtualism within the same eucharistic prayers.[30] In the nineteenth century this came to be understood as a middle way between the extremes of Catholicism and Calvinism. Today, the question of Christ's presence in the Eucharist is answered by Anglicans saying Christ is present in the consecrated bread and wine, by the Spirit, but how that comes to be is carefully not defined.

Rome's Counter-Reformation—Trent

The Protestant Reformation was met by the Roman Catholic Church with its Counter-Reformation, solidified at the Council of Trent held between 1545 and 1563. In matters of the supper, the Council reaffirmed the Fourth Lateran Council and declared the doctrine of transubstantiation a dogma of faith: "By the consecration of the bread and wine there takes place a change of the whole substance of the bread into the substance of the body of Christ our Lord and of the whole substance of the wine into the substance of his blood. This change, the holy Catholic Church has fittingly and properly called Transubstantiation."

It was Rome's way of safeguarding Christ's presence as true, while at the same time confessing that there was no change in the empirical appearance of the bread and wine. However, rather than impose the

---

29. *Book of Common Prayer*, 873.
30. Holy Eucharist I, in Episcopal Church, *Book of Common Prayer*, 333–40.

Aristotelian theory of "accidents" and "substance" that had emerged under the philosophy that undergirds the theology of St. Thomas Aquinas, Trent used the term *species*, meaning "appearances." To appearances it was bread and wine, but to the eyes of faith it was truly the substance of Christ's body and blood.

Trent's definition remained Rome's position until the Second Vatican Council (1962–1965) where its position on transubstantiation was slightly modified and restated in the *Catechism of the Catholic Church* and the *Compendium of the Catechism of the Catholic Church*. The latter asked, "What is the meaning of *transubstantiation?*" It answers, "*Transubstantiation* means the change of the whole substance of bread into the substance of the Body of Christ and of the whole substance of wine into the substance of his Blood. This change is brought about in the eucharistic prayer through the efficacy of the word of Christ and by the action of the Holy Spirit. However, the outward characteristics of bread and wine, that is, the 'eucharistic species,' remain unaltered."[31]

Sacramental Protestantism

The last one hundred years in the classic churches of the Reformation have been a time of liturgical renewal, especially since the Second Vatican Council did so much to lower barriers to communication, understanding, and cooperation—if not full communion. Alongside Vatican II was the work of the Protestant World Council of Churches (WCC) and its Faith and Order Commission. The WCC began its work in Lausanne in 1927. Following Vatican II, the Faith and Order Commission met at Accra (1974) and Bangalore (1978), and came to completion in Lima (1982).

Seeking to leave behind the hostilities and misunderstandings of the past, the WCC reemphasized its mission "to proclaim the oneness of the Church of Jesus Christ and to call the churches to the goal of visible unity in one faith and one eucharistic fellowship, expressed in worship and common life in Christ, in order that the world might believe."[32] In pursuit of this goal, the WCC's Faith and Order Commission included a steering group on the two sacraments and the nature of Christian ministry.

The group reached back to capture the work of Lausanne in 1927, while being post-Vatican II, and continued its work in Accra and

---

31. "Compendium of the Catechism," §283.
32. World Council of Churches, *Baptism, Eucharist and Ministry*, v.

Bangalore. It fashioned a document that might lead to ecumenical consensus. But such ecumenical consensus could not be achieved. Short of that consensus, the commission, meeting in Lima, Peru, in 1982, presented its document *Baptism, Eucharist and Ministry*, which was then adopted by the WCC. *BEM*, as it is popularly known, explores the growing agreement and the remaining differences in the fundamental areas of the church's faith and life.

Baptism, Eucharist and Ministry

In its preface the World Council of Churches commission writes:

> This Lima text represents the significant theological convergence which Faith and Order has discerned and formulated. Those who know how widely the churches have differed in doctrine and practice on baptism, eucharist and ministry, will appreciate the importance of the large measure of agreement registered here. Virtually all the confessional traditions are included in the Commission's membership. That theologians of such widely different traditions should be able to speak so harmoniously about baptism, eucharist and ministry is unprecedented in the modern ecumenical movement. Particularly noteworthy is the fact that the Commission also includes among its full members theologians of the Roman Catholic and other churches which do not belong to the World Council of Churches itself.[33]

It is that "significant theological convergence" that has continued to take place since *BEM* that has informed the sacramental theology that is being employed here as we seek to understand atonement theology in the first quarter of the twenty-first century. For there is, among those who study the worship of the church, a recognition of differences as a matter of history, culture, and language, as opposed to differences as a matter of contemporary biblical and sacramental theology.

There is also the recognition that the longer we probe the questions, the more we find ourselves saying much the same thing, though with different language. To that end, Roman Catholic, Lutheran, Reformed, Anglican, and many Orthodox find themselves sharing fundamental understandings and convictions about baptism and Eucharist as we seek to embrace our oneness in Christ today.

---

33. World Council of Churches, *Baptism, Eucharist and Ministry*, vii. This work included representatives from the Orthodox churches.

Free Church Evangelical Protestantism

In the world of Free Church Evangelical Protestantism, the theology of Zwingli prevails, save for a few churches whose theology is grounded in the work of John Calvin. The Zwinglian notion of sign, symbol, and devotional practice dominate that free church world. Baptism is a rite by which believers profess their faith and offer commitment and devotion. Bread and wine, usually the "unfermented wine" of grape juice, are signs and symbols that are means for remembering what Christ did for sinners—devotional and subjective, rather than objective and transactional.

Pentecostalism

In Pentecostalism—the one truly unique church movement to emerge out of the twentieth century—the focus on the work of the Spirit in life is most experienced subjectively in what is called "the baptism of the Holy Spirit." It is a moment in which the Spirit is manifest in a person through various displays of the Spirit's presence, the sine qua non being prophesying and speaking in tongues—the two manifestations of the Spirit's presence in the churches of Paul's day.

Prophesying takes place in corporate worship as one speaks out, often in tongues, followed by an interpreter speaking (translating) the prophecy into the vernacular. Speaking in tongues, commonly known as glossolalia—the more common phenomena—takes place both in corporate and personal worship and is a gift for personal edification and spiritual nurture.

For Pentecostals, baptism and the supper are ordinances to be kept because Jesus commanded them. The real sacramental moment in the life of Pentecostals is the baptism of the Holy Spirit as it manifests itself in tongues and other subsequent displays.

Eastern Orthodox

Finally, let us briefly look at the Orthodox Churches of the East, which, because of the great schism of the eleventh century, were spared the influences that effected the churches of the West. For the Orthodox, the Holy Eucharist, as it is named, is "the sacrament of sacraments," also known as the "sacrament of the church." It is the center of the church's life of thanksgiving—thus Eucharist, coming from the Greek word *eucharisto* for "to give thanks."

It is also known as Holy Communion. In it, a mystical union between God and the baptized community comes about. In the meal, through Christ and the Holy Spirit, believers are joined and made one with the Triune God and one another, one with all who are in Christ, and one with all people and things in Christ.

The Eucharist is the main liturgy of the Orthodox churches and is celebrated each Lord's Day as well as on special days of commemoration (feast days). In monasteries it is celebrated daily, while in churches it is usually reserved for the Sunday liturgy. The Eucharist is given to all members of the church, including infants who have been baptized and confirmed—the latter taking place as a part of the baptismal liturgy. In it, Orthodox Christians understand themselves to be receiving the true body and blood of Christ who is real and present to and in them mystically in and through the bread and wine that is offered to God in Christ's name and consecrated by the Spirit.

Though much of the history of eucharistic theology in later Western church was developed to explain how this can be, the Orthodox see that emphasis and theological debate as unfortunate. It has led to what is *real* becoming symbolic, mystical, intellectual, or psychological symbols. Bread and wine become things through which the gathered are called on to "think about Jesus" or "commune with him in their hearts," rather than totally giving themselves over to be united with God in worship through the Eucharist and the transformation that promises.

Eucharistic Commonality in the Twenty-First Century

Despite the various philosophic and cultural differences across the church over the last two thousand years, there remains an astounding unity of conviction about the Lord's Supper. First, we do it because Christ commanded it of his faithful as a means of being fed by and on him as the bread of life for the life of faith. In it, he is again sealing the forgiveness of sins God offers to the world in Christ.

To drink the cup of salvation is to participate in what it promises. It is a means of nourishment for the faithful as we continue our journeys of discipleship, with their difficulties, challenges, and triumphs. It is a source of consolation in our failures. More, it is God's means of nurturing us with Christ and maturing us into Christ, as St. Paul said, "from one degree of glory to another," until we reach the very fullness of Christ himself (2 Cor 3:13). We will return to this in chapter 13 when we explore "Growing in Christ."

The West calls this *sanctification*—being made holy. The East calls it *theosis*—being filled with the presence of God until we become the godly ones we were created to be. It is atonement realized and actualized—how we know our at-one-ment with Christ, and through Christ, by the Holy Spirit, our at-one-ment with the Triune God.

Irenaeus and Athanasius said God became one with us in Christ so that we can become one with God in him.[34] It was their way of understanding God's action to put right what went wrong in God's good creation, especially as the biblical writers portray it in Genesis—what went wrong, why humanity could not fix it, and what God did about that to redeem and restore creation.

Why was it Jesus died? It is to that story that we now turn.

---

34. Athanasius, *De Incarnatione*, 269. More precisely, Athanasius said, "For he [the Word of God] became man that we might become divine."

Chapter 4

Why We Need Atonement—The Problem

A TWENTY-FIRST CENTURY ANSWER to the question of why Jesus had to die leads us into a breadth of subjects and questions that must first be incorporated and addressed. These questions are about creation, good and evil, freedom to choose, failure, sin, what sin is, where it comes from, and who is responsible for it. Interestingly, many of those foundational questions are embedded within the first eleven chapters of the book of Genesis, so named for its opening word, *bereshit*. It means "in the beginning."

When the Hebrew Scriptures were translated into the Greek Septuagint (LXX), rather than use the Greek word for beginning (*arche*), they chose *genesis*. *Genesis* means "origin" and is the word that appears in LXX at Gen 2:4a. Today many English translations render it "generations" or "the account." Either way, we are reading what biblical scholars call the "prehistory" or the prehistoric portion of the Bible, dealing with the questions that lie at our beginning and origins, answered through the telling of mythological stories.

A word about myth: as it is used here, myth is not a falsehood or untruth. Myth is a truth told through a fictitious story to tell a truth about life. One of my seminary professors used to tell us that in the Bible, myth is used to help us understand what is "too true" simply to be described by prose. The Bible begins with two such mythological accounts of creation—only two of the many that appear across the pages of the Bible.[1]

---

1. The others are found in Job 26, 28, 38; Pss 8, 19, 33, 89, 102, 104; Prov 8; Jer 4, 10; Isa 11, 28, 40, 45; Hos 2; John 1, and Rev 2.

The Biblical Story of Creation—Two Versions

Genesis 1

The Bible opens with a priestly version,[2] probably written after the return from exile in Babylon between 539 and 450 BCE, telling us about the world's origin and beginning. Again and again, it tells us how good God made things. Out of a formless void covered in darkness and water, God speaks, and all things come into being: light, the heavens, earth, vegetation, sun, moon, stars, swarming creatures in the sea, and birds in the air. All of this is good.

At the zenith of this creative extravaganza, God says to those surrounding God in the heavenly court, "Let us make humankind in our image, according to our likeness, and let them have dominion" over all of this (Gen 1:25–26). God creates humanity in God's image. Male and female, God creates them and blesses them. Then God commissions them, saying, "Be fruitful, multiply, fill, and subdue the earth, and have dominion over the fish of the sea and over the birds of the air and over every living thing that moves upon the earth" (Gen 1:28b).

Notice that this is not the "Adam" and "Eve" that appear in the next creation story—the older of the two. This more recent priestly version has left them out. Here, humankind is the zenith of God's creation with the plants and fruit of the trees being given as food for all that creep upon the earth. Yet only humanity is made in God's likeness and image, what theologians call the *imago Dei*.

Imago Dei does not mean that humans look like God, though the earliest understandings of the term probably thought so, given how unique humankind is within the realm of creation. It surely meant and continues to mean that people are God's representatives in the world and to all else that God created—especially to one another. As such, they are to care for creation as God cares for them. Thus, they are given power and freedom to share, be gracious and cooperative, explore, create, and bear responsibility. These special divine gifts are created for purposeful tasks. Those include being creation's caretakers on behalf of God, sharing in God's rule over creation, and being God's co-creators. Herein lie humanity's ability to explore the created order and its power to fashion beauty, as well as to bring forth new and useful things out of the earth.

---

2. The Hebrew Bible has been through several editorial revisions, and the latest was by the priesthood following Israel's return from exile.

There is, however, a more important understanding of this unique divine gift to humanity that is far more profound than physical or representational. We might call it humanity's *spiritual capacity*. More explicitly still, created in God's likeness and image, humanity has been given the capacity for a unique relationship with God—a role given to no other creature in creation. It is to humankind, and to them alone, that God speaks, interacts, and promises. Consequently, humans are the only ones in creation who can speak for God or speak on God's behalf.

Other portions of creation can witness to a Creator and its divine order, but only humans have the capacity to reveal something about who and what God is. Because they can freely enter friendship, fellowship, communion, and communication with God as God has purposefully designed them to be, they are the ones ordained to speak to and for God.

On the sixth day of creation, God pronounces it all "Very good!" (*meod tob*)—God's creative project is now complete. On the seventh day, in good priestly fashion, God observes the Sabbath—God rests. There is not one negative word in this entire story. And though the creation is permeated with God's goodness and bears God's fingerprints, the creation is not God. Rather, it is all God's handiwork (Ps 19:1).

What Genesis 1 Tells Us

What truths does this story suggest? First, creation was not a cosmic accident; it is intentional. The Big Bang may have been the method God chose but is not its *source*. Cosmologists and physicists can tell us about what happened thereafter, but getting behind that last nanosecond prior to the Big Bang, and to its source, is the task of theologians.

Second, the story tells us that creation has a divine order, is good, has balance and life. In addition, it is fertile, bringing forth life in abundance with purpose. Its vegetation is not coincidental—it is given to support all life. Everyone and thing here is vegetarian, as there is no death within this new realm—all is verdant life. Women and men are an integral part of creation, not above it, but of the same stuff. God gives them responsibility for populating the earth, filling it, subduing it, and having dominion over all that is upon it. They are blessed to do so; they will realize that blessing as they do.

Finally, whether God formed creation by bringing order out of the formless void and its chaos, as most ancient Near Eastern creation stories tell in their own creation myths, or whether God created even that formless, watery void out of nothing and then brought it into further existence—as much of Christian theological tradition has maintained—it really does not matter. As the psalmist said long before this account was written, "By the word of the Lord the heavens were made, and all their hosts by the breath of God's mouth" (Ps 33:6). The point is this: creation is not an extension of God's being. God is God, and creation is creation. "For [God] spoke, and it came to be; [God] commanded, and it stood firm" (Ps 33:9).

Genesis 2

The second version in Gen 2 is the older of the two and extends into chapter 3. It is the creation story told by those in ancient Israel who named God Lord, the synonym for the four Hebrew consonants that form the name God gave to Moses at the burning bush—YHWH (Exod 3:13–15). It was written about 950 BCE, during the reign of Kings David and Solomon.

> In the day the Lord God made the earth and the heavens, no plant or herb had yet sprung up—for the Lord God had not yet caused it to rain and there was no one to till the ground, but a stream would rise from the earth, and water the whole face of the ground—then the Lord God formed a man from the dust of the ground, and breathed into his nostrils the breath of life; and the man became a living being. (Gen 2:4b–6)

Here, the order of creation is reversed. God forms a creature from the dust of the earth—*adam*, the name of the clay—and fashions that clay into a male figure of the same name. God then breathes into the figure the breath of life, transforming lifeless clay into a living being. The man comes from the earth but receives his breath from God. Linked to the soil for sustenance, he is also linked to God for his every breath.

God creates a home for the man, plants a garden in Eden—the root meaning of Eden is "fertility"—and places the newly created man within it. With Adam watching, the Lord brings forth the rest of creation as a gift to him. Out of the ground God causes to grow every tree pleasant to sight and good for food. The Lord God places the man in the garden of Eden to till and keep it.

Among all the trees are two special ones that God has placed in the middle of the garden. The first is named the tree of life—its fruit when eaten produces life. We will later learn that the life it produces is endless. The second tree is "the tree of the knowledge of good and evil." Its fruit produces knowledge, both good and bad. Here is the first time the word bad or evil (*ra*) appears. But with that, God issues this warning: all in the garden is for the man, all except one thing: the fruit from the tree of the knowledge of good and evil. "In the day that he eats of that tree he shall die" (Gen 2:17).

Until now, all has been good and without limitation. And, of course, the lack of limitation also suggests freedom—Adam is free to choose. But mention of this tree introduces two new dimensions to the story. The first is constraint. Until now, all in the garden was for the man. The second new thing is the idea of something opposed to good: evil. With that warning observed, all is still good in the garden of paradise, save one thing. "It is not good that the man should be alone" (Gen 2:18).

God determines to make the man a "helpmate" as his partner. Notice the seeming simplicity the biblical storyteller utilizes to make some particularly important points. God goes back to the earth for material to fashion the various potential helpmates—all of them come from the earth, like the man—the animals of the field and the birds of the air. God brings them to the man, who names them—a sign and act of the man's authority over them. But even in this extravagance of creativity, no creature is found fit to be man's helpmate—his partner.

Finally, God causes an anesthetizing deep sleep to fall upon the man, and in an act of divine surgery—this is a story, after all!—takes a portion of the man of the earth to form a partner. Is the portion a rib or side?—*tsela* can mean either.[3] With that side, the Lord brings forth a new human being, one made of the same "stuff" as Adam, but different. Not only is she made *from* the other and *for* the other, but they are made *for one another*—designed to help one another in so many ways. This is not simply the man's helpmate; this is his other half—a full partner. She is the

---

3. The same word appears in Exod 25:12–14 to describe the sides of the ark of the covenant and in 1 Kgs 6:15 to describe the sides or ribs of the temple walls. My former parishioner, colleague, and friend, Dr. George Landes, of blessed memory, who was professor of Hebrew and cognate languages at Union Theological Seminary in New York, insisted that here in Genesis, "side" was much a better translation than "rib" and far more in keeping with the spirit of the author. And when asked "Which side?," George slyly replied, with a slight grin, "Well, which is the same and which will be different—the front or the back?"

only one who can help take away what is not good about the man being alone. And, though the man has been in God's presence from the beginning, not even that has been enough to take away his aloneness.

Adam's response makes exactly that point. God has finally gotten it right; high fives all around! She is bone of his bone and flesh of his flesh. She shall be called woman, for she has been taken not out of the clay of the earth but out of man himself. She is not his subordinate over whom he is to have dominion but made of the very same stuff he is. She is his partner and equal in all things. With that, the narrator adds this word: it is for this reason that "a man leaves his father and mother and clings to his wife, and they become one flesh" (Gen 2:24). This union is not simply in the sexual sense. They are to be one in all they were created to be and do.

We are told, almost as an afterthought, that both are naked and were not ashamed. Here, nakedness is both literal and metaphorical. Not only is this the power of oneness that spouses know in their intimacy as well as in the routines of working together, but it also alerts us to the fact that there is nothing in all this that would hint of anything inherently wrong with either of them. There is no reason for anything but the joy of unity, partnership, and fellowship, and enjoying the blessings of the good creation. All of this is as good, as was the case in the first story.

Both creation accounts tell us of what later will be spoken of as the bliss of paradise.[4] The garden has been planted with all that is needed for life. All the creatures in it have their place and purpose, and there is peace among and between them all. Every green thing in the garden is theirs for their food, even the tree of life. From it they may take its fruit, eat, and live.

What Went Wrong and Why?

Even paradise has its limits if it is to remain paradise. In this case it is the fruit of the tree of the knowledge of good and evil that has limits. If those limits are not respected, they will bring forth some things that do not yet exist. The most obvious has already been announced—death. Therefore, that tree's fruit, and only it, is off limits to them. But whether it is the lure of that prohibition—for who of us likes to be told we cannot do something—or questions of what may lie behind God's exclusion of

---

4. What theologians call the *prelapsarian* period of human life—before the fall.

this particular tree's fruit, the temptation is simply more than the two can abide. It is much too fascinating for them to leave alone.

Genesis 3

Enter the serpent! We are told that the serpent was more "crafty" and "shrewd" than any other wild animal that the Lord God had made. But notice, first and foremost, the serpent is a creature like them—a wild one, to be sure—but nothing more nor less. That the serpent will later be associated with Satan, or equated with the devil as a source of evil, is a history we will later investigate and how and why that came to be. Here, the serpent is simply that—one of the creatures God made, one who fits within the order of creation. And though more crafty, shrewd, sensible, or prudent than any of the other *wild* creatures,[5] that is also true about the man and the woman. The serpent here has no unfair advantage over the couple.

Lest we miss the point the story is trying to make, this talking snake is not the personification of evil. It could be an ancient symbol of wisdom or the mystery of desire. Certainly, that is how others in the ancient Near East looked at serpents. In addition, it might well be our narrator warning about the potential for anything within God's good creation to draw us away from God as source, truth, and the only One worthy of our trust and worship. For that is precisely what happens here. The serpent in this story is almost a neutral observer.[6] It presents itself as interested in what God has said about this new place in which it also now finds itself, together with the man and the woman.

Many have called the serpent the first theologian; notice the first words out of its mouth: "Did God say?" Many a sermon has been preached on the dangers of asking for clarification of God's prohibitions, equivocating about them, or striving to twist them to conform to one's own desires. Here the serpent asks the woman an open-ended question about the trees in the garden.

On its face, the question seems less about a particular tree than simply a question designed to draw the couple into deeper conversation

---

5. The Hebrew *arom* can mean all of that and is also used to speak of humans. See Prov 12:16, 15:5.

6. Fretheim, "Genesis," 360.

about God and what God said to them.[7] "Did God say you shall not eat from *any* tree in the garden?" Notice it is a negative question, not only introducing the notion of prohibition but more, the nature of God's provision—can it be trusted? And notice that the serpent's question is one that cannot be answered with a simple yes or no. It demands expansion and explanation—things we theologians love to do!

Why the serpent asks the woman rather than Adam is a curiosity, as both are present. Yet, she was not there when the Lord issued the prohibition. Perhaps that is the reason the serpent chooses her. Yet, she knows the answer and seems eager to correct the serpent's false assertion that none of the trees are available for food. "We may eat of the fruit of the trees in the garden, but God said, 'You shall not eat of the fruit of the tree that is in the middle of the garden, nor shall you touch it, or you shall die'" (Gen 3:2–3). Wait; she has said too much; much more than God said. Any attorney will tell you that saying anything more than yes or no in a deposition always leads to trouble.

Offering more than is asked for always leads to danger, especially when the one asking the question is "crafty." Clearly, she has overstated the prohibition. God said nothing about touching the tree—either doing so or not—only not eating its fruit. Adam has clearly passed on the prohibition correctly, at least to that point. Is he the one who said too much, and she is only repeating what she heard from him? What has caused this new dynamic about God's prohibition? Anxiety, confusion, defensiveness, even hyperbole now lie beneath this conversation. Is that what comes from pondering what those words "you shall die" might actually mean?[8]

No matter, crafty as it is, the serpent opportunistically uses the man and woman's curiosity to excite their desire by telling them a double lie. Though God has told them that to eat of its fruit means death, the serpent insists they will not die. Rather, God knows that if they eat of its fruit their eyes will be opened, and they will be *like* God, "knowing good and evil" (Gen 3:1–5).[9] The serpent's clear implication is that God is jealous of this divine prerogative and that divine jealousy alone lies behind God's

---

7. "You" in the text is plural; Adam is listening in!

8. Fretheim, "Genesis," 360.

9. This is a definition of divine wisdom. One of my seminary professors, Diogenes Allen, regularly pointed to this verse to remind us that God is the only one wise enough to know good from evil and, therefore, the only one who can manage both for God's good purposes. See Gen 50:20.

prohibition. The question has nothing to do with divine providence, protection, and managing evil on their behalf. What it does is raise the question of whether this God can be trusted. Do they want to obey this God?

"So, when the woman saw ... that the tree was desirable to make one wise, she took from its fruit and ate; and she gave also to her husband" (Gen 3:6). Their eyes are opened. At least the serpent did not lie about that. But now they know something heretofore they did not—they are naked. But more, they know something else entirely new—shame! They rush to clothe themselves, to paste on fig-leaf loin cloths. Later, when they hear the sound of the Lord walking in the garden, they go into hiding.

Something has gone wrong—very wrong—and they know it. The former blissful communion they had known with one another is gone; it will soon turn to mutual accusation and blame. In the place of their bliss, new emotions appear: anxiety, confusion, and fear. Too soon, that turns to blame as they turn on one another, each attempting to fault the other while trying to escape the guilt of their own actions. But this story is about more than the two of them. Their actions have now begun to reverberate throughout creation, most openly manifest in what will take place in the following eight chapters.

A Not So Simple Tale

So much is going on here; clearly, there is nothing simple about this mythological story! First, we are told what it means to be "like God"—to have one's eyes opened and to know good and evil. Remember, here, the word know is *yada*—the Hebrew verb that runs the gambit of meaning from "be informed, understand, get, acquainted, aware, experience, discern, realize, to have sexual relations, to be intimate friends," and so on.[10] Here, it initially seems to mean what we call knowledge, information that she presumed would make her wise; at least, that is what the storyteller suggests. Is that what is at issue—wisdom? If so, from the broader perspective of Scripture, this seems less a prohibition against the couple having wisdom than it is a warning about how true wisdom is to be acquired in this world.

"The fear of the LORD is the beginning of wisdom," say both the psalmist and the wisdom writers (Ps 111:10; Prov 1:7; 4:11; 9:10; 15:33;

---

10. Bible Hub, "3045. Yada."

Wis 6:17; Sir 1:14).[11] The word rendered "fear" (*yirah*) means to stand in awe, respect, honor, and obedience to what is given. It does not mean dread, to be afraid, panic, fright, anxiety, misgiving, or any of the negatives that are too often associated with that word today. So, the first thing we might say is that wisdom was being sought in the wrong place and in the wrong way. It had already been given in the initial prohibition by the One they are to honor, respect, obey, listen to, and hold in awe. But all of that had been set aside by their desire to be like God—to be God's equal—one free to ignore God and God's word.

Notice what the serpent said about "being like God"—not only are their eyes opened to see realities of good and evil, but the two will soon learn something more: though "like" God, they are not God! Being like God is not being God. Only God can truly distinguish between good and evil, as well as manage them productively. When Genesis comes to its conclusion, it is clear that matters in this world are not always what they seem (Gen 50:20). What initially appears bad can turn out to be good, while what seems good to our eyes can often lead us into evil, just as the narrator of the story is telling us here.

The one telling the truth in this exchange with the serpent is the serpent—that they will know both good and evil. But time and again, they will get them confused and make the wrong choice. It seems God is the only One able to manage such knowledge in ways that are productive and life-giving.

Death and Dying

Why did the Lord tell them that from the day they ate of the fruit of the tree of the knowledge of good and evil they would surely die? They have eaten the fruit but have not yet died? Did God lie to them or, if not lie, fail to tell them the whole truth? Or might it be that this is a long-term death sentence that will take time to unfold? Either way, God clearly warned them of what would come of their disobedience.

Was the serpent suggesting God has ulterior motives in not telling them the full truth? If so, what might those be? Is there something God does not want them to know that the serpent knows? Or is it simply that in their infancy, they could not understand the whole truth if told it?

---

11. In Proverbs, wisdom is personified as Lady Wisdom, the first of God's creations, (Prov 8:22–36), insisting that it begins with listening, seeking insight, and prizing her.

Would the truth be so beyond them that all God could do is say no? Was God being a parent, preserving these newborn infants from dangers they could not otherwise perceive, issuing a prohibition, and sealing it with a terminal threat? It seems so.

Two other observations: first, God said nothing to them about being "like God." Those were the serpent's words. And nothing was said by either God or the serpent about being "made wise." These are the narrator's words ascribing motivation to the woman. The couple's *desire* was to be made wise, to be made like God. What is it the narrator is trying to tell us about the role of desire in all of this?

Desire—In What We Take Pleasure

What drives the couple's choice is desire—at least, that is what the narrator tells us. They seem to think the fruit will give them pleasure. Whether it was to be like God, to be made wise, or simply to be free to make their own choices, what drove them was the compulsion of desire. That is precisely what the fourth-century theologian Athanasius labeled this—the compulsion of desire.[12] For him as an ascetic monk, it was the sensual desires of carnality: food, drink, sex, bodily pleasure. For our day, desire may well include those that Athanasius named. However, today, there is a much wider universe of things we desire with compulsion: wealth, power, fame, security, and for some, even escape—all driven by desire.

When these things become the focus of our desire, they can be equally compulsive and corrosive. Our desire for things other than God leads us to allow them to displace God. When we do that, we give to them what rightly belongs only to God—awe, respect, honor, trust, and obedience—our worship. That not only violates God's first and second commandment of no other gods and no idols (Exod 20:3–6), it releases in those things a power the Bible calls evil. The couple now know both good and evil as well as its confusions. No wonder they go into hiding, filled with shame and feeling guilty.

Freedom?

Nothing here has been said about freedom and the problems associated with its misuse. Too often, when considering the outcomes in this story,

---

12. Athanasius, *Contra Gentes*, 9–13.

the objection is raised, "Why did God give us freedom in the first place if it is going to lead to this?" The implication in the objection is that all of this is God's fault from beginning to end. Without freedom, none of this would have happened. So too for God's culpability in creating the snake—why did God do that? We shall consider these questions in a bit. For now, notice there has been no compulsion here, no coercion on the serpent's part. It did not make the couple do anything. As for being "crafty," remember that it was the most subtle of the *wild animals*, but not more so than the man and the woman. They were equally equipped with craftiness. All the serpent did was ask a question about God, God's word, and God's trustworthiness. What drove the primordial couple to disobedience was the compulsion of their desire.

The Fall?

Some have spoken of this as *the fall*, as though it were an actual moment in real rather than demythologized time—"the original sin" that was passed on to all humanity that followed from them. Others, more in keeping with the framework of mythological prehistory, can speak of it as a fall from innocence—"the serpent tricked me" (Gen 3:13)! Others can name it "the sin at our origins." Whatever it is, God did not create it. Rather, the storyteller suggests that this is what comes from the desire to be like God.

In such moments, sin powerfully emerges in life. The story also reminds us that whenever we attempt to be more than we were created to be—our own gods, sovereigns, or masters—we fall short of who we were created to be. We overreach, with acts of disobedience, and miss the mark. Each of these is an expression of what the Bible calls sin.

There is yet another biblical definition for sin—separation. Sin separates us from God, the source and sustainer of life, and we begin to die. Sin separates us from one another, and our relationships begin to die. And the most telling manifestation of sin in the twenty-first century—it separates us from ourselves! Today, this separation from ourselves fuels psychiatric care and counseling practices, the self-help industry, and many a self-proclaimed guru. It leads many to attempt escape through cults, alcohol, cocaine, opioids, or, more tragic still, the ultimate escape of suicide. Those who think sin is old-fashioned, not real, a religious "hangover," or something that no longer exists, are being as naïve and misled as our primordial parents in this ancient story.

Why the Snake amid the Gift of Freedom?

Why the snake? More fundamentally still, why freedom, especially if freedom could enable the couple to be disobedient? First, we recall that behind this lies the familiar suggestion that God is somehow culpable in all of this and responsible for what went wrong. Why did God create the man and woman with the freedom to choose and the serpent with such craftiness? Did God create evil? Another version of this line of thinking is the question "If God is good, why does evil exist?" It is what philosophers and theologians call the theodicy question. If God and God's creation are good, why evil, and from where does evil come? If God did not create it, why does God permit it?

First, why the serpent? Earlier we said the serpent is not a symbol for the source of evil. Nor is it ever spoken of as being coercive or controlling of those around it—much less evil. The serpent is simply one of God's wild creatures, fashioned out of the dust of the earth, like all the other wild creatures. It is neither human nor divine. In fact, in the story, the serpent has no power over anyone save itself. It is in many ways quite neutral in the dialogue, simply asking questions. Rather than being out to seduce the couple or force them to rebel against God—neither of which the serpent does—the snake seems to be one whose purpose is to move the story forward by testing the couple's intention and integrity, to see what they will do with their lives, their freedom, and the gift of creation.[13]

It is a trickster. It lied to the couple, and they fell for it. That could well be the reason for God's punishment of it with a double curse. First, it, among all the wild animals, must go all its days on its belly, eating dust—an act of humiliation. Second, there will be great enmity between the serpent and the woman, its offspring and hers. They will strike at its head, while its offspring, confined to the ground, will be able to strike only at their heels. Clearly, humanity will have the advantage.[14]

Those Christian traditions over the centuries that have equated the serpent with the devil have interpreted this cursing text messianically. They see from the woman's "seed" the promise of a messiah-liberator who

13. Fretheim, "Genesis," 365.
14. Fretheim, "Genesis," 362–63.

will crush (*shuph*) the devil and destroy its power. This began as early as the second century, especially in those forms of atonement theology that saw the cross as first and foremost the defeat of the devil. This continues to be the case today for many conservative Christians.

More modern commentators point out, the word for seed here is a collective noun and more probably refers to Eve's immediate offspring Cain, Able, and Seth, rather than a far-distant messiah. However, it was certainly a useful text in an age that believed in the devil as the root and source of evil in the world, an evil the messiah would destroy. As for the verb bruise (*shuph*), it is used for both the serpent and the woman's offspring and may better be seen as witness to the endless bruising struggles humanity has had with temptation in its various forms. Regardless, it can be said, that in God's curse, humans clearly have the advantage in gaining mastery over the serpent. Bruising one's head is definitely more consequential than bruising one's heel.

Today, most biblical scholars equate the snake with "the satan" as he appears throughout the Hebrew Bible—the tempter. There, the satan is portrayed as a sort of heavenly quality control agent—doing its work on God's behalf. It appears when it entices David to take a census (1 Chr 21:1). It is the one who seeks God's permission to test Job (Job 1:9–12; 2:4–6). It is found standing before God with the prophet Zechariah, there as the prophet's accuser (Zech 3:1–3). All of this is in service to God's best interests. More will be said later about how the satan came, by the time of the New Testament's writing, to be equated with the devil. For now, let us return to the couple and what comes of their choices.

Sin—Whence and Whither?

The story tells us that sin has entered the world with profound consequences—evil and death—all because of the couple's disobedience. More tragic still, the couple cannot now undo it, impairing not only themselves but all who will follow them. And though the serpent in its craftiness did lie to them about not dying but being like God, they will know death, not just their own but death in all its forms.

As for being like God and knowing good and evil—yes, they will know both—that is, they will *experience* both.[15] But unlike God, they will not know what to do with evil or how to manage it. More damning still,

---

15. The foundational meaning of the Hebrew *yada*.

far too often they will find themselves unable to distinguish one from the other or confusing one for the other. They will make bad choices, mistaking evil for good and vice versa, thus explaining that same malady of confusion and bad choices that emerges among their descendants, for whom this story was written. Such is one of the powers of sin in the world.

Thus begins the long history of humanity's participation in evil under the guise of thinking they are pursuing good. In the fifth century, St. Augustine of Hippo saw it as humanity's self-imposed bondage to sin. The theme continued in the church through St. Thomas Aquinas, and at the Reformation became known in Lutheran and Calvinist churches as "total depravity." In 1775, Samuel Johnson commented on "the unhappy failure of pious resolves" when he was reported as saying, "Sir, hell is paved with good intentions."[16] By the next century, that had become a proverb that says "The road to hell is paved with good intentions."

Banned from Eden—Punishment or Providence?

This immediate episode of prehistory ends with God expelling the man and woman from paradise. This is, however, less an act of personal punishment than of divine providence. It is God's way of preserving the rest of creation. Given the couple's knowledge and their inability to use it wisely, as well as their propensity for doing evil while seeking to do good, they must be banished from paradise for creation's sake. They must be shut off from the tree of life, lest they eat of its fruit and perpetuate sin's chaos and death forever. The Lord drives them east of Eden and places a cherubim armed with flaming sword to guard the way to the tree of life (Gen 3:22–24). The Lord does so for the sake of the rest of creation.

Thus we have the breach between humankind and God that the Bible calls sin. From this point on, humanity will fall short[17]—short of who God created humanity to be, short of what God expects of them, and short of why God made them in God's likeness and image. Thus, the communion and fellowship God initially intended when making humankind in God's own image have been breached, marred, and shattered. They will remain so until God acts to enable them to be restored.

---

16. Boswell, "Life of Samuel Johnson."
17. *Chattath*—to miss (a goal or way), go wrong, fall short, sin.

Sin Is More Than Personal

This breach is not simply between humankind and God. By the next chapter, brother turns on brother with deadly violence. It is here that the word sin first appears in the story, when God names it such (Gen 4:7). Notice, sin is not so much Cain's act—though his action certainly was filled with sin—indeed, it was sin-full. But it was more. As the Bible describes it, *sin* is not simply an event in the past that harmed someone or something; it is a *power that contaminates and distorts life and finally destroys it*. Sin is now personified and understood as a force lurking at the door of everyone's life. It constantly seeks to distort and contaminate life as well as to overcome and enslave it, until sin's work is complete in death.

Even so, God tells them they must master and rule over it (Gen 4:7).[18] It will take eons of years for that to happen. Until then, the Hebrew Bible is filled with chapter after chapter of failure to do so. It portrays God continuing to meet self-acknowledged and penitent failure with compassion and forgiveness. Yet, it also promises the day when one will come as God's servant, who will master it and do so for all (Isa 42:1–4; 49:1–6; 50:4–9; 52:13—53:12).[19]

The Rest of the Story

As the primordial history of Gen 1 through 11 unfolds, the caustic power of sin prowls at the door of human lives, desirous of human complicity. It spreads repeatedly in the primeval story, regularly acting itself out in human life, until Gen 6 tells us that "the Lord saw that the wickedness [*ra*] of humanity was great on the earth . . . every inclination of the thoughts of their hearts was only evil continually" (Gen 6:5). The Lord was sorry and regretted making humankind on the earth, for all they did was grieve God to the heart (Gen 6:6).

The story continues; God ventures, through a flood and a righteous man named Noah and his family, to start over (Gen 6:1–7). Yet, no sooner is Noah back on dry land, tilling its goodness, than the destructive power of sin expresses itself once more, rupturing that family's relationship and moving beyond Noah's family into the nations. Finally, sin is so

---

18. Note, however, how long it will be until a human appears who can do so.

19. These are the four "servant songs" of Isaiah, interpreted by the church from the first century onward as referring to Jesus, his life, his ministry, his suffering, and his saving work.

comprehensive and humanity's desire to make a name for themselves so consuming, God must confuse the people's language to limit the capacity of what they can do. As the story tells it, different languages are God's built-in obstacle to control the unified violence that could emerge out of the human hubris, its disposition to wickedness and misguided attempts to be like God.

The next eight chapters of Genesis is the story of the power of sin unfolding in human life. It lies at our origins. Not only does it tempt us to take what is God's alone and make it our own, it entices us to give what rightfully belongs only to God to other things. Thus, we make them idols—false gods—which, when worshiped by us, turn demonic in lives.

If something is to be done about this, it must come from somewhere other than sinful humankind; it must be initiated from God's side of the relationship. Until something is done to deal with sin's ability to separate us from God, and us from ourselves—until reconciling atonement takes place—humanity will live trapped, searching for the dominion of life that only God can give and living under the dominion of death, which is both the power and the work of sin.

From Primordial History to God's Provision

Genesis brings all its primordial prehistory to a close in chapter 12. There, God attempts a new beginning. God appears to Abram and says,

> Go from your country and your kindred and your father's house to the land that I will show you. I will make of you a great nation, and I will bless you, and make your name great, so that you will be a blessing. I will bless those who bless you, and the one who curses you I will curse; and in you all the families of the earth shall be blessed. So, Abram went, as the LORD had told him. (Gen 12:1–4)

So begins the story of God's covenant with Abram, putting in place the promise of blessing that will emerge in God's good time through one of Abram's children. The story begins here and makes its way through the rest of the book of Genesis. Still, it remains a story of one failure after another. Sin is still at work wreaking havoc among God's people.

Abram takes things into his own hands more than once. Confusing evil for good, he and his wife Sarah try to force the promise, putting it at risk again and again. God responds, out of God's steadfast love and mercy, bringing blessing out of Abram and Sarah's failures.

Abram, now Abraham[20] and near the end of his life, finally has learned to trust God. When confronted with God's testing command that he make Isaac a sacrificial offering to the Lord, Abraham responds (Gen 22:1–19). He takes the heir of the promise on a distant journey to Mt. Moriah, telling him they are going there to offer a sacrifice to the Lord.

Isaac sees the wood, knife, and fire for the sacrifice but twice wonders aloud about the animal. All Abraham will say is "God will see to the lamb"—the Lord will provide (Gen 22:8, 14).[21] Determined to demonstrate his obedience, Abraham builds the altar with Isaac, lays the wood on it, and then binds Isaac in preparation for slaying him. At the last moment, God stays Abraham's hand and provides a substitute—a ram caught in the thicket. God says to Abraham, "Now I know that you fear God, since you have not withheld your son, your only son from me" (Gen 22:12b).

Known in Judaism as the *akedah*—the binding of Isaac—the story tells us many things. The traditional Christian understanding is that God was testing Abraham's trust and obedience but was always prepared to intervene in the end, regardless, just as Abraham twice told the boy. But the story is about more than Abraham's obedience and trust. It is also about God's provision in the covenant and God remaining true to God's word. God did "see to it," in providing the ram in the thicket as a substitute for Abraham's firstborn son. But that provision was about more than the ram; it was the first of many of God's provisions to ensure the covenant promise coming to fulfillment. We will look more closely at this incident in the next chapter, when we consider how sacrifice functioned in Israel's life with God.

Sacrificial Worship and Substitution

Embedded in this story is another provision. Sacrifice had long been a means of worshipping the Lord. It is as old as the story of Cain and Abel, was repeated by Noah in the priestly version at the end of the flood, and

---

20. God gives Abram a new name when promising that he will become the ancestor of a multitude of nations. He goes from being Abram ("exalted") to Abraham ("ancestor of a multitude"). See Gen 17:5.

21. In v. 8 it is "God will provide"; in 14, it is the Lord. In both, the verb is *yir'eh*.

was Abram's response upon reaching Bethel, acknowledging God's faithfulness to the promise (Gen 4:3; 8:20; 12:8). It is what Abraham thought he was doing in binding Isaac. But now the covenant reveals two new dimensions to sacrifice.

From the beginning, sacrificial gifts had been a means for worshipping the Lord. Following this event on Mt. Moriah, two new dimensions emerge. First, sacrifice embodies God's gift of substitution. Something of lesser value can be offered as a substitute for something or someone of greater value, just as the ram was a substitute for Abraham's son, especially the firstborn of God's promise. Second, and more important still, the binding of Isaac is understood as God's prohibition of offering any human life as sacrifice in worship, especially firstborn sons. Though such practice was common in the ancient Near East among Israel's neighbors, and officially it is condemned by the prophets Jeremiah, Ezekiel, and Micah, there are more than hints in Scripture that early in Israel's life it may have also taken place among them.[22] Judges records the rash vow of Jeptha that leads to his sacrifice of his daughter (Judg 11:30–39). The combined book of Kings includes four references to the practice, three described as "ma[king] his son pass through the fire" (1 Kgs 16:34; 2 Kgs 16:3; 17:17; 21:6); so too for 2 Chronicles (2 Chr 28:3; 33:6). The most well known comes from Ps 106:37–38. Ever after, this story of Abraham and Isaac stands as witness that such worship is not only rejected by the Lord; it is an abomination.

All of this will find its way into Israel's unique understanding of the role and purpose of sacrifice in its daily life as it sought to live into the covenant God had made with their father, Abraham. It was a system Israel understood given to them by the Lord for worship that offered tribute, expressed gratitude, reconciled differences, maintained communion, and wiped out the corrosive result of sin, all as a means of being and remaining at-one with God.

Over the years, as the church grew further and further from its Jewish roots, sacrifice would increasingly be misunderstood and misinterpreted, leading to a pagan rather than biblical understanding of atonement. Consequently, we need to take a fresh look at sacrifice in Israel's life with God as contemporary biblical scholarship understands it today. Failure to do this in the past has badly distorted most atonement theology. To that we now turn.

---

22. Dewrell, *Child Sacrifice*, 191–93.

Chapter 5

Sacrifice in Israel's Life with God

FEW THINGS IN THE Bible are as complicated, debated, and frequently misunderstood as sacrifice, especially when it has to do with the theology of atonement. To understand sacrifice biblically, particularly as it is applied to Jesus and his work of atonement, we must first look at how sacrifice was used in Israel's life as it worshiped the Lord. It was hardly uniform over the years.

We catch a glimpse of sacrifice as it was first understood in the prehistory of Genesis. Cain and Abel bring offerings to the Lord, one from the fruit of the ground, the other from his flock.[1] Noah builds an altar, offering every clean animal and bird as a burnt offering to the Lord.[2] As the historical section of Genesis begins in chapter 12, God calls Abram, and Abram goes. Arriving at Bethel, Abram builds an altar to the Lord after God appears telling him that God is giving the land to Abram's offspring. Moving on to the hill country, Abram builds a second altar and calls on the name of the Lord.

Jacob, Moses, Joshua, Gideon, Samuel, David, and Solomon are all reported to have sacrificed to the Lord in many separate places and for varying reasons, as sacrifice developed in form and meaning. From sheer worship, as it seems to have been for the patriarchs, it began to seal covenant acceptance, as for Moses at Sinai. It also became thank offerings

---

1. Why God had regard for Abel's rather than Cain's is not explained, despite the wealth of homiletic speculation that has been attributed to this event.

2. Note that this is the priestly section of the book of Genesis, probably written at the time the Second Temple was constructed.

of well-being on various occasions. David sacrificed abundantly, bringing the ark of the covenant to Jerusalem. At the dedication of Solomon's Temple, sacrifice was well established and used in abundance, if not excess (2 Chr 7:5).

Sacrifice in the Ancient Near East

The study of the religious practices of the people of the ancient Near East (ANE) has found sacrifice common among all those peoples as *the central act of worship* in their temples. Scholars theorize at least four possible purposes behind these worshiping sacrifices: to provide food for the gods, to assimilate the life force of the sacrificed animal while offering it to their gods as food, to effect union with the god, or to give a gift to the god to induce the deity's aid for some particular purpose. Though each of these findings might, at first reading of the Hebrew Bible, seem appropriate for the children of Israel, a close look at how sacrifice is presented in those Scriptures reveals a development away from the practice of its neighbors to one unique to Israel.

For the most part, for the Hebrews, offering a sacrifice meant joyously giving something of value to the Lord. The Hebrew word for what was offered to God is *qorban* and means "brought near." In religious context, it means more specifically "that which is brought near to the altar of God."[3] In similar manner, the English word for sacrifice comes from the Latin *sacer facere*, which means "to make something holy."

The general word for sacrifice in Hebrew is *zebach*, from the verbal root *zbch*, which means "to slaughter" or "slit the throat." It is the way all domestic animals were slaughtered for use, whether food for domestic consumption or an offering to the Lord. It was the most nonviolent, painless, and humane means of killing an animal. Of the four motivations that have been identified as practices in the ANE, contemporary scholarship has concluded that the primary purpose of sacrifice in Israel was this joyous gift or offering being given to God as an act of worship, which in Hebrew is *abad*, the word for work or service offered to God.

Initially, sacrifices in the Bible were acts of individuals or families, whether a formal rite of ancestral devotion to the gods or god of the household or a clan ritual feast remembering its dead. Such a ritual may

---

3. Kaiser, "Book of Leviticus," 1005.

be behind the sacrifice the Lord tells Samuel to use as a cover for going to Bethlehem in search of the new king who will be David (1 Sam 16).

Later, in David's tactical strategy with Jonathan to escape Saul's murderous plans to kill David, David asks Jonathan to explain his absence at the king's table, saying he has had to return to Bethlehem for the family's annual sacrificial feast (1 Sam 20:6, 29). Other sacrifices could be spontaneous responses to some gracious action on God's part or specified actions that were required for some condition—taking and completing a specific vow, the birth of a child, gratitude for a crop, healing, or making a covenant with others.

Sacrifice after the Sinai Covenant

In the age of the patriarchs, sacrifice took place in the open air, on earthen altars or altars built of uncut stone. They were an expression of worship—awe at being in or near God's presence. Before the exodus, worshiping God with sacrifice took place wherever God was encountered. According to the narrative in the book of Exodus, the Lord is depicted as dwelling in the tabernacle established under the Mosaic covenant made at Mt. Sinai—a sanctuary of God's own design thought to mirror the Lord's dwelling in the heavens (Exod 25:8—27:19).[4] The tabernacle's portable altar was five cubits square and three cubits high,[5] made of acacia wood covered in bronze, with four upturned corners called horns. The altar was for making burnt offerings to the Lord and was part of God's design for the tabernacle (Exod 27:1-8).

On this altar, sacrifice was to be offered to the Lord daily. It bore the power of God's holiness, and to desecrate it in any way was punishable by death (Exod 28:43). By now, only those ordained to the priesthood were permitted to perform the actions around the altar involving sacrifice. The sons of Levi were no longer able to officiate at sacrifice but rather were appointed to care for the tabernacle: its movement, setup, maintenance, deconstruction, overall care, and so on. But it was only the sons of Aaron,

---

4. Here one finds the instructions for building the tabernacle, the ark of the covenant, and all the tent's furnishings.

5. A cubit was the distance of one's forearm, approximately eighteen inches or half a meter, making the altar approximately 7.5 feet square and 4.5 feet high, large enough for domestic animals' consumption by fire.

themselves sons of Levi, who were ordained as priests to perform sacrificial actions within the tabernacle on behalf of the worshipper.[6]

The advantage of the tabernacle was that it was portable. God could travel with the people to the land of promise. During the people's travel to the land of Canaan, the tabernacle was always at the center of the camp, immediately surrounded by the Levites, then by the rest of the people. The daily sacrifices conducted by the priests on its altar were at the center of the people and their lives.

One Last Fateful Rebellion

Upon reaching the door to the land of promise, the Lord charged Moses to select a leader from each of the twelve tribes who, under the leadership of Joshua, would spy out the land. The men found it truly a place of milk and honey—abundant grain and rich in fruit. But its people were strong, the cities fortified. More foreboding still, they had seen the descendants of Anak—a race of giants (Gen 23:2; Josh 15:13). The spies felt like grasshoppers among them. Only Joshua and Caleb remained steadfast, believing that having the Lord with them, they would prevail.

The report of the other spies sent panic through the camp that broke out in rebellion. The people pleaded with Moses to take them back to Egypt. When Moses refused, they sought a new leader among themselves, threatening to stone Moses, Aaron, Caleb, and Joshua. The LORD appeared, threatening to destroy the people with pestilence, disinherit them, and start again with Moses. But Moses interceded with the LORD, on the people's behalf.

Moses reminded God of God's promise of being "slow to anger and abounding in steadfast love, forgiving iniquity and transgressions, but not clearing the guilty" (Num 14:18). What would the Egyptians think; God brought them into the wilderness to destroy them? The LORD relented. Yet none of those who rebelled would enter the land. God consigned the Israelites to forty years of wilderness wanderings (Num 13:1—14:45). The prophets Amos and Jeremiah tell us there were no sacrifices offered among them during that time (Jer 7:22; Amos 5:25). Only after the death of that generation of rebels, and the people's subsequent entrance into the land of promise, were sacrificial offerings resumed (Exod 15:1-31).[7]

---

6. All Aaronic priests were from the clan of Levi, but not all Levites were priests.

7. Though cast at the time of settling into the land, the text shows the clear hand

Sacrifice in the Promised Land

Upon settling into the land, there were numerous sanctuaries and shrines in which sacrifice was now offered, sometimes pejoratively referred to as "high places" where earlier Canaanite peoples had worshiped. These were present in Gibeon, where the tabernacle was located for some time, Bethel, Shiloh, and finally Jerusalem, once David moved the ark of the covenant there. David's decision to do so was a strategic one. By now, it was the ark of the covenant rather than the tabernacle's altar that had become the witness of the Lord's presence among them. Nonetheless, sacrifices continued to be offered in those earlier worship sanctuaries as well.

Though David wanted to build a house for the Lord, it would be his son Solomon who would build the first temple. At its dedication, we are told that the glory of the Lord descended upon it. God's presence filled the house so mightily that the priests could not enter it to conduct their ministries (1 Kgs 8:11; 2 Chr 7:1–5). The king and all the people offered sacrifice before the Lord—twenty-two thousand oxen and one hundred twenty thousand sheep.[8] Clearly, God was now living among the people in Jerusalem. The temple would be the center of priestly sacrifice daily, evening and morning, on behalf of the people, as well as for the people's other offerings.

Sacrifice during the Exile

Some four hundred years later, when Solomon's Temple was destroyed by the Babylonians in 587 BCE, it was abundantly clear to everyone that the Lord no longer lived among them. God's house was gone. Yet sacrifice continued. Those left behind continued to offer daily sacrifices on the ruins of the temple's altar. Yet, if you read Ezekiel, the priest/prophet of the Babylonian exile, the Lord seems to have gone into exile with them, as it is God's glory that appears there to Ezekiel, yet without a place for sacrificial worship (Ezek 3:23; 8:4; 9:3; 10:4, 18, 19; 43:2, 4–5; 44:4).

Cyrus, king of Persia, in the first year of his reign (538 BCE), issued the edict allowing the Jews in exile to go home and rebuild their temple, even providing funds for doing so (2 Chr 36:22–23; Ezra 6:3–5). As the

---

of the priestly editor to ensure the sacrificial instructions were in keeping with the sacrificial practice of the Second Temple.

8. Second Chronicles is clearly hyperbolic speech on the part of the writer.

exiles arrived, they gathered with others in Jerusalem at the remains of Solomon's destroyed temple. There, they built a new altar on the foundations of the old. Thus, even before the foundation of the Second Temple had been laid, the returned people resumed making burnt offerings to the Lord, evening and morning. In addition, they kept the new moon offerings and the sacred festivals of Passover, Weeks, and Tabernacle. The Day of Atonement would not be observed until the Second Temple was dedicated.[9] But through it all, the people's joyous gift or offering of work and service (*abad*) to the Lord continued to be at the center of Jewish life.

Basic Sacrificial Actions—Food for the LORD

Like all the Semitic people of the ANE, the children of Israel believed that what made the gods immortal and different from themselves was the special food and drink with which they were nourished in the heavens. The psalmist speaks of it as the "bread of angels," whereas Revelation will later speak of heaven's "waters of life" (Pss 78:25; 105:40; John 4:14; Rev 21:6; 22:1, 17). When the gods left their heavenly abode to be among their people in their temples, they left this sustenance behind. Consequently, it must be supplied by worshippers through daily sacrifice, lest the gods return to their heavenly home for nourishment.

Whole Burnt Offering—*Olah*

For Israel, that nourishment was offered in a daily evening and morning whole burnt offering (*olah*—"that which goes up in smoke"), as well as in the special offerings on each Sabbath, on the new moon of each month, at Passover, the Feast of Weeks, and Rosh Hashanah (beginning of the new year). Each was an occasion when the priests joyously offered God such nourishment. All but the animal's hide was consumed by fire, the hide being given to the priest for his service. The sacrificial foods were cattle, sheep, goats, and birds. Other offerings would include food stuffs: grain, flour, olive oil, fruit, and wine. Often these were comingled with incense to make the smoke a pleasing aroma.

---

9. See the books of Ezra and Nehemiah for the chronicle of the return, including the beginning of the temple, the local interference to keep it from being built, and the role of King Darius in assuring that it was.

Chief among all this sacrificial nourishment for the Lord were the blood and the fat (suet) of the cattle and sheep being offered. These were thought to be sources of special vitality and energy for God. In addition, because the offering was for the Holy One, the animal must be the very best available—clean and without birth defect or other blemish or injury. So too for the other foods brought as sacrifice. They must be the finest grain, fruit, and drink, and they must be free from any "leaven." Leaven is fundamentally the initiation of a process of decay, which would make the offering impure. All these, whether the whole animal, or simply a representative portion of other offerings, were turned into smoke on the altar to form "a pleasing odor for the Lord" (Gen 8:21; Exod 29:18, 25, 41; Lev 1:9, 13, 17, etc.—sixteen times in Leviticus and eighteen times in Numbers). It was the burning of the gift—turning it to pleasing smoke—that was the identifying mark of all sacrifice offered to the Lord, *not the animal's slaughter.*

There were sacrifices, such as the whole burnt offering, that were solely food for the Lord (Exod 24:5–8; Lev 3:14–17; Num 7:15; 15:8; Deut 32:37–38; 1 Sam 2:15). There were sacrifices of well-being, thanksgiving, and covenant-making, in which the food was shared by God, the priest, the supplicant, and often the supplicant's family and friends (Num 6:17; 7:17).[10] There were sacrifices of purification, in which, except in two cases, the food—both the meat of the animal as well as the produce offered—was shared only between God and the priest officiating at the sacrifice (Num 6:16; 7:22).[11] Sacrifice thus played a double role: it was an offering and service to God, but it was also a means of sustaining the priests, who otherwise had no other source of income.

Sacrificial Actions

Whatever the type or occasion for the sacrifice, it followed these steps: the worshippers selected the animal or other gifts appropriate to the particular offering (not all sacrifices were animals). The gifts were presented to the priest, the offeror laying a hand upon it as an act of identifying the offering as the supplicant's own. If it was an animal, the supplicant quickly killed it while the priest collected all the animal's blood to use it according to the requirements of that particular sacrifice.

---

10. These chapters record the sacrifices offered at the temple's dedication.
11. Only the priests were sanctified enough to withstand God's presence.

If the sacrifice was one of the first three—whole burnt (*olah*), cereal (*minha*), or well-being (*zebah selamim*)—and not a purging sacrifice, all the blood was returned to the Lord by pouring it out on the burnt offering altar. If it was a purgative sacrifice, some of the blood was smeared or sprinkled on various cultic objects before the rest of it was poured on the altar for consumption by the fire. While the priest prepared the fire to burn the portion of the animal being offered to the Lord—whether whole or just the fat, vital organs, and blood—the worshippers prepared the animal: they skinned, cut up, and washed the animal's flesh in preparation for its burning, separating the portions to be burnt as an offering to the Lord from those prepared for the priest or for the priest and the worshippers' consumption.

Unless it was a whole burnt offering, once the priest had turned the Lord's portion to smoke, the rest of the animal was boiled in preparation for the sacrificial feast, whether for the priest alone or the priests, worshippers, and their families and friends. If not a purifying sacrifice for a priest or the whole community, the hide of the animal was given to the priest as payment for his services. If a purifying sacrifice, the hide was burned outside the camp.

If the sacrifice was a cereal/grain offering (*minha*), it was presented to the priest, who took a portion of it, added incense, and "turn[ed] this token portion into smoke on the altar, as an offering by fire of pleasing odor to the LORD" (Lev 2:1–3). The remainder of the cereal/grain was for the priests' or worshippers' consumption as part of the larger sacrificial feast.

The Other Side of Sacrifice

In the Hebrew mindset there was another dimension to sacrifice beside service to God and occasions for giving thanks. Sacrifice preserved God's presence among them. If corruption crept in unabated, the Lord would withdraw. God was first and foremost, the Holy One of Israel. Therefore, as God's people, they too were to be holy—set apart—a theme that resonates repeatedly in Leviticus and Numbers (Lev 11:44–45; 19:2; 20:7; and so on).[12] To assure God's participation in the meal, worshippers must first deal with those things that had the capacity to pollute God's house.

---

12. The command appears eleven times in Leviticus and three in Numbers. Deuteronomy 23:14 commands the entire camp to be holy, lest God see something

Any contact with impurity of whatever sort, whether physical or moral, any violation of religious or social taboo, any action that missed the covenant stipulations for behavior between them as Israelites, was regarded as a breech against their entire community, a member of it, or God. It generated a contamination within them that must be purified, lest God withdraw. The contamination was the miasma of sin or uncleanness that threatened the sanctuary, the people, and the offender's "whole essential self"—a person's *nephesh*, often translated "soul"—but designating the whole person and their life force.[13]

Until those contaminations were dealt with, one of two things would result: God's holiness would consume the contamination and the people with it, or God would withdraw from the sanctuary and the people so that God's holiness would not destroy them. Until the worship place and the violator's *nephesh* were cleansed and regenerated, they were damaged goods, falling short of the mark, needing and awaiting a process of purification or being made clean. Thus, there was in Israel's daily life an overriding and constant concern for purity—whether physical or ritual. That meant the need to purge, purify, or eliminate anything that might give God offence or cause God to withdraw, thus destroying their relationship.

How could the people of Israel approach God in a way that their contamination by sin or impurity neither destroyed them nor caused God to abandon God's holy sanctuary among them? In addition, what could restore the sinful or impure body—personal or corporate—and make them once again whole and fit for communion with God and one another? The answer is sacrifice or, more correctly still, *the entire sacrificial system*. For behind the priestly understanding of the sacrificial system lies God's forgiving and steadfast love freely offered and assured by God's eternal covenant promise to the people of Israel (Exod 34:6; Pss 25:10; 85:10; 86:15; 89:14; 98:3). Sacrifice did not procure God's forgiveness and love. Sacrifice recognized and responded to God's steadfast love in a variety of situations to blot out and purge the contaminated spaces and purify the sanctuary from the corrosive and damaging effect of sin and impurity of various kinds.

---

indecent and turn away from them.

13. Gaster, "Sacrifices," 151.

More Than Food for the LORD

Another challenge to understanding the role of sacrifice in Israel's daily life is that there was not just one kind of sacrifice; there were five, each for a different purpose. Though all five had common factors, each also had its unique provisions based upon what the sacrifice was and why it was being offered.

Of the five, the first three were about worshipping God and were completely voluntary. They were joyful expressions of praise, thanksgiving, well-being, and concord. Except for one of the three—the two daily whole burnt offerings to God—they also involved the people feasting on what had been offered. Once the portion reserved for the Lord—the animal's fat and organs, and portions of the grain, oil, and wine—had been turned to smoke on the altar, the remaining portions of the sacrifice were shared with the priests, the worshipper, and family and friends as a joyful feast. These three sacrifices had nothing to do with sinful behavior, purging sin's corrosive residue, or making restitution to anyone. They were simply celebrations of the blessings of being at-one with the Lord as God's covenant people.

Purifying-Purging Sacrifices

The other two sacrifices of the five did deal with people's sinful behavior—violations of commandments—and the sacrifices were prescribed and mandatory. The first (*hattat*) dealt with the individual's infraction and required a particular animal according to the violator's standing in the community. The other (*asam*) was for sinful behavior that had harmed another. This sacrifice involved not only the person who had committed the sin but the one affected by it, through some harm or loss. Both forms of sacrifice purged the corrosiveness introduced into the people's common life and worship space and wiped it out.

Of the five sacrifices stipulated in Torah,[14] only these latter two have anything to do with sin. Yet, neither of them is about procuring or receiving God's forgiveness. Both are about *expiation*, the sacrificial blood wiping out or away the contamination brought about by the violation and purifying Israel's worship space. Neither applies the purging blood to the

---

14. See Lev 1–7: *ola* (whole burnt), *minha* (cereal), *zebah selamim* (well-being), *hattat* (purification), and *asam* (guilt offering for reparation and purification).

perpetrator. Of the two, only one has anything to do with paying for the sin—the latter one. In the sole case of this "guilt offering" (*asam*), a payment of reparation for the transgression is required to be made to the one who was abused. In none of Israel's sacrifices is a payment being made to God! The portions of the animal consumed by the fire are not payments, but offerings of thanksgiving for God's forgiveness and restoration.

Consumption of the remaining portion of the sacrificed animal in these two cases was reserved for the sacrificing priest alone. In the *asam*, in addition to there being a particular animal—a ram—prescribed for the purgative sacrifice, the violator was also required to make reparation for the wrong done by repaying those violated with what had been taken from them, along with an additional monetary fine.

Here is one of the places where Israel's sacrificial practice was unique within the ANE. For their neighbors, sacrifice was concerned with keeping their temples free from demons, devils, and other powers of evil that could drive away their gods. For Israel, there was only one source of evil that could drive God away—that *within the human heart*. Only people and their errant behavior could pollute the sanctuary and thereby drive out God from their midst. They must maintain their holiness.

Maintaining Holiness

Holiness was either given as an attribute of one's status as a priest or Levite or was determined according to the person's rank within the community: first the high priest, then other priests, followed by the Levites, then princes, chieftains, and finally the common Israelite. For each of these, the impurity of an offence could be blotted out by the enactment of a *hattat*, but the higher the rank of the offender, the more costly and valuable the animal prescribed for the sacrifice. Once offered, and the sacrificial blood appropriately applied to the worship space, holiness was restored to the space and the offender.

If the source of defilement was an illness or something like contact with mold, impurities following one's menstrual cycle, sexual intercourse, childbirth, or another bodily emission, the defilement could be purged, and restoration to purity achieved, through acts of containment rather than sacrifice, what today we would call quarantine. After the passage of a set of time and ritual washing, one was examined by a priest and restored to community.

Purging the Contamination of Torah Violation

Contamination came from *accidental* and *unintentional* violations of a law. This included accidental contact with blood, not fulfilling a vow because of forgetfulness, or some other event. It could be breaking a commandment or keeping a commandment that itself led to defilement, such as preparation of a corpse for burial or some other form of personal pollution. Violations by ordinary individuals contaminated the outer sanctuary, its altar, and courtyard. Communal breaches were more destructive still and contaminated the inner shrine between the outer court and the holy of holies. The contamination included all ritual appointments in those spaces—the incense altar, candlesticks, and the table for the showbread. Infringements of a priest were the most serious. They contaminated the most sacred place in the tabernacle (temple), its inner sanctum, often called the "holy of holies," where, until its loss at the destruction of the First Temple, the ark of the covenant rested.

In each instance, regardless of the perpetrator, the violation must have been *unintentional* and accompanied by a realization of guilt and a verbal confession of sin by the one who trespassed (Lev 5:5). Once the sacrificial blood of the designated animal was appropriately applied, the purgation and purification necessary to maintain God's presence was complete. Turning the fat and organs into smoke pleasing to the Lord was an appropriate act of thanksgiving for the purification. If the violation had been that of a priest, the rest of the sacrificial animal was taken outside the city and completely burned.

The Bible never tells us exactly how blood purges, rubs out, expunges, and expiates the unclean residue of sinful behavior—only that it does. It cannot be overemphasized that it is the *pollution* created by errant behavior that is wiped out or purified, and that it has to do with Israel's worship space, not with the perpetrator. Sacrificial blood from the *hattat* and the *asam* was never applied to people to wipe out their action or restore their *nephesh*.

As to why blood does expiate sin's contamination, the Bible's answer is because "the life is in the blood" (Lev 17:11). For the Israelites, blood was the seat, source, and carrier of life, and it belonged to God. Therefore, it is holy. Because it is holy, it has power not only to give life but to cover (*kpr*) or expiate impurities created by human failure and sin that threaten life. Similarly, this explains why blood cannot be consumed. Blood has the power to give and sustain life, the power to purge the impurities that threaten life, and the power to purify what has been purged. After its use for purification, the remaining blood was placed on the altar and consumed by its fire, as the blood belongs to God alone who is the giver of all life.

Acts of Containment for Severe Sin

The priestly code regularly uses the phrase "when one sins unintentionally" or "unwittingly" (Lev 4:2, 22, 27; 5:15, 18; 22:14; Num 15:27, 28, 29; 35:11, 15; see also Deut 4:42; 19:4; Josh 20:3, 9).[15] Another way to say it would be "to have acted mistakenly" or to have "erred accidentally." This is not a distinction between "known" and "unknown" sins but between those that were not deliberate or intentional. The opposite would be "high-handed" sins—those that are intentionally defiant, mocking what God requires through Torah, or intentionally infringing upon God's holiness and therefore "blasphemous" (Num 15:30). "Unintentional" sins have no resolve to rebel against commandments or deliberately disobey God for one's own benefit. It is these unintentional sins that the sacrificial systems cover.

It is the high-handed or blasphemous sins for which there is no sacrifice. These were more severe both in their intentionality and their consequence, and therefore far more dangerous to the community. Because there was no sacrifice for intentional or unrepentant sin, those who committed them were dealt with by exclusion, containment, or outright elimination. They were "cut off" from the people.

Being cut off could be for a temporary amount of time—for an unintentional murder or other act that had a particularly destructive impact on the community that required time to heal. This is what lies behind the provision for the cities of refuge. These were six cities in the land—three on the west side of the Jordan and three on the east—to which someone who had unintentionally killed another could flee for safety from an otherwise legal blood avenger (Num 35:10–15; Josh 20:1–9).

At other times, the behavior was so severely high handed that it was dangerous to the whole community and required extreme action. Blasphemy or intentional and flagrant violation of a commandment

---

15. The Hebrew word is *shegagah*, often translated "error" or "inadvertence." It is a mistake, and the idea of "intent" is not part of the word. The Deuteronomy and Joshua texts refer to the cites of refuge set aside for those who kill someone unintentionally or accidentally, to protect them from blood vengeance.

meant being totally cut off through death. Otherwise, the behavior would spread and its contagion become destructive to the entire community.

To modern ears, the purity and expulsion/containment laws may be hard to understand. They can seem not to make sense, to appear arbitrary or even harsh. But given what was believed to be at stake for Israel—preserving God's protective, regenerative presence—arguably, that was not the case. The people were to work to avoid all physical impurity when possible, and when not, to undertake the proper means of purgation to be able to remain fully a part of the community. Because the temple was a place of intense holiness for Israel's Holy One, anything that pointed to or revealed the frailty of mortality was forbidden within its inner sanctum.[16]

It was the priesthood and its sacrificial apparatus that enabled the two worlds of holy and the common to interface. They provided a remedy for sin and its impurity and were a joint effort between the priests and the laypeople. It was also those laws that maintained the radical difference between Israel as God's holy people and the nations around them that worshipped other gods. Being God's holy people meant being separate—the foundational meaning of the Hebrew word for holy—*qodesh*—and these laws became the means for that and a mark of Israel's distinction.

Day of Atonement

What about those sins that were intentional? What about the pollution created in the sanctuary and among the people by flagrantly sinful members of the community who were not even permitted to offer sacrifice before being cut off? What purged the sanctuary of the effects of those transgressions or other high-handed sins? Once a year, there was a ritual enacted by the high priest on behalf of all Israel—the day of purgation known as Yom Kippur—what we have come to call in English the Day of Atonement (Lev 16:1–34).

All year long the transgressions of the people had been polluting the sanctuary. Though the pious among them brought sin and guilt offerings of purification for their inadvertent actions, there was still plenty of behavior that was not inadvertent and for which a purgative activity or offering had not been made. As the ten-day New Year's celebration came to its climax each fall, the high priest entered the tabernacle on behalf of the people, changed out of his normal priestly garments, washed his body

---

16. Anderson, "Introduction to Israelite Religion," 1:281.

in clean water, changed into special linen clothing, and then returned to the entrance of the tent.

At the tent's entrance, the high priest was presented with a bull and two goats (Lev 16:6–10). Over the goats he cast lots: one for the Lord and the other for the *Azazel* goat, this latter commonly known as the scapegoat. Both the bull and the one goat upon which the Lord's lot fell were offered by the high priest as a *hattat* sacrifice. The bull was a purgation *hattat* offering for the high priest and the entire priesthood—his "house"—while the goat was a purgation *hattat* offering for the people; but each in proper order, the bull first.

Upon the slaughter of the bull, the high priest gathered the bull's blood, took a censer of coals from the burning altar along with two handfuls of crushed sweet incense, and brought them to the curtain between the shrine and the inner sanctum. Entering the inner sanctum, he placed the incense on the coals of the censer to create a cloud that would cover and shield him from the ark and its gold lid, the *kapporet*. Though English Bibles often call it "the mercy seat," one renowned Jewish scholar suggests a better translation is the "place of atonement."[17] The high priest would then take some of the blood of the bull and smear it on top of the lid, and then sprinkle blood seven times in front of the ark. He then retreated to the inner shrine, sprinkling blood seven times before (not on) the curtain separating the shrine from the inner sanctum. After sprinkling the blood of the bull seven times before the curtain, he would smear blood on the horns of the incense altar in the shrine. Thus, each of these had been purified of the impurity brought about by the high priest and his priestly colleagues.

Having made a purification offering for himself and the other priests, the high priest now made one for the people. Leaving the sanctuary and returning to the people, the high priest slaughtered the goat designated for the Lord as a *hattat* for the people. Collecting the goat's blood, the high priest would reenter the holy of holies and repeat all the blood manipulation on behalf of the people. When these dual purging *hattats* for the priests and the people were completed, the high priest would then mix together the remaining blood of the two *hattat* sacrifices, the high priest's bull and the Lord's goat for the people. The priest would then move to the outer shrine, smearing and then sprinkling the mixed blood

---

17. Milgrom, *Leviticus*, 167.

of the goat and the bull on the horns of the outer altar and dashing what remained on the altar's sides.

Thus, the whole sanctuary—the holy of holies and its adjacent shrine, with the incense altar and the outer altar for the burnt offerings—was purged of all the contaminants produced both by the priests' and the people's uncleanness and transgressions, including those willful and flagrant violations by the people who had been cut off. The smearing of blood was understood to cleanse the sanctuaries and their appurtenances, while the sprinkling of blood sanctified and reconsecrated them.

The Second Goat

With the sanctuary's inner sanctum, shrine, and altar purged and reconsecrated, the high priest returned to the second goat. Placing both hands on the animal's head, the high priest confessed over it all the iniquities of the people of Israel, all their transgressions and all their sins—inadvertent and high handed—placing all on the head of the animal in a rite of transfer. Thereafter the goat was led away into the wilderness by someone among them designated for the task. As the second goat was led away, the high priest returned to the sanctuary, took off the special linen clothing, leaving it there, bathed, and again dressed in his priestly vestments, while the goat bearing all the sin, iniquity, and transgression of the priests and the people was taken into the wilderness and there set free (Lev 16:23–28).[18]

Dressed again in priestly vestments, the high priest would emerge from the sanctuary and offer the fat and the vital organs of both the bull and the first goat as burnt offerings to the Lord. The rest of the two animals was taken outside the camp and their skin, flesh, and dung completely consumed by fire, as was done with all *hattat* offerings having to do with the priesthood or community. The one consigned the task of burning the animals then had to wash his clothes and bathe his body in water, as contact with the dead animals had rendered him unclean. Only after the washing of clothing and his body could he return to the camp; so too for the person who had led the scapegoat *Azazel* into the wilderness.

---

18. Initially, the *Azazel* was simply a means of conveying the sin, iniquity, and transgression of the people away from the camp. There was no notion of this being done to punish the *Azazel* (Milgrom, *Leviticus*, 169).

The uncleanliness of the sanctuary created by all the people's sin, unwitting or high handed, had been purged. The sins that were the occasion of that uncleanliness had also been removed from among them. They had been transferred to the scapegoat who carried them away from the sanctuary, camp, and people, into the wilderness. All had been dealt with. With the sanctuary purified and reconsecrated, God's presence was assured for the beginning of a new year.

All Sacrifice as an Act of Atonement with the Lord

From what we have seen, it can be said that all sacrifice in Israel's cultic life was a means of providing closer communion between God and God's people. Acknowledging God's holiness, seeing to God's care through gifts of pleasing smoke, giving thanks, making vows and covenants, repenting for failures, making amends with fellow Israelites in God's presence, or simply eating and drinking with one's family and friends in the joy of God's presence were the motivations behind these offerings. All of this could take place because of and within the sacrificial cult. Consequently, all sacrifice was at some level a so-called "sacrifice of atonement"—a means of entering God's holiness and presence on God's terms.

The Sacrifice of Isaac—An Exception?

Long before the exodus, and God's claiming the life of all firstborn sons as God's own, God tells Abraham to take his son Isaac—firstborn with Sarah, and heir to the covenant promise—and offer him to God as a sacrifice. This terrifying story has an interesting and complex history. Some scholars are convinced that in Israel's earliest stage of development, especially during the Israelites' initial entry into the land of Canaan, they practiced human sacrifice, mimicking the religious behavior of their neighbors by offering their firstborn to the Lord as a means of ensuring future fertility. Others think that if such sacrifice took place, it was in worship not of the Lord but in an apostate act to seek the help of one of the pagan gods.[19] Whatever, clearly something of this sort lies behind the story of Abraham and Isaac, which in Judaism is known not as the *sacrifice* of Isaac, but as the *akedah*—the *binding* of Isaac.

---

19. See Dewrell, *Child Sacrifice*, for his view and the three different circumstances in which he believes child sacrifice may had taken place in pre-exilic Israel.

Throughout Genesis, Abraham has proven himself less than exemplary in his faith and trust in God. Despite the visionary encounter of God making a covenant with Abraham in Gen 15 and repeated promises, Abraham is far from confident of the truth of the covenant promise God has made to him. Finally, Isaac, whom God has identified as the son of the promise, is born to Abraham and Sarah. But now, God commands Abraham to take Isaac to the land of Moriah and offer him there as a burnt offering on one of the mountains God will show him (Gen 22:2). Abraham responds with an obedience that is, frankly, heretofore uncharacteristic but now terrifying. Clearly, Abraham intends to sacrifice his beloved son Isaac to the Lord.

When twice asked by Isaac about the absence of a sacrificial animal, Abraham twice simply replies, "God will see to the sheep," generally translated into English as "God will provide" (Gen 22:8, 14). Among the things that can be said about this is that it is a sign that Abraham has finally grown to the full stature of faithful obedience and trust. The story, after all, begins, "God tested Abraham." That said, there is extensive and diverse scholarship on what the story means, and, consequently, opinions range widely as to what is taking place here.

The traditional Christian view is that God was testing Abraham, always prepared to intervene in the end, just as Abraham twice promised the boy. After binding Isaac, with knife poised to slay him, Abraham hears God's voice and the command not to do so. Abraham looks up to see a ram caught in a thicket by its horns. Abraham takes the ram and offers it as a burn offering to the Lord (Gen 22:12–14). Just as Abraham was about to prove his commitment to God, God intervened. Here then, the story is about more than obedience and trust. It is also a story about the provision of God, and God's provision of an animal as a substitute for the firstborn within the sacrificial cult.

God remains true to God's word; Isaac will be the heir of the promise, and God's promise to Abraham will be kept. Humanity, like all of God's creatures, belongs to God. But humanity bears the image of God and is therefore of a different order within God's creation. Human life is precious and worthy of being redeemed. God's claim on all firstborn sons remains, but now, the binding of Isaac introduces a new factor into the equation—substitution. God provides an animal to be offered in sacrifice as a substitute for the firstborn. In addition, ever after, this story stands as witness to God's absolute aversion to human sacrifice.

The Passover Lamb

We now come to one of the more misunderstood cultic actions in Israel's worship life—the slaying of the Passover lamb, commonly called a sacrifice. Technically, it is a cultic action to ward off evil, which scholars call an *apotropaic* ritual. Though it may at first appear to be a sacrifice, it was only so designated much later, in the Second Temple, when the priesthood insisted that all Passover lambs be slaughtered by the priests at the temple. Imagine the impact that decision had on Israel's ability to observe the mandatory commemoration. To have a lamb, one must be in Jerusalem, as, indeed Jesus and his disciples had come to Jerusalem to observe his last Passover. More on that later. If one looks closely at the rite, we discover significant differences between the ritual that preceded that first Passover in Egypt and the sacrifices of lambs that were part of the various sacrificial offerings we have looked at in this chapter.

The First Passover

Exodus chapter 12 tells how on the threshold of Israel's redemption from slavery in Egypt, the Lord told Moses to have each household in the community, on the tenth day of the month, select an unblemished, male, one-year-old lamb—either a sheep or a goat—and take it into the household and keep it until the fourteenth day of that month. On that last day, all Israelite families were to kill their lambs, each at their own homes, at twilight. They were then to take some of the lamb's blood and put it on the doorposts and lintels of their houses.

The Lord was preparing the final act that would judge both the gods of Egypt and Pharaoh's refusal to let the Israelites go. God promised to move through Egypt that night and strike down all the firstborn in the land, both humans and animals. The blood on the Israelites' doorposts and lintels would be a sign, and when seen, God would pass over that house so that no plague would strike them or anyone in the household.

After using the lamb's blood to mark the door, the household was to roast the animal whole with fire and eat it with unleavened bread and bitter herbs, while dressed and ready for a quick departure. Whatever might be left after the meal was to be burned. It was the Lord's Passover—an event that would bring about the Israelites' redemption. Thereafter, the ritual was to become an annual feast to the Lord commemorating God's action to liberate them from slavery in Egypt. It was to be kept throughout their generations and celebrated annually as a permanent memorial and ordinance (Exod 12:1–14).

Several things clearly distinguish this meal of liberation from Israel's historic sacrificial meals. First, it takes place in the Israelites' homes rather than in a designated sanctuary. The animal is slain by the head of each household without the involvement of a priest (the priesthood did not yet exist!). Never is any portion of the slain animal offered to the Lord as *qorban*. Rather, all the animal is consumed by the members of the household as a commemoration of liberation from slavery. Whatever of the meal remained was to be burned, but as a means of disposal, not as a sacrifice offered to God.

There is no blood manipulation that could be conceived of as purging the contaminants of sin or consecrating anyone or anything. This was simply a mark of identification to ward off the evil of death. The only possible connection here would be the power of blood as a life-force—it also has the power to ward off evil and death. But it has nothing to do with sin.

Finally, the entire ritual was to be a perpetual ordinance for remembering what God had done for them—freed Israel from bondage of slavery in Egypt. It was not until after the exile that the Passover lamb came to be thought of in sacrificial terms. Once the passover lambs could only be slaughtered at the temple and by the priests, rather than by the heads of households, it did not take long for the killing of the lambs to be associated with some form of sacrifice.

Rejection of Sacrifice?

Under the influence of nineteenth-century Protestant German scholarship, the notion emerged that prophets such as Amos, Hosea, Micah, and Jeremiah were rejecting outright the validity of the temple cult, seeing it as fundamentally the adoption of a pagan practice of offering a sacrifice to propitiate their gods' wrath. Indeed, that was one of the assumptions in the sacrificial cults of Israel's neighbors.[20] This notion of sacrificial propitiation seems to have made its way into most nineteenth-century conservative and moderate Western Christian thought, with only the most liberal churches rejecting it. But rather than see these prophets' critique as a wholesale rejection of sacrifice, it seems more correct to see their critique as a means of warning against the abuse of sacrifice, calling

---

20. Collett, "Book of the Twelve," 412.

on Israel to accompany its sacrifices with repentance, integrity, justice, steadfast love, and covenant faithfulness.

God's worship and service have always demanded the accompanying ethics of justice, mercy, kindness, and walking humbly with God. It is that continuing steadfast faithfulness to God's covenant promises and stipulations for which the prophets continually called. Contrary to the nations around them, who typically regarded the forgiveness of the gods as something that automatically emerged from their propitiatory sacrifices, Israel understood that apart from acknowledgment, confession, and commitment to ethical change, there was no purging or at-one-ment taking place in their sacrifices. They would be violating the holy things of God. Neither the prophets, priests, nor psalmists would disagree about that (1 Sam 15:22–23; Isa 1:11–14; Amos 5:21–23; Mic 6:6–9; Jer 7:21–23; Ps 25:4–11).

Sacrifice as Worship, Not Appeasement

Never within the biblical witness to the sacrificial cult as scholars understand it today is there the notion that sacrifice placated or propitiated an angry deity—either paying God back for a failure or mollifying or pacifying God's wrath. Even as King David pleads with God to save the life of the child born to him through Bathsheba, he does not offer God a sacrifice. Rather, he fasts, weeps, and debases himself by lying prostrate on the ground day and night until the child dies, seeking God's graciousness and mercy in the matter (2 Sam 12:15–23).

The prophets regularly railed against the notion that sacrifice could purchase God's forgiveness and saw it as the height of apostasy. Yes, that might be true of the pagan religions that surrounded Israel in antiquity, as well as some of those of the Greco-Roman world of the third century BCE and first century CE, but not so for the Israel of the Second Temple and Jesus' day. Forgetting, or simply not knowing this, has led to much bad Christian atonement theology.

Sacrifice was a means of rejoicing in God's presence, giving thanks for God's steadfast love and forgiveness in the face of disobedience, when one had somehow violated or fallen short of God's stipulated expectations for being a member of God's people. It was this sacrificial cult and the at-one-ment it helped maintain that, as much as anything, gave Israel its identity. How the *hattat* and *asam* sacrifices—regularly translated "sin offering" and "guilt offering" respectively—in the Christian understanding of sacrifice evolved into being a payment to God for one's sins, much less the sins of the world, is a story for another chapter. For now, it is important to note how foreign that notion would have been to Jews of Jesus' day. Perhaps that is why the apostle Paul never speaks of Jesus' death as either *hattat* or *asam* and avoids sacrificial categories to speak of the meaning of Jesus' death.

Chapter 6

New Testament Application of Sacrifice to Jesus

THE NEW TESTAMENT TREATS sacrifice (*thysia*) and offering (*prosphora*) far differently than the Hebrew Scriptures. In the Hebrew Bible, sacrifice is a cultic action and God's gift. It is the Lord's means of making atonement to enable Israel to continue to worship and serve God, and to enable Israel to attend to God's "needs." It purges the contamination that accrued to the sanctuary because of the priests' and people's sins and creates a context for covenant-making and fellowship with God that is a realization of "at-one-ment." In the New Testament, sacrificial language appears only metaphorically as its writers use the various images from Israel's sacrificial cult to interpret the *meaning* of Jesus' life, death, and resurrection rather than to create a descriptive narrative of what it was.

Sacrificial imagery from Israel's worship practice is only one of the means of interpreting Jesus' offering his life in pursuit of his divine vocation, and a minor one at that. Images and metaphors of sacrifice are used far less than those from Roman law, commerce, politics, sports, military, diplomacy, and social relationships. The single exception to this is the book of Hebrews, which was written to Jewish Christians, probably in the mid-first century, while the Second Temple was probably still standing and sacrifice was still being offered in Jerusalem. Those for whom Hebrews was written understood the form and function of sacrifice in Israel's life and would not see Jesus' death as a "payment for sin." They would understand it to be dealing with sin itself and its corrosive effect on human life. More about that when we take up the book of Hebrews, below.

The Gospels

The Gospels never portray Jesus offering a sacrifice at the temple. Though Jesus' time in Jerusalem is largely spent in the temple, when there, the Gospels' concentration is on his teaching others who had come there for the festivals or to offer their own sacrifices. His rage at the abuse of the sacrificial system, not unlike that of the latter prophets before him, is evident in his driving out the money changers, vendors, and their animals that were available for sale as potential offerings. It is an event of such importance that it appears in all four Gospels (Matt 21:12–13; Mark 11:15–19; Luke 19:45–48; John 2:13–22). Yet, like the prophets, it is not the sacrificial system itself that Jesus is decrying but the way sacrifice, and the temple itself, were being abused.

It is quite true that in Jesus' teaching, he embraces the prophetic vision, that "to obey is better than sacrifice" (1 Sam 15:22), that the Lord desires righteousness and justice more than sacrifice (Prov 21:3), and "delights in loyalty rather than sacrifice, and knowledge of God rather than burnt offerings" (Hos 6:6). His teaching on the priority of reconciliation with one another over religious obligation (Matt 5:23–24), and God's desire for compassion and mercy rather than sacrifice, are all in accord with the prophetic traditions of sacrificial critique we have looked at in the previous chapter.

On the other hand, Jesus does not condemn sacrifice. We can safely assume that as a faithful Jew he attended sacrifices when in the temple. In one telling passage, found in each of the Synoptic Gospels, after healing the leper whose impurity had kept him from the temple, Jesus employs the sacrificial system by instructing the healed man to show himself to the priest and "offer for your cleansing what Moses commanded" (Mark 1:44; Matt 8:4; Luke 5:14). It was the priest's responsibility to determine if the healing were complete and the man could reenter Jewish society. The sacrifice that "Moses commanded" was a well-being sacrifice of thanksgiving!

Jesus never speaks of himself directly as a sacrifice, though many have assumed he is doing so when he speaks of giving his life as "a ransom for many" (Matt 20:28; Mark 10:45). However, the word ransom is not the language of the sacrificial cult. It is the language of commerce and is related to buying back what formerly belonged to you, or freeing those who have become enslaved, the way God ransomed Israel from Egypt. We shall see that when Jesus speaks of offering his life as a ransom for many, he is presenting it to free the world from slavery to the power of sin and death, not as a payment to God or the devil for sin or release from it, much less a payment that is both penal and substitutionary. More on this later.

Jesus is never spoken of in the Gospels as a sacrifice, though distorted readings of John the Baptist's naming him the Lamb of God have certainly led to that notion (John 1:20). The title, as we have seen, evokes the image of the Passover lamb, not a sacrificial lamb, and certainly not a lamb used in a purification *hattat* sacrifice, so commonly mistranslated in English Bibles as a "sacrifice for sin." Passover is Israel's annual reminder of God's power to free from slavery. It was not in any way a sacrifice to purge the corruption of sin, much less pay a penalty for sin itself.

When John calls Jesus the Lamb of God, he is not designating Jesus as someone who is going to have his throat slit for his blood, have that blood smeared over the cultic objects from the inner sanctum to the outer altar for the burnt sacrifice, the remaining blood poured out on the altar, and then his body burned outside the city gate, as happened to a lamb or bull slaughtered for New Testament *hattat*, to purify the altar. Rather, we hear John speaking in the metaphorical sense, saying that in and through Jesus, God is somehow taking away "the sin of the world." In Jesus' self-offering he is purging the cosmos of what has created and seeks to continue to create alienation from God, the rest of creation, and especially humankind. Jesus is not dying *for sinners* or *in their place*. He is dying to defeat the power of sin and death.

Was Jesus a Scapegoat?

The term *scapegoat* for the animal used in the Day of Atonement ritual was coined by William Tyndale in 1530. It was his attempt to explain in English the meaning of the second goat—*Azazel*—so named because it was designated to carry the people's sins into the wilderness of Azazel. The term was subsequently adopted for the same use in the later King James Version. Tyndale's scapegoat, largely due to the influence of English Christians' belief in substitutionary atonement, came to mean those who symbolically took on payment for the sins of others. Today, it has come to mean "one who bears the blame for the mistakes of others,"[1] doing so unwillingly. Because these distorted images of the *Azazel* in the Day of Atonement ritual have been misused to interpret the meaning of Jesus' death,[2] it is important that we recall six significant distinctions that emerge in the rite called Yom Kippur as we talked about it in the previous chapter.

First, the goat designated for Azazel—Tyndale's scapegoat—is not offered as a sacrifice. The goat is not slaughtered, and there is no blood manipulation.

Blood manipulation in the Day of Atonement liturgy is limited to the bull and other goat ("the LORD's") sacrificed for purification of the inner sanctums of the temple. There is no sacrificial slaying of the *Azazel* so that its blood might be included in those purgations. In addition, the goat designated *Azazel* is never presented as an offering to the Lord. That designation goes to the first goat, which is sacrificed on behalf of the nation. Moreover, laden with the sins and transgressions of all the people, and the impurities that would have been transferred onto it, the *Azazel* would have hardly been acceptable as an offering to even a demon, much less to the Lord!

The *Azazel* is not a vicarious substitute for Israel and its failures—the goat was not being punished, much less put to death. It was simply the "vehicle to dispatch Israel's impurities and sins to the wilderness/netherworld,"[3] a form of containment and delivery to elsewhere—away from the people.

As the high priest acknowledged and confessed *all the iniquities and transgressions* of himself and the people over the first goat, he turned all sins, including the high-handed ones—even intentional sins—into

---

1. *Webster's New World Dictionary*. This latter distortion is the dominant assumption of the atonement theology of the French literary critic René Girard and his mimetic theory of atonement, and one of the reasons his theory is so far from the mark of what is taking place in Jesus' self-offering. For Girard, Jesus saves by becoming a victim and thereby overturning once and for all the scapegoat mechanism in cultures.

2. Sklar, *Leviticus*, 213. See also Fleming Rutledge's discussion of the subject, *Crucifixion*, esp. 247–49. Though Rutledge concludes that "the scapegoat image makes little direct imprint in the New Testament" and notes that it "seems to be the province of the theologians rather than the biblical scholars, which suggests there needs to be more cross-conversation between the two," she continues to pursue that tack in attempting to defend penal substitutionary atonement theory (Rutledge, *Crucifixion*, 248).

3. Milgrom, *Leviticus*, 169.

inadvertent sins, thereby qualifying them for sacrificial expiation. That means that their pollution had been purged in the sacrifices of the bull or the first goat.

Finally, the subtle distinction between impurities and iniquities requires closer attention. They are not synonyms for one another. Impurities refer to the effect of Israel's iniquities on the sanctuary, the miasma of pollution created by Israel's actions. The blood of the bull and the sacrificed goat purged the impurities of the sanctuary from its very inner sanctum all the way to its outer court and burnt offering altar.

Iniquities refer to the acts themselves, those that created the miasma and their lingering effect on the *Israelite community*. It was these iniquities—the sinful acts of the Israelites—that the *Azazel* goat bore away from the people and the camp, taking them into the wilderness.[4] On the Day of Atonement, the two actions must go together. For it is not enough to expiate impurity; its cause must also be dealt with. This is what happens as the scapegoat is sent into the wilderness, carrying all the wrongs that have been placed on it by the high priest's confession and act of transfer.

It is easy to see why Christian theologians, especially those who understand so little about the sacrificial system and how it served Israel, could jump to the conclusion that Jesus was such a scapegoat. Yet, even then, only through first equating the goat *Azazel* with the suffering servant of Isaiah (Isaiah 52:13—53:12) could such a connection be made. From the perspective of the Day of Atonement itself as described in Leviticus (Lev 23:27–32), there is simply no warrant for it.

Place of Atonement: That Troublesome Greek Word

The place on the Ark of the Covenant where the high priest smeared the blood of first the sacrificial bull and then of the sacrificial goat is called in Hebrew *kapporet*. It is all but universally rendered "mercy seat" in most English translations. However, there is an emerging scholarly consensus, following the work of Hebrew scholar Jacob Milgrom, that the term is, in his words, "untranslatable, so far" but can "hardly be rendered 'mercy seat/throne' or even 'cover,' and is best translated, '*place of atonement.*'"[5] The blood of the bull and the goat that was smeared upon it and then sprinkled in front of it seven times accomplished what the blood of a

---

4. Milgrom, *Leviticus*, 171–72.
5. Milgrom, *Leviticus*, 167; emphasis added.

hattat did in Israel's sacrificial system when smeared on sanctuary objects: purge, expiate, and purify. The sprinkling of blood purified the inner shrine and rededicated that space for the Lord. It is the place God provided and where God made atonement to give Israel a fresh start for a new year.

When the Hebrew Scriptures were translated into Greek, the word *kapporet* became the Greek noun *hilasterion*, with its associated verb form, *hilaskomai*. In the book of Hebrews, *hilasterion* is simply the word used to describe the place on the ark of the covenant where the blood of the *hattat* was smeared on the Day of Atonement, as we have already said, most often translated "mercy seat," which Milgrom's scholarship now tells us is inadequate. *Hilasterion* appears in the New Testament just twice, once from Paul and once from the author of the book of Hebrews (Rom 3:25; Heb 9:5). It appears in a related form (*hilasmos*) in only two other places, 1 John 2:2 and 4:10. Paul's only use of *hilasterion* is in Romans 3:25, and his use of it there is complex. He writes to the Romans, God put Christ "forward as a *hilasterion* that becomes effective through faith in his blood." I have intentionally used the Greek here to avoid its confusing history of translation.

A review of this text in English Bibles reveals the disagreements and misunderstandings of what this cultic word should mean in English. Translations range from "propitiation" (ESV, KJV, and NAS), to "reconciliation" (GEN), to "expiation" (RSV, NAB), to "place of sacrifice where mercy is found" (CEB), to "seat of mercy" (TNT, NJB), to "sacrifice for reconciliation" (NJB), to, finally, the most popular in the modern versions: "sacrifice of atonement" (NIV, NRSV). This latter rendering in most modern English translations is at best a compromise of confusions and is highly misleading. The term never appears in the Hebrew Scriptures, and in the Greek translation of the Hebrew Scriptures (LXX), *hilasterion* is never used as a name for any of Israel's sacrifices. Modern New Testament scholarship suggests *hilasterion* means "a means of expiation, a place of expiation"—Jesus as the remover of sin, which disrupts or obstructs relationships between God and sinners.[6]

Consequently, just as *hilasterion* has an interesting history in translation, it also has an intriguing history of interpretation. When initially beginning the research for this book, I went to the gold standard of Kittel's *Theological Dictionary of the New Testament* and learned that the

---

6. Bauer, *Greek-English Lexicon*, 375. See also Danker, *Concise Greek-English Lexicon*, 175.

word in classic Hellenistic literature does indeed have to do with propitiation. However, when used in the LXX and the New Testament, it means expiation, as suggested by the two Greek lexicons just cited. The choice between these two vastly different meanings was first made by the KJV. Firmly entrenched in the doctrine of penal substitutionary atonement of the sixteenth and seventeenth centuries, the KJV rendered Rom 3:25 "whom God hath set forth to be a propitiation through faith in his blood."

More recent translations, less under the constraint of doctrinal positions and better informed by Hebrew cultic practice, have moved, as did the RSV, to "whom God put forward as an expiation by his blood." After the late twentieth-century explosion in new English translations, a look at the several ways *hilasterion* has been rendered in contemporary English Bibles demonstrates the continuing confusion over the word's meaning. Again, doctrinal positions still have a way of dictating translation decisions. The groundbreaking NET rendered the text "God publicly displayed him at his death as the mercy seat accessible through faith." Other modern translations range from "expiation by his blood,"[7] to "propitiation by this blood,"[8] to "a sacrifice of atonement,"[9] to, most recently, "a place of sacrifice where mercy is found."[10] All the recent translations still reveal their ambiguity and discomfort with what the word means.

We have already seen why "a propitiation for sin" is inappropriate—God is not being placated in Israel's sacrificial system, and certainly not as the New Testament uses the term. We will explore this more later. All atonement for Israel is God's work and emerges out of God's grace that has already "passed over" former sins! In that vein, "an expiation" would be the closest and most consistent translation—wiping out. In truth, it may be the older Geneva version that remains the best: "Whom God hath set forth to be a reconciliation." What is clear is that "sacrifice of atonement," in the cultic sense, is wrong and leads to wrong conclusions. It was not the killing of the sacrificial animal that was the essence of sacrifice but the manipulation of its blood that scrubbed out and purged the impurity created by sin and not the sin itself. To be sure, the phrase "by his blood" tempts us into thinking of this as a sacrifice, leading to the most recent trend of "sacrifice of atonement." It is more plausible to see not only this

---

7. RSV (1946).
8. KJV (1611/1769), NAS (1977), NAU (1995), ESV (2021).
9. NRSV (1989), NIB (1984), NIV (2011).
10. CEB (2011).

but most of the New Testament references to Jesus' blood as a metaphor for his death—"faith in his saving death"—not unlike the way "the cross" also functions for Paul as a reference to Jesus' saving death (1 Cor 1:17; Gal 6:12; Phil 3:18) as metaphorical references to his saving death.

In Rom 3:25 Paul is speaking of the righteousness of God that is revealed in Jesus' ultimate act of offering himself to deal with what has kept humankind from being reconciled to God. Why would Paul speak of faith in an object like blood, even that of Jesus? Faith for Paul is not in blood or even the cross, but in God and God's action in Christ, and the righteousness *of God* that is revealed in Jesus' death, resurrection, and ascension. Faith here is in God's righteousness.

Biblical scholar Christian Eberhart encourages us to remember that the *kapporet/hilasterion* was the *place* where the high priest smeared the blood of the bull and the goat as purification *hattat* offerings on the Day of Atonement to purge it of sin's contamination. He suggests that the better and more consistent translations of Rom 3:25 should be "whom God put forth as a place of atonement."[11] Eberhart reminds us that it is typical of Paul's theology of salvation that he makes God the "agent [of salvation by] 'putting forth' Jesus as the place of atonement."[12] Jesus is the One God has put forth—from the foundation of the world, according to Ephesians (1:4)—whose blood not only purges the contamination of the sin of the world but wards off evil and death, and has power to give new life to those who have faith in him.

There is, as the gospel hymn sings, "power in the blood."[13] But there is more power in Jesus' blood than expiation, mercy, or forgiveness. Life is in the blood! This makes what follows in the next Romans verse even more clear: "This was to show God's righteousness, *because in his divine forbearance he had passed over former sins; it was to prove at the present time that [God] is righteous and that [God] justifies the one who has faith in Jesus*" (Rom 3:25b–26a RSV; emphasis added).[14]

---

11. Eberhart, *Sacrifice of Jesus*, 115. I am highly indebted to Dr. Eberhart and his work on sacrifice, and commend his book to any who would like to explore this more deeply. Like this work, it is intentionally written for nonspecialists, especially pastors and laypeople.

12. Eberhart, *Sacrifice of Jesus*, 115.

13. Jones, "Would You Be Free."

14. Notice that God is the subject of the justifying act. It is God who justifies, not Jesus. Nor does one's faith in Jesus justify one. Justification is all God's work.

Whatever else Paul may mean here by "justify," he is not using the word *hilasterion* to mean a sacrifice to propitiate God for the sin of the world, the sin of humanity, or that of individuals. It most probably means "puts in right relationship with God those who trust in Jesus." The other place *hilasterion* appears is in the Letter to the Hebrews, which we will look at momentarily.

First, let us look at 1 John 2:2 and 4:10, where the cognate of *hilasterion*—*hilasmos*—is used. What we have said about Paul's usage of *hilasterion* can apply here as well. The word has to do with forgiveness and is better translated as "place of atonement" as in Romans, as "reconciliation," or with the general term "expiation" as does the RSV. Tyndale translated the word "to make agreement" for our sins.

The New Testament uses *hilasterion/hilasmos* only in these four cases, and rather than portray Jesus as a sacrificial victim for sin, they more correctly convey the traditional Jewish concept of Jesus being the "place of atonement." Jesus is the One God has given us as the incarnation of God's grace, mercy, and forgiveness, the place where God is making atonement/reconciliation with humanity. God is present as one of us in Jesus, who is *dealing* with sin; *reconciling*, enabling humanity to be at-one with God in him; and—the function of blood most often forgotten—*giving new life*!

The Book of Hebrews

It is the book of Hebrews that deals most directly with the cultic imagery of sacrifice in relationship to Jesus. The unknown author of this book, so steeped in the knowledge of the Jews' Scripture in the Greek of the Septuagint and the Jewish sacrificial cult of Jesus' day, is writing to second-generation Jewish Christians who know both but are considering abandoning Jesus as the Christ because of the hardship it is bringing them in daily life. They seem to be ready to return to the Torah and its cultic life, centered in the Judaism from which they have come. The author skillfully and beautifully uses the language of Israel's sacrificial cult to demonstrate that what God has done in Jesus is vastly superior to all they have come from. It is *their* (Jesus and God's) mutual offering of Jesus' life to deal with the sin of the world that makes it vastly superior to the old sacrificial system.

Hebrews presents Jesus' death in the context of the sacrificial cult of Israel but identifies him *not as a sacrificial animal*—certainly not the Lamb of God, much less as a powerless victim[15]—but as God's Son. He is "the exact imprint of God's very being who sustains all things by his powerful word" (Heb 1:3). In Jesus, God is cleaning things up, dealing with sin, once for all. Note that the Greek text does not say "our sin" as do the three older English translations.[16] Rather, it says "sins"—the sins of the world. Jesus is the place of atonement, as the *kapporet* was that place on the ark of the covenant where God made atonement with Israel. He is not a "sacrifice of atonement" as the NRSV translates 2:17, nor "that he might make atonement for the sins of the people," as both the NIB and NIV render it. Rather, the Greek text calls him "a merciful and faithful high priest in the things of God, to expiate (*hilaskesthai*) the sin of the people." It is the power in his blood that is offered to absorb, purge, and expunge the pollution of the *sin of the world*!

This theme emerges at the very beginning, as the author puts the words of the psalmist in Jesus' mouth, saying, "Sacrifices and offerings you have not desired, but a body you have prepared for me; in burnt offering and sin offerings you have no pleasure" (Heb 10:5–6; Ps 40:6–8). This, alone, should alert the careful reader to the fact that this book is not about Jesus as a sacrifice for sin. "Then I said, 'See, God, I have come to do your will, O God'" (Ps 40:7). It was the early church's habit to read the psalms prophetically—foretelling the preexistent Christ's incarnation, his work, and what he had come to accomplish. It is what theologians call "reading the psalms Christologically."

Understanding Jesus as the preexistent Christ, the author addresses the incarnation and portrays the necessity of the Word becoming human in Jesus to become one of us to become an eternal High Priest, after the order of Melchizedek (Heb 5:10). God's eternal Son is incarnate in Jesus to become one of us in all things. Jesus experiences the fullness of what it means to be human: growth that is physical, emotional, and spiritual, with a developing sense of identity and purpose. He faces the reality of life's hard choices, the fears about their consequences, including the fear of death. As he opens himself increasingly to embrace his divine vocation

---

15. The phrase "both victim and priest," popular in Roman Catholic and Lutheran theology, and repeated in hymnody after the seventeenth century, has no foundation in Scripture. It is a pious mistake, a concept developed on a false understanding of sacrifice in Israel's life.

16. Geneva, KJV, Tyndale.

and identity, he experiences the suffering that comes with living in this world as God's child.[17]

The man Jesus becomes more perfect until reaching his ultimate purpose as the eternal High Priest. He sheds his own blood to purge and purify (*katharismos*) sin's pollution. Though the high priests of Israel were required, on the Day of Atonement, to first offer a purification sacrifice (*hattat*) for themselves before offering one for the sins of the people, not so for the sinless Jesus. Having learned obedience through what he suffered, and having been made perfect, there was no need for Jesus to offer a sacrifice for himself. Rather, Jesus offers (*anaphero*) himself to God and, in doing so, suffers death, "so that by the grace of God he might taste death for everyone" (Heb 2:9) and become the source of eternal salvation for all who obey him (Heb 5:5–10; 7:27).

Jesus is not offering himself to God as a sacrificial substitute for humankind. He has "appeared once for all at the end of the age *to do away with sin* by the offering of himself" (Heb 9:26; emphasis added). The word behind "to do away with" is *athetesis*, which is a legal term for annulment, for something that is no longer in force, having been cancelled or abolished.[18] It is in this sense that Jesus' death is sacrificial—it has been offered on behalf of sin to break its enslaving power over life.

According to Hebrews, having made for all time a single offering on behalf of sins (*huper harmation*), Jesus entered "through the curtain (that is his flesh)" into God's heavenly sanctuary—the holy of holies—and sat down at God's right hand (Heb 10:12, 20). This is the archetypical place of authority. From there, Jesus now continues his ministry. As David Moffitt has written, "in Hebrews forgiveness is not granted by Divine fiat or legal declaration but comes by way of Jesus' sacrificial offering taking away sin."[19] We will turn to that more fully in the next chapter.

Jesus' death was "sacrificial" only in the sense of it being his self-offering to God to deal with sin. Jesus is anything but a sacrificial victim here. He *gives* his life to create life. Once again, the phrase "both victim and priest," though appearing as early as Origen, and popular in Roman Catholic and Lutheran theology, has no foundational basis in Hebrews. The animals slaughtered in Israel's sacrificial cult were never considered victims. They were gifts to God. Popular in some eucharistic piety, the

---

17. Johnson, *Hebrews*, 51–56.

18. See *athtesis* in Friberg, *Analytical Lexicon*; Danker, *Concise Greek-English Lexicon*.

19. Moffitt, "Hebrews," 534.

phrase has absolutely no basis in the Levitic understanding of sacrifice, by Paul, or in the book of Hebrews. For Hebrews, Jesus' death becomes the means of his ultimate entry into God's heavenly sanctuary/presence, so that he can continue to exercise his eternal priesthood on behalf of humanity.

Jesus does so "through the curtain (that is, through his flesh)" (Heb 10:20). Just as the earthly high priest entered the earthly inner sanctum through the curtain that separated it from the shrine, Jesus has entered God's heavenly sanctuary through the curtain of his body's death. He sits at God's right hand in all his risen glory. But he is doing more than simply sitting there awaiting his dispatch back into the world to take up his role as judge of the living and the dead, as he will one day do. Until then, Jesus continues to exercise his priestly ministry as intermediary and intercessor on humanity's behalf. The book's message is that, if those for whom it is being written renounce Jesus to return to their former ways, they will abandon him. In doing so, they will cut themselves off from his continuing ministry. Moreover, there will be no sacrifice sufficient to cover their sin of abandoning him.

The book of Hebrews uses sacrificial language metaphorically to make the point that Jesus' self-offering as high priest, and his intercessory presence before God, now render the sacrificial cult of Israel obsolete. Blood sacrifice is no longer effective or necessary. Jesus has not only dealt with the miasma of pollution created by sin, but he has also put away the power of sin and death to separate humanity from God.

From here, the author of Hebrews moves on to establish a New Testament theology of sacrifice not unlike that which is found in the writings of Paul. Sacrifice becomes day-to-day, practical discipleship in a world hostile to such living, offered to God out of the presence and power of the risen Christ (Rom 12:1–2). Hebrews exhorts its readers, saying, "Let us continually offer a *sacrifice of praise to God*, that is, the fruit of the lips that confess his name" (Heb 13:15; emphasis added). Our witness to Jesus—who he is, what he has done, and what he is now doing—is a sacrifice of the lips that renders praise and thanksgiving to God. This is especially true for those living in times of hardship and persecution because of their commitments to him.

The letter exhorts the Hebrew believers to continue to trust Christ, for all time and times. Early on, the author had urged his readers to "approach the throne of grace with boldness, so that [they] may receive mercy and find grace to help in time of need" (Heb 4:16). The word approach is the technical term for what the priests did in the temple as they moved to the altar to offer sacrifice.[20] It is now Christ who "is able to save those who approach God through him, since he is always making intercession for them" (Heb 7:25). "Jesus Christ is the same yesterday and today and forever" (Heb 13:8). They are to make their "approach with a true heart in full assurance of faith," believing that God not only exists but rewards those who thus seek God in faith. Jesus is the One who enables humanity to approach and be at-one with God (Heb 4:16; 7:19; 7:25; 10:22; 11:6).

To willingly persist in sin after having received this truth is perilous indeed. There no longer remains a sacrifice for such sin—only a fearful prospect of judgment (Heb 10:26–27). The only sacrifice that is real now is a sacrifice of praise and thanksgiving to God, the "fruit of the lips" that confess Jesus' name. That is the day-to-day practical Christian life, following Jesus, opening oneself to his presence in life, and daily living out of it as he in life progressively opened himself to becoming who he was destined to be—the author, pioneer, victor, and finisher of our faith.[21]

Beyond the book of Hebrews, the word sacrifice, in its actual cultic meaning, is used extraordinarily little in the New Testament and only once by the apostle Paul. Let us then turn to Paul and his witness to who Jesus is and what he did, as Paul was proclaiming his gospel before the four Gospels were written and in circulation.

The Apostle Paul

Paul was the most literate, well-educated, and, arguably, the most religious and sophisticated of any of the other eleven apostles. He was deeply versed in Israel's religious history and culture, especially in first-century Jewish apocalyptic thought. He was a Pharisee. Gamaliel had schooled him, and he was something of a religious prodigy (Acts 22:3). He was advanced in Judaism beyond many of his same age (Gal 1:4). But Paul was not an eyewitness to the life and ministry of Jesus, nor even to his crucifixion. As he tells us, he was born too late for that (1 Cor 15:8). Rather, as he repeatedly insists, it is his encounters with the risen Christ that are the validation of his apostleship and the foundation and *source* of his gospel. This means that, above all, Paul was what today we call not only a charismatic but, first and foremost, a mystic.

20. Daly, *Sacrifice Unveiled*, 62.
21. Daly, *Sacrifice Unveiled*, 63.

Paul's letters were written, for the most part, to the churches he founded, as well as to the church in Rome. His letters are arguably the earliest and the most important New Testament material for a faithful understanding of God's work of atonement in and through Jesus. Unfortunately, too often Paul is read from a position of doctrinal presupposition, without an understanding of what lies behind his use of various images as metaphors, the different arenas of life from which those images come, and how they functioned in those worlds. Among the challenges to reading Paul, one of the most significant is to understand which of these various worlds he inhabits is being used to express his convictions about Jesus.

The Challenges of Reading Paul

Paul was first and foremost a Jew. He knew that world and its sacrificial cult as a means of worship from the inside, in a way none today could know it. He was highly educated, not only in Torah but also in Hellenistic philosophy and rhetoric, and he was comfortable and skilled with allegory and typology as interpretative tools to help proclaim the gospel.

Paul freely used all of these as he moved in and out of both Greek and Jewish worlds. As a Pharisee, he had full command of the Pharisaical system of biblical exegesis as well as its conviction of two forms of the law, one written and the other oral. He was deeply immersed in the apocalyptic worldview of the Judaism of his day, expecting the full breaking in of the new age of God's reign upon Jesus' return. Until then, he knew himself to be a participant in God's unfolding reign as part of God's new creation "in Christ"—one of his favorite metaphors for living in union with the risen Lord.[22]

Paul could look back into his Judaism and see things through the lens of Christ and find in them meanings that, heretofore, were hidden to him. From his experience with worship in the temple in Jerusalem, he understood *corban*, the various five forms of sacrifice in worship as occasions of atonement, the difference between expiation and propitiation, the role of the scapegoat on Yom Kippur, baptism, covenant meals, Passover, and the meaning of the Passover lamb. What is often forgotten about Paul is that he was still a practicing Jew. In other words, Paul

---

22. The phrase appears some fifty-eight times in the undisputed letters of Paul.

understood sacrifice in its first-century Second Temple context in ways we can never understand it.

Paul was born a Roman citizen, with all the privileges and perspectives that citizenship brought to him in the first-century CE Greco-Roman world. As a tentmaker, he could provide for himself in almost any cultural setting. He was extremely well traveled, a citizen of the world and familiar with its various cultures and images. All these worlds, gifts, and perspectives get employed by Paul as he uses the full range of linguistic and literary tools at his command to announce his gospel.

The challenge for us in reading Paul's mixture of these images is knowing the difference between sacrifice for worship of adoration, thanksgiving, and well-being; sacrifice as exchange and purification; sacrifice as reparation; and the other cultic metaphors he uses, especially his phrase "living sacrifice." These are not made specific by Paul or further explained. He evidently felt no need to do so, as both he and his readers knew he was speaking metaphorically, not literally. They all understood the cultural contexts and the point of contact made by the image that causes a metaphor to work in the first place, something most readers of Paul today do not have readily at hand.

Paul's Use of Sacrifice

The fact that Paul is writing, for the most part, to gentile churches[23] may well explain why he rarely, if ever, uses *thusia*, the Greek word for sacrifice, to proclaim Jesus' work or explain his saving death.[24] Gentile readers

---

23. The church in Rome was comprised of both Jews and gentiles, and probably traces its beginning to the day of Pentecost, when Jews from Rome were in Jerusalem for the festival, became believers in Jesus, took that experience back home with them, and became the beginning of the church where Peter is later active and martyred. On the other hand, many scholars today think Paul is writing to the church that became dominant in Rome, after the Jews were expelled from Rome by Emperor Claudius, somewhere between 41 and 53 CE. That would make it a gentile church. Still others are convinced Paul is writing to a mixed Jewish and gentile church that emerged when Jews returned to Rome once the ban has been lifted. If so, Paul is encouraging the gentile Christians to welcome back the Jewish Christians; if not, Paul is seeking to pave the way for the returning Jewish believers' full acceptance into that congregation they had initially founded but had been forced to leave. Others believe the exiled Jews have already returned and that is creating some of the tensions that Paul addresses in the last two chapters of the book.

24. The one place it does appear in reference to Christ is Eph 5:2, possibly a deutero-Pauline text that says, "Live [walk] in love, as Christ loved us and gave himself up

unfamiliar with Jewish sacrificial practices would only distort sacrificial imagery from their own cultic perspectives, the way it would begin to be distorted in the Greek-speaking churches within a hundred years of the destruction of the Second Temple, and especially by the Western churches since the Reformation.

Paul's Theology of Sacrifice

Though Paul avoided the word sacrifice (*thusia*), using it only once, and there, quoting the tradition (1 Cor 5:7), he clearly had a theology of it. In his letters, he incorporated much of the imagery of the sacrificial cult of Israel as he preached Christ crucified and risen, but always metaphorically rather than literally. First, of course, was his understanding of the sacrificial nature of Jesus' death as a liberating moment and event not unlike Passover. As we have seen, he could write to the Corinthians, "For our paschal lamb, Christ, has been sacrificed"(1 Cor 5:7). But behind that was his conviction that Christ's mission was to be God's resolution of the blight and plague of sin in life—a second Passover—and thereby reveal and demonstrate God's righteousness in redeeming the world from sin (Rom 1:17).

God sent Christ into the world to be the One who dealt with sin on humanity's behalf. "For our sake he made him to be sin who knew no sin, so that in him we might become the righteousness of God" (2 Cor 5:21). The language Paul is using here is not legal but that of cultic ritual transfer—a reversal is taking place—an exchange. Behind that were not only images of the Hebrew *hattat* purification and reconsecration, as well as the Day of Atonement with the transfer of the nation's sin onto the goat sent into the wilderness, but also images of reversal. Christ became sin so that humanity might become what they are not—the righteousness of God. Or God sent God's "own son in the likeness of sinful flesh, and to deal with sin, he [Christ] condemned sin in the flesh" (Rom 8:3). A similar cultic transfer combined with mixed metaphors appears in Galatians as Paul writes, "Christ redeemed us from the curse of the law by becoming a curse for us" (Gal 3:13).

Paul's only other use of sacrifice—*thusia*—is to refer to his own life and the life of his readers. He *never* uses it to speak of Christ's death.

---

for us, a fragrant offering and sacrifice to God." Again, the text is not urging its readers to become cultic sacrifices but, like Christ, to offer themselves to God in love.

Thusia is always used as a metaphor for living faithfully "in Christ." Paul urges the members of the Roman church to "present [their] bodies as a living sacrifice, holy and acceptable to God, which is [their] spiritual worship" (Rom 12:1). He addresses the Corinthians concerned about whether they can faithfully eat meat sacrificed to idols, speaking negatively about the pagans who offer sacrifices to demons rather than to God, warning the Corinthians not to participate in such worship, lest they thereby join themselves to demons (1 Cor 8:1–13, 10:20–33). He speaks of himself being poured out as a libation[25] over the "sacrifice and offering" of the Philippians' faith and later speaks of their gift to him through Epaphroditus as a "fragrant offering, a sacrifice acceptable and pleasing to God" (Phil 2:17; 4:18). Beyond that, Paul does not use the word. He had a more appropriate vocabulary at hand.

Other Pauline Images of Atonement

From Paul's experience of the first-century Greco-Roman world, he had a multitude of options for forming his arguments. We have already mentioned those from the realm of economics—*redeem, ransom, exchange,* and *save*. This economic language had a history of theological use in Judaism in understanding God's intervention on Israel's behalf—especially *redeem/redemption*.

From the political-diplomatic-judicial worlds, Paul could use the imagery of *reconciliation, recapitulation,* and *liberation*. From Roman law court, he used the images of *justify, condemn, acquit, liberate, adopt, set free*. Paul's knowledge of Hellenistic philosophy enabled him to utilize the notion of the *noble death* of those who died for their people, country, or a noble cause. In Greco-Roman culture, *self-sacrifice* was especially *salvific*, as exemplified in the plays of Euripides, and thought to have vicarious saving power.

The notion of the saving power of self-sacrifice was not simply present in Hellenistic culture. It had become, under Hellenistic influence, very much a part of more recent Jewish history and thinking during the time of the Maccabees. Those third-century BCE Maccabees who gave their lives to maintain Torah under the murderous rule of Antiochus

---

25. Libations of wine or "drink offerings" were regularly added to and poured over burnt offerings (Exod 29:38–41). Here Paul is using the image as a metaphor for the possibility of his own martyrdom. He would gladly add his life of sacrifice to theirs.

Epiphanes IV were understood to have vindicated the whole nation of its sin by their death.

The slaughtered Maccabees were martyrs, and martyr's blood was as purifying as that of unblemished animals in cultic sacrifice, whether for the sins of the people or the land itself, as it became ransom for the sin of the nation (4 Macc 6:29; 17:10, 21–22). Consequently, Paul could speak of Christ "dying for us" or "for our sins," (Rom 4:25; 5:8; 1 Cor 8:11; 15:3; Gal 1:4; 1 Thess 5:10) or Christ dying for the weak and ungodly but, again, never as a sacrifice (Rom 5:6). Paul not only used these various images from their differing contexts, but to make matters even more complex, he often mixed them together in a single verse—piling one on top of another, adding nuance and shades of meaning—as he drove his arguments home to make his point.[26]

Given Paul's skill in drafting his letters, with his masterful architecture of argument, his deep immersion and dexterity in Second Temple Judaism, his knowledge of Greek philosophy, and his fluency in rhetoric and prose, care needs to be taken to examine and understand the logic of each image within its own context before bringing it together with other images and shaping them into a unified theological thought. The result can be theologically breathtaking, as anyone who has read Paul's letter to the Romans in one sitting, with critical interpretative tools at hand, soon discovers. On the other hand, failure to do so has led to some awfully bad atonement theology, which is precisely Finlan's point.

Paul's Mixed Metaphors

The one place Paul does link Christ to sacrifice we have already mentioned when, in his Letter to the Corinthians, he writes, "For our paschal lamb, Christ, has been sacrificed." It is a classic illustration of Paul mixing images and metaphors to serve his purpose of exhortation.

Paul is in the process of castigating the Corinthians for their toleration of the man reported to be having sexual relations with his father's wife. Paul not only pronounces judgment on the man but on the entire congregation, reminding them that "a little yeast leavens the whole batch of dough." Sin is never just personal! He continues:

26. See Finlan, *Problems with Atonement*, 5–7, for a more technical discussion of Paul's use of mixed metaphor from multiple arenas of life. Finlan's work has been most helpful and influential in the development of this chapter, and I commend it for those who want to follow these themes in Paul more deeply.

> Clean out the old yeast so that you may be a new batch, as you really are unleavened. For our paschal lamb, Christ, has been sacrificed. Therefore, let us celebrate the festival, not with the old yeast, the yeast of malice and evil, but with the unleavened bread of sincerity and truth. (1 Cor 5:7–8)

Let us look at this more carefully. Using the background of both Passover and the Feast of Unleavened Bread (which immediately follows Passover), preparation for which requires the elimination of anything containing yeast, Paul appropriates the image of yeast/leaven as a metaphor for sin.

> Clean out the old yeast [*image for sin*] so that you may be a new batch [*new life in Christ and his church*], as you really are unleavened [*sinless in him*].

To drive his point home, Paul portrays Christ as the paschal lamb. The lamb's slaughter in Egypt on the eve of the first Passover was an image of being freed from slavery. And, as we have seen in Leviticus, the paschal lamb *is not a sacrifice, much less one for sin.* When Paul says "Christ has been sacrificed,"[27] he is simply saying that in Christ's offering himself up to death, he has initiated a new Passover, opening a door to new life beyond the grip and slavery of sin. If the Corinthians are to be true to the faith, they must live that way. Consequently, Paul continues,

> Therefore, let us celebrate the festival, not with the old yeast, the yeast of malice and evil [*the sexual immorality infecting the community*], but with the unleavened bread of sincerity and truth.

This not only demonstrates Paul's ability to adopt and mix metaphors for his purpose but may also be an example of Paul's use of typology.

Typology takes an event from the past, in this case, from Hebrew Scriptures, and presents it as a preview or type of what is to come. Typologically, Paul seems to be saying that the Passover lamb was a type of Christ whose blood has functioned as means for liberating and identifying, as well as shielding his own people.[28] What we have then is a rhetorical flourish intended to demonstrate not only the soundness but

---

27. Note, he does not add "for us" as has been popular to do in some communion liturgies at the breaking of bread.

28. Another example of Paul's use of typology is his description later in 1 Corinthians of Christ as the spiritual rock that followed the Israelites through the wilderness giving them "spiritual drink" (1 Cor 10:1–4). Once again, the use of typology comes amid Paul chiding the Corinthians for their idolatry.

the superiority of Paul's argument. Using images from cult, economics, politics, and law, it is a linguistic and theological masterpiece.

The primary point here is Paul's criticism of the church's acceptance of the sinful behavior among them, not that Christ was somehow sacrificed to forgive their sin. But when these series of images are simply lumped together and read to mean one and the same thing, and read without any serious understanding of what they mean in their own worlds and contexts, let alone what they might mean when conflated with others, the result is extraordinary distortion that leads to not only bad theology but theories of atonement that are scripturally wrong and have no biblical basis.[29]

To make matters even more challenging, Paul frequently tied cultic metaphors to those from other realms of life. To the Corinthians, he could write, "In Christ, God was reconciling the world to himself, not counting their trespasses against them" (2 Cor 5:19). Though he does not say why their trespasses are not counted against them, we can know from our understanding of Israel's cult. The reason the trespasses were no longer counted is the miasma they created has been purified and their actions have been transferred and borne away. Reconciliation was the result of all of that and now a reality.

Other Pauline Terms Explaining Christ's Work

Reconciliation in the gentile world is primarily a diplomatic term, which becomes in argumentation a social metaphor, not a cultic one. When Paul writes to the Corinthians to remind them that they have been "bought with a price" (*agorazo*) (1 Cor 6:20; 7:23), he is making double use of the imagery behind *agorazo*: the gentiles will hear the language of the marketplace—especially the ransom price to free a slave—while those Jews among them, now Christian, will hear of the price of Israel's redemption from Egypt. So too for the legal metaphors Paul mixes with the image of Jesus' blood—here an image for his death in much the same way the cross is an image of shameful death. Jesus' self-offering death justifies humankind (Rom 5:9), *justify* being a legal term that means acquitted.

Justification is also a relational term, meaning put into proper relationship with another once again. "As one man's trespass led to condemnation for all, so one man's act of righteousness [his death] leads

29. Finlan, *Problems with Atonement*, 37–38, 61–62.

to justification and life for all" (Rom 5:18). Behind this lies Paul's understanding of Jesus as the second Adam, sent by God to undo Adam's transgression and its impact in and on life, and thus set us in a right (justified) relationship with God, so as to begin again. This concept is called recapitulation, and we will look at it more in the next chapter.

Paul could at the same time write, "Now that we have been justified [put in a right relationship with God] by his blood [death], we will be saved through him from the wrath of God" (Rom 5:9). Notice the future tense in Paul's argument about salvation from God's wrath. Jesus' death was not a once and done thing on Good Friday afternoon that automatically saves those who simply believe in it. Rather, Jesus' death puts believing humankind in a proper relationship with God. Out of that restored relation, they can grow increasingly like Christ as his sisters and brothers in the new creation. Living lives centered in Christ, they are empowered to deal with sin and death now, and will, at his return, be "saved through him from the wrath of God."

Paul can also use the language of the sacrificial cult to speak of God's presence in believers' lives transforming them into God's new and holy temple (1 Cor 3:16–17)—the place where God lives. Sometimes Paul seems to be speaking to his readers as individuals and at others as a community, as if to say it is not just one or the other—both are true. It is not just that God is living in them as the new temple; rather, God's indwelling presence in Christ is making them holy.

Paul can also use the cultic term of tabernacle or temple to describe Christians' lives as the places God lives and is at work in them continuing the work of redemption. He can write to the Galatians, "I have been crucified with Christ; and it is no longer I who live, but it is Christ who lives in me" (Gal 2:19–20). Paul died with Christ in the waters of baptism and has been raised to new life, empowered by the risen Christ who he knows now lives in him.

The most obvious way Paul uses sacrificial metaphor is to talk not about the cross but about his life as an apostle and the quality of life faithful believers are to live. And so, he writes to the Corinthians:

> We are afflicted in every way, but not crushed; perplexed, but not driven to despair; persecuted, but not forsaken; struck down, but not destroyed; always carrying in the body the death of Jesus, so that the life of Jesus may also be made visible in our bodies. For while we live, we are always being given up to death

for Jesus' sake, so that the life of Jesus may be made visible in our mortal flesh. (2 Cor 4:8–11)

Or to the Romans:

> I appeal to you therefore, brothers and sisters, by the mercies of God, to present your bodies as a living sacrifice, holy and acceptable to God, which is your spiritual worship. Do not be conformed to this world, but be transformed by the renewing of your minds, so that you may discern what is the will of God— what is good and acceptable and perfect. (Rom 12:1–2)

Is it any wonder that Paul's gospel met resistance, even in his own day? Was it simply too radical and bold? Was it too mystical for those who had not known his visions or had had none of their own? Was it too "this-world" oriented with its assumptions about the goodness of creation and life, ideas and convictions that the Greek world could not accept? Was it so mixed in its metaphors and various other cultural appropriations that it was difficult for lesser minds to grasp? That certainly seems to be what the Second Letter of Peter, written some twenty to thirty years after Paul's death, is saying (2 Pet 3:16).

Sacrifice after Paul

It is no surprise then that those who followed Paul after his death found themselves writing in his name, attempting to explain him more fully. They did so to extend his influence in new cultural contexts and issues or to appropriate his authority to address new questions or challenges. On the other hand, there were also those writers who sought to tame, adjust, simplify, or reduce Paul's thought to something more easily digested or accepted within cultures that found Paul too radical, and to do so in Paul's name. Among those letters that do this are the Pastoral Epistles.[30]

The epistles of 1 and 2 Timothy and Titus are called the Pastoral Epistles because unlike most of Paul's authentic letters—save Philemon— they are not written to a church but are from an older pastor addressing

---

30. Finlan, *Problems with Atonement*, 37–38, 61–62. Finlan provides a much more detailed and annotated discussion of this reducing faith to dogma trend in the last third of the first century. This may also include the letters to the Ephesians and Colossians, both of which are in question because, through their theology is "Pauline," their vocabulary seems not to be so. They seem to many a bridge between those letters Paul did write and the clearly pseudo-epistles of the Pastoral Epistles that bear his name.

a younger one. They show a concern for church management and governance that was not yet in place in Paul's day, much less a concern to Paul. In addition, these letters reveal a clear movement *away* from Paul's first-level proclamation of the gospel as the revelation of God's righteousness revealed in Jesus Christ, to *doctrine about Christ*.

Paul's emphasis upon Christ's cross, resurrection, people of the new creation, and expected imminent triumphal return, and the good news they bring shift in the Pastoral Epistles. There, the concerns are about the delay of Christ's return, persecution being endured, and the fate of those who do not embrace Christ as Lord or of those who have fallen away from the faith once embraced. The warnings against false teachers and instructions to maintain sound doctrine suggest the various forms of Greek gnostic philosophy and thought that began to emerge in the church in the late first and early second centuries, some forty to fifty years after Paul.

Constraining Paul—A Classic Example

Within these later texts written in Paul's name, there are moments in which Paul flatly contradicts himself. Having declared in Galatians that in Christ there is neither male nor female (Gal 3:26), in these later letters there are prescribed gender roles that Paul seems not to have observed if we read not only the book of Acts but also the farewell sections of his authentic epistles—especially Romans. However, the Pastoral Epistles reaffirm, through Paul's voice, the gender norms and household codes that would certainly make Paul less offensive to the culture of the day, and even more acceptable to those who were now exercising ecclesiastical leadership.[31]

Can women speak in church? In Romans, Paul acknowledges his indebtedness to Phoebe, whom he names a servant (*diakonon*) of the church in Cenchrea (Rom 16:1). He speaks of his reliance on Priscilla with her husband Aquila, who not only hosted a house church in Ephesus but also took Apollos aside to correct him and explained the faith to him more accurately (Acts 18:24). And, of course, there is Junia, Paul's relative, who

---

31. The irony of this is that it is precisely these portions of the Pastoral Epistles that are so offensive to many of today's readers—especially women—and have given Paul such a bad name among them.

was also a fellow prisoner with him. He names Junia "prominent among the apostles" and in the faith before him (Rom 16:7).

Yet, in 1 Timothy, Paul is presented as saying, "Let a woman learn in silence with full submission. I permit no woman to teach or to have authority over a man; she is to keep silent" (1 Tim 2:12). Clearly, Paul is being toned down to be more palatable to a church increasingly led by men. And though that same theme does appear at the end of 1 Cor 14:34–35, many scholars today—save the most conservative—recognize this as a later editorial revision inserted to make the Corinthian text compatible with 1 Timothy, and more acceptable to a Hellenistic culture offended by women in leadership.[32] In other words, even authentic Pauline texts got modified to fit the needs of the church leadership during this period of scriptural development![33]

Metaphor Reduced to Doctrinal Formula

The good news Paul sought to convey in his various salvific, redemptive, and new creation metaphors is reduced in the Pastoral Epistles and turned into doctrinal formulas. Finlan writes, "Paul's subtleties are lost on his successors who fuse together and freeze his metaphors. Redemption becomes the controlling figure. Even sacrifice is understood in terms of redemption."[34] "Redeemed at a price" begins to dominate late first-century Christian thought.

Paul's "while we still were sinners Christ died for us" (Rom 5:8), emerges in Ephesians as "in him we have redemption through his blood" (Eph 1:7). "Redemption through his blood" soon has little to do with the power of blood to purge, purify, and give life, or a martyrdom that is redemptive for the nation, and instead becomes a doctrine about blood sacrifice for sin that is more pagan than biblical. Paul's "Christ died for our sin according to the scriptures" (1 Cor 15:3), by the time of 1 Timothy has become "Christ Jesus . . . gave himself a ransom for all" (1 Tim 2:6).

By the time of 1 Peter, sacrificial language has become even less metaphorical and more literal:

---

32. Brown et al., *New Jerome Biblical Commentary*, 811–12. Finlan, *Problems with Atonement*, 64.

33. Our task is not to sit in judgment on those who made the changes for whatever their reasons but simply recognize them for what they are, and be free to discard them for what they are—inappropriate for our day.

34. Finlan, *Problems with Atonement*, 64.

> You know that you were ransomed from the futile ways inherited from your ancestors, not with perishable things like silver or gold, but with the precious blood of Christ, like that of a lamb without defect or blemish. (1 Pet 1:18–19)

As the church entered the second century of its life, the focus began to shift. Paul's "saving faith" as a life dynamically lived out of a right relationship with God, in and through Christ, empowered by the Spirit, increasingly began to disappear. In its place there began to emerge what would become an overriding concern with believing right teachings about Jesus, who he was, his death, why it was necessary, and what it accomplishes for those who believe in him.

It is time for us to look at the theories of atonement that emerged in the church in the next two thousand years as it has continued to wrestle with understanding what God was doing in Christ. To that we will now turn.

Chapter 7

Atonement Theories

Post-Apostolic Church to Reformation

JESUS' PASSION, DEATH, RESURRECTION, and ascension had taken place. It was not an accident of history. It was central to what God was doing in and through him. Post-apostolic church leaders attempted to explain what this meant based on five principal sources: the Hebrew Scriptures translated into Greek (LXX), the Letters of Paul, the Letter to the Hebrews, the emerging Gospels, and the writings that now make up the last portion of the New Testament, especially the book of Revelation. Rome had destroyed the Second Temple in 70 CE, thus ending the sacrificial cult in Judaism. The church had become increasingly made up of Greek-speaking gentiles, with little or no knowledge of Israel's Scriptures—especially in their original Hebrew—its religion, or history.

Post-Apostolic Church

As the church moved into its second century, the question of who Jesus was and what he had done were leading to other controversies. What did it mean that he was the Son of God? What did it mean to say "Jesus is Lord!," given the various associations "Lord" had among both Jews and gentiles? Was he the incarnation of the One who had appeared to Moses—the I AM? Or was he simply God's most faithful human servant, raised from death to the designation of Son of God? The term had, of course, also been used by the Roman emperor Augustus. On the other hand, was Jesus *truly* human, or did he simply *appear* so, divinity dressed in the guise of human flesh? The questions we reviewed in chapter 3 were now increasingly being asked. To answer them, the emerging theologians wrote about how they understood what God had done in Jesus, using their emerging Scriptures to do so.

Ransom

Both Matthew's and Mark's Gospels record Jesus saying that he was giving his life "as a ransom for many" (Matt 20:28, Mark 10:45; also 1 Tim 2:6). In the first-century world with its familiarity with slavery, the word ransom could be used in one of two ways. As a noun, it was the fee paid to free someone, whether from slavery or from being a prisoner of war. As a verb, it was the action taken by someone to set another free, as God had ransomed Israel from Egypt's grip.[1] For roughly the first fifty years after the resurrection, this latter image of Jesus' death as an action setting humanity free from slavery to sin and death was the dominant one.

As the church's Jewish roots receded and the Greco-Roman gentile worldview became dominant, ransom began to be understood differently. By the time of the writing of 1 Timothy, ransom had moved from saving action to payment.[2] A ransom was the expense of redeeming prisoners of war, slaves, or property within one's clan that had been lost to pay a debt in the world. In a gentile world that knew nothing of Israel's sacrificial practice and its unique use of such language, sacrifice became less an image of something joyfully offered to God, as it had been in Judaism—the image the author of Hebrews had used symbolically—but increasingly was literalized and seen as an act of killing something that paid the ransom's price. Jesus' words that he had come to give his life a ransom for sin were no longer heard as an action he was taking to free sin's grip on humanity but as the payment of his life through his sacrificial death to pay for that sin.

But to whom was the payment made? The initial answer was to the tempter, satan—by now free of any Hebrew constraint, conflated into the adversary who was at war with God over human souls—the devil. The

---

1. In fact, even the two Gospel texts can be read as Jesus' freeing, redeeming, liberating action rather than a payment. It is 1 Tim 2:6 that makes it a noun.

2. It is one of the textual reasons biblical scholars question the letter's being written by Paul. As we have seen, that is not Paul's theology.

devil had taken humanity captive at Adam's fall in the garden. The devil had, thereafter, some legal right or claim over humanity that needed a payment for them to be released from his grip. It was Origen (184–253) who saw God paying a ransom to the devil for Adam's sin and humanity's redemption.

Other emerging theologians began to ask why the devil should deserve a ransom payment for such treachery. Some answered that God had given the devil permission to hold sinners in bondage as payment for their failed behavior in Eden. Any act of liberation on God's part without some payment would violate that agreement, and God must be true to God's word. Not until a ransom was paid could the agreement be nullified and humanity freed. However, that raised another question. If a ransom price was to be paid, and the devil does not deserve it or have claim to it, to whom must it be paid? This suggested that God, not the devil, was the recipient of Jesus' offering.

Defeat of the Devil

Others thought that so long as the devil held only sinners in bondage, he was keeping his end of the bargain, but when he went after Jesus, he exceeded his rights within the agreement, claiming and killing a sinless one, and the deal was off. In this view, God drew the devil into a trap, tempting him with Jesus, whose divinity was hidden behind his humanity. When the devil claimed Jesus in death, he got more than he bargained for and truly got his due. He was defeated by Christ in that encounter, and the result was humankind were released from the devil's grip.

This was the first in a series of attempts to show how Christ had triumphed over the devil in his crucifixion and death. It would later come to be known as *Christus Victor* in multiple forms. Even St. Augustine (354–430) followed this line with his bold analogy of the cross as a divine mousetrap. Whether Jesus was bait on the mousetrap, as St. Augustine suggested, or a worm on a fishhook, as Gregory of Nyssa (335–394) portrayed it, either way, the devil had been deceived, just as the serpent had deceived Adam and Eve. In that divine tête-à-tête, the devil had been defeated and deprived of his due and grasp. It was one thing to try to seduce the primordial couple, another the Son of God. The devil had overplayed his hand, was caught, defeated, repaid for his treachery, and lost his dominion over humanity.

For the next nine centuries, the conversation moved back and forth primarily between these two forms of the theory. And though other theories of atonement would be developed and considered, the ransom theory continued to be the dominant one and explored in some detail by many of the church's theologians, well into the eleventh century.

Recapitulation—Irenaeus (130–c. 202 CE)

Irenaeus was a second-century bishop in the south of France and the first post-New Testament Christian writer to appropriate Paul's theology of incarnation. He believed that atonement and redemption took place through God becoming human in Jesus the Christ. Irenaeus was also the church's first "biblical theologian," known for his extensive work with identifying and normalizing various books as Christian Scripture, especially the books of the New Testament. He is the earliest Christian writer, following the New Testament authors themselves, whose writings we have today.

Irenaeus was a student of Polycarp,[3] who was said to have been a student of the apostle John. It was Irenaeus who first insisted that it was the beloved apostle who wrote the Gospel of John and was, in fact, John himself. Irenaeus used John's Logos theology foundationally in his own work as well as in his reading of Paul. Driven by his belief in the unity and goodness of God, Irenaeus held the conviction that everything that happened in and to creation was part of God's overall good plan for its salvation.

God intentionally created the world as a difficult place, where people were confronted with hard, moral decisions that, if made properly, would enable them to mature increasingly into the fullness of God's intention for them when God created them. Though they were initially formed immature in God's image—as Adam and Eve were immature—obedience would lead to maturity and, finally, into the fullness and blessedness of the image of God they had been created to become.

Adam and Eve's disobedience brought sin and death into creation and, through their disobedience, corruption that not only entered the world but marred and distorted the divine image in which humanity had been made, ever after passing on that "flaw" to humankind. However,

---

3. First- and early second-century CE bishop of Smyrna, who died at the stake as a martyr.

long before creation, God had known this would be. Consequently, the preexistent Logos would become incarnate in Jesus Christ as a means of salvation, correcting Adam's failure, remaking and restoring creation.

Irenaeus reasoned that because God is immortal and incorruptible, Christ, when united to a flawed humanity through the incarnation, would be the reconciler between God and humanity, and would also nascently convey and transfer his divine qualities to humankind. Those qualities would begin to emerge in humanity, over time, eventually spreading into all human life like a benign but saving, good infection. And though the essence of this salvation was through a process of maturing, it took place in Christ's incarnation, not in humanity's final achievement of maturity. That maturity would finally come in God's own time, but the problem had been addressed by the incarnation and would not be reversed.[4] Jesus had become what we are so that he might make us to be what he is, a theme that would become central to the atonement theology of Athanasius in the fourth century CE; T. F. Torrance in the twentieth century; and, most recently, Kathryn Tanner in this one.

Did the cross have a role to play in this? Yes, Jesus' obedience unto death as God's Word was God's victory over sin and evil, absorbing them into God's economy to be transformed into good. During his passion, Jesus' soul was handed over to Satan as ransom. However, ransom here is not a payment to Satan, as was beginning to emerge in atonement theologies of the day. Satan, failing to see the bond between Jesus' soul and God the Father, unwittingly took Jesus' soul to Hades, where, with its divine power, it freed all held captive there, taking them, now liberated from sin and death, with him in his ascension.

The cross was Christ's act of redeeming—"the price of the victor's toils endured that we might be free, not a price paid to omnipotence or to any lesser power."[5] God had not simply provided a way of escape from the devil; God had redeemed the universe, restored nature through nature, so that in the end, all that came from God would finally return to God.

Highly influenced by Paul, Irenaeus believed the incarnation of the Logos in Jesus made him both a reconciler and the new Adam, the One in whom God was redoing, restoring, and redeeming human life.

---

4. Irenaeus believed that Jesus lived to be much older than thirty or thirty-three, as he is portrayed in the Synoptic Gospels, and did not die until in his fifties, which in Irenaeus' day was the age at which "old age" was thought officially to begin; consequently, Jesus recapitulated the entire lifespan of humanity.

5. Richardson, "Exposition of the Faith," 351.

It is called a recapitulation model of atonement—God in Christ doing over, improving, and expanding humanity into the fullness of God's intentions. Neither sacrificial nor juridical, Jesus, as the new Adam, undid what Adam had done.

Athanasius (296–373)

During the Nicene controversies of the fourth century, St. Athanasius had, following on the work of Irenaeus, written on the incarnation as the means of God's restoration of a fallen humanity. If a king, who is a man, does not allow the realms he has founded to become subject to others and escape from his power—as was being argued in the ransom theory—will not God have much greater pity on his creatures? They had once partaken of the image of God but in foolishness despised the grace given to them and turned away from God. Would not God act to restore it in them?

> What then was God to do, or what should have happened except that he should renew again that which was in his image, in order that through it men might be able once more to know him? But how could this have been done, unless the very image of God were to come, our Savior Jesus Christ? . . . So the Word of God came in his own person, in order that, as he is the image of his Father, he might be able to restore man who is in the image. In any other way it could not have been done, without the destruction of death and corruption. So he was justified in taking a mortal body, in order that in it death could be destroyed and men might be again renewed in the image. For this, then, none other than the image of the Father was required.[6]

As his argument draws to its conclusion, Athanasius writes, "God became one of us in Christ, so that we could become one with God in him."[7] This will become foundational to the atonement theology for the churches of the East and their concept of theosis.[8]

---

6. Athanasius, *De Incarnatione*, 165–66.
7. Athanasius, *De Incarnatione*, 269.
8. The belief that Christians can experience a union with God in Christ and become increasingly like him until the image of God in them is fully restored. It is sometimes called *deification*. However, it does not mean they become God or merge with God but that they grow fully into God's image in them.

The Exemplar Model

Another form of thought that emerged, especially in the Eastern church with its emphasis on the Christian life as one of moral transformation in Christ, was the image of Jesus as *exemplar*. This was as old as the Gospel of John, with Jesus saying that when he was lifted up, he would draw all people to himself (John 12:34; 8:28; 3:14). Jesus' innocent self-giving trust in his Father in the face of hatred, corruption, duplicity, violence, suffering, and death was both a model for how we are to live our own lives and a source of inspiration, providing the power to do so. When that lesson is properly internalized, it has power to lead people to live similar lives of triumph over sin and death.

This model, so important to Eastern Christianity, was also central to the theology of St. Augustine. It would later become known in the Western church as the *moral influence* or *subjective* theory of Jesus' death—subjective because of its influence on humanity.[9] Because of the great schism between the Eastern churches and the West in 1054, Orthodox theology was not influenced by any of what followed the break and has remained anchored in the recapitulation theory of Irenaeus and Athanasius to this day.

From Medieval Thought to the Reformation

As the Christian faith moved beyond the first five to six hundred years of the writings of its formative theologians and more deeply into the medieval church, these models continued to be discussed, with the ransom theory the easiest to understand and, therefore, the most popular. Shortly after the great schism between Eastern Orthodoxy and the Roman Catholic Church, there came on the scene in the Western church a brilliant young Italian monk named Anselmo d'Aosta, a philosopher and theologian, who would become the archbishop of Canterbury (1093–1109). He is known to history as St. Anselm of Canterbury. His three major ideas in Christian thought are what philosophers call the ontological argument for the existence of God ("that than which nothing greater can be thought"), theology defined as "faith seeking understanding," and the satisfaction theory of atonement.[10]

---

9. Those theories considered "objective" are theories in which God was the object of Jesus' saving action.

10. See T. Williams, "Saint Anselm."

Satisfaction—Saint Anselm (1033–1109)

Anselm wanted to leave behind, for good, the notion of Jesus' death as a ransom paid to the devil. It had come to dominate most conversations about what Jesus had done and why God had become incarnate in him. Anselm's extreme dissatisfaction with the ransom theory, in any of its forms, led him to author a philosophic essay designed to convince nonbelievers of God's incarnation in Jesus and why the incarnation was necessary. Using the method and logic that would form the foundation of scholastic philosophy,[11] he wrote *Cur Deus Homo* (Why God Became Human). Written in Latin, it was designed for a reader with little or no knowledge of the Bible's narratives or background, much less its overarching story, and was based on feudal law, not the grace of the gospel.

In feudal law, a breach of a noble's honor could be dealt with in one of two ways. Honor could be restored by payment of some means of satisfaction—money, some other form of property, or indentured service. But if the offender could not make suitable payment for the dishonor, then the alternative was for the offender to be punished.[12] It was one or the other, but it was never both.

In a world where society's well-being depended upon such balance in relationships and one's status in life determined the amount of recompense required to right a wrong, what was required for satisfaction of a serf's dishonor was one thing. Satisfaction of a lord's dishonor was quite another. But if the one dishonored was God, something altogether more extravagant was required!

Vicarious Satisfaction

All of this produced a theory that asserts that in humanity's fall into sin, sinful men and women had irreparably violated God's honor. In that breach, a debt to divine justice had been incurred that must be paid to restore justice in the world. Sin could not simply be forgiven—remember, the theory assumes the feudal system, *not the gospel!* God cannot forgive the debt. It must be "satisfied" either through recompense or punishment. If not, God would cease to be just. More, only one who was sinless could offer something that would "satisfy" that debt and restore

---

11. The philosophic foundation that would dominate the teachings of the church through the medieval universities of Europe from 1100 to 1700.

12. Fiddes, *Past Event*, 96–97.

God's honor. Otherwise, the balance of divine justice that kept the world in equilibrium would be forever destroyed. Only someone God's equal could pay the debt.

Therefore, it was necessary for God to become human, the eternal Word becoming incarnate in the sinless man Jesus, to pay the debt owed to God. Having no debt of sin to pay for himself, Jesus could make an offering or take an action suitable to satisfy and restore God's honor. Thereafter, God and humanity could again be at-one, as they were before Adam's sin. Jesus' death was not satisfaction of the debt of his own sin—he was sinless. Nor was he being *punished* for the sin of humanity through this satisfaction. He was simply satisfying humanity's debt vicariously—in its place.

The theory became known as *vicarious satisfaction*. It was quickly embraced and would continue to be a dominant theme in atonement theory in the Western church for the next thousand years. However, subsequent appropriations of it would bring modifications—especially when introducing the notion that satisfaction for the breach of honor was not enough. Sin must be not only satisfied; *it must also be punished*. That would bring to the theory meanings that Anselm never intended, often giving him a black eye, especially today, in certain quarters of Protestantism.

Moral Example—Peter Abelard (1079–1142)

Anselm's answer quickly became popular. It continues to lie behind much if not most conservative atonement thought to this very day. However, it flew in the face of other theologians and philosophers[13] who were strong adherents of the older exemplar theory. Among them was Anselm's younger contemporary, Peter Abelard, with whom the *moral influence theory* has come to be associated. Though often attributed to Abelard, the theory has its roots in the Gospel of John and the Orthodox churches of

---

13. Fourteenth-century theologians Duns Scotus (c. 1270–1308) and William of Occam [Ockham] (c. 1285–c. 1349) are two examples. Rejecting ransom, satisfaction, and moral theory, they proposed the "acceptance theory." God is omnipotent; therefore, there are no laws to which God must conform. God binds Godself to Godself but is dependable, because God does so by eternal decree. God could have decided to free humanity in any way God chose. For reasons known only to God, God chose to accept the torture and death of Jesus as atonement for all humanity. All "satisfaction" is God's arbitrary choice.

the East and may be found in the writings of second-century theologians such as Irenaeus.

Over against Anselm's new satisfaction theory, Abelard held that Christ's death had nothing to do with the satisfaction of God's violated honor or of maintaining a balance of divine justice in the cosmos. The devil was guilty of an injustice that left him no right except punishment. Further, the idea that satisfaction for sin was necessary for God's embrace, and that the death of the Son, sent by the Father as Redeemer, was the only way that forgiveness and atonement could take place, was patently unbiblical and totally unacceptable. There was no biblical basis or evidence to justify Anselm's theory, and plenty of occasions in Scripture that suggested otherwise.

God could pardon without requiring satisfaction. God is God and can do as God chooses. A loving God would not make such a choice. The death of the Son was not something demanded by the Father. It was a mutual decision between Father and Son intended to be an example of God's love for humanity, to impress them with that truth and, in that awareness, to influence them to live similar lives motivated by love.

Jesus' passion and death were intended not only to soften but to transform human hearts in order that they could live lives of repentance in conformity with the life and teachings of Jesus. The incarnation was not simply to give the world Jesus' teaching and example but also a redemptive self-offering by the Triune God, which would allow God to take humanity unto Godself and be the means of their transformation.

Finding its roots in the writings of Paul, and contrary to the term that has come to identify it, Abelard's teaching holds that the purpose of the incarnation was not to *morally influence* but to *change* humankind. In his passion, Jesus paid no penalty for sin. Rather, he died a martyr at the hands of sinful humanity to reveal a love so supreme that it has the power to transform. It acquired for women and men the freedom of the children of God, liberating them from slavery to sin and drawing them to God. No longer slaves to the power of sin, they can become slaves to God's love. They no longer need to do things out of the fear of God. Recognizing God's love revealed to them in Jesus, they can live faithfully in life, through and out of their love for God.

From Anselm and Abelard to Aquinas

The thirteenth century gave the Western church one of its greatest theologians, Thomas Aquinas (1225–1274), doctor and saint of the Western church. Though Aquinas is often thought of as Anselm's heir, thereby building upon Anselm's theology of atonement, it is important to remember that Aquinas was deeply immersed in biblical texts as he worked on his monumental *Summa Theologica*. His understanding of the incarnation was shaped primarily by what Scripture teaches, not Anselm's theory of satisfaction.[14] Consequently, his writing on atonement is multifaceted and interprets the incarnation in ways like those theories that have been labeled *Christus Victor*, moral exemplar, and recapitulation, as well as Anselm's theory of satisfaction.

For Aquinas, the problem was less one of sin having to be paid for and more the problem with human nature itself. God created humanity to participate in the divine life through love and knowledge, ordering all things in life to God as their beginning and end and dealing with them out of that stance and reality. Humanity, however, had chosen otherwise, desiring things other than God. Herein was their sin.

Contaminated by sin, human nature had been so badly distorted that humanity could not extricate themselves from sin's power. They were therefore damned by sin's grip on life unless that sinful nature was repaired and restored by the atonement. Thus, the incarnation. It was not to pay for sin or enable God to forgive sinners. As Irenaeus argued, the incarnation addressed human nature itself and transformed it. God sent the Son into the world in Jesus as a *remedy* for what the sin of its first parents had done to humanity's nature—not as a *payment* for that sin. Here Aquinas agreed not only with Irenaeus but also with Athanasius, Augustine, and Abelard.

Aquinas also believed God became human in Jesus to make *satisfaction* for the sin of the world. But Aquinas' use of the word satisfaction was quite different than the way Anselm had used it. For Anselm, satisfaction was *a matter of necessity* to preserve God's justice. Aquinas disagreed at several levels. With Abelard, Aquinas believed God could forgive sin

---

14. Raith, "Thomas Aquinas' Pauline Theology," 169. Raith challenges the notions that St. Thomas Aquinas was Anselm's heir and substitutionary satisfaction was the heart of Aquinas' atonement theology. He points out a much broader range of atonement theories in Aquinas and is a valuable corrective to much Protestant thought about him. What I write here on Aquinas is highly indebted to Raith's work as well as to other resources on Aquinas listed in "For Further Reading."

freely, or with a lesser form of satisfaction. God could make satisfaction for sin in any way God chose. In fact, God could do so without any act of satisfaction at all!

For Aquinas, satisfaction for sin had nothing to do with Jesus doing something to kindle or enable God's forgiveness, nor with restoring God's violated honor. Nor was it to deal with some other necessary constraint on God. Satisfaction meant doing something *to restore humans and their sinful nature to a state of harmony with God* so that they could know, love, and participate in the divine life. It was something *done freely by God out of God's love and mercy*. It was the love of God for humanity coming to them in the grace of Jesus Christ to transform its sinful human nature.

Aquinas did agree with Anselm, however, on one thing—humanity's sin had violated God's justice. It had brought about disorder in God's world. That did demand satisfaction. That satisfaction—to restore God's violated justice—could be accomplished in one of two ways. The first would be through punishment that was prescribed, involuntarily imposed, and personal. The second means was *penance*—punishment that was *voluntary*, shareable, and intended to satisfy God's justice. Aquinas considered voluntary penance vastly superior to imposed punishment. It was intended to address the injustice, its aim was to restore the relationship between the wrongdoer and the one who had been wronged, and it was voluntary. Penance was a morally good response to sin.

Satisfaction through Penance

The satisfaction God chose was Jesus' voluntary suffering in his passion. It was penance in humanity's place. It addressed God's violated justice regarding the debt of original sin and made satisfaction to God for the sin of the world. It also revealed the abundance of God's mercy—the depths of Christ's love and God's desire for sinners' salvation. It did so in such a way that sinners could be moved to love God in Christ in return, transforming and restoring them into those who loved God above all else in the world. God was both requiring justice and providing satisfaction for sin in Jesus, not in his incarnation, nor in his death, but through his voluntary *passion*. Jesus' *suffering*—not his death!—was the satisfaction needed to make atonement and restore humanity as lovers of God.[15]

---

15. With sin having been satisfied by Jesus' suffering, Jesus' death produced a treasury of merit upon which the church could subsequently call. This would lead to the

Thus, Jesus, in innocent, voluntary suffering, did two things. He made an offering to God far greater than any debt of human sin, thereby addressing God's violated justice. It was atoning in that it enabled humanity to come to know and share in Christ's love, thereby having their sinful nature transformed. As they come to know and love God as God desires, they step free from bondage to guilt and the debt of punishment for violating God's justice. Thus, people can live lives of love for God and neighbor, which has been God's intention for them from the beginning.

Aquinas' theology would become the official theory of atonement in the Roman Catholic Church during the Counter-Reformation at the Council of Trent between 1545 and 1563. It remains the standard Catholic understanding on atonement today. In the Protestant house, his thought would have a different impact, especially on Martin Luther and John Calvin. It unlocked the gates on Jesus' suffering on the cross not only as satisfaction, payment, and revelation of God's love for humanity but as the *means* of its redemption.

The Reformation

Martin Luther (1483–1546)

For all of Luther's influence, weight, and leadership in the Reformation and the Protestant theology that emerged from them, there was little new or controversial in his theology of atonement. As an Augustinian theologian and biblical scholar, he inherited the logic of Anselm refined and modified by Aquinas and the understanding that Christ's suffering was satisfaction for sin. But Luther's thinking about Christ's death was even more powerfully shaped by his reading Scripture—especially the letters of Paul—and Paul's understanding of what was taking place in Christ on the cross.

The scholastic theologians before Luther approached things from the perspective of faith seeking understanding, employing reason to speculate about what was possible and fitting for God to have done. Luther was interested in what God *had actually done* and rejected the scholastics' speculations. For him, God and Christ were synonymous—a paradoxical union of human and divine in the God-man Jesus Christ.[16]

Reformation controversy over the use of indulgences to cover an individual's sins.

16. Luther, *Small Catechism*, art. 2.

God was in Christ reconciling humankind to Godself. This is as clear a statement of Luther's doctrine of atonement as we might find in his writings. The word atonement, of course, is English. The German word Luther used for Christ's work is *versöhnen* (reconcile) or *Versöhnung* (reconciliation) with the key to its meaning in 2 Cor 5:19, "God was in Christ reconciling the world to himself."[17] Unfortunately, all too often in English translations of Luther's writings, *versöhnen* and *Versöhnung* are rendered "atone" or "atonement" rather than "reconcile" or "reconciliation."

God had totally joined humanity in the incarnation, and on the cross, God in Christ had taken sin and death upon Godself. The demands of God's righteousness in the face of human sin, and the grace of God's love for humankind, were at work through Christ's reconciling sacrifice as a death that swallowed death.[18] Christ suffered and died there to defeat the devil, redeem humankind, and set humanity free to be God's own in Christ. As God's own, humanity could live into this reconciliation through faith in Christ and his work rather than attempt to do so by their own good works. People could be clothed in Christ's righteousness and live lives of love for God and for their neighbor.

John Calvin (1509–1564)

John Calvin was a second-generation reformer, barely eight years old when Luther nailed his ninety-five theses to the chapel door. But Calvin was destined to become Luther's successor as the second most influential theologian of the Protestant Reformation and its first systematic theologian.

Initially, Calvin prepared for the priesthood, with a solid grounding in Latin and philosophy gained as a young student at the University of Paris. But after his father's altercation with their local bishop, Calvin was sent off to study law. Through his study of law, he found himself drawn into the humanist movement sweeping intellectual Europe, with its passion for the study of ancient, classical texts in their own languages. He learned Koine Greek—the language of the New Testament—and continued his studies in law and literature, publishing his first scholarly work at the age of twenty-two, a commentary on Seneca's *De Clementia*. By then

---

17. Hagan, "Luther on Atonement," 252.

18. "Wie ein Tod den andern fraß" (How one death the other ate), from Luther, "Christ lag in Todesbanden." My thanks to Paul Westermeyer for this hymn reference.

he had broken with the Roman Catholic Church to fully embrace the Reformation and its biblically centered Christianity.

When religious conflict in France exploded into violence and the persecution that followed the Placards Affair in October of 1534, Calvin fled France, ending up in Basel the following January. There, in 1536, he published the first of five editions of his *Institutes of the Christian Religion*. The *Institutes* is a work that would dominate the rest of his life and form the foundation of Reformed theology.[19]

The subject of the atonement was not one of controversy for Calvin. The scriptural evidence was abundantly clear to him. He quotes Scripture exhaustively in the *Institutes*, as well as the churches' earliest theologians—especially Augustine—with whom he had strong affinity. On the other hand, he had an equally strong antipathy to speculative theologies. With Augustine, he believed the atonement was the result of God's love for humankind.[20] With Anselm and Aquinas, he agreed that God's justice, which had been violated by human sin, required satisfaction—Calvin was, after all, a lawyer as well. But, for Anselm and Aquinas and the medieval mentality of the other scholastics, satisfaction meant something vastly different than it now meant for Calvin.

From Vicarious and Forensic Satisfaction to Personal Punishment

In the medieval world, as we noted earlier, the violation of the personal honor of another could be redeemed in one of two ways: by some form of satisfaction or by punishment, but never by both. By Calvin's day, the ancient Roman view of criminal law had replaced feudal law. That meant that every infraction of the law required punishment—there were no other alternatives—justice simply demanded it. Believing sin inherited through Adam's original sin, all humanity was guilty; therefore all humanity must be punished for it. Bringing his legal training to bear on the question, the only satisfaction Calvin could comprehend for human sin was some form of *personal punishment*.[21]

---

19. In addition, Calvin was writing biblical commentaries, sermons, confessional statements, and correspondence with other Reformers. All of that was an expression of his life as Reformer, pastor, and the first systematic theologian of the Reformation.

20. Calvin, *Institutes*, 2.16.4.

21. Calvin, *Institutes*, 2.16.1.

This meant that Jesus had to take on and suffer God's righteous judgment and wrath on sin—the penalty demanded by the law for each sinner—so that God's justice could be accomplished.[22] Until that debt to God's violated justice was paid, God remained humanity's enemy. Like Luther, the sinless Son was personally experiencing God's wrath for sinners in their place. It was in bearing God's wrath in sinners' place that Christ satisfied the demand of God's law and propitiated God's wrath. With God's law fulfilled and wrath appeased, God and humanity were reconciled, and God could now be gracious and favorable to humanity and rightly show grace to those for whom Christ died—the elect.[23]

Here is another shift in the development of the concept of atonement—a uniquely Protestant one. For Anselm and Aquinas, Christ's death was satisfaction for the general penalty for sin. Therefore, it was applicable to all humankind. For Calvin, Christ's death was a specific penalty for the sins of particular individuals rather than of all humankind. Christ's death was for all who were to be saved, to be sure, but only for those predestined for salvation—the elect.

Though salvation was limited to the elect, it was unlimited regarding sin—no sin was too great to be expiated by Christ's sacrifice.[24] As a sacrifice, it both expiated sin (wiped it out) and propitiated (placated or appeased) God's wrath but, again, only for the elect. And though the elect are saved by becoming united to Christ through faith, they do so by God's grace, not of their own initiative. In God's wisdom and grace, they have been predestined to faith and its saving union with Christ.[25]

The problem here, as one eminent contemporary Reformed theologian has pointed out, is Calvin portrays the death of Jesus as what changes God's disposition to predestined humanity.[26] It suggests that God was humanity's enemy until Jesus' death reconciled humanity to God. But if that were the case, why would God send the Son to redeem the elect in the first place? In addition, it is humanity that is God's enemy, not vice-versa. As Paul writes in Romans,

> But God proves his love for us in that while we were still sinners Christ died for us. Much more surely then, now that we

---

22. Calvin, *Institutes*, 2.15.6; 2.16.1.
23. Calvin, *Institutes*, 2.16.4–6; 2.17.3–4.
24. Calvin, *Institutes*, 2.12.3–5.
25. Calvin, *Institutes*, 3.21.1.
26. McCormack, *For Us*, 26.

have been justified by his blood, we will be saved through him from the wrath of God. For if while we were enemies, we were reconciled to God through the death of his Son, much more surely, having been reconciled, we will be saved by his life. (Rom 5:8–10)

According to Paul, all of this was done as proof of God's love for us, and done while we were still estranged and at odds with God. It is humanity's hostility to God, born of rebellion, that is the problem, not God's hostility to humanity. But for Calvin, the love of God seems to have dropped out of the atoning work of God in Christ. Atonement seems less about fulfilling God's love and desire to be at-one with an estranged humanity, than satisfying God's righteousness by placating God's wrath. Only until God's wrath is propitiated—satisfied—can God and humanity be one.

Though this would subsequently be called *penal substitutionary atonement*, the term does not really fit nor do justice to Calvin's larger thought on God's atoning work in Christ. In the end, for Calvin, atonement is the result of God's mercy and grace revealed in Jesus Christ and nothing more.[27]

Scholastic Calvinism

Calvin's sixteenth-century treatment of atonement set the stage for what his seventeenth century Dutch Calvinist successors[28] would do with it, turning it into what is now generally known as penal substitutionary atonement. This happened as Calvin's theology became ossified and compartmentalized by second and third-generation Calvinists, and through controversies over several of Calvin's theological views. The result of those controversies then became "canonized" in confessional documents of various Reformed traditions.

Examples of this are the Canons of Dort, the Heidelberg Catechism, and the Westminster Confession of Faith. The Canons of Dort were approved to resolve the Arminian disagreement among the Dutch (see below). The Heidelberg Catechism was written to counter Roman Catholic teachings that came from the Council of Trent as well as to commend the Reformed faith to its skeptical Lutheran neighbors in the Palatinate.

---

27. Calvin, *Institutes*, 2.16.7.
28. A second and third generation of Calvinists.

The Westminster Confession of Faith was written to unite the Church of England and the Church of Scotland, a failed effort that was destined to become the sole doctrinal confession of Presbyterians for the next 321 years.

Not Just the Elect —Jacob Arminius (1560-1609)

Jacob Arminius was a Reformed Dutch theologian who taught at the University of Leiden. His high view of Scripture, insisting on only those things that could be proved from the Scriptures, and his high view of God's grace caused him to begin to question aspects of Calvinism—especially predestination. He taught that God's grace, obtained through God's redemption in Christ, was preventing or prevenient, that is to say, divine grace that is said to operate on the human will prior to that will turning to God. This divine grace has been conferred on all humanity by the Holy Spirit—not just the elect. Turning to God is not achieved through human effort but by this "preventing grace" of God.

The view came to be known as Arminianism, and soon had a group of Dutch Calvinist supporters known as Remonstrants. A year after Arminius' death they issued Five Articles of Remonstrance, identifying five points of Calvin's teachings with which they disagreed.

The Remonstrants

The Remonstrants' articles began by rejecting Calvin's "unconditional election"—that God elects some unconditionally regardless of their conduct or faith.

- Article 1 says that election is conditional upon faith in Christ, and that God elects to salvation those God knows beforehand will have faith in Christ.

- Article 2 challenges Calvin's "unlimited atonement," asserting that Christ died for all, though salvation is limited to those who believe in him.

- Article 3 is often seen as reaffirming Calvin's concept of "total depravity"[29] but is, in fact, affirming humanity's fallen state and

---

29. Total depravity for Calvin did not mean "rotten to the core" but, rather, something was rotten that kept humans from living truly and faithfully. Depravity means

consequent inability to do any good—much less "attain to saving faith"—thereby laying the foundation for what follows in article 4.

- Article 4 rejects the notion that God's grace is "irresistible"; humanity has the free will to resist the prevenient grace of God.
- Article 5 refines the Calvinist view on the perseverance of the saints, arguing that it may be conditional upon the believer remaining in Christ. They later became convinced that Scripture did teach that true believers could fall away from faith and perish eternally as an unbeliever.

The five articles fanned the fire of controversy that continued until 1618–1619 when a Calvinist Synod was convened in the Dutch city of Dordrecht, often referred to in English as Dort. The purpose of the synod was to condemn Arminius' theology, declare its adherents' "anathema" (those to be shunned), and further define as orthodox the five points of doctrine that had been disputed. The result was the Canons of Dort were not only a refutation to the Five Articles of Remonstrance but an extended and "authorized" Reformed teaching on each of those points. They were asserted to be in accordance with what the Scriptures teach and designed to expand on their meaning and offer comfort and assurance to believers. Calvin's theology was becoming Calvinism.

Moral Government Theory—Hugo Grotius (1583–1645)

Hugo Grotius, a younger contemporary of Arminius, was a Dutch lawyer and scholar in the fields of philosophy, political theory, and law. He was a civil servant, diplomat, poet, playwright, and theologian. As attorney general of Holland, Grotius found himself caught up in the political-religious conflict between the strict Calvinists and the Remonstrants, with an affinity for the latter because of his commitment to and support of religious tolerance. When asked to draft an edict to express the state's policy of toleration during the conflict, he wrote that the only basic theological tenets necessary to preserve civil order were belief in the existence of God and of God's providence. Otherwise, differences on theological doctrines should be left to private conscience.

"twisted." As Kant wrote, "Out of the crooked timber of humanity, no straight thing was ever made" (see Guyer, "Crooked Timber of Mankind"). My gratitude to Elder Curtis Field for this reminder and quote.

Enter the ideas of Faustus Socinus (1539–1604), an Italian theologian from what is now called the radical left-wing of the Reformation. He was anti-Trinitarian, denied the preexistence of Christ and the doctrine of original sin, and rejected a propitiatory view of atonement. As Socinus' works began to be embraced in Holland by followers of Arminius, Grotius wrote *Defensio fidei catholicae de satisfaction Christi* (A Defense of the Catholic Faith Concerning the Satisfaction of Christ). Using language drawn from his expertise in law, natural philosophy, and his general view of God as a moral governor of the universe, Grotius developed what is known as the *governmental (or moral) theory of atonement*. Jesus' sacrificial death took place so the Father could forgive sinners while still maintaining a just and moral rule over the universe.

For Grotius, Christ's suffering was a real and meaningful substitute for the punishment humans deserved, but contrary to Calvin, Jesus' death paid the penalty for no one's sins. It was *not a punishment* for sin. What it did was demonstrate what sinful humanity deserved at the hands of the just Governor and Judge of the universe. In Jesus, God publicly demonstrated divine displeasure with sin through the propitiatory suffering of God's own sinless and obedient Son. Christ's suffering and death served as a *substitute for the punishment humans* might *receive*. But, if humans turn from sin, God will forgive them. Jesus' sacrificial death enabled God to forgive while still maintaining just rule over the universe. Thus, linked to Arminius notion of preventing grace, humanity could choose to accept Jesus' work and God's grace.

Grotius' theological writings were published by Oxford University in 1692. They came to be accepted in varying degrees in England by people such as Puritan leader Richard Baxter (1615–1691). They then made their way to the Harvard and Yale Colleges' libraries, to have an impact on the New England theology that emerged out of the First Great Awakening (1730s–1770s). They prospered in the United States in nineteenth-century Methodism and among New England Congregationalists, some Anglicans, and, in the twentieth century, Pentecostals. Here was a Protestant alternative to Luther and Calvin that would take full root in nineteenth-century atonement thought in all but Reformed and other conservative Protestant churches. To that we now turn.

Chapter 8

Atonement Theories from the Enlightenment to the Early Twentieth Century

The Enlightenment

THE ENLIGHTENMENT ERA OF the seventeenth and eighteenth centuries, characterized by the empiricism that was brought on by the scientific revolution, had its impact on atonement theology.[1] Challenging the mysticism and religion of the Middle Ages, it radically changed the way humanity thought about themselves, God, and the world. The subsequent age of reason brought about a new confidence in the power of human reason to understand the nature of God, the universe, and humanity, unaided by revelation or theological confessions. That resulted in a series of critiques on religion in general, but especially on the Christian church and its beliefs.

God, if there was a God, was unknowable. But given the human mind, there was no need for revelation. If there was a God, it was the impersonal one of Deism—"the prime mover itself unmoved."[2] This religion of reason rejected Christianity and its revealed truths about God and humanity. It produced a sustained attack on Scripture as revelation, miracles, prophecy, and religious rites, all which were deemed superstition. Atonement theories of satisfaction or substitution, whether

---

1. The Western European Enlightenment is generally dated beginning in the mid-1600s until the late 1700s.
2. See Scandalon, "Aristotle."

forensic or penal, were rejected altogether, except in the most conservative Christian churches.

Nature was the new source of knowledge; the senses the primary tools for seeking it. Clear-cut human reason could reveal all that needed to be known as it looked at the world. Feelings became an important source for evaluating the unseen world of religion and faith. The focus shifted from humanity's salvation in a heavenly future world to its perfection through reason in this one. Enlightenment thought challenged the authority of both the church and the monarchy and their power over life, and opened the door for political revolution that led to a separation between church and state.

Enlightenment theologians brought the moral influence theory back into the discussion within Protestantism, but with a far more liberal perspective now that the church had been stripped of its coercive power. Jesus' death was not necessary to remove sin. Its value was its subjective impact on people, especially their feelings. Jesus offered his life to influence the hearts and minds of those who learn of it and, upon learning, are moved to repentance and trust in his moral way of life revealed in his life and death. Denying the idea that Jesus was anything more than a man, his death was simply that of a man with nothing more theologically important about it. His death had no *objective* effect on God. Though reaching back to Abelard, this new "subjective" or "moral" view was not Abelard's. It was the product of Enlightenment theological thought.

Nineteenth Century

Friedrich Schleiermacher (1768–1843)

Friedrich Schleiermacher was a German Reformed pastor, theologian, biblical scholar, and philosopher known for his attempt to reconcile the Enlightenment's criticisms with traditional Protestant Christianity, and the alienation of the modern world from the entire Christian Tradition.[3] He is often called the father of modern theology. At the age of eighteen, he wrote to his father, a Reformed pastor:

> I cannot believe that [Christ's] death was a substitutionary atonement because he never expressly said so, and because I cannot believe that it was necessary. For it would be impossible

3. Gerrish, "Schleiermacher," 644.

for God to desire the eternal punishment of those whom he had obviously not created perfect, but for the pursuit of perfection, since they are not [yet] perfect.[4]

The following year he writes:

> I cannot believe that he who called himself the Son of Man was the true, eternal God; I cannot believe that his death was a vicarious atonement.[5]

Humanity needed perfection, not punishment.

The task of philosophy was to relate God to the world and to oneself. That begins when one becomes aware of oneself as part of a vast system of nature, not only intuiting that system but also seeing that entire system represented in one's own self-consciousness. When that happens, one realizes one's absolute dependence on the active reality beyond the world. That reality Schleiermacher called God. Since God can only be known indirectly, God is the "whence" of this feeling of absolute dependence. This "God consciousness" is the essence of religion and an essential element of human nature.

Jesus is not the incarnation, or inbreaking of the divine into the mundane. He is the divinely ordained fulfillment (*telos*) and perfection of human nature because he lived all his life out of his absolute dependence on God, a potent force within him that can be shared. This is what made him without sin.

Sin and perfection are not two successive stages but two possibilities that coexist in the human nature of every man and woman.[6] Jesus' life opened the possibility of humanity's perfection. When Jesus' disciples first encountered him, they experienced his uniquely powerful consciousness of God, and it was communicated to them so they too could begin to live out of it. This was, for Schleiermacher, redemption. In such fellowship with Jesus, they had entered a way of life beyond the curse of sin and on the way to perfection.

Though Jesus' life opened the possibility of humanity's perfection, to do so he must have manifested his God-consciousness in the face of all opposition. Consequently, he was tempted in every way as we are, yet without sin (Heb 4:15). His death on the cross was his ultimate

---

4. Stratis, "Friedrich Schleiermacher," 739.
5. Gerrish, *Prince of the Church*, 25.
6. Gerrish, "Schleiermacher," 645.

faithfulness to his vocation as the second Adam and a moment of supreme revelation—the proof of his blessed existence. The result was not a transaction between God and humanity—something Schleiermacher repeatedly calls a "magical" view of the atonement.

Jesus' redemptive activity was the founding of a real, historically redeemed community. With him, something entirely new entered human history—human perfection as God had intended. This created not just new people but a new humanity and a new world—a corporate life where believers are assumed into Jesus' unique consciousness of God. It is this corporate life that works against the corporate life of sin.

Psychology and sociology have entered the atonement conversation. They would dominate liberal Christian thought well into the twenty-first century. At the other end of the theological spectrum was the classic Reformed orthodoxy of Charles Hodge.

Penal Substitutionary Atonement—Charles Hodge (1797–1878)

Charles Hodge taught systematic theology at Princeton Theological Seminary for fifty years. His three-volume systematic theology, which devoted more than sixty pages to the theme "Satisfaction of Christ," was vastly influential. Not only did Hodge directly teach theology to several thousand Presbyterian and Congregational ministers during his fifty years of instruction, but he also trained several generations of professors of theology. His systematic theology text continued to be used and exercised enormous influence well into the early twentieth century. It continues to be espoused as orthodox atonement theology in conservative Reformed circles today.[7]

Hodge taught that God could not simply pardon sin. Though some, like Abelard, claim that God, being God, can do anything God wants, for Hodge, that would require God to stop being just, which God cannot do. Rather, like Calvin, before divine forgiveness can be offered, there must first be satisfaction for divine justice. That justice demands that sin be punished. It can be pardoned, in consistency with divine justice, only if legal (forensic) penal satisfaction is first paid.

Hodge believed this is what God was doing in Jesus. God gave himself in the person of his Son, Jesus, who by the Son's own sacrificial choice took on his sinless self the punishment of God's wrath against sin, doing

---

7. Rutledge, *Crucifixion*, 488.

so in the place of sinners. Jesus suffered the full wages of sin—death and abandonment by the Father—all to give justice its legal due. Only after the penalty for sin had been legally extracted from the Son by the Father could God forgive humankind their sin. But such pardon was still limited to only the elect. It became one of the pillars of what has been called Protestant orthodoxy, and also known as Old School Princeton theology.

At the heart of Hodge's teaching is a legal concept that assumes a universal moral law, which, though readily understood and accepted in his day, is no longer tenable, much less acceptable. Today, the imposition of a penalty upon the innocent—as with a false conviction—is considered both scapegoating and the height of injustice. It is one of contemporary theologians' chief criticisms of penal substitutionary atonement, though not their only one.

Hodge depended heavily upon a notion of blood sacrifice of which few if any of his readers had any understanding, in which he regularly confused propitiation with expiation, and which most biblical scholars today discredit. Though Hodge quotes Scripture extensively in support of his arguments,[8] giving the impression of its being biblical, he is, in fact, like Anselm, reading his Bible through the lens of the philosophy of the justice system of his day and superimposing over that a theological system of atonement that, in fact, allows God's justice to eclipse and overcome God's love.

John McLeod Campbell (1800–1872)

John McLeod Campbell was a minister of the Church of Scotland and a Reformed theologian whose atonement theology put him at odds with his church's seventeenth-century confessional standard, the Westminster Confession, and its doctrine of limited atonement.

Appointed minister to the Parish of Row on the Clyde coast of Scotland in 1825, he soon discovered his parishioners' troubling lack of any Christian assurance. Theirs was a Christianity that was joyless, depressing, legalistic, and focused on providing safety from God's wrath. There was little evidence of peace, joy, assurance of faith, and confidence in God's love revealed in Jesus Christ. Rather, they were burdened by a doctrine of conditional grace: "Only if we do this, and don't do that, can

---

8. Chiefly Isa 53:4-6, 10-11; Rom 3:23-26; 2 Cor 5:21; Gal 3:10, 13; 1 Pet 2:24, 3:18.

we come to the enjoyment of salvation."[9] God's forgiveness for them was a reward for their repentance, rather than the cause and reason for it. But were they up to authentic repentance, and how could they know?

Campbell observed that regardless of what he preached, they only heard it as an additional demand on them to try harder. They did not question the power of Christ to save. Their doubts were about themselves—their ability to meet those conditions.[10] That, and the double-predestination Calvinist theology of the day[11]—that Christ died only for the elect—was the source of their misery. How was one to know if one was predestined to salvation or damnation?

As McLeod read the church's earliest theologians as well as Luther and Calvin, he believed that atonement was for all and that salvation was guaranteed for *all believers*; the New Testament proclaimed and assured that. He began to preach two doctrines: universal atonement and the assurance of faith. He was soon charged with heresy for his disagreement with the Westminster Confession on limited atonement, and in 1830 the General Assembly found him guilty, applying the next to most severe form of ecclesiastical discipline—disposition: he could no longer serve as a minister of the kirk.[12]

Deprived of his ministry in the kirk as well as his means of living, he served as an independent evangelist in the Scottish Highlands. In 1833, he became minister of a large, independent chapel that had been built for him in Glasgow by sympathetic and supportive close friends.

In 1856 Campbell published *The Nature of the Atonement*. From his reading of Irenaeus and Athanasius, Campbell approached atonement based on the incarnation. One cannot separate the birth, person, and work of Jesus from his death—they were a whole. Looking closely at Christ, one discovers a life and mind of a perfect, obedient Son toward God, and a perfect Brother toward humankind. In his life, Jesus fulfilled the law to love God wholeheartedly and to love his neighbor selflessly.

By the fact of the divine incarnation in him, Christ's life was one of atonement, lived vicariously in all humanity's place—a perfect and complete reconciliation. Christ represents God to humanity, bringing God's

---

9. Campbell, *Nature of the Atonement*, 3.

10. Campbell, *Nature of the Atonement*, 3.

11. A theory developed after Calvin, aided by his successor, Theodore Beza, who theorized that even before decreeing Adam's fall, God had determined who would be redeemed and who would be damned.

12. The most severe would have been excommunication.

word of forgiveness, and represents humanity to God, dealing with God on behalf of humanity as its High Priest and Intercessor.[13] It was not just his death that saved. The Son of God became human so that through the Spirit, humanity might participate in his Sonship and, through that Sonship, have communion with God.

Campbell was working to change the dominant view of atonement theory in Scotland and most Reformed theology. He was seeking to move from a legal framework of atonement, which dominated Reformed thought, to a filial and familial one based on God's love for God's children. It would have a profound influence on subsequent Scottish theology.

Søren Kierkegaard (1813–1855)

Søren Kierkegaard was a Danish philosopher, theologian, and social critic whose work crossed the boundaries of those disciplines with one ultimate driving purpose: to renew Christian faith within nineteenth-century Christendom in Denmark.

Initially studying theology, philosophy, and literature, Kierkegaard soon attacked them and the Danish church for misrepresenting what he believed the highest task of human existence—*becoming oneself in an ethical and religious sense*. Philosophy, literature, and the church were leaving out the most important part of human experience—*existence itself*. The human condition could be explained only by living in reality—experiencing its joys, pains, confusions, hopes, fears, guilt, and dread. That is what mattered, not some philosophic ideas about all of that. Existence was more important than ideas.

At the age of twenty-five, Kierkegaard had an experience of indescribable joy that reconciled him to the Christian faith and made faith something for which he would live and die the rest of his few years. From then on, Kierkegaard was a man of deep, almost mystical faith, wrestling with life's fundamental questions, which he believed could not be answered rationally. The only way to live through the pain and dread of existence was through faith. But such faith was not a mental commitment nor conviction about doctrine, nor was it the positive religious feelings of the German idealism he so disliked. Faith was a passionate, personal commitment to God in the face of life's uncertainty—a long, slow, lifetime process of *becoming* a Christian.

---

13. James B. Torrance, in Campbell, *Nature of the Atonement*, 13.

Incarnation—The Absolute Paradox

Central to this faith was *the absolute qualitative difference between God and human beings.* Any fusion between God and humanity was impossible—rationally anathema. The radical difference between them made *any* communication between God and humanity impossible. Yet this impossibility came about in the incarnation. *Jesus was the absolute paradox of the unification of the divine and the human.* Only this God-man could allow for communication between God and humanity—at-one-ment. This was Jesus' salvific role; he is this impossibility actualized.

The pain and dread of existence is the realization that over against God we are always in the wrong—always in sin. The fear of not finding forgiveness is devastating. But knowing and believing this, we have faith that, by virtue of the absurdity of the God-man paradox, humans can be at-one with God. The absurdity is believing that, for God, even the impossible is possible, including the forgiveness of the unforgivable. Those who accept God's forgiveness completely—sincerely, inwardly, contritely, with gratitude and hope—open themselves to the joyous prospect of beginning anew.

There can be only two possible attitudes toward this claim: faith or offense. What one cannot do is believe this based on reason. One must *choose* faith and suspend reason to believe in something higher than reason.[14] It is the most important task in life. Only thus does an individual have a chance to become a true person—a true self—the lifework of a human, work that God judges for eternity.

The only obstacle to this joy is refusal or resistance to accepting God's forgiveness. God can forgive the unforgivable but cannot force anyone to accept it. For Kierkegaard, the only guilt God cannot forgive is refusing to believe in God's greatness.

Relatively unknown outside of Denmark in his lifetime, Kierkegaard would become a major influence on existentialism and much Protestant theology in the twentieth century.

Abelard Revisited—Horace Bushnell (1802–1876)

Horace Bushnell, sometimes called the father of American Protestant liberalism, was born and reared in nineteenth-century rural New England

---

14. Though this is popularly referred to as "the leap of faith," Kierkegaard rarely used the phrase.

(New Preston, Connecticut), growing up and working on a farm and then in a factory. It was a time of raging religious controversy. The Second Great Awakening in America was in full force with its camp meeting and nineteenth-century emphasis upon emotions, freedom of choice, and perfectionism.

Central in this new movement were frontier evangelists, who with a message of Arminian "free will" to choose good or evil and to embrace or reject a loving God, placed the emphasis upon conversion. But now it was one's *personal decision* for salvation. That required repentance, removing sin from oneself and one's society, and living a life increasingly free from sin, to grow into perfection that was "saving." This was the religious and emotional climate into which Bushnell was born and reared.

Bushnell joined the Congregational Church at nineteen, and two years later entered Yale College with plans to become a Congregational minister, graduating in 1827. By now, religious doubt, fired by the religious controversies of the day, seems to have changed his plans. He taught school for a time, served as editor of a commerce journal, and began to study law at Yale.

In 1831, a spiritual revival swept through the campus. Though Bushnell was now qualified for the bar, his thoughts returned to ministry. He enrolled in Yale Divinity School, where he graduated in 1833. Thereupon, he was ordained the minister of North Congregational Church in Hartford, where he served for twenty-eight years, retiring in 1861 because of ill health.

Bushnell's power was as a thinker, preacher, and a literary figure. He challenged the orthodoxies of the day and pointed to a new way of thinking theologically about the Christian gospel. He broke ranks with those who viewed theology as an exacting science, an intellectual attempt to prove things through demanding logical deduction, and he criticized the way theology was using language.

His theology was both original and mediating, seeking grounds of consensus in a time of divisive rancor in theological debate between Hodge's Old School theology of Princeton and the newer schools of theology. These latter were emerging out of Europe—primarily Germany—with their "scientific" approach to theology and the Bible. Included in these newer schools was the writings of the Unitarians on the far left of the Protestant spectrum.

Bushnell challenged cornerstone theological convictions of the day: Trinity, atonement, conversion, and the relation of the natural to the supernatural. In the debate between predestination and free will, he could see the truth on both sides of the argument, as well as their distorting limitations. He could say a limited yes to both, which was unacceptable to both sides of the argument. He rejected speculative theology, insisting that the test of a doctrine must be experiential, for only experience can transform one's character and behavior. Yet he vigorously opposed the methods of revivalism. Children of believing parents should be reared so that they never know themselves other than Christian.[15]

Bushnell believed theology was an attempt to describe that which was beyond the ability of thought or language to capture with precision. He pressed for language, including that in the Bible, to be read as analogy, metaphor, and symbol. Only these could truly evoke the truths about God that otherwise cannot be expressed. When reduced to literalism, these truths are turned into destructive distortions. The historical context of words was crucial for understanding them, while changing situations require new definitions, as the meanings of words change.

Bushnell critiqued the distortion and confusion that had crept into the words sacrifice and atonement, as well as the misapplication of propitiation and expiation to sacrificial imagery, distortions that continue to plague atonement discussions today and leave people wondering about God's character.[16] He rejected both the penal substitutionary theory of the Calvinists and the governmental theories of the Methodists, arguing that they reflect a lack of understanding of the biblical concepts of sacrifice behind the New Testament's use of its imagery to speak of Christ's death.

Heir to the thinking of Abelard: the Son of God did not come in flesh to satisfy the righteousness demands of God regarding human sin. He came to give humanity an example of divine love and awaken human love in return. There is no wrath in God on account of human sin; Christ's life and suffering reveal God's fatherly heart to humanity to convince them they need not fear God because of their sin. Love was the basic principle in Christ's vicarious sacrifice and love was its power.

Christ's vicarious sacrifice was effective not because it changed God's mind about sinful humanity but because it exercised moral influence on humanity to change and seek out God's love and forgiveness and therein

---

15. He would become a major influence on the church, turning its attention to the education and nurture of its young people.

16. Bushnell, *Vicarious Sacrifice*, ch. 2.

find power for transformation. *Atonement then is a change wrought in us, a change by which we are reconciled to God.*[17]

Like Kierkegaard, Bushnell believed that it is one's experience that establishes truth, not doctrine or creed. Religious truth must appeal to the emotions and conscience, which neither the governmental nor penal substitutionary theory did. Rather, they were repugnant and lacked both the beauty and the power necessary to give new life, the latter theory having much that revolted the soul and raised a chill of revulsion within people.

The moral influence theory was "a kind of truth not likely to be realized without experience. It still seems to be a truth overdrawn, unless it is drawn out of the soul's own consciousness to some degree."[18] It must be put to the test of one's own experience. Bushnell's experiential theology deeply appropriated the moral influence theory. It subsequently became a dominant atonement theology of the Congregational Church and remains so today.

Walter Rauschenbusch (1861–1918)

Walter Rauschenbusch, commonly named the father of the social gospel movement in America, was pastor of an American German Baptist church in the Hell's Kitchen area of New York City for eleven years. Thereafter he taught New Testament and church history at Rochester Theological Seminary. An evangelical liberal, he was an heir of the theology of Schleiermacher, German Pietism, and Horace Bushnell. Though not utopian, he believed in the "immense latent perfectibility of human nature."[19]

Upon graduation from Rochester Theological Seminary in 1886, Rauschenbusch began his work in Hell's Kitchen. There he saw firsthand the privation of urban poverty, the victimization, and the abuses of capitalism on the poor—especially on children through the abuse of child labor. He became a social activist. Though he had entered ministry to

---

17. Bushnell, *Vicarious Sacrifice*, 38. Emphasis is added to draw attention to Bushnell's limitation of "objectification" and the need to see "the propitiation of God" symbolically, rather than as the penal and governmental arguments do.

18. Bushnell, *Vicarious Sacrifice*, 54.

19. Rauschenbusch, *Christianity and Social Crisis*, 422. See Schwarz, *Theology in Global Context*, 145.

save souls, he found himself striving to save bodies and make reparation for American society and its social evils.

Evil was embodied not in individuals but in "suprapersonal entities" that were embedded in political and socioeconomic institutions. Militarism, individualism, capitalism, and nationalism served the "kingdom of evil" rather than the kingdom of God. It was from these entities that sin emerged in societies corporately and spread to its members individually. Both needed redemption by bringing them under the influence of Christ: his love, teaching, life, ministry, courage, and integrity, as he faced his society's threats, even unto death.

Rauschenbusch's doctrine of atonement is based on two modern concepts: personality and solidarity. God had become human in Jesus Christ to mediate and proclaim the kingdom of God, a society based on love rather than selfishness, and to demonstrate the power of love in a world captive to evil and sin.

Jesus' death revealed four things. The cross was the ultimate and conclusive demonstration of the power of sin in human life; it convicted both society and its members of its sin. At the same time, the cross was the supreme revelation of God's love for all humanity. It changed the spiritual situation for humanity, putting God's approval on self-sacrifice and service. Jesus' vicarious suffering becomes a source of inspiration and courage for those defying evil in the world. Finally, his death makes it clear that belief in Jesus and the God who sent him is prophetic rather than priestly.

All of this requires those who believe in him to become like him, considering everyone as a subject of love and service. Adopting Jesus' personality—his devotion to the principles of compassion, justice, and mercy in God's reign, remaining unwaveringly committed to them, even in the face of deadly opposition, along with his solidarity with all humanity—would bring about atonement.

Rauschenbusch rejected both ransom and satisfaction theory as an offense to Christian convictions about the love and mercy of God. They were alien from the spirit of the gospel. He viewed the ideas of substitution, imputation, and merit through suffering and death as post-biblical, and foreign to the gospel as well. He observed that throughout the history of the church, the various theories, terms, and analogies of the atonement have been taken from contemporary life rather than Scripture, and thereby have distorted the gospel.

Though Rauschenbusch says nothing about Abelard, he was highly influenced in seminary by Horace Bushnell's experiential theology and embraced a more fully developed moral influence theory as a model for the atonement of society.

Following Schleiermacher's understanding of reconciliation, Rauschenbusch argued that it is in looking, listening, and following Jesus that humanity learns to take on Jesus' personality and stand in solidarity with the suffering and the oppressed. Humanity comes to understand and love God. God sees God's life in Jesus taken up by humanity as its example takes root, grows in them, and begins to mature into God's kingdom. But this is a lifelong task. There is no perfection of humanity in this life—only progress toward it.

Protestant Thought's Deep Divide

As the nineteenth century drew to a close, Protestant Christian thought on atonement was deeply divided. Conservative Protestant denominations held to the Reformation's "objective" views of satisfaction and penal substitutionary atonement, with a renewed rigidity buttressed by their seventeenth-century confessional documents. Liberal Protestant churches continued to embrace some form of moral influence theory in both individuals and society, using psychology and social theory to make their case. Moderates were truly in the middle; the moral influence theory seemed to have too little force to effect a real change in human nature, while the legalisms of penal substitutionary atonement linked to predestination produced the "joyless" religion that McLeod Campbell had worked to change.

The impact of German scholarship in biblical studies had started theologians thinking afresh about who Jesus was and what he did, sending them on a new quest for the "historical Jesus." Søren Kierkegaard, though largely unknown outside of Denmark during his day, had begun making his impact on modern theology, especially atonement theories. As Rauschenbusch had observed, that brought to the fore the new disciplines of psychology, sociology—and even literary theory—as interpretive tools.

Nineteenth-century idealism and romanticism about social progress producing the perfection of humanity and a universal brotherhood did not fare well in the wake of the Great War. Theories of evil and sin began to erode as the idea of demons and the devil were considered medieval in all but the more conservative circles. Sin for conservatives was both personal and highly moralized, while liberals blamed it on society. Individuals were its victims. In place of a personification of evil, most theological language simply spoke of "the powers of evil" at work in the world.

Dominance of German Liberal Theology—Adolf Harnack (1851–1930)

The dominance of German theologians well into the beginning of the twentieth century brought with them the "higher criticism" of biblical texts, challenging their veracity. Miracles were rejected out of hand. History was the new source of authority, and historians like Adolf Harnack were its "high priests." Rector and professor of church history at the University of Berlin, Harnack's lectures were enormously popular and influential. Published in English in 1901 under the title "What Is Christianity?,"[20] many scholars think them to be the best example of liberal Protestant thought at the beginning of the twentieth century.[21]

Harnack approached Christianity and Scripture as "scientific" history and characterized his own work as a "critical-historical" study. He believed critical-historical study could present Christ in such a way that it would lead one to true faith in God, the Father of Christ. Notice, it was faith in God, not faith in Christ. Christian faith must focus on the Father whom Jesus preached, not Jesus himself. Jesus was merely a human being.

Jesus was, indeed, a great ethical teacher whose teachings were spiritual, not political. If followed, they could lead one into the absolute best of human religion. But theology that focused on dogmatic statements about Jesus—who he was and what he had done—was a mistake. They led one the wrong way. Creedal statements like Nicaea and Chalcedon were wrong, as were doctrines like the virgin birth, the resurrection, and the ascension. Harnack would remain an active and influential theological figure for another twenty-five years.

---

20. *Das Wesen des Christentums*, published in 1900.

21. Hastings, "Twentieth Century," 720. For those interested in the rapidly changing landscape of Christian theology in the twentieth century, both Protestant and Catholic, Hastings' essay is an invaluable, comprehensive, yet succinct resource.

Harnack's Critics

Harnack had his critics, to be sure! The German Lutheran Church of Harnack's birth rejected his teachings and did its best to thwart them, trying to deny him a place at the University of Berlin. That planted the seeds of antagonism between the established church and many in the theological world, creating a rift between traditional Christian belief and academic thought.

As Harnack's influence spread throughout the Christian world, the same dynamics would take place in England and the United States. In America, it would spark an anti-liberal antagonism that produced a series of tracts espousing doctrines believed to be fundamental to Christian faith, entitled *The Fundamentals* (1910–1915).[22] The tracts were based on the scholastic Federal Calvinism of Reformed theology. It would produce a fundamentalist-modernist divide in American Protestantism that would remain a constant presence in the United States through the rest of the century and into the next.

In the Roman Catholic Church, Harnack's critics there had already been largely marginalized and silenced, having been charged by Rome's magisterium with "modernism." But Harnack's most vigorous challenge would come from his German colleague at Berlin, Ernst Troeltsch, and the brilliant musician-turned-theologian from Alsace-Lorraine—Albert Schweitzer.

Ernst Troeltsch (1865–1923)

Troeltsch wrote on the philosophy of religion and the philosophy of history. He was a member of the history of religion school (*Religionsgeschichtiche Schule*) that had emerged at the University of Gottingen in the late 1880s. It was an academic discipline dedicated to investigating ancient texts to understand the worlds they represented. It compared Christianity to other religions, demonstrating what Christianity shared with other religions, and viewed it as but one of many, challenging its claim to absolute truth. Troeltsch realized that history could never produce evidence for Harnack's claim about Christianity. Faith could not be established based on history.

---

22. The inerrancy of Scripture, the virgin birth of Christ, penal substitutionary atonement, the bodily resurrection of Christ, and the reality of Christ's miracles.

Albert Schweitzer (1875–1965)

The other person who discredited Harnack was Albert Schweitzer. He challenged the various liberal, secular, romantic views of Jesus that had been created in theology by the German historical-critical method over the previous 130 years, as well as the traditional Christian view of Jesus espoused by the established church of his day. In 1906 Schweitzer summed up his theological work on the history of the life of Jesus, criticizing the liberal view put forth by scholars in the first quest.[23] It was later published in English as *The Quest of the Historical Jesus* (*Geschichte der Leben-Jesu-Forschung*).

The quest had sought to separate what the apostles said about Jesus ("the Jesus of faith"), and what Jesus had said about himself ("the Jesus of history"). Its methods rejected all supernatural event simply as myth and utilized the historical-critical method to study biblical texts, determine their veracity, and construct a "Jesus of history." These "historical" lives of Jesus varied in many ways. They were often extremely romantic in nature, highly psychological, and made Jesus more a man of the nineteenth century than a Second Temple Jew of the first century. Some of these "lives of Jesus" supported Christianity, while others attacked it.

A conservative German counter movement to the liberal quest emerged among a group of theologians who dwelt on the unusual nature of Jesus' ministry and teachings. One scholar developed the idea of "the messianic secret" in the Gospel of Mark to explain why Jesus, as the Messiah, never claimed to be so.[24] Others saw in Jesus two quite different people, one the son of an unknown builder in Nazareth who was a political revolutionary, and the other the Son of God and Lord of the world, rising after death. Schweitzer criticized both the liberal and conservative views; neither was valid. Each was re-creating Jesus in their own intellectual image. Harnack and his school had turned Jesus into a moral teacher who embodied the late nineteenth-century bourgeois Protestant thought in Europe. The Jesus Schweitzer had discovered in his historical and theological research was anything but what the post-Enlightenment,

---

23. The first quest for the historical Jesus is thought to have been initiated by German historian Samuel Reimarus (1694–1768) whose *Fragments* was published after Reimarus' death by G. E. Lessing in 1774–78. A second quest, also known as the new quest, emerged in 1950, fired by new biblical scholarship emerging out of the discovery of the Dead Sea Scrolls, but waned within two decades. In 1985, a third was begun by a group of American theologians and laypeople known popularly as the Jesus Seminar.

24. Johannes Weiss (1863–1914).

liberal, romantic, Protestant world was looking for.[25] As Schweitzer read his New Testament, he concluded that John the Baptist and Jesus were unique, eschatological men in their time who set the end times in motion "by acting, by creating eschatological facts."[26] Both proclaimed, "Repent, for the kingdom of heaven is at hand" (Matt 3:2; Mark 1:15).

> Soon after that comes Jesus, and in the knowledge that He is the coming Son of Man lays hold of the wheel of the world to set it moving on that last revolution which is to bring all ordinary history to a close. It refuses to turn, and He throws Himself upon it. Then it does turn; and crushes Him. Instead of bringing the eschatological conditions, He has destroyed them. The wheel rolls onward, and the mangled body of the one immeasurably great Man, who was strong enough to think of Himself as the spiritual ruler of mankind and to bend history to His purpose, is hanging upon it still. That is His victory and His reign.[27]

Schweitzer then concludes the results of his study, writing,

> The Jesus of Nazareth who came forward publicly as the Messiah, who preached the ethic of the Kingdom of God, who founded the Kingdom of Heaven upon earth, and died to give His work its final consecration, never had any existence. He is a figure designed by rationalism, endowed with life by liberalism, and clothed by modern theology in an historical garb.
>
> This image has not been destroyed from without, it has fallen to pieces, cleft and disintegrated by the concrete historical problems which came to the surface one after the other.[28]

Yet, lest we think this is the end of the story for Schweitzer or Christianity, he continues, "Jesus means something to our world because a mighty spiritual force streams forth from him and flows through our time also. This fact can neither be shaken nor confirmed by any historical discovery. It is the solid foundation of Christianity.[29]

Reading the apostle Paul, Schweitzer found Paul to be a mystic for whom faith was a matter of living and "being in Christ." Faith was

---

25. Hastings, "Twentieth Century," 722.
26. Schweitzer, *Quest of Historical Jesus*, 242.
27. Schweitzer, *Quest of Historical Jesus*, 242.
28. Schweitzer, *Quest of Historical Jesus*, 259.
29. Schweitzer, *Quest of Historical Jesus*, 261.

a mystical union of dying and rising with Christ, first through baptism, then dying and rising with him daily throughout their lives.

> It is not Jesus as historically known, but Jesus as spiritually arisen within men [and women] who is significant for our time and can help it. Not the historical Jesus, but the spirit which goes forth from Him and in the spirits of [them] strives for the new influence and rule, is that which overcomes the world.[30]

Leaving a career in theology behind, Schweitzer went back to the university to study medicine. His dissertation was entitled "The Psychiatric Study of Jesus," and it defended Jesus' mental health. Medical degree in hand, in 1914 he went off to establish his hospital at Lambaréné, Gabon, Africa, to live out his own quest to follow Jesus.

Gustav Aulén (1879–1977)

Gustav Aulén was a Swedish Lutheran minister who taught dogmatic theology at Lund University until becoming bishop of Strängäs in the Church of Sweden in 1933. Three years before leaving his teaching post to become bishop, he gave a series of lectures, first in Sweden, then in Germany, which were translated into English the following year under the title *Christus Victor*.

Aulén was convinced that the traditional understanding of the history of the doctrines of the atonement was badly in need of thorough revision because it had focused primarily upon the work of Anselm and, to a lesser degree, that of Abelard. Though these theories of atonement had received a great deal of attention by theologians, he believed that in many ways atonement's source material in Scripture had been seriously misinterpreted or simply ignored. In his lectures and the book that they became, he set out to correct that.

Aulén's work divides the whole of atonement theology into three main types: Anselm's satisfaction theory, Abelard's moral example theory, and a third that he calls the "classic theory"—*Christus Victor* (Christ the Victor). Aulén traces this latter theory back to the church's earliest theologians. He recognizes Anselm's satisfaction theory as the real beginning of a thoroughly thought-out doctrine of the atonement but believes Anselm, in his desire to leave ransom theories behind, had repressed the old mythological account of Christ's work as a victory over the devil.

30. Schweitzer, *Quest of Historical Jesus*, 261.

Therefore, Anselm had missed the opportunity for a more physical and contemporary idea of salvation, one not constructed out of medieval philosophy or legal theory.

Anselm had put forward a notion of sin as transgression of law, and a theory of deliverance from the guilt of sin through satisfaction of that law. Aulén called Anselm's theory *objective* atonement, because in it, God is the "object" of Christ's work. Reconciliation comes through the satisfaction of God's justice.

Abelard's moral example theory Ansélm labeled *subjective*, doing so because it is a concept that explains the atonement as something that is addressed to women and men and brings forth a change in them rather than a change in God and God's attitude toward them. He then argues that after the eleventh century, these two theories—objective and subjective—with some variation, have dominated theological thought on the subject, with Anselm's satisfaction theory being the dominant of the two.

Aulén concludes his review by asking if this is at all a sufficient understanding of the Christian doctrine of atonement. It has overlooked "the classic idea" of *Christus Victor*, Christ's victory over "the powers" that separate humanity from God.[31] Neither objective nor subjective, it is "dramatic": its central theme is the divine conflict and victory of Christ over the powers in God's drama of salvation.[32] Christ fights against and triumphs over the evil powers of the world that have humanity in bondage and suffering. In Christ's action and victory, a twofold atonement is taking place.

First, the drama and battle are cosmic. Christ's victory over the hostile powers brings into being a new relation between God and the world—reconciliation—at-one-ment. Second, because the hostile powers are carrying out God's judgment on sin, they are unwittingly acting as servants of God's will, extracting the sentence of the divine Judge of all. Triumph over them "is regarded as a reconciling of God Himself; He is reconciled by the very act in which He reconciles the world to Himself."[33]

Aulén believed this theory markedly superior to either the objective or subjective ones because it is God's work from beginning to end, while the objective and subjective theories place too much emphasis on the work of humanity in making atonement. In addition, it was the dominant

---

31. Aulén, *Christus Victor*, 13.
32. Aulén, *Christus Victor*, 14.
33. Aulén, *Christus Victor*, 14.

idea of Christ's work in the infant church, its New Testament, and the predominant idea of atonement in the church for its first thousand years.

Though Christ's victory began to be pushed out in the Middle Ages after the church's embrace of Anselm's teaching on satisfaction, Aulén believes it emerged afresh, both vigorously and profoundly, in the preaching and writing of Martin Luther. For Luther, the devil was not simply an idea about evil and its power but its very incarnation. God, in Christ and his cross, had taken on the devil and defeated him, reconciling humanity to God in that defeat.[34]

Aulén observed that Luther's successors, however, returned to satisfaction theory. Consequently, it became the dominant view in orthodox Lutheran and Reformed Protestantism, while the subjective exemplarist view diverged further still, through nineteenth-century liberal Protestant thought, focusing on psychological and sociological processes that bring about a reformation in humanity and society and its atonement with God.

A Third View—*Christus Victor*

Aulén's work has become the third dominant stream of atonement theology in the last one hundred years, though subsequent reflection has recognized not one but three different streams of Christ's victory in the history of the church's thought. The first, as we saw at the beginning of chapter 7, is the work of Origen, who saw God paying a ransom to the devil for Adam's sin. The second, slightly different than Origen's, was God offering Jesus to the devil, not as a payment for the release of captive and sinful humanity but as a trick to ensnare and defeat the devil.[35] The third, Aulén's "classic theory"—*Christus Victor*. In the battle between the forces of good and evil, evil appears initially triumphant in Jesus' death. However, evil is ultimately defeated and conquered by the sovereignty of the Triune God in Jesus' resurrection and ascension.

Unfortunately, Aulén missed altogether the second-century incarnational recapitulation theory of Irenaeus and its further development by Athanasius and failed to explore the deeper scriptural roots of the

---

34. See Aulén, *Christus Victor*, ch. 6, "Luther," 72–77.

35. This latter version of atonement theory most recently appeared in C. S. Lewis' *Chronicles of Narnia*, specifically in *The Lion, the Witch and the Wardrobe*. The lion Aslan allows himself to be slaughtered by the witch, who does not know "the deeper magic." In her taking Aslan's life, she loses her power over Narnia, and the "deeper magic" restores Aslan and the land to life.

exemplar theory in the Gospel of John. In addition, more recent scholarship has challenged Aulén's assertion that the version of *Christus Victor* that he identified with Luther, was, in fact, what was at work in Luther's atonement theology. One Lutheran scholar has argued that Luther did not have a "theory" of atonement.[36] Rather, he was a biblical theologian working with the death and resurrection of Jesus as Scripture witnesses to its meaning in multidimensional ways and not with a theory at all.

---

36. Hagan, "Luther on Atonement," 252n3.

Chapter 9

Twentieth-Century Atonement Theologies—Incarnation Recovered

Donald M. Baillie (1887–1954)

DONALD MACPHERSON BAILLIE, PROFESSOR of systematic theology at the University of St. Andrews from 1934 until his death in 1954 became a twentieth-century pivotal figure in atonement theology. At a time of theological upheaval, as the liberal Protestant German schools of theology encountered the withering critique of Swiss Reformed theologian Karl Barth and the neo-orthodox theology that emerged from that, both in Europe and the United States, Baillie wrote what he called "an essay for the current time."[1]

The quest for the historical Jesus was still reverberating well into World War II, with the theological camps divided between the "Christ of history" and the "Christ of faith." Liberal Protestant theology was focused on the Christ of history and what one could learn about the historical Jesus, setting aside dogmatic assertions about who he was. Language describing him as God incarnate, God's Son, Lord, Messiah, Savior—the divine attributes described in the historic creeds—was simply the language the church used, long after Jesus' death, and was not reliable. The only authentic Jesus was the Jesus of history. But one could not discover the real Jesus of history through the Gospels. They were simply the constructs of the church, often in conflict with one another, and could tell us nothing about the real Jesus.

---

1. Baillie, *God Was in Christ*, 8.

For the Christ of faith camp, history was superfluous. What was truly important was the salvation Christ brought to humanity that is initiated by faith, not the Jesus from Nazareth who lived and did ministry in Galilee. Historical information about him was unimportant for faith, as he was more than simply a man who entered history. Some, like Schweitzer, had argued that the Jesus of history could never be discovered. He would always be a reflection of the seeker's highest ideals, for good or for ill. The Christ of faith was the only way forward for the church, especially since most of that historical information was not available to contemporary Christians.

The neo-orthodox Protestant theology of Karl Barth that emerged after the First World War challenged all of these. It stressed God's absolute transcendence, spoke of (in Kierkegaard's words) the "infinite qualitative distinction" between the human and the divine, the otherness of God, and insisted that all we could know about God must come to us through God's self-revelation in Christ as it is encountered in and through Scripture.[2] That must be the sole source of Christian doctrine.

Stepping between Camps—Christology

Stepping between these camps and its leaders, many of whom were Baillie's theological contemporaries, colleagues, and friends, Baillie utilized Paul's now familiar words to the Corinthians about reconciliation: "God was in Christ" (2 Cor 5:19 KJV). If theology (talk of God) is to be done properly and be authentic, it must have a credible Christology (who Jesus is as "the Christ" of God) that is taken seriously, and to have such a Christology, it must hold together the Jesus of history and the Christ of faith.

> A true Christology will tell us not simply that God is *like* Christ, but that God was *in* Christ. Thus, it will tell us not only about the *nature* of God, but about His *activity*, about what He has done, coming the whole way for our salvation in Jesus Christ; and there is no other way in which the Christian truth about God can be expressed.[3]

Baillie challenged both the Christ of history and the Christ of faith camps, insisting that any authentic and credible confession that Jesus is

2. Tietz, *Karl Barth*, 127, in reference to Barth's *Römerbrief* (second version).
3. Baillie, *God Was in Christ*, 66–67; emphasis original.

the Christ of God who saves must also understand him as the Christ who inhabited historical time and space and saves those who live in historical time and space. It is only by understanding that the Jesus who is confessed as the Christ lived a life like the rest of humanity—their joys, sorrows, needs, etc.—and by knowing what kind of life that was, that will enable the church's confession of him as the Savior to have credibility, as well as tell us what we can say about God.

> Whatever Jesus was or did, in His life, in His teaching, in His cross and passion, in His resurrection and ascension and exaltation, it is really God that did it in Jesus: that is how the New Testament speaks. It becomes most striking of all in connection with the reconciling death of Jesus. When his early followers spoke of His death on the cross as a supreme expression of love for men [and women], it was not so much of the love of Jesus that they spoke of as the love of God who sent him.[4]

Baillie's modest essay did not fit the theological camps and labels of his day. It became far more controversial than he had expected. Liberal Protestants of Europe were troubled by his dogmatic convictions about saving belief in Jesus. The neo-orthodox saw him coming to different conclusions about Jesus than their own. He reintroduced the incarnation as critical and central to atonement theology and put that theology back on track to be driven by biblical witness rather than philosophies, especially those of history *or* religion.

Reconciliation— A Trinitarian Corrective—Karl Barth (1886–1968)

In the Reformed house, a Swiss pastor and biblical theologian who had already sent shock waves across liberal Protestant theology, began to untangle the deficiencies in the way Calvin and the Reformed tradition had erred in their focus on atonement as satisfaction of God's wrath rather than as an expression of God's love—God's *holy* love.

---

4. Baillie, *God Was in Christ*, 67–68.

God's Holy Love

The holiness of God's love is what makes it different than any other form of love and what makes it divine. In such holy love God seeks after sinful humanity, but does so not as humanity's equal or enemy but as their Lord—One whose will stands over against all other wills, allowing nothing to stand in its way.

This means that God's love and grace are not only irresistible but that they will inevitably reach their goal.

> God's will to love the creature will not be stopped by the will of the creature to resist that love. God's love will reach its goal, even if the path to that end lies through condemning, excluding, and annihilating all resistance to it. God's love turns to wrath when it is resisted, but not for a minute does it cease to be love even when it expresses itself as wrath.[5]

Why? For Barth, atonement's goal is reconciliation: the renewal of relationship and fellowship driven by God's love, righteousness, and mercy.

Regardless of humanity's bondage to their desires and their resistance to and rebellion against God, God's reconciling pursuit is driven by divine love and mercy for humanity that is also righteous. This is what distinguishes it from all other forms or sources of love, mercy, or righteousness. It allows God to remain faithful to Godself as righteous Judge.

Barth was unwilling to repeat the error of Reformed theologians post-Calvin who made the death of Jesus a sacrifice of atonement that was offered to satisfy and propitiate the wrath of God's righteousness. Rather, Jesus' death must be seen as God's righteous love in action (Rom 1:17; 5:6–8).

Christ's Death Is Not about Punishment

Barth noted that the idea of punishment in relation to Christ and his cross was inconsistent with the New Testament witness, where Jesus' death is God dealing with sin, not satisfying a desire for vengeance and retribution. The idea of an atonement in which Jesus suffered our punishment so that humanity is spared it themselves, or that in so suffering he "satisfied" or offered satisfaction to the wrath of God so that sinful

---

5. McCormack, *For Us*, 28–29.

humankind did not have suffer that wrath, is "quite foreign to the New Testament."[6] Barth writes:

> The decisive thing is not that [Christ] has suffered what we ought to have suffered so that we do not have to suffer it, the destruction to which we have fallen victim by our guilt, and therefore the punishment which we deserve. This is true, of course. But it is true only as it derives from the decisive thing that in the suffering and death of Jesus Christ it has come to pass that in his own person [Christ] has made an end of us as sinners and therefore of sin itself by going to death as the One who took our place as sinners. In His person He has delivered up us sinners and sin itself to destruction.[7]

God Dealing with Sin

For Barth, it is sin and the sins of humanity that form the disruption in God's creation that makes necessary the atonement. It is an at-one-ment that opens humanity to a new peace with God, the restoration of the covenant, and the redemption and salvation of humanity, and does so as the work of God's steadfast love and mercy. It is sin that must be dealt with, removed, and overcome in God's act of reconciliation. The very heart of the atonement in Christ is overcoming sin—dealing with it—not providing for its forgiveness.

God has been forgiving sin from the beginning. That did not start at the cross. As Barth notes, in the New Testament, the forgiveness of sins is rarely related to the death of Jesus.[8] Rather, it was to fulfill God's judgment on sin that God became human in Jesus and that Jesus as the God-man took humanity's place and did so to end sin's power to separate humanity from God. Christ did that by destroying sin's power. That work was not simply Christ's. It was the work of the of the Holy Three in cooperation with One Another, out of the Holy One's love for and primal determination never to be God apart from humankind. "The concept of God without [humankind] is indeed as anomalous as wooden iron."[9]

---

6. Barth, *Doctrine of Reconciliation*, 246.
7. Barth, *Doctrine of Reconciliation*, 246.
8. Barth, *Doctrine of Reconciliation*, 248.
9. Barth, *Humanity of God*, 72.

T. F. Torrance (1913–2007)

Fellowship with the Triune God

Thomas Forsyth Torrance was a minister of the Church of Scotland and professor of Christian dogmatics at New College in the University of Edinburgh for twenty-seven years. Born to missionary parents in Chengdu, Sichuan, western China, he lived the first thirteen years of his life there, and then returned to Scotland to attend Edinburgh University. Upon graduation from New College in 1937 he took up research at the University of Basel, on "The Doctrine of Grace in the Apostolic Fathers," under the supervision of Karl Barth. That research was interrupted when, at the behest of John Baillie, Torrance taught at Auburn Seminary for a year (1938–1939) and returned to England just as the war was breaking out. As there was a waiting list to be a chaplain and he could not, at the time, return to Switzerland, Torrance moved to Oriel College, Oxford, to continue work on his dissertation for Basel. Thereafter, in 1940, he was ordained by the Church of Scotland and served the parish in Alyth Perthshire, taking leave between 1943 and 1944 to serve as a chaplain ministering to Scottish soldiers, first in North Africa and then in northern Italy. After the war he returned to Alyth, and from there in 1947 was called to the Beechgrove Church Aberdeen. In 1950 he was called from parish ministry back to the University of Edinburgh to the chair of church history. Two years later, he transferred to the chair of Christian dogmatics, where he remained for the rest of his teaching career.

At New College, Torrance became a pioneer in the study of theology and science. It is the theological work for which he became best known and received the Templeton Prize in 1978. He reasoned that what bound together science and theology was their shared commitment to the objects of their disciplined reflection. Science dealt with the world created by God, and theology with the world's Creator. But God was more than a distant Creator. God is the constant Reconciler and Redeemer who became incarnate in Jesus, God's Son, within the time and space of creation to make atonement and reconcile to God a rebellious humanity under the power of sin.

Classically Reformed, Torrance was a consummate interpreter of Scripture, which was foundational to his dogmatic thinking. This would shape him as one of the leading theological thinkers of the twentieth century. He was also a prolific writer, editor, and translator of others' theological work. Having been a student of Barth, he translated and edited Barth's thirteen-volume *Church Dogmatics* into English, as well as Calvin's New Testament *Commentaries*. He remained an involved minister in the Church of Scotland the rest of his life, actively engaged in ecumenical dialogue. He was moderator of the General Assembly of the Church of Scotland 1976–1977. Two years later he retired from university teaching but continued lecturing and publishing. His extensive work on the Trinity took him into conversation with Orthodox theology and made him instrumental in the agreement between the World Alliance of Reformed Churches and the Orthodox Church on the doctrine of the Trinity.

Nicene Orthodoxy

Heir of both H. R. Mackintosh and Karl Barth, Torrance read Athanasius all his theological career. Torrance's mature theology of atonement is rooted in the Nicene insistence on the unity of God's being and act in Jesus.

> Following, then, the holy fathers, we unite in teaching all men to confess the one and only Son, our Lord Jesus Christ. This selfsame one is perfect both in deity and in humanness; this selfsame one is also actually God and actually man, with a rational soul and a body. He is of the same reality as God as far as his deity is concerned and of the same reality as we ourselves as far as his humanness is concerned; thus, like us in all respects, sin only excepted.[10]

Father and Son are one—undivided—what One does, so too does the Other. The Triune God is made known exclusively in Jesus Christ, who is both God for humanity and a human being for God, the two fused in one "person." There is no unknown God "behind" Jesus. Christ is the grace of God given to humankind, and at the same time, he is humanity's faithful response to God's grace. In Jesus Christ we experience not only the duality of God and man in the unity of one person, but the unity of Christ's person as man and God, and his act in God's work of salvation. This is foundational, in that it lies at the heart of who Jesus is and what he does in atonement.

---

10. For the full statement, see Monergism, "Definition," or Kelly, *Early Christian Doctrines*, 399.

God's Judgment on Sin—God's Wrath

Sin is separation from God—alienation—the result of rebellion that severs the two-sided relation "in which the creator gives existence and life to the creature, and in which the creature depends on the creator for existences and life."[11] This, however, is about more than existence. The creature is to have *fellowship* with God, sharing in God's light, life, and love.[12] God opposes, contradicts, and judges the creature resisting in sin. That is humanity's guilt. God's judgment on sin is what is meant by *the wrath* of God. God's wrath is the negative side of God's holiness and love. Out of God's holiness and love, God must judge and reject sin. If God simply condoned sin, God would "abdicate from being God, would un-God himself."[13]

Yet, God does not leave humanity to themselves or alone in the darkness of sin. Through the incarnation, and in the person and work of Jesus Christ, God takes up humanity's cause as God's own. Atonement in Jesus is not simply one moment, as on the cross. It is the creative and continuous "dynamic event" of God's incarnation in him.[14] It begins in Jesus' conception, birth, life, ministry, passion, death, resurrection, and ascension, and continues with his giving of the Spirit in and to the new creation.

Jesus is humanity responding faithfully to God, and God reaching out to humanity in Jesus. He is vicariously all humanity acting before God for humanity's sake, and God acting in Jesus for God's sake. It was not Jesus' death that saved so much as his life. Scripture talks about Jesus' life as salvific, not just his death. As a human being, he lived a perfect, God-pleasing life of faith and obedience in humanity's name and on our behalf before God.

Salvation comes not from Jesus paying a price for sin. It is his living a life as a perfectly faithful human before God in all circumstances—especially the assault of sin—that is in itself a salvific event. As the perfect human being before the Father, he established an unbroken and perfect fellowship between God and humanity on our behalf. In Christ, and through his perfect and unbroken fellowship, humanity can participate in Christ's fellowship with the Father. One must not think of his person

---

11. Torrance, *Incarnation*, 247.
12. Torrance, *Incarnation*, 247.
13. Torrance, *Incarnation*, 249.
14 Torrance, *Incarnation*, 67.

apart from his atoning work, or his atoning work apart from his person. He is, in his person, God's work of salvation—the atonement.[15]

The sin that threatened God's relationship with humanity is dealt with through the expiation of sin and guilt. Torrance looks at this through the lens of the New Testament conception of redemption and the price of that redemption—ransom—a theme Jesus used to speak of his giving of himself (Matt 20:28; Mark 10:45). All of this, Torrance sees prefigured in Israel's history and sacrificial cult.

Sacrifice in Israel—God's Provision and Forgiveness

God's forgiveness of Israel was not the *result* of its sacrifice. Its sacrifice bore *witness* to God's provision and forgiveness. God was not being acted upon by a sacrificial offering. Atonement does not come from offering something to a hostile, angry God to appease God. Torrance believed all appeasement theories fundamentally pagan. Christ's death did not cause a change in God, for none was needed. Rather, what was needed was the *expiation* of humanity's sin, which could take place only at God's hand, as it did for Israel. Torrance utilizes the Old Testament's sacrificial terms of *padah, kipper,* and *go'el* to describe how this takes place.

One aspect of atonement for Israel was "rescue," which Torrance links to the Hebrew root *pdh*. *Pdh* refers to a "mighty act of God bringing deliverance from oppression, as in the redemption of Israel out of Egypt."[16] Deliverance came by the provision of redemption through substitution, an animal for a human life. Jesus' death was not a ransom offered to the devil. It was the *redemption* of sinners from captivity to sin, death, and judgment, as God had done with Israel at Passover in Egypt and continued to do through the Day of Atonement. Torrance termed this aspect of atoning action "dramatic" because it is "sheer intervention on the part of God in human affairs."[17]

Another dimension or aspect of atonement had to do with "covering." Torrance links the Hebrew root *cpr* to this. *Cpr* indicated the "expiatory form of the act of redemption by which the power of sin and guilt between God and man is broken and done away with, while propitiation

---

15. Torrance, *Incarnation*, 37.
16. Torrance, *Trinitarian Faith*, 170.
17. Torrance, *Trinitarian Faith*, 170.

is effected between them."[18] Propitiation is used by Torrance to express the fact that the chasm between God and man has been bridged by God and is an act in which estranged parties have been reconciled, God drawing near to humankind and humankind being brought near to God.[19] Propitiation is priestly mediation, not appeasement. Once again, God is acting. Though the priest offered this form of sacrifice, it is witness to the fact that it is God who is making atonement and blotting out Israel's sin. It is God who by God's judicial and merciful acts makes atonement between Godself and humankind, and blots their sin and restores them to favor and holiness before God.[20] This is the "priestly" concept of redemption and one in which God is always the actor, never the one acted upon.

The third aspect of atonement is the concept of redemption, in the Hebrew Bible, *g'l*. *G'l* refers to redemption out of destitution or bondage, or forfeited rights undertaken by an advocate. The *goel* is someone related to the one in need through kinship or other form of affinity, or by covenant love. The *goel* does what the one in need cannot do for oneself—stands in for them and redeems them.[21] In Jesus Christ, God came to be our brother, flesh of our flesh and bone of our bone—our *Goel*—to restore in us what was lost in our sin and lead us back to union and fellowship with his Father. Torrance calls this *ontological atonement* because it brings about an existential change in our being.

Each of these three is but *one aspect* of the complex movement that is atonement and what God is doing in Christ's atoning action. The three must be seen working simultaneously together, as they are "profoundly interrelated aspects of divine redemption."[22] They are like the strands in a threefold cord. One must not emphasize one over the other or overlook any of the three. All are present in Christ's atoning work.[23]

---

18. Torrance, *Trinitarian Faith*, 170.
19. Torrance, *Atonement*, 68.
20. Torrance, *Trinitarian Faith*, 170–71.
21. Torrance, *Trinitarian Faith*, 171.
22. Torrance, *Trinitarian Faith*, 170.
23. These dimensions of atonement mirror what the Reformed thinkers called the "triple office" of Christ: Christ is Prophet, Priest, and King.

Incarnational Atonement

Incarnational atonement means that it is God who bears humanity's sin, becomes human, taking humanity's place, and stands with humanity under divine judgment. God the Judge becomes the man Jesus, the Judge who is judged and bears God's own judgment upon the sin of humanity.[24]

God, as Jesus, so identifies with humanity that he abases himself, substitutes himself in humanity's place, puts himself between humanity and God the Father, taking all of humanity's shame and guilt upon himself. He does so not as a third person but as One who is God himself, the very God against whom humanity had sinned and rebelled. As this man, he stands in humanity's place. This is Christ both identifying with us and intervening on our behalf. In identifying with us he meets the full assault of our evil and takes the full contradiction of our sin upon himself.

God's wrath—the result of humanity's sin and rejection of God's love—is poured out against sin and death, destroying and overcoming them in Christ's death. This means that God's wrath is purposeful. Torrance calls it the "wrath of love" and characterizes it as similar to the way a loving parent might react fiercely against an attacker who seeks to harm their child. God's wrath is for us, not against us.

Jesus Christ enters the conflict between humanity and God and takes that conflict upon himself, bearing it to save us.

> Therefore, he met the full opposition of our enmity to God, and the full opposition of God to our enmity and endured it with joy, refusing to let go of God for our sakes, and refusing to let go of us for God's sake. In laying hold of us as sinners, he judged our sin in himself and reconciled us to God, and in laying hold of God he received [God's] judgment of us upon himself and offered our humanity in himself to the Father.[25]

Atonement Embraced Sacramentally

This atonement continues and is entered into and embraced sacramentally through the Spirit that the ascended Christ has sent to his own. Baptism is being clothed in Christ, dying with him to sin and death, and rising with him to new life beyond the power of death. Eucharist is the

---

24. Torrance, *Atonement*, 184–85.
25. Torrance, *Atonement*, 151.

risen Christ's means of feeding us on him, to sustain, nurture, and enable us to mature in him as members of his new creation. For we are not saved by Jesus *from* something but *for* something—life in God's new creation.

Through the Spirit, in union with Christ, we are lifted into fellowship with the Triune love of God where our existence and our fellowship are actualized. There God draw us into God's holiness and sanctifies us with it, bringing about an *ontological change in our being*.[26] Yet God's work of atonement is not done but awaits Christ's final return, when all things are redeemed.

Jürgen Moltmann (1926-)

The Crucified God

Jürgen Moltmann is a German Reformed theologian, professor emeritus of systematic theology at the University of Tübingen, and one of the most widely read, important, and influential theologians of the late twentieth century. Reared in a secular home with no Christian influence, he set out to study science and mathematics but was drafted by the German army at the age of sixteen, becoming an air force auxiliary in a battery in the center of Hamburg. During an RAF firestorm bombing of Hamburg, a friend standing next to him was torn to pieces by a bomb that left Jürgen untouched. It shaped the rest of his life and theological career. He writes, "That night I cried out to God for the first time, 'My God, where are you?' The question 'Why am I not dead too?' has haunted me ever since."[27] The following year he was sent to the front lines in the Belgian forest, and there, in 1945, Moltmann surrendered to the first British soldier he met.

It was in POW camps (1945–1948), while reflecting on the horrors and devastation of World War II, that he met Christian chaplains and was given a New Testament with the Psalms. That introduced him to the Christian gospel and Christian theology. In the camps, he participated in the Student Christian Movement, became a Christian, and continued to read theology. Upon release, he began theological studies at the University of Göttingen, where he would be highly influenced by its largely Barthian theological faculty. He has described his theology as post-Barthian.

---

26. Torrance, *Atonement*, 373, 376; emphasis added.
27. McDivitt, "Creation and the Spirit."

In 1952 Moltmann received his doctorate, focusing upon Reformed theology in Germany and France, and for the next five years was pastor of the Evangelical Church of Bremen-Wasserhort. Thereafter he entered academic life, first at an academy in Wuppertal, then in 1963 at the University of Bonn. Four years later he was appointed professor of systematic theology at the University of Tübingen, where he remained until retirement in 1994. His early work is a theological trilogy: *Theology of Hope* (1964), *The Crucified God* (1972), and *The Church in the Power of the Spirit* (1975).

In *Theology of Hope*, Moltmann focuses on the hope the resurrection brings when one is bound to Christ in faith. But that hope is first and foremost grounded in Christ crucified. There is where God is to be found, recognizing that the present reality in this world is not God's intention for humanity. Consequently, hope in life is not for the perfection of the present, driven as it is by the sin that emerges out of humanity's hopelessness. Authentic hope is for the fulfillment of the promises of God—hope for God's lordship, peace, and righteousness—the kingdom of God on this earth. Such hope and faith are essential if one is to find consolation in suffering or live in and protest things in this world that are so corrupt and distorted, things so different than what God intends for creation.

In his subsequent book, *The Crucified God*, Moltmann utilizes the Barthian dialectical method[28] to interpret the cross as the suffering of the Triune God who is love, suffering unto death for all who suffer and are godforsaken. Therein is the foundation of his Trinitarian doctrine of the atonement.

The Love of the Triune God

God is love[29] and Triune: three persons—Father, Son, and Spirit—within the one loving reality that humanity names God. God's work of atonement is first and foremost an "event" within the Triune life of God that expresses not only the mutual love of Father, Son, and Spirit for Each Other but their love for the world as it comes into expression through the

---

28. Dialectical theology begins with the conviction that God is unknowable to humans without God's grace and direct revelation. All attempts to know God through human reason meet impossible contradiction. Reason must give way to faith revealed in Jesus Christ and to find the truth about God, which transcends the yes and no of other theological methods.

29. First John 4:7–8, 16–17.

mystery of Jesus. God, in the person of the eternal Son, fully enters the limited, finite situation of human life to become the man Jesus.

> The mystery of Jesus . . . is the incarnation of eternal, original, unchangeable being in the sphere of temporal, decaying, transitory existence, in which [humans] live and die. If the mystery of Jesus is the eternal presence of God amongst [humanity] then the salvation of the world is also to be found in him. God became [human] so that [humans] could partake of God. [God] took on transitory, mortal being, for that which is transitory and mortal to become intransitory and immortal.[30]

The depth of God's love for the world is revealed in what God does within Godself to accomplish this incarnation and its intended purpose.

> Not only does [God] enter into [the limited finite situation of humanity, God] descend into it, but [God] also accepts it and embraces the whole of human existence with [God's] being. . . . [God] lowers [Godself] and accepts the whole of [humanity] without limits and conditions, so that [everyone] may participate in God with the whole of [their] life.[31]

Thus, God in the eternal Son limits and denies Godself to fully assume the person of Jesus, the man-God, the reality that is witnessed to in the name Jesus Christ.[32]

The Cost of Such Love

God as true love so loved the world that God gave the eternal Son for the world (John 3:16). The verb for gave in this well-known verse is *didomi*—"to give." Moltmann understands this giving in the way the Gospels and Paul employ the compound of that verb, *paradidomia*, meaning "to give over" or "to hand over" (Matt 26:2; Luke 18:32; John 18:36; Rom 1:24, 26, 28; 8:31–32; Gal 2:20). God the Father handed over to the world God the Son in Jesus, and did so for the sake of the sinful, corrupt, and otherwise godforsaken world.

---

30. Moltmann, *Crucified God*, 88. Note his paraphrase of Athanasius, *De Incarnatione*, 54. Words in brackets here and henceforth in all quotations are my modification to make the dated 1974 text inclusive.

31. Moltmann, *Crucified God*, 276.

32. This is Moltmann's understanding of Phil 2:7, more commonly called *kenosis*, from the Greek verb *kenoo*, meaning "to empty" or "make void."

Within that world, the Jewish religious leaders believed Jesus was a dangerous religious rebel, challenging its Torah-based Judaism, while embracing and proclaiming the outcast of its world as acceptable to Israel's God—the One he called his Father. Further, his claim to forgive sinners made him a blasphemer. Torah says such a person must die (Lev 24:14, 16, 23). Rome, on the other hand, saw Jesus as a political threat, a zealot, and a potential revolutionary. Thus, in this religious and political collaboration, Jesus was crucified outside the walls of Jerusalem between two zealots.

Jesus goes to the cross out of love for the Father and the world. Yet, Mark and Matthew report that in his crucifixion, Jesus cries out in the words of Ps 22:1, "My God, my God, why have you forsaken me." Moltmann sees this as pivotal to what is happening in the crucifixion and witness to the truth that not only did the religious, political, and inner circle of Jesus' followers abandon Jesus in death, but even the One he called Father. Jesus dies in total abandonment for all the abandoned of the world. He dies godforsaken for all the godforsaken of the world. The Father, in his love for the godless world, gave up the incarnate Son, forsaking him for all in the world who are godforsaken.

The Paradox of God's Love

The paradox of divine love lies at the heart of Moltmann's theology of the atonement: the love of the Father for the Son and for the world, and the love of the Son for the world and for the Father. The incarnate Son's love for humanity is expressed in Jesus' total identification with the godforsaken, going to the cross for their sake while also expressing his love for his Father in total fidelity, obedience, and trust of his Father—even as he experiences his Father's abandonment. The Father's love for the godforsaken causes God to forsake the Son on behalf of the world.

Through this bond of paradoxical love, Jesus suffers his dying in separation and isolation from his Father, doing so for all who likewise know godforsakeness. Likewise, God the Father suffers death as well, but not in the same way as the Son. As God the Son suffers his own dying in union with Jesus, God the Father suffers with the Son, as a human parent suffers with a child in sickness unto death. But the Father suffers even more as the Father suffers the eternal Son's death in Jesus. The Father suffers death's separation, loss, grief, and sorrow, thereby taking death and all that goes with it into Godself. God the Son is crucified and dies in Jesus Christ; God the Father suffers the crucifixion as the Father of the crucified Son.[33] The crucifixion is "a trinitarian event between the Son and the Father."[34] It is a deep division within Godself. God has abandoned God and contradicted Godself.

The paradox here is not the death of God but that in the mutual surrender of the Two, "God was at one with God and corresponded to Godself."[35] Consequently, as the Father and Son are most deeply separated in forsakenness, at the same time, they are most inwardly united in their love and their surrender to this event. Moltmann suggests the formula in this paradoxical way: "God died the death of the godless on the cross and yet did not die. God is dead and yet is not dead."[36]

The solution to the seeming absurdity that God is dead on the cross and yet not dead is resolved by abandoning the simple deistic concept of God as monad[37] and remembering the more defined Christian understanding of God in Trinitarian terms—Three in One. Moltmann reminds us that when Paul says to the Corinthians "God was in Christ reconciling the world" (2 Cor 5:19),[38] he is referring not only to the Father who abandons the Son and gives the Son up for the world but also to God the Son who is abandoned and forsaken on behalf of the world, as both are persons within the Godhead. One has died, the other has not. God is crucified in and with the death of the Son who dies in and with the crucified Jesus.[39] It is the death of God the Son *within* the Triune God.[40]

---

33. Moltmann, *Crucified God*, 255.

34. Moltmann, *Crucified God*, 245.

35. Moltmann, *Crucified God*, 244.

36. Moltmann, *Crucified God*, 244.

37. A single unit, indivisible; from the Greek *monas*, meaning alone.

38. A careful reading of the text with its footnote will reveal two different ways of translating this verse: "God was in Christ reconciling the world," as Moltmann and many older translations render it (Tyndale, Geneva, KJV), as well as many modern ones (NAS); and "In Christ, God was reconciling," as the NRSV, RSV, ESV, and NIV translate it. In truth, the Greek of the text can be authentically translated either way.

39. This must not be confused with the "death of God" theology that began with Nietzsche in the nineteenth century and became briefly popular, especially in America, in the mid-twentieth century, as an expression of protest over the increasing secularity of the 1950s and 1960s.

40. Moltmann, *Crucified God*, 204.

The Center of All Christian Theology

The death of Jesus on the cross and his death within the Triune God, makes the cross "the *center* of all Christian theology."[41] For from this event between the Father and the Son, held in unity by their mutual love for One Another and for the world, comes the spirit of God's love—God's grace—the Spirit who is released into the world, the third person of the Godhead. Until now, the Spirit has been the bond of love between the Father and the Son. At Jesus' death, the Spirit is released into the world as the Spirit of divine love.[42] It is the Spirit, the "Lord, the giver of life,"[43] who justifies the godless, fills the forsaken with love, and even brings the dead alive.

Because God does not spare the Son, all godless are spared; for though they are still godless, they are not godforsaken.[44] And even though they are dead, death cannot exclude them from this event that has taken place on the cross—a death for all godforsaken—a death God suffers within Godself that is for them.[45]

Resurrection

As the cross divided God from God to the utmost degree of enmity and distinction, the resurrection of the Son abandoned by God unites God with God in the most intimate of fellowship.[46] And though cross and resurrection must be seen together as what the New Testament tells us God was doing in Christ and what happened to Christ in those three days, they must not be understood as "facts on the same level." The cross is a historical event that happened to the God-man Jesus on Good Friday. The resurrection is "an eschatological event." But it is not eschatological in the sense that eschatology has been traditionally thought of—something that is relegated to the end of time and has no relationship to the present. It is an event that has happened in the world and has power in this world now, not simply at "the end."[47]

---

41. Moltmann, *Crucified God*, 204.
42. Moltmann, *Crucified God*, 244.
43. Third article of the Nicene Creed.
44. Moltmann, *Crucified God*, 242.
45. Moltmann, *Crucified God*, 244.
46. Moltmann, *Crucified God*, 152.
47. Moltmann, *Crucified God*, 204; see also 177.

The Transformation of the World—The New Creation

Jesus' resurrection by God must never be thought of as a private or isolated miracle for Jesus' vindication or authentication. Nor can Jesus' resurrection be regarded as a fortuitous miracle in an unchangeable world. It is the beginning of the end of history in the midst of history, the beginning of the eschatological transformation of the world by its Creator.[48] It is the anticipation of God's future, God's new creation beginning in God within history. Jesus' resurrection has nothing to do with life after death or the revivification of the dead.

Resurrection means a qualitatively new life beyond death, a life that will never know death again. It is eternal life.[49] Thus, "the resurrection of the crucified Christ reveals God's righteousness in a unique way, namely as grace which makes righteous and as the creator's love of the godless."[50] This means that eternal life is not a reward for one's own righteousness—whether personal or through faith—and eternal damnation the fate of the unrighteous. It is "the law of God's grace for the unrighteous and self-righteous alike."[51]

The future of a new world of righteousness lived in the presence of God has already dawned in one person—Jesus Christ, the God-man—amid the world's history of death. All who hear and believe this word move from a "distant expectation of an uncertain future, to a sure hope in a new future of God which has already dawned in that one person."[52] Faith in the risen Jesus means living, in this transitory world of death, out of the powers of the resurrection and the new world of life that has dawned in him. Believers no longer live in the unredeemed world of death. "There is already true life in the midst of this world's 'false life,' though only in communion with the one who had been crucified by that world and its 'false life' and was raised beyond it to a life beyond mortality to eternal life. The future has already begun."[53]

---

48. Moltmann, *Crucified God*, 162.
49. Moltmann, *Crucified God*, 162.
50. Moltmann, *Crucified God*, 176.
51. Moltmann, *Crucified God*, 176.
52. Moltmann, *Crucified God*, 171.
53. Moltmann, *Crucified God*, 171.

Chapter 10

Feminists and Liberation Theology

Feminist Theologians

THE SECOND HALF OF the twentieth century marked an increase in women making an impact on theology, not just in America but across the Christian world, especially in its Protestant expressions. These feminists forced theologians to begin to rethink what they were saying about God in multiple ways, not the least of which was the language being used to speak of God. The challenge was especially strong in languages such as English, which are gender specific and lack neutral singular nouns and pronouns for people.

This becomes a significant problem when one attempts to speak of God. Consequently, one of the first great gifts of the women theologians was forcing the discipline to rethink the language Christians were using to speak of and try to understand the Triune God as God the Father, God the Son, and God the Holy Spirit, as well as the language they were using to describe people.

Language for humans was relatively easy—keep nouns and pronouns plural. Language about God was more complex—God within Godself and God as revealed to humanity.[1] Consequently, feminists helped bring Trinitarian theology back into the whole of theological converse. However, the gifts to theology of these women have been more profound than the issues of language or resurgence of Trinitarian thought.

---

1. Theologians speak of the former as the immanent Trinity and the latter as the economic Trinity.

The feminists have brought not only their experiences and perspectives but also their challenges to the way theology had been done in the church for nineteen hundred years. It had been commonplace to reject the notion that all mainstream religions were inherently male dominant—the word man being thought to be collective rather than gender specific, and He (note the uppercase *h*) as appropriate to God because, as was often said to justify the practice, "we all know that God is beyond gender." Beginning in the 1960s that assumption started to change.

Based on the history of patriarchy found in Scripture and the church, a small group of women began to demand that their churches and academies not only respect their intellect and scholarship but also hear their voices. Those voices had to do with far more than language about God. They demanded that theologians (almost all white male) respect their experience and perspectives as women, their ability to speak of God, and their descriptions of God's work in the world.[2]

Liberation Theology and Its Role

These female reformers also found themselves being influenced by a theology emerging out of Latin America. Highly shaped and encouraged by the events and theology of Vatican II, several theologians began writing what quickly became known as liberation theology. This theology incorporates Marxist political philosophy[3] with Christianity and insists upon activism on behalf of the marginalized, poor, or otherwise oppressed. Such activism, liberationists insist, is essential to Christian life if one is to remain faithful to the God revealed in Jesus Christ.

Leaders in this movement in the southern hemisphere include Peruvian priest Gustavo Gutiérrez, Brazilians Ivone Gebara (an Augustinian nun) and Leonardo Boff (a former Franciscan priest), Uruguayan Juan Luis Segundo (a Jesuit priest), and Argentine José Miguez Bonino, the latter a Methodist minister. It was in 1968 that Father

---

2. Among these, the more notable were Mary Daly, Rosemary Radford Ruether, Letty Russell, Catherine Mowry LaCugna, and Elizabeth Johnson in the US; Kari Børresen and Elisabeth Gössmann in Europe; Ivonne Gebara in Brazil; and Ahn Byungmu in South Korea.

3. They often prefer the term *Marxian* to avoid the implications of Communism. It is its essential association with Marxist thought that brought Rome's condemnation of the work, especially from then-Cardinal Ratzinger, who later became Pope Benedict XVI.

Pedro Arrupe, superior general of the Jesuits, coined the phrase "God's preferential option for the poor." The phrase was later picked up by the Catholic bishops of Latin America. In South Africa, Allan Boesak (Dutch Reformed pastor) was developing a theology addressing apartheid, while Kwame Bediako (Ghanaian Christian theologian) worked to relate Christian faith to traditional African culture.

In the United States, James H. Cone produced the groundbreaking books *Black Theology and Black Power* and *A Black Theology of Liberation*. They emerged from his experience as a Black theologian in America as well as the dawn of the Black Power and civil rights movements in the sixties. His role as professor on the faculty of Union Theological Seminary in New York City made the seminary a place hospitable to the newly emerging liberation theology, especially its feminist proponents, such as his faculty colleagues Euro-feminist Dorothee Sölle, African American Jacquelyn Grant, Cuban American Ada Maria Isasi-Diaz, and African American Delores Williams, as well as second-generation feminists, prominent among them South Korean Hyun Kyung Chung.[4]

What had been dominantly the domain of white males was no longer so, as not only white females but also women of other color and cultural traditions incorporated their own experiences into their theologizing. That soon became a critique of the feminist movement itself. At its earliest levels, feminist theology had been focused only on concerns of white, middle-class, Western women.[5] To be authentically feminist, they argued, that must change.

Thus, feminist liberation theology moved from concerns over language and gender to the more complex relationship of theology with gender, race, class, ethnicity, and economic conditions, as well as other concerns. The result is a multiplicity of theologies that now include not only feminist but also womanist (women who are not white, though predominately African American), *mujerista* (Hispanic), and *minjung* (Asian), and are no longer limited to Christianity but may be found in Buddhism, Hinduism, Sikhism, Neopaganism, and Bahá'i, as well as Judaism and Islam.[6]

---

4. Sölle, *Christ the Representative*; Grant, *White Women's Christ*; Isasi-Diaz, *En la Lucha/In the Struggle*; D. Williams, *Sisters in the Wilderness*; Chung, *Struggle to Be the Sun Again*.

5. As in fact, mainline theology in the West in general had been focused and filled with white, middle-class values and thought.

6. For a much broader and inclusive description of feminist theology and its impact

One of the dynamics that has emerged among those feminist theologians who have chosen to remain Christian has been the revision of traditional theological themes in ways that take seriously women's experience. This has meant revisiting classic concepts in theology such as God (the Holy Three who *are* the Holy One),[7] the role and necessity of God's only child being the Son, the implication of the Son being Savior, Christology, sin, atonement, the meaning of the cross, redemption, and the nature and identity of the Holy Spirit. All have been subject to feminist critique.

Feminist Atonement Critique

Almost all the atonement theories we have reviewed have come under severe critique and rejection by feminists and others who deem the theories to have contributed to women's subjugation, abuse, and oppression, as well as justifying child abuse. We have already visited much of that critique of traditional atonement thought, which, not coincidentally, emerged at the same time as feminists' theologies and owes much to their work.[8] As the last seventy-five years have seen Christology and the incarnation reemerge as central to atonement theology, the feminists have raised objections, primarily because of the perceived problems that incarnation in male form create.

This has led to questions like, can a male Savior save women?[9] Is there an importance to maleness in Jesus that is greater than his being fully human? For instance, the Roman Catholic Church continues to insist that Jesus being male means that only men can serve as priests.[10] Others have responded that a male Savior can save women, but only if his being male is not raised to become a theological principle critical to salvation. Today, most feminist theology focuses on Jesus' life and work as a liberator

---

on the discipline, as well as its most influential leaders, see Linda Hogan, "Feminist Theology."

7. Gail Ramshaw coined this phrase in her search for language that is gender-free and faithful to the Christian gospel.

8. See Trelstad, *Cross Examinations*, esp. "Cross in Context" and part 1, 17–124.

9. Reuther, *To Change the World*, 45–56.

10. Though initially an assumption in mainline Protestantism, the last fifty years have seen that give way to full inclusion, not only to women but, in many traditions, to homosexual, bisexual, and transgendered believers, largely thanks to the feminist movement.

of the oppressed and outcast, on his liberating practice as a model for faithful discipleship, or as the incarnation of God's wisdom, Sophia, who is personified in Hebrew Scripture as a woman (Prov 8:22–24).

Many liberationists, feminist or not, now avoid the category of atonement, choosing to focus on the saving work of Jesus among the poor and the oppressed. For some, Jesus' death has meaning as the death of One whose life was "identified with God's life" and thus whose cross is "God's definitive expression of love."[11] For others, especially among feminist liberation theologians, the emphasis is upon Jesus' experience as example. Jesus is the One whose suffering is like no others and whose sacrifice ends all sacrifices. As Messiah, he is obedient unto death, giving his life for others, giving hope to the otherwise hopeless because of the power of sacrificial love.

For others, it is not Jesus' death that is significant but his life; the cross is an "image of defilement, a gross manifestation of collective human sin." Jesus does not conquer sin's temptation on the cross but does so in the wilderness. It is his life that conquers sin in life, not his death.[12] The cross is simply a tragic accident of sin-filled history.

Kathryn Tanner (1957–)

Unique among these feminist theologians is the contemporary American theologian Kathryn Tanner, to whom we now turn. Tanner is an example of some of the finest and most rigorous contemporary theological thought on atonement, incorporating feminist critique and offering a theory of atonement based on the incarnation that addresses feminist, womanist, *mujerista* (Hispanic), and *minjung* (Asian) concerns, while maintaining a classic Trinitarian understanding of God.

Tanner earned her BA, MA, MPhil, and PhD degrees from Yale University, where she first began her teaching career in its department of religious studies. Thereafter she moved to the University of Chicago where she was professor of theology for the next 16 years. While there, she delivered the 2007 Warfield Lectures at Princeton Theological Seminary on the subject of atonement, which were published three years later as *Christ the Key*. That same year she returned to Yale as professor of

---

11. Sobrino, *Jesus the Liberator*, 606.
12. D. Williams, "Black Women's Surrogacy Experience," 31.

systematic theology, where she continues to do "constructive theology"[13] as the focus of her research, writing, and teaching. A confessing and practicing Christian[14] (Episcopalian), Tanner relates the history of Christian thought to contemporary issues of theological concern using social, cultural, and feminist theory, and is one of this century's more important theologians.

Atonement—The Center of All Christian Theology—Its Inner Heart

Rather than write off atonement as a cruel doctrine, or avoid it, as many liberationist theologians have done, Tanner makes atonement central to all Christian theology, in large part following Karl Barth's Christology. She quotes T. F. Torrance, saying, "Union with God in and through Jesus Christ who is one and the same being with God belongs to the inner heart of the atonement."[15] Influenced by early church theologians Irenaeus (130–202), Athanasius (296–373), and the Cappadocian theologians Gregory Nazianzun (329–390), and Gregory of Nyssa (335–394), Tanner argues that atonement begins at the incarnation, but is central to Jesus' entire life, ministry, passion, death, and resurrection. It comes from God's gracious desire to be in an intimate relationship with humanity.

God as Creator and Gift-Giver

God is the Creator, doing so through God's Word and Spirit. Both of the latter have remained in the world, nurturing, and sustaining it since creation, while the first person of the Godhead is transcendent over creation and all its creatures. Yet, God is not only Creator but also the Giver of all good gifts. Those divine gifts do not limit human freedom but are intended to complement, enhance, and enable humankind to grow into

---

13. A reconceptualization of what formerly was called systematic theology, constructive theology no longer attempts to build a theological "system" around one coherent philosophical theory. A term that emerged in the 1980s, especially among feminist theologians, it recognizes that all theological works are "constructions. " Constructive theology resists such systemization and insists on multiplicity and openness to the new, and is dynamic, often attempting bridge-building between theology and other disciplines.

14. Not all theologians are these days.

15. Torrance, *Trinitarian Faith*, 159; Tanner, *Christ the Key*, 252.

being who God has created them to be. Among other things, this means that human nature is not fundamentally flawed by a fall. God has created humanity in God's image in order to have a relationship with humankind. This image is what distinguishes humans from all the other of God's creatures.[16]

God's Image—Weak and Strong

Initially, the image of God in humanity is "weak." It awaits strengthening through the appropriate use and participation in God's other good gifts. Humans are highly "plastic," malleable, and open to everything in their environment. Consequently, they are neutral—neither predisposed to nor opposed to God. The image in them is so weak that they do not even have a desire for God.

Humans have been created in this way so that they can "participate" in God, receive God's good gifts, and have the image in them strengthened by divine nourishment. As they do so, they will reach the fullness God intends and desires for them and in that fullness enjoy communion with Godself through full participation in the divine life God wills for them.

Falling into Sin

In humanity's initial weakened state, they fail to pay attention to God's gifts, stray, and fall victim to sin in the world seeking nourishment that is not good for them.[17] Under those influences, they see God's good gifts as nothing more than the result of their own work and fall into the sin of pride. Inattentive to God's gifts of Word and Spirit, these gifts become lost to them.[18]

Thus, humanity enters the downward spiral of a world in which sin separates them from God. This exposes them to all the tragedies and horrors of life polluted by sin and death. Having turned their backs on God's presence in the world, people have lost access to the divine, are unable to avoid or resist the power and influence of sin, and, in fact, choose sin by cooperating with it.

16. Tanner, *Christ the Key*, 1.
17. Tanner, *Christ the Key*, 69.
18. Tanner, *Christ the Key*, 34.

Losing the ability to know and love God, and living under sin's influence, all human action is ruined. Everything humans do, even their pursuit of good is done in the wrong way—done without the one thing necessary for every authentic good in life—God's own goodness through the gifts of Word and Spirit.[19] Under sin's corruption, without the divine nourishment of Word and Spirit, life becomes a kind of death.

Incarnation—Christ the Key and Paradigm

In humanity's dire state, if God's desire for relationship with them and the fullness of God's good gifts are to be realized in them, God must attach humanity to Godself. This, the transcendent God, out of God's grace, does by sending the eternal Word, via the Spirit, to be incarnate in the man Jesus.

More correctly still, the second person of the Triune God *assumes humanity* in Jesus bringing God's desire for a relationship of fellowship into being.[20] God does this in all of humanity's frailty, weakness, sinfulness, suffering, and finitude. It must be thus if a "participation" is to take place that will ultimately restore, strengthen, and maintain the divine image within humanity. In this unique union of Jesus and the Word of God, God has assumed humanity into Godself in the God-man Jesus, a perfect bond in which the divine and human natures become one.

Hypostatic Union

This union the church has, since the council of Chalcedon (451 CE), named *hypostatic,* a union in which one nature does what the other nature does in undivided fashion. These two natures—divine and human—are fused into one at Jesus' conception in Mary, and remain so, being essential to everything Jesus is and does throughout his life.

Jesus is the image of God within humanity in the strongest sense, the perfect human imaging of God, because of the presence of the second person of the Trinity within him. He is sustained and driven by the Spirit, as the Word and Spirit work within him to lead and drive him to live out his divine mission. Thus, he is not only the paradigm of what the image

---

19. Tanner, *Christ the Key*, 63.
20. Tanner, *Christ the Key*, 13.

of God is to be within all humanity but also God's gift and the means of humanity growing into its fullness.

This perfect imaging of God in humanity is manifest from Jesus' birth on through his maturation, calling, baptism, temptation, ministry of proclamation and healing, welcoming the outcast, eating and drinking with sinners, being condemned by religious leaders, being arrested as a religious and political subversive, and so tried and executed.

Whereas most other atonement theories based on the incarnation seem to isolate the importance of the incarnation to Jesus' birth, in fact, God's incarnation of the Word in Jesus is at work throughout his entire life and saving work.[21] God is making atonement through the Word incarnate in Jesus at each step of Jesus' life, as Jesus and the Word come to know the fullness of what it means to be fully human in a sin-filled world, yet remain fully attentive to God, remaining the perfect image of God in which all humanity have been created. From birth through death, the divine and the human have been one.[22]

Though theologians have often looked at the hypostatic union as a means of explaining the role the divine nature has upon Jesus in his life, Tanner is far more radical and comprehensive in explaining the union's role in Jesus and what she understands it to accomplish. The second person of the Trinity in assuming Jesus' human nature has assumed not only his humanity into itself but *all who share Jesus' humanity*. The Word is now present in all humanity as well as in Jesus.[23] "Via the hypostatic union, we are wrapped around with something we cannot get rid of, something that therefore inevitably makes itself felt in all that we go on to become."[24]

Incarnation as the Mechanism of Atonement

Incarnation is not atonement; otherwise, humanity would have been saved at Jesus' birth.[25] Incarnation is the *mechanism* of atonement, the *explanation* of how atonement takes place in and through Jesus, and his

---

21. Tanner, *Christ the Key*, 259.
22. One is reminded of Irenaeus and his idea of God recapitulating every phase of human life in Jesus' life.
23. Tanner, *Christ the Key*, 36.
24. Tanner, *Christ the Key*, 72.
25. Tanner, *Christ the Key*, 261.

entire life and death. Incarnation is "the mechanism"[26] God uses to effect atonement in and among a sinful humanity. It is the entire process of Jesus' birth, life, death, and resurrection—not just one immediate saving moment on the cross—that effects atonement.[27]

Christ is key because he is the center for connecting humanity with God, and God with humanity. Before Christ came, humanity's participation in sin meant the divine image was foreign to them. Now that the Word has taken humanity to be its own in Christ, humanity can be knit into the Word incarnate in Christ as never before. In Jesus, God takes into Godself the full scope of what it means to be human, doing so to defeat sin's power and enable humanity to come into communion with God in and through Jesus. As humans enter into that communion with and through Jesus, drawing near to the perfect image of God revealed in Jesus Christ and clinging to what they are not, they find the image of God within them maturing and growing stronger.

As humans participate in Jesus Christ, God conquers sin and death within them by taking their sin and death into Godself. God does so to heal them.[28] Yet, unlike Christ's human nature, humanity's weaknesses and faults still exist. These will have to be purged in the process of people participating in Christ throughout their life so that they may someday rise to the full holiness of Christ's own life through their attachment to him.

It is through such "participation" in Christ that humanity's image of God within them is changed from weak to strong, and people, in that process, find themselves being not just healed, but transformed.[29]

Once our human inclinations and dispositions are turned to Christ, they have no power to alter the unity we have with Christ. This unity did not come about by our own choice or inclination; therefore, it cannot be affected by any fall back into sin. The Word's making itself one with us in Christ is God's gift and remains with us regardless of how much we might fall back into sin.[30] While humans waver in their attachment to Christ, Christ nonetheless remains in them and is their unshakeable hope. So

---

26. A recurring phrase Tanner uses to express how atonement is brought about.
27. Tanner, *Christ the Key*, 261–62.
28. Tanner, *Christ the Key*, 298.
29. Tanner, *Christ the Key*, 16.
30. Tanner, *Christ the Key*, 72.

knit to him, people no longer need fear the loss of the divine image in them.[31]

As humans continue their participation in Jesus Christ, bearing the hardships and challenges of belonging to him, they are healed of their pasts. They are changed and matured into their identities and destinies as strong images of God as that image is revealed in the man Jesus and in the resurrected and glorified Christ. Thereby they become that life themselves.[32]

The Cross

On the cross, Christ is standing in humanity's stead, bringing about their salvation. The cross is a precondition for this salvation, the means of the Word assuming all of humanity's experience in the sinful world—its betrayal, abjection, suffering and death—doing so to heal and save it.[33] This is the meaning of his dying "for us"—it is for our benefit, for our healing.

The cross is not a *forensic* death, one of legal substitution to pay for humanity's sin so humanity does not have to pay for its sin themselves.[34] The cross is God's act of solidarity, through Word and Spirit, with humanity caught in sin and its suffering. The cross is God's ultimate protest against sin and death, God's no to it, and God's action to do something about it.

Resurrection

Christ's resurrection is God's resolute answer to humanity about death. As Christ's coming and life have been atoning, his death and resurrection are instructive—the power demonstrated in Jesus' resurrection tells us of our future and provides us hope for our own final consummation. Atonement unites the being of humanity with the being of God in Christ, and Christ in God. In that union, what is alien to both God and humanity are exchanged, the one taken on by the other.

The exchange is not one of *moral* standing before God, as though those who have been separated from God by sin are now placed in a

---

31. Tanner, *Christ the Key*, 36.
32. Tanner, *Christ the Key*, 16–17.
33. Tanner, *Christ the Key*, 257.
34. Tanner, *Christ the Key*, 257.

justified relationship. What justified humanity before God happened long before the cross—the self-emptying of the eternal Son to assume humanity in Jesus. Rather, the exchange atonement accomplishes has to do with humanity's very being itself.

As the Spirit sent the eternal Word to be incarnate in human flesh and be one with it, so the Spirit now comes to humanity through the resurrected and glorified humanity of the risen Christ to attach us to him—one with him—in faith hope and love.[35] Jesus Christ, the resurrected and glorified One, continues to give himself to us through the Spirit so that we can continue to be conformed to him. In doing so, the character and identity of our life is remodeled—it is changed—transformed for the better.[36] As a result, human beings become more fully themselves. Thoroughly reworked and driven by God's power, humans are more fully human. They can now know the truth and choose the good as God meant them to do in first making them—lead lives that participate in Christ.[37]

Participation in Christ

Attached to Christ by the Spirit, we gain the power of the Spirit to imitate Christ and have our lives renovated because of what Christ is—God's righteousness—rather than what we are or are doing. It is about what God is doing, which means that the sacraments are critical to participation in Christ.

Baptism is the work of God's Spirit; it establishes our link with Christ and causes it to take place within us. The Spirit does not simply join us to Christ in baptism, it enters within us as the power for new life. It is the power to shape us into Christ's life and make us over into him.

Eucharist is where the gifts of the Son and the Spirit are most strongly available to us for our nurture. It is food to sustain, energize, and enable us to live new lives in Christ. We bring bread and wine consecrated in the name of the risen Christ, and the Spirit lifts those gifts to the risen Christ.

> Christ is the celebrant (Heb 3:31) who takes our gifts to the altar in heaven for the Father's blessing and approval; they come back to us as Christ's own body and blood, filled with every grace and

---

35. Tanner, *Christ the Key*, 14.
36. Tanner, *Christ the Key*, 16.
37. Tanner, *Christ the Key*, 297.

blessing of the Spirit, and by blending that flesh with our own we become like Christ—Spirit filled [children of God].[38]

It is through repeated engagements in the Eucharist, receiving the life-giving power the consecrated bread and wine bring to us by way of the Spirit, that our lives are nourished, strengthened, enhanced, sustained, and transformed into Christ's life as we become more and more like him. What we receive in the Eucharist is not simply the *risen* Christ. We receive *all of his life* from birth, ministry, passion, death, resurrection, to his ascension as God's life-giving sacrifice for us and for our nourishment.[39]

The Continuing Work of the Spirit

The Spirit does its work, shining through what we humans do. It does not come on the scene when or until human processes fail, as though the Spirit and its work are a "miraculous" intervention in human affairs. The Spirit works in and through very natural and human processes to do its work. Divine powers appear in and through the regular human happenings of life.[40]

Jesus' divine glory appeared, not alongside his humanity but shown in and through it, but with its very own distinctive character. His divinity was the form or organization of the whole. So too, in his resurrected flesh, his humanity is not removed or obliterated. His humanity is now glorified complete with his wounds—the eternal life of his full, finished humanity.

Out of sin and death, its conflicts, sufferings, and losses in our lives that all but render the Spirit invisible, there comes what one would never expect nor predict: "a new human manner of existence, human lives re-formed, reworked as a whole by the Spirit into a life-giving, Spirit-filled form."[41]

---

38. Tanner, *Christ the Key*, 201.
39. Tanner, *Christ the Key*, 272.
40. Tanner, *Christ the Key*, 300.
41. Tanner, *Christ the Key*, 301.

Critique and Displacement of Other Atonement Theories

Taking the incarnation seriously throughout Jesus' life, death, and resurrection not only sets aside and replaces all vicarious satisfaction and penal substitution theories, but it also addresses the problems of the latter from both the feminist and non-feminist points of view. Consistent with liberationists' concerns, atonement can no longer be limited to the cross. Atonement is being at-one with the divine in Jesus, which is as true everywhere else in Jesus' life as it is on the cross. That is what is saving about his life.[42]

This divine atonement with humanity through incarnation in Jesus also undercuts any legal or contractual understandings of how the cross saves. More, it refutes the notions that salvation is a reward for Jesus' obedience. The cross is not a self-sacrificial death on the part of Jesus offered to God to release sinners from a debtor's prison.[43]

The Distortion of Sacrifice

Until now, Tanner has been addressing feminist and womanist worries about atonement theologies and, with them, stressing the essential nature of Jesus' life and ministry as central to his work of atonement. Now that she has reviewed those concerns, she turns to what has been, since the medieval church, a huge distortion in atonement theology—the image of sacrifice.

Tanner shares the feminist and womanist concerns about how the image of sacrifice has been used since the medieval church to laud self-sacrifice, especially among those who have so little to give up. She also understands how the entire concept of sacrifice has been so badly distorted, misunderstood, and disconnected from its biblical meaning, first in the Hebrew Scriptures and then in the New Testament, and as a consequence, has distorted what God is doing in making atonement in and through Jesus. We do not need to revisit that, as much of what she says we have already examined in chapters 5 and 6, in "Sacrifice in Israel's Life with God" and "New Testament Application of Sacrifice to Jesus."

In short, Tanner finds in the ritual sacrifices of Israel no evidence that they are a contractual payment to make satisfaction with God. The

---

42. Tanner, *Christ the Key*, 256.

43. Tanner, *Christ the Key*, 256. For Tanner's full feminist critique of other atonement theories, see ch. 6, "Death and Sacrifice," in *Christ the Key*, 247–73.

notion of the cross as a propitiatory sacrifice misses the biblical cultic understanding and operation of sacrifice in many ways.

A Helpful Way to View Sacrifice

There is one way the concept of sacrifice may be helpful: if one understands sacrifice as an act of redemption that follows from God's decision to be incarnate in Jesus. God's decision to make humanity God's own in Christ causes God's sacrificial action on the cross to take center stage. There, it becomes what God does for humankind, not what humans or even "the perfect human" does for God.

On the cross God is sacrificing Godself on humanity's behalf, doing so to destroy sin and death, and effect humanity's salvation. The One who dies on the cross is not just a man but is God as well. "God is both the One sacrificing and the One sacrificed. The whole act is God's."[44] The sacrifice is not directed here to God but from God to human beings. Humans are not offering anything to God; God is giving to us.[45]

One more thing: though the humanity of Jesus is suffering under the weight of sin and death, more is going on there. Death is being sanctified—made holy—transformed from death to life. But it is not death that is doing the sanctifying. It is the living-giving power and properties of the Word "sanctifying Jesus' humanity, healing his wounds, raising him from the dead, and bringing him back to community with his disciples."[46]

But death here is not bringing about the transfer of the sacrificed One to God, the transfer of this particular human being named Jesus into God's possession in the realm of the divine. Rather,

> Death itself (along with sin, rejection, and conflict) . . . is being transferred to God by way of the already given fact of God's assumption of mortal flesh. Dying suffering humanity is God's own because this humanity is that of the Word incarnate. Here God purchases us, in the sense of acquiring us as [God's] own people, through the life-giving blood of Christ in the way God always acquires a people—through a covenantal communion with them (1 Pet 2:9; Titus 2:14; Acts 20:28).[47]

---

44. Tanner, *Christ the Key*, 268.
45. Tanner, *Christ the Key*, 268.
46. Tanner, *Christ the Key*, 269.
47. Tanner, *Christ the Key*, 270.

The function of sacrifice in Israel's life was to allow Israel to cleave to God within God's covenant. This sacrifice of incarnation is the same—it gives us covenantal communion with God. But in the incarnation God cleaves to us long before the expiatory sacrifice of the cross. This is what overturns sacrifice and makes Jesus the sacrifice that ends all sacrifice (Heb 10).[48]

Being Living Sacrifices

Tanner concludes by reminding us that humans are not to offer sacrifices to God. It is God who has and continues to make gifts to us for use on our behalf—gifts which we receive in praise and thanksgiving. We are to put those received gifts to use for the good of ourselves and others: for the satisfaction of human needs, for the reversal of the effects of sin on human life, for service to the neighbor. As we do, we ourselves become living sacrifices (Rom 12:1), the only sacrifice proper for humanity to offer God. No other sacrifice is necessary, for God needs nothing.[49]

---

48. Tanner, *Christ the Key*, 271.
49. Tanner, *Christ the Key*, 272.

Chapter 11

What God Has Done in Jesus Christ

CHRISTIAN ATONEMENT THEORIES HAVE, as Rauschenbusch observed, been captive to the movements of their day, finding expression through various philosophies, sociologies, psychologies, and even literary theory. Increasingly, this has led the subject of atonement away from the biblical narrative. In this chapter we will return to the Scriptures to follow their descriptive thread, attempting to make sense not only of what was happening in Jesus' crucifixion but how that is related to the much larger story of God's promise to Abraham.

Starting Over with Abraham and Sarah

God's promise to Abraham, often put at risk by him and forced by Sarah, moved through the patriarch's family with varying degrees of threat, ending with Jacob/Israel's progeny, generations later, in slavery in Egypt. God raised up Moses and acted at Passover to redeem the people from slavery and lead them from their captivity through the Red Sea waters to Mt. Sinai. There God renewed the covenant with Abraham, incorporating Israel within it.

The Faithlessness of the Covenant People

Yet, repeatedly, the people resist, follow other gods, or try to serve both the Lord and the gods of their neighbors. Throughout the long history of their faithlessness, God judges them and then renews the promise. The story involves the former prophets, such as Samuel, kings—primarily David—and the latter prophets, especially Jeremiah, Isaiah, Ezekiel, and Daniel.

At Solomon's death, because of the burden of his expansive building program, as well as the religious syncretism[1] that entered the nation through his foreign wives, the kingdom was torn in two—Israel in the north and Judah in the south. Israel seemed especially prone to worshiping foreign gods. Following Solomon's example, its kings took foreign wives—Jezebel being the chief example among them—and soon the kings were building temples to their wives' gods. It would not be long before the people were worshiping those gods along with the Lord. God's judgment on the Northern Kingdom of Israel came through King Sennacherib of Assyria who conquered Israel in 722/1 BCE and relocated its people across his lands. Thus, the people and nation were absorbed into Assyria. Israel vanished thereafter.

Exile

Things in the south were little better. One hundred twenty-four years later, in 597 BCE, Nebuchadnezzar conquered the Southern Kingdom of Judah. A major portion of the nation's leadership was forcibly deported to Babylon, while Judah's king remained in Jerusalem, but now as Nebuchadnezzar's subject. In this period of increasing subjugation to Babylon, Jeremiah announces a time of God's judgment on the nation for its faithlessness, followed by a time of redemptive renewal through a remnant. After the judgment, God will establish a new covenant with the people, writing God's law on their hearts (the center of volition), and transform their hearts of stone to those of flesh. They will each know the Lord, who will forgive their iniquity and remember their sins no more (Jer 31:31). Judean leadership ignores Jeremiah, then imprisons him, and continues its attempts at rebellion. After several failed Judean efforts at revolt, in 587 BCE Nebuchadnezzar destroys Jerusalem, burns Solomon's Temple to the ground, and takes Judah's king in bondage to Babylon where he and his royal line will be executed.

Thereafter the leadership of the nation will remain in exile for forty years, with only an unnamed group of Judeans left behind on the land.

---

1. The amalgamation of different religions, cultures, or schools of thought into one's culture and worship.

Whereas the Assyrian king spread the exiles across Assyria, causing their absorption into its people and culture, Nebuchadnezzar settled the Jews in one place, allowing them to develop a community with its own religious practices and national identity. They spoke of themselves as "children of the exile" and lived in doubt and despair. Had the Lord forgotten or simply abandoned them?

As their exile continued, the conviction among them emerged that it was their own rebellion, abandonment of Torah, and religious impurity that had brought this on them. God had judged them, but Second Isaiah announces, "Comfort!" Their time of punishment is over (Isa 40:1). God is about to redeem them once again.[2] The exiles will return, the people will be restored, and a new temple will be built, as God returns with the people to dwell again among them in Jerusalem. Therein, Second Isaiah includes four poems about an Israelite whom God will raise up, one who will become God's special servant to bring about the people's redemption (Isa 42:1–4; 49:1–6; 50:4–7; 52:13—53:12).

Ezekiel, a priest as well as a prophet who was among those taken to Babylon, continued his prophetic work there, speaking of God's liberation of the *whole house of Israel.* The Northern Kingdom, which had disappeared into Assyria as it was conquered, and the nation of Judah wounded by the exile would again be made one. God would reestablish both nations, who seemed like those who had died and were without hope, their dead, dry bones, now scattered over the whole land of promise. God's spirit would revive the people, stand them on their feet, and unite the former two nations again into one people, land, and nation. They would again have a single king—one shepherd, great David's greater son—and would never again be divided or defiled by the apostasies, idols, and other transgressions that had led to their exile (Ezek 37:1–28).

---

2. Scholars today identify at least two, and possibly three, different writers in the book of Isaiah: Isaiah of Jerusalem, the eighth-century prophet in Jerusalem for whom the book is named; Second Isaiah, whose words interpret the meaning of the exile some forty-five years after it began and announce God's coming liberation and the peoples' return; and, possibly, Third Isaiah, writing as the people return, to find the circumstances less glorious than they had envisioned.

Judah's Return from Exile: A New Political Crisis Creates New Expectations

Cyrus the Great, the Persian king, invaded and conquered Babylonia in 539 BCE, doing so for his own religious reasons.[3] A deeply devout man, Cyrus believed the Jew's god was one of the gods on the side of the forces of good. Cyrus believed the Lord had appeared to him in a vision, commanding that he rebuild the temple in Jerusalem. Consequently, Cyrus ordered that it be done and that the Jews be allowed to return to Jerusalem. Thus, the children of Israel were released and began to return to Jerusalem in 538 BCE.[4]

As the exiles returned and the building of the temple began, prophets began announcing the coming of one who would be a prophet like Moses, a priest like Aaron, and a king like David, who, as God's anointed one, would be God's servant as Isaiah had promised. This one would bear the promise and be commissioned and empowered to be the blessing long promised through Abraham. This one would be the faithful son of Abraham, the faithful Israelite, the one who would be a blessing to all the nations, just as God had promised Abraham long ago.

The spirit of the Lord God[5] would rest upon him, anointing him to bring good news to the oppressed; bind up the brokenhearted; proclaim liberty to captives and release to the prisoners; proclaim the Lord's favor, the day of vengeance of God; and comfort all who mourn (Isa 61:1–2). God will work through those who have taken Judah captive. Indeed, God has raised up Cyrus, not a Jew but still named God's anointed shepherd, and done so to carry out God's promise and purposes (Isa 45:1–13). God had never been limited to working solely through Israel, any more than God is limited to working solely through the church. God is the Sovereign of all and at toil in and though all working out God's providence.

Jerusalem was rebuilt, the foundations of its temple laid once again (Isa 44:28). But Cyrus' purposes were religious only. The Jews would remain only a religious state, itself a political vassal, first to Persia, then

---

3. A follower of the Persian prophet Zarathustra, Cyrus brought Zoroastrianism and its dualistic concept of the world to the ancient Near East. He believed the conflict between good and evil was about to come to a cataclysmic and cosmic end, deciding finally who ruled the cosmos.

4. Not all Jews in Babylon returned. A portion remained behind to be absorbed into Babylonian religions.

5. In Hebrew this is *adonoi YHWH*, and therefore the sacred name, usually rendered Lord, is here rendered God.

later to the Greek rulers—first Alexander, then at his death Ptolemy, then Seleucid Mesopotamia—and finally, after a brief rule by the Hasmonean dynasty, a client state of Rome.

The Jews would never again have their own king, and the power of leadership was usurped into the priesthood. The priesthood would consolidate its power within a religious state under Roman rule but then would find itself forming leagues with those who governed as a means of self-preservation. It would set loose the corruption within the priesthood that such leagues with power inevitably bring. Rome brought with it the Pax Romana, a peace that they would brutally enforce against any who would disrupt it. Through it all, Israel continues to look for its promised anointed one, the messiah, who as the prophet Moses long before promised, would be their liberator.

The return to Jerusalem and their homeland is less glorious than the returning exiles envisioned. It is filled with hardships, disappointment, and obstacles, as the optimism of Second Isaiah turns once again to despair. Aware that behind the exile lay the nation's apostasy and the abandonment of Torah, the priesthood leads the people into a new period of religious legalism. The Zoroastrian dualism learned in Babylon will take root and turn Satan from God's chief prosecuting attorney into God's adversary—the devil, the lord of evil. And the Persian notion of an impending final clash between these powers of good and of evil would be incorporated into the Jewish expectation of the day of the Lord. It would become a day of both judgment and redemption, and thereafter the expectation of a new aeon of God's reign of justice and peace.

When the Persian Empire gave way to Alexander the Great, Israel became subject to the political forces that followed—first Greek and then Roman. It is during the cataclysmic days of Greek Seleucid subjugation, under Antiochus Epiphanies in the second century, that a new prophetic voice, Daniel, emerges, utilizing a new form of theological language appropriate to the new dualism—apocalyptic—expecting an imminent end that will also be a new beginning.

Written sometime between 167 and 164 BCE, the book of Daniel, with an anonymous narrator, is set in the sixth century BCE, during the Babylonian captivity, and falls in two distinct sections (chs. 1–6 and 7–12). The first portion portrays an exiled Jew and his friends who face great hardship because of their loyalty to the Lord as faithful Jews. In each crisis, the Lord saves Daniel and his friends. Through it, Daniel rises to a position of power because of his God-given wisdom and ability to interpret dreams. As God saved Daniel and his friends through his observance of Torah stipulations, so too God will save Israel.

The second half of the book comes after this series of folklike tales and turns prophetic. It consists of dreams, with angelic visions that describe the sufferings of the nation under Antiochus and the subsequent Maccabean revolt. In this second section, Daniel is an apocalyptic prophet, one of Israel's wise sages who has responsibility to teach the people righteousness. Now the book is structured as a divine revelation of the end of time—the day of the Lord—when God will intervene in history to judge and usher in the final kingdom. The dead will rise, some to everlasting life to share in this earthly kingdom of God's eternal justice, righteousness, and peace. Others will rise to everlasting judgment and shame. This is the first overt statement in the Hebrew Scriptures of the concepts of resurrection and immortality.

It is with this as backdrop that Second Temple Judaism found itself now under Roman occupation. The expectation for a coming messiah, who would politically liberate the nation and usher in an everlasting golden era for Israel, became more urgent. It is into this political-religious milieu that Jesus is born.

The Promise Is Borne

God takes on flesh and enters this world in what the apostle Paul calls "the fullness of time," not as God but as a man named Jesus (Gal 4:4; Eph 1:10).[6] God comes as a child of humanity—"Son of man" is the term Jesus most preferred when speaking of himself. He is born of a poor young woman, a Jew, a son of the promise God made to Abraham, a faithful son of Abraham, and a righteous son of Adam.[7] God comes as a liberator like Moses, the new prophet Moses, ushering in the end of the age and leading a new exodus (Matt 21:11; Luke 1:76; John 6:14; 7:40). God comes as the suffering servant foretold by Isaiah. God comes as the King who

---

6. The name Jesus is important, as it is a variant of Joshua, which means "God saves." See Matt 1:21 and Luke 1:31. The word "Christ" is less a name than a title—the Greek for messiah. By the mid-first century CE, when Paul is writing, the names have been conflated, with the verb "to be" being silent. To say "Jesus Christ" is to say, "Jesus is the Christ" or "Jesus is the Messiah." Conversely, "Christ Jesus" means "Messiah Jesus."

7. Note the two different genealogies, one in Matt 1:1–16, emphasizing the "son of Abraham," the other in Luke 3:23b–38, emphasizing the "son of Adam."

is great David's greater Son, whose reign is unfolding and will be everlasting. God comes as the anointed One, a second Adam, undoing what the first Adam had gotten wrong. God comes in One through whom all the people of the earth will be blessed. God comes as the paschal Lamb who takes away the sin of the world that has kept it in bondage, setting all people free. God comes as the eternal High Priest after the order of Melchizedek. God comes as Lord of life. All of these are biblical images and prophetic promises that have set the context for "the fullness of time" that lies behind Paul's announcement.

If the witness of the New Testament is to be taken seriously, "fullness of time" means even more. It began from before the foundation of the world, when the Triune God, knowing what would come from creating humanity with the gift of freedom, decided within Godself to become one with humankind, to be at-one with humanity, to reverse what would go wrong through humanity's abuse of its gift (Eph 1:4; Matt 13:35; 25:34; John 17:24; 1 Pet 1:20; Rev 13:8; 17:8).

By the time Jesus appears, the people's expectations for their messiah-king have been so shaped by the political ways and aspirations of the nations around them that they not only miss his coming but ultimately reject him and engineer his death at the hands of their oppressor, Rome. Yet, the Christian gospel proclaims none of this as an accident or tragedy of justice. Rather, this was God at work, the eternal Word of God becoming incarnate in Jesus of Nazareth by God's Spirit, to do what needed to be done to be true to God's promise of "Never again!," first spoken after the flood (Gen 8:21; 9:11; 9:15).

Commentators on Genesis 8 and 9 often argue that God's "never again" in those texts meant that God expected more of the same or that God had simply decided to put up with this state of evil.[8] But something more costly lay behind that vow—most especially to God. For the Triune God had decided within Godself, from "before the beginning," to do more than simply put up with the evil in the human heart. God had decided to do something about evil itself and its work of sin and death.

God decided to take evil, sin, and death into Godself and defeat it and its power to defy God and God's love for the world. God decided, as Ezekiel had long before announced in exile, to replace the heart of the first Adam with that of the second, thereby giving God's people a new

---

8. Westermann, *Genesis 1–11*, 456; Von Rad, *Genesis*, 133–34.

heart and new spirit, removing the heart of stone, and replacing it with a heart of flesh (Ezek 36:26). And now we watch that begin to unfold.

God's "Never Again!" Unfolds

God comes into God's creation through God's eternal Son, the Logos through whom all creation came into being—God's eternal Word, now, by the Spirit, incarnate in Jesus. The One through whom all things were made becomes one of what was made. The eternal Son/Word/Logos is not simply present in Jesus as a thought, idea, aspiration, or even promise. The eternal Son of the Triune God is so fully a part of him to make him both man and God—the incarnate God-man. They are one; there is no separation between them. What Jesus does, the Logos does, and vice versa. The Logos has not displaced Jesus' humanity; the Logos has become human in him.

Yet, Jesus is not some "superhuman," with gifts and trait unlike the rest of the humanity. In assuming human flesh, the Logos, divine, eternal Word, has given up all its prerogatives and powers. It has emptied itself of them (Phil 2:5–7). Jesus is not operating with "divine superpower" through any portion of his life. He is no different than any other human. It must be so if he is to be one of us, who has become one with us, so that in him, we can become one with the God who sent him. He must take on all that humans experience: suffering, confusion, doubt, betrayal, even death. Once we are joined to him, he brings us "just as we are" into the presence of God for our redemption, healing, and transformation. What makes Jesus different is that he is the one human able to maintain his perfect focus on and devotion to the One he calls Father. He will allow nothing to separate him from God. Something it will take the rest of humanity their lifetimes to do.

Jesus is God's Beloved, the One John the Baptist named the Lamb of God who takes away the sin of the world. That means not just our sins but *the sin of the world!*—that in life which seeks to separate us from God and obscure the fact that God is present among us and has always been so (John 1:29, 36). This Jesus, God's living Word, emerges in the world where sin has had dominion and legitimate claim on all of humanity since the beginning. But that sin has no claim upon Jesus. He alone has not indulged in the idolatries and rebellions against God that have separated God's people from God and from each other from the beginning.

He alone is sinless; despite its repeated attempts, sin has never made him its captive.

At his baptism, Jesus hears his identity announced and confirmed. As he emerges from the baptismal water, the Spirit of God who brought about his conception in Mary, who has been at work in him as he has matured and grown in strength and spirit, now descends upon him in a moment of revealing declaration heretofore unknown to him. A voice from heaven announces, "You are my son, the beloved; with you I am well pleased" (Mark 1:11; Luke 3:22).

One might expect miraculous fanfare. Such an announcement would seem to be an appropriate prelude to a divinely driven and occupied life—a royal life par excellence. But no, the Spirit who has descended upon him must lead him in the next step of his mission. Immediately, the Spirit drives Jesus into the wilderness to sort out what has happened, what he has heard, to encounter the tempter, and to internalize what it means to be on a mission in this world as God's Child sent to redeem the creation he had made.

Will Jesus remain steadfast where Adam failed? Or will he seek to save his own life in the face of this temptations? He does remain steadfast and faithful, each time refusing in any way to displace God, place his trust elsewhere, or seek his own advantage, security, or peace. He will allow nothing to come between him and God. It is what the church means when it confesses him to be "sinless." It is not that his mother never found him with his hand in the cookie jar without permission; sin is far more profound than such moralisms. Jesus is like us in all things, in all the moments of glory, tragedy, anxiety, and fear. "In every respect [he] has been tested as we are, yet without sin" (Heb 4:10). Never does he abandon his trust in the One he calls Father. The tester's temptations have failed, with a simple "Away with you, Satan!" (Matt 4:10).

Jesus emerges from the wilderness victorious and, with those initial tests behind him, takes up his public ministry announcing, "The time is fulfilled, and the kingdom of God has come near; repent, and believe in the good news" (Mark 1:9; Matt 4:17). It is his challenge for people to turn from a life of self-sovereignty and embrace God's gracious sovereignty in their lives.

His message is addressed to everyone in the land, from the temple priests to the actively religious Sadducees and Pharisees, from the tax collectors in league with Rome to the common Israelite, from the respected synagogue leader to the social outcast. All are called on to repent, as John the Baptist had earlier called on the people to do. But there is a difference here that we must note.

Jesus especially identifies with those that the religious system of the second and first-century Judaism of the Second Temple had made outcasts: the poor, those living under the burden of illness, under the limitations of sight, speech, or hearing, or the shame of madness. All of those encumbered with the forms of blight that the culture understood to be God's payment for their sin are embraced and welcomed. Jesus not only welcomes and ministers to all of these, announcing their sins forgiven, but seems to give priority to them in his ministry.

Jesus seems to prefer sinner to saints—prostitutes to priests. He eats meals with them, forgives their sin, breaks its power and dominion in their lives, and releases them from its blight. He demonstrates his sovereignty over the powers of evil, silencing demons who recognize him, then casting them out. He heals the sick, curing the deaf, lame, blind, speechless, and the dying. He even raises the dead, not just once but multiple times.[9] His ministry is both a call to new life and the gift of it.

Initially, Jesus is welcomed gladly by all but the religious authorities. There is reason enough for them to vilify him. They are the ones who have the most to lose if life is lived his way. And of the others? Who would not want to be near a healer, a charismatic preacher, a marvelous teacher? But as it becomes clear that he has come to do more than build a supportive group of followers who are to be privileged for being on "the inside," those following him increasingly turn away from him.

His teachings seem unreasonable, too demanding, or simply impossible. Humanity, confronted with a God of loving acceptance face to face and with the opportunity to welcome God as Lord of life, in their hearts' bondage to sin, refuse to know, acknowledge, or accept God's visitation (Luke 19:44). Rather, they do what sin always does—they seek to destroy anyone who brings life into this world.

As Passover approaches, Jesus leads his band of followers to Jerusalem. He has told them repeatedly that he must go there to die at the hands of their religious leaders. Yet each time, his followers, lost in themselves and their own concerns, are confused and fail to understand what he means. When he speaks of dying and rising again, they are completely baffled (Matt 27:63; Mark 8:31; 9:31; 10:34; Luke 18:33; 24:7). Was it their hardness of heart or the wiles of the tempter that kept them confused and

---

9. Jairus' daughter (Mark 5:22–43), a widow's son in the town of Nain (Luke 7:11–15), and his friend Lazarus (John 11:1–44).

unable to comprehend who he was and what he meant? Or had they not yet understood him, and themselves were still catering to their own self-sovereignty, hoping their status would be increased by being associated with him (Mark 10:35–41; Matt 20:20–21)?

Jesus enters Jerusalem in triumph, cloaked in the symbolism of their coming king. He goes immediately to the temple. There he confronts the corruption that the evil of the human heart always brings to religion. He drives out the money changers, enrages the religious officials, delights the crowds, and continues to preach his call for repentance and the gospel of God's love, forgiveness, and acceptance.

As that week unfolds, it becomes clear to the religious officials that they must do away with Jesus. If not, the movement he is drawing to himself will cause the Romans to come to do away not only with him but with them and their religious privilege as well. The high priest announces that is it better to have him die for the people rather than risk an uprising that would bring Rome's means of keeping the peace down on them in crushing ways (John 18:14). Combining religion and politics in its always unholy alliance, they develop a strategy that will send Jesus to the cross at the hands of Rome.

A New Passover Begins

That Thursday, as Passover approaches, Jesus gathers his followers for the Seder commemorating Israel's redemption from Egypt and ransom from slavery. Evening comes, and the meal begins. At the end of it, Jesus takes bread and wine, speaks of them as his body and blood, and institutes a new covenant for the forgiveness of sins. It is a covenant sealed in his blood, just as the covenant with Moses and Israel had been sealed in the sacrificial blood at Sinai. They are to eat the bread designated as his body, and drink the cup of wine named his blood, as a means of entering, remembering, and becoming one with him, embracing this new covenant of forgiveness with and in him. They are to do so until he comes again.

From that meal, Jesus takes his closest friends to a familiar garden in nearby Gethsemane for prayer. Soon, one of his followers, having betrayed Jesus to the religious officials, leads their soldiers to Jesus, identifies him with a kiss, and Jesus is arrested. In the chaos that follows, all his band of followers, save one, flee into the night. Only Simon Peter hides in the garden by the fire and, when recognized as Jesus' friend, denies it, not once but three times, just as Jesus had said he would (Matt 26:34; Mark 14:30; Luke 22:61).

In what follows, Jesus does not resist but offers himself to fulfill his mission of redemption, to ransom, set free, and save humanity from our slavery to sin. We know the story and need not say more than that he goes quite willingly and silently to the cross, not as a victim or captive but in accordance with his own understanding of his vocation. Rome thinks it is in control. Little does it know the power behind all this that is being unwittingly served by its lust to stay in control.

Jesus is the Servant of God—God in the flesh—offering up his life to contain, consume, overcome, expiate, purge, and defeat evil, sin, and death. Born to die, Jesus is *so* fully human that he knows what it is to be betrayed, die unjustly, cruelly, abandoned, and alone.

What Is Happening on the Cross?

On the cross, Jesus encounters the full power of evil, sin, and death, taking them on himself. Not only does he suffer evil's physical violence, but he also discovers for the first time in his life another dimension to sin's savagery that he has never before known—its power to separate even him from God. From noon until 3 p.m., he hangs between heaven and earth surrounded by mocking, ridicule, and rejection, and must do so surrounded by something even more devastating—the silence of God.

The Synoptics' Perspective

If we follow Mark's and Matthew's portrayals of the events (Matt 27:46; Mark 15:34), it is clear Jesus knows the full weight of abandonment—what it means to die in desertion. He has been left behind to bear the worst that sin can inflict—death—and to do so in the silence, if not the absence, of God.[10] But even in that silence, Jesus' impulse and response

---

10. The two are not the same, though God's silence here is often interpreted as God's absence. David H. C. Read, of blessed memory, my predecessor in New York City and dear friend, when preaching a Good Friday sermon on Jesus' cry of dereliction, made the point that the Father's silence here does not mean God's absence. Rather, sometimes, when encountering such suffering and horror, there is simply nothing one can say. The Father suffers with the Son in silence, every bit as much as Jesus' mother is suffering, and both are present.

remain faithful. He reaches out to God, praying Ps 22, as he expresses his sense of abandonment. Yet he also knows that before that psalm comes to its conclusion, it turns from despair to confidence in God's power to hear, answer, and save.[11]

If we follow Luke, we find that Jesus, after asking for forgiveness for those taking his life, spends his last three hours veiled in darkness, with Rome's warning sign, "This is the king of the Jews," posted over his head. There he is surrounded by two thieves, one of whom heaps scorn upon him, while the other proclaims Jesus' innocence and asks Jesus to remember him when he comes into his kingdom. At Jesus' final moments of life, rather than cry out as if abandoned, he acknowledges God's presence, calls him Father, and hands over and entrusts his spirit to God (Luke 23:32–46).

In all three of these Gospel presentations, Jesus hangs at his most precarious hour in the darkness of God's silence, undergoing what Christian mystics have called "the dark night of the soul." It is sin, doing all that it can to convince him and us of God's absence. In the lowest depths of human existence, sin does its ultimate to obscure God's presence and takes Jesus' life.

John's Unique Perspective

John has a quite different perspective that we need to keep within our focus as well. According to him, Jesus recognizes the coming of death as the fulfillment of why he has come. Throughout John's telling of Jesus' passion, there is a solemn, almost magisterial dignity to Jesus.

Here, Jesus is not the victim of mob violence or a religious-political conspiracy. That is the way Matthew, Mark, and Luke tell this story. There, Jesus is the victim—despised and forsaken and "esteemed stricken, smitten of God and afflicted"—as the poem in Isaiah speaks of the servant, a text that surely influenced the Synoptics' account of Jesus passion and death (Isa 53:3).

For John, Jesus is God's Son, the Messiah and Servant, and as such, he is also the Logos.[12] As the Logos, and though bereft of his divine pre-

---

11. In Mark and Matthew only the first verse of Ps 22 is quoted. See Psalm 22:21b–31; the psalmist has been heard, answered, and now praises God for vindication in undeserved suffering.

12. The *logos*, in Hellenistic Greek thought, was the divine ordering and unifying principle of the cosmos.

rogatives set aside at incarnation, he remains steadfast and in absolute control of his mission up to the very moment he hands his life back to his Father. This means that John understands that there is divine agency at work in all that Jesus does, and he tells the events to emphasize that. It is as though this had been planned, seen, and ordained within the Godhead as a covenant between and within *them* from before the foundation of the world (John 14:17; Eph 1:4). Jesus hands his life over; it is not taken from him. Just as he had earlier said, he lays it down himself; no one takes it from him (John 10:17–18).

Even the speed with which Jesus dies seems to be a matter of his own control. Here, in John, there is no cry of dereliction or abandonment. And here, there is even more than Luke portrays. After consigning his mother to John's care, Jesus' final words are "It is finished"—mission accomplished! Jesus bows his head and hands over his spirit.[13] That is not just a metaphor to say "he died." He *handed it over*.

To whom did Jesus give it? To whom has his spirit been entrusted? To his Father, of course; but why? So that the Spirit could be given to you and to me. He had said the Spirit could not come so long as he was with us (John 16:7). The Spirit was, after all, the bond between the Son and the Father throughout Jesus' life. The means of his conception, it descended most fully upon Jesus in his baptism and sustained him throughout his life and ministry. Jesus had said he would not leave us desolate but give us another comforter—the Spirit (John 14:8). It will soon become the bond, not only between the Holy Three of the Holy One but also between the Triune God and all faithful humankind, through Jesus by the Spirit.

Jesus' Dying

Whichever version of the events one chooses, the point is this: Jesus does not resist but accepts his vocation, laying down his life, as he told us he would, to take it up again. It is the charge he received from his Father, and he is being faithful to it, but he is doing so of his own accord (John 10:18).

Nor does Jesus respond in kind, returning evil for evil, unleashing his power on the enemy. Nor does he call upon twelve legions of angels (Matt 26:53) to bring it all safely to an end, employing their heavenly

---

13. The word translated "gave up" is *paradidomi* and means "to hand over, to give, to deliver, to entrust."

powers of destruction against evil and sin on his behalf. Who could fault him had he done so?

Certainly, the "ruler of this world" (John 12:31, 14:30, 16:11) would delight in such a destructive conflagration. It is how this world thinks we must respond to evil and teaches us to do, believing in the redemptive power of violence. But think of the carnage his doing so would bring. Yet, as in the wilderness, the Tempter has no power over Jesus. Jesus is doing what he does so the world may know God's ways, and that his obedience to death is an expression of his love for the Father (John 14:31). But more, it is an expression of *their* love for the world.

One other thing: notice that the devil and Satan are absent in Jesus' entire passion. They appear nowhere in the biblical narrative. Why is that? Because this is about more than them. It is about sin and taking it away. This is God's work. The Lamb of God who takes away the sin of the world is doing just that. This is faithful fulfillment of God's righteous intent to reverse what went wrong at the beginning. This is God's "never again!" And this is what it costs God to say that.

God is taking sin and death into Godself to *absorb* it, *purge* it, *purify* it, *extinguish* it, *eradicate* it, take it away—to defeat it. God's holiness consumes it within Godself. It is in that pursuit that Jesus suffers his way into his identity. In doing so, he takes within himself evil's ultimate weapon—death. There he deals with it, disarms it, and does so *without using violence*—one of evil's most effective tools! He absorbs it, silencing it, disarming it, robbing it of its power, and, in his full innocence, dies to complete the ministry for which he was born. His death has fulfilled his promise of life and becomes a source of new life for a new humanity, life empowered by the Spirit of God.

The Blood and Water of His Death

A spear is thrust into Jesus' side to assure he is dead. Water and blood flow from the wounds of his lifeless body. Only John includes this information and does so with meticulous care, insisting on its veracity, because he was an eyewitness—the only eyewitness passion narrative of the four Gospels.[14] Why has John done this?

---

14. In the Synoptic Gospels, everyone except the women abandons Jesus, fearing for their own lives, though Luke does say "all of his acquaintances, including the women who had followed him from Galilee, stood at a distance, watching these things" (Luke 23:49). Only John's Gospel records the presence of a disciple, the "beloved

Elaborate theories have emerged around this incident, supported by various forms of medical evidence.[15] Preachers in the next four centuries of the church will see this as John's reference to the two sacraments of baptism and Eucharist, both of which are instituted by Jesus at his command in the other Gospels but neither of which is directly mentioned in John's Gospel.[16] Augustine will speak of the sacraments of water and blood having flowed from our Lord's side at this time. The custom of mixing water with wine in the Eucharist will come from it.

As interesting as these explanations are, we really must return to Jesus' own words in this Gospel to understand what John is telling us. Jesus had promised living water to quench thirst (John 4:14; 7:37–38) and that his blood would give life, expiate, and forgive sin, wiping it out for those who receive it through the consecrated cup (John 6:38–53).[17] From him both water and blood now flow, forming those rivers of living waters, which, you will remember, was Jesus' way of speaking of the gift of the Holy Spirit and the blood of the new covenant (John 7:38–39). But let us not get ahead of ourselves.

For now, all must wait as the Passover Sabbath unfolds, and all—even God—observe it in grief. Atonement is not yet complete in his death; it is still unfolding. As in life, Jesus was in solidarity with the living. Now in death, he is in solidarity with the dead. Despite what has often been written about this time,[18] and various activities proposed by epistle writers on Jesus' part, Jesus is simply dead and the eternal Son of God with him.[19]

---

disciple"—John—at the foot of the cross with the women. It is there that just prior to his death, Jesus consigns his mother to John's care (John 19:25–27).

15. See Raymond Brown's survey of the various medical suggestions of how both water and blood could flow from a dead body (R. Brown, *Gospel According to John XIII-XXI*, 946–47).

16. John reports that the Pharisees heard that "Jesus is making and baptizing more disciples than John" but quickly corrects that rumor, stating, "It was not Jesus himself but his disciples who baptized" (John 4:1–2). Of course, the sixth chapter of John is filled with sacramental and eucharistic images, but the commission to baptize in Jesus' name and the formal institution of the supper appear only in the Synoptic Gospels.

17. In Matthew, Jesus speaks of the cup as "my blood of the covenant, which is poured out for many for the forgiveness of sins" (Matt 26:28).

18. What the creed calls his descent into hell.

19. Balthasar, *Mysterium Paschale*, 148–81; A. Lewis, *Between Cross and Resurrection*, 239–55; Moltmann, *Crucified God*, 203–78.

The Sabbath of Grief

It is a Sabbath rest of deepest grief, not simply for Jesus' disciples but, most of all, for God. The eternal Father and the Spirit have lost the Son. It is not just the man Jesus of Nazareth who lies dead on that cold stone shelf in the garden tomb. The eternal Son of the Father, the Word of God who became incarnate—one in being with Jesus to deal with sin—is dead as well.

The eternal Word is not hovering secretly in the corner of the tomb to reenter Jesus' lifeless body early Sunday morning. This is not a charade. The eternal Son of God has died with Jesus the Son (Phil 2:8). As Jesus came to experience death for all, so now God is experiencing death as well, suffering death within Godself.

There is no Word of God on this day, and no Word from God on Holy Saturday—all is as silent as death. Evil, sin, and death have done their worst. They have unleashed all their power against the Son, and God has taken all of that into Godself. God has not only experienced what it means to lose a beloved Son, suffering his death. In doing so, God has tasted death Godself. The Triune God has taken in evil, sin, and death within Godself, and rather than return evil for evil, ever after sending it reverberating and ricocheting throughout the rest of the cosmos, has absorbed it, silenced it, consumed it, extinguished it. As Martin Luther later said, this is a death that swallows death.[20]

God has so loved the world that God has died for it (John 3:16). God has done it to deal with evil once and for all. God has done it as God's answer to the theodicy question that philosophers delight in raising—vindicating divine goodness and providence in the face of evil.[21] Taking sin into Godself, God is expiating it, satisfying the just requirement of the law, requiring of Godself what God would not allow Abraham to do with Isaac. The eternal Son is dead, and the Father and Spirit experience that death within the Godhead, spending Holy Saturday in deepest grief.

---

20. Luther's hymn text, "Christ lag in Todesbanden": "Wie ein Tod den andren frass" (How one death the other ate).

21. Theodicy, the word coined by Gottfried Wilhelm Leibniz (1646–1716) in 1710, means literally "justifying God." It is the vindication of God as absolute Good in view of the existence of evil in the world, an answer to the question of why, if God is good, evil exists, why God permits it, the insistence that God is not its author, and why God does not do something about it.

The Power of God in Weakness—Resurrection

On that Saturday of silence, evil, sin, and death seem the victor. But the Sabbath past, God's rest is over. Evil's victory and God's defeat are turned inside out. *Evil* is reversed, transformed to *live*, and what it means to live has new meaning. In the depths of death, lifeless in the tomb, and at the nadir of human weakness, God's power comes to perfection in the lifeless body of Jesus (2 Cor 12:9).

The Father and Spirit raise the dead Son from death to life, eternally beyond evil, sin, and death's grip and power. The God-man Jesus has left that behind and is returning to the Father and the Spirit, doing so once and doing so for all. As Jesus had been in solidarity with the dead in his death, he remains in solidarity with them in his resurrection, as those formerly imprisoned in Hades—the abode of the dead—now rise with him as well (1 Pet 3:19).

This is not resuscitation; this is resurrection. Resuscitation is what Jesus did for Lazarus and for the widow's son, and what was done in those biblical stories about Elijah and Elisha restoring to life those who had died. This is different. *God has raised Jesus to life beyond death, never to die again, raised the God-man back into the Godhead*, to life that is eternal, bringing Jesus' humanity with him.

This is why Jesus died. This is what makes him Savior, Redeemer, and the One who ransoms-frees humanity from the power of sin to separate them from God. And though Jesus' tomb is now empty, the story does not end here. Raised to life beyond death, at the "Father's" right hand, he has power to share his risen life with all those joined to him.

Signs It Has Happened

Atonement is still unfolding. For God not only raised the Son back into Godself but also manifested the Son alive and sent him back to his own. Those resurrection appearances among his own are fleeting indeed, and what one renowned theologian has called "appearances in withdrawal," which are a moment of reappearance as well as "simultaneously a farewell."[22]

The shortest resurrection appearance is the one in Matthew. There, when the eleven disciples see him, he commissions and blesses them and

---

22. Balthasar, *Mysterium Paschale*, 214.

promises to be with them to the end of the age (Matt 28:16–20). The most prosaic of the resurrection appearances is in Luke, the longest of the Synoptic Gospels (Luke 24:13–50).

Two disciples on the road to Emmaus fail to recognize the risen Jesus until he breaks bread among them and then vanishes from their sight, only to appear again to them later that evening when they have returned to the others still gathered behind locked doors in their hiding place. Jesus opens their minds to understand the Scriptures, saying,

> Thus it is written, that the Messiah is to suffer and to rise from the dead on the third day, and that repentance and forgiveness of sins is to be proclaimed in his name to all nations, beginning from Jerusalem. You are witnesses of these things. And see, I am sending upon you what my Father promised; so stay here in the city until you have been clothed with power on high.

Thereafter Jesus leads them to Bethany, blesses them, and while doing so "withdrew from them and was carried up into heaven."

John's Gospel is the fullest account (John 20:1–29; 21:1–23).[23] At Jesus' first encounter with a disciple—and notice that it is Mary Magdalene in the garden—she is warned not to hold him; he has yet to return to his Father. Later that evening, the disciples gathered behind locked doors because of their fear, Jesus is suddenly standing among them, showing them his hands and side, commissioning them, and giving them the Spirit. But Thomas is not present. Jesus reappears a week later when Thomas is present. Upon seeing him, Thomas responds with "My Lord and my God!"

The so-called epilogue to John reports the reunion with the disciples at the Sea of Tiberias, while they are fishing. John, the beloved disciple, is the first to recognize Jesus. At John's announcement, Peter leaps into the sea, swims ashore, and Jesus' poignant reunion and reconciliation with Peter takes place.

Paul's Letter to the Corinthians, written much earlier than the Gospels, will report multiple appearances of the risen Jesus, first to Peter, then to more than five hundred people at one time—most of whom are alive as Paul writes—then to Jesus' brother James, then to all the apostles, and "last of all, as to one untimely born, he appeared also to me" (1 Cor 15:5–8). In addition to this report, if we read Paul's letters and Luke's

---

23. Verse 24 is the author's signature and points to the conviction that at its foundation, John is an eyewitness report.

report in Acts carefully, we discover that the risen Lord appears to Paul multiple times, not simply on the road to Damascus.

All of this, says Hans Urs von Balthasar, "is at the service of a deeper and more definitive presence."[24] This is not a distant God hiding anew from humankind, but rather, the one who became human in "the incarnation, reflecting the 'glory of God' and bearing 'the very stamp of [God's] nature' (Heb 1:3)." This is the one who promised not to leave us desolated but to be with us always. Balthasar concludes, "The appearances of the Risen One are a kind of down-payment towards this abiding presence, and indeed of the ceaselessly self-renewing advent (*parousia*) of the definitive Word of God in the Church."[25] In the risen Jesus, the Christ, God is appearing as the One who became one with us that we might become one with God in him.[26]

Where to from Here?

This is not simply about Jesus' resurrection from the dead nor union with God "in" him. It is also about the renewal of life and creation, the eighth day of creation. It is the establishment of a new humanity, with hearts of flesh rather than stone, those in whom the divine image is being restored. It is about the birth of a world where sin has been dealt with by God and is not only forgiven but its power to enslave and separate is overcome and broken.

God, who made covenants with Noah and promises to Abraham and Jacob, who chose and bound to Godself a people, the children of Israel, even as they failed, wandered, went into exile, and then returned to become exclusive and religiously rigid,[27] this God, time and again, reveals a commitment to be God for God's own sake, for God's word's sake, and for the sake of God's world. Each time, God reveals God's desire and determination to be one with humanity—the zenith of God's creation—because of who God is: merciful and gracious, slow to anger, and

---

24. Balthasar, *Mysterium Paschale*, 214.
25. Balthasar, *Mysterium Paschale*, 215.
26. Athanasius, *De Incarnatione*, 269.
27. The religious legalism that appears on the pages of the Gospels was a product of post-exilic Judaism under the aegis of the priesthood and its attempt not again to fall into the behaviors that led to the exile.

abounding in steadfast love and faithfulness (Exod 34:6; Num 14:18; Neh 9:17; Pss 86:5, 15; 103:8, 145:8; Joel 2:13; Jonah 4:2).

Hearts of stone that embrace this forgiveness and steadfast love find themselves being turned to hearts of flesh. The evil inclinations that have dominated human hearts have met their match in the power of God in a covenant so radical that it can only be called new. God reveals the risen Jesus as the Christ (Rom 1:4), the second Adam, the firstborn of God's new creation, the One in whom the old humanity is born again from above, the One in whom God's new humanity comes into being.

Children of God will be born by grace through faith in the faithfulness of Jesus. In the waters of baptism, they will be made sisters and brothers of Christ. In those waters they will put him on and by the power of the Spirit become part of the new humanity destined to emerge in the world on God's behalf. Now vested and empowered by God's Spirit, they can live out of the power of the risen Christ as they continue to be transformed more fully into Christ and his glory, as Paul said, "from one degree of glory to another" (2 Cor 3:18), until they reach the fullness God destined them for from the beginning.

Is Forgiveness of Sin Enough?

It should now be obvious that Jesus' birth, life, ministry, passion, death, and resurrection—the new Passover—are about more than the forgiveness of sins. That has been God's way with humanity from the beginning. God did not forgive the sins of humanity at 3 p.m. on Good Friday afternoon as Jesus handed over his spirit. But God did deal with what lay behind them.

Nor is this about proving there is life after death, though it does say much about how eternal life emerges through death. Nor is this about the Father demanding the death of the Son to restore God's honor. And most certainly, this is not about Jesus having to pay a penalty on our behalf because we cannot pay it ourselves.

Jesus' passion, death, and resurrection are certainly not reconciliation between God and hostile humanity so that, when death comes, those who believe this story can be snatched away to live with God in heaven forever. And this Passover is about far more than the defeat of Satan or the devil—though, indeed, it is also that.

This is God's new three-day passover revealing God's love and leading to a new exodus to a new land of promise, to be sure. But this is even about more than the revelation of God's love for the world. It is all of these, to be sure, but so much more.

Evil, sin, and death have been swallowed up in victory. The power of God came to perfection in human weakness, locked in the bonds of death, just as it continues to do so today. For God is pouring the same Spirit, by whom Jesus was raised from death, on a humanity being made new in the risen Lord. God is giving receptive women and men this power, which transforms hearts of stone into hearts of flesh and restores the image of God within them, which sin had so tragically distorted. God is doing all of this so they may become members of God's new creation, living in their lives at-one with God in Christ, out of the power that comes from such living. To that we now turn.

Chapter 12

God's New Creation

One Has Died for All

IN THE RISEN CHRIST, God is starting over. Jesus is not only the risen Lord and Christ, the One who defeated sin and death, and the One in whom humanity is finally reconciled to God; he is the firstborn of God's new creation.

In his Second Letter to the Corinthians, Paul writes:

> For the love of Christ urges us on, because we are convinced that one has died for all; therefore all have died. And he died for all, so that those who live might live no longer for themselves, but for him who died and was raised for them. From now on, therefore, we regard no one from a human point of view; even though we once knew Christ from a human point of view, we know him no longer in that way. So if anyone is in Christ, there is a new creation: everything old has passed away; see, everything has become new! All this is from God, who reconciled us to himself through Christ, and has given us the ministry of reconciliation; that is, in Christ God was reconciling the world to himself, not counting their trespasses against them, and entrusting the message of reconciliation to us. So we are ambassadors for Christ, since God is making his appeal through us; we entreat you on behalf of Christ, be reconciled to God. For our sake he made him to be sin who knew no sin, so that in him we might become the righteousness of God. (2 Cor 5:14–21)

This classic text is packed with information across a broad range of concerns about what Jesus' death meant and accomplished. It introduces not only the concept of reconciliation, but also an exceptional change in reality—God's new creation—and what it means to be included within it for all who claim Jesus as Lord and live their lives "in Christ."

Once again, we see, as we did in chapter 6, Paul's use of sacrificial language. We are reminded how complex and interrelated the linguistic tools at Paul's disposal are as he argues his case. He begins with the exchange language of the cult: "One has died for all," the same thing he says in slightly different ways to the Corinthians (1 Cor 15:3), Thessalonians (1 Thess 5:9–10), and Romans (Rom 5:6–8). However, he does not mean Christ dies for us in a substitutionary sense. Christ does not die "in our place so we don't have to." Rather, Christ dies on behalf of us all. Actually, Paul says *hyper panton*—for all (Rom 5:18; 2 Cor 5:15)! Jesus dies *to make a difference for all humanity*. Christ died in solidarity with humanity and *for them*—not in their place.

Christ did for us what we could not and cannot do for ourselves. Christ died to defeat the power of sin and death that rule over humanity, as we saw in the last chapter.[1] But now, moving beyond the defeat of the power of sin and death for us, comes something more astonishing still. After writing "one has died for all," Paul immediately adds, "therefore all have died" (2 Cor 5:14b).

Paul assumes that believers die to sin with Christ in his death, something he makes even clearer when writing to the Roman church (Rom 5:15; 6:3–8). Whether Paul means "all [*believers*] have died" or the even more astonishing "all [*humanity*] have died" is a hot debate among biblical scholars, and not ours to resolve here. What we do know is that Paul is arguing that the sinful self—the old Adamic self in each of us—was crucified with Christ, so that the body of sin might be destroyed in us. Christ, in his death, has destroyed what within humanity held it captive to the domination of sin.

Humanity is no longer enslaved to sin. Sin is still present in the world, no doubt about it. And yes, believers are still subject to it. That is why classic Christian liturgies include a daily confession of sin. That said, those in Christ are *no longer enslaved to it!* We have a choice. Do believers often still make wrong choices? Absolutely! That is what confession

---

1. Sampley, "Second Letter to Corinthians," 92.

and repentance are about in the Christian life, followed by accepting and living into God's goodness, mercy, and forgiveness.

It can also be argued that it is God's goodness, mercy, and forgiveness—God's steadfast love—that enables us to confess our sin in the first place. Certainly, that was true for Israel, as we saw earlier. Certainly, that is how the Reformers understood it. But notice that this is less about forgiveness, or even purgation of sin, than it is about Jesus' triumph over the *power* of sin. Jesus' triumph over sin is for all, especially all who claim him as Lord and Savior.

Paul makes the same argument with the Galatians when he insists that, "being crucified with Christ," he also died to the law as well as sin's power to use the law to enslave him. He is no longer under sin's power (Gal 2:19). Christ did this so that those who have died with him in the waters of baptism and now live on the other side of his death might live not for themselves but for Christ. For those who have died with Christ are freed from sin so that they may walk like Christ in newness of life, living not for themselves but out of and for him who died and was raised for us all!

Reconciliation

We have been using the word reconciliation a good deal. Might it help to remember that reconciliation is both *diplomatic* and *financial* language? Here Paul uses it metaphorically to say that the barrier of sin that has kept humanity separated from God and from one another has been dealt with in Christ's death and resurrection. It has been removed, creating a new relationship, status, and vocation for us.

Reconciled life in Christ is not a mutual action between humanity and God. This is all God's work; we have not done anything to bring it about. Even believing or having faith in all of this is a gift of the Spirit, not our doing. It is the Spirit within us that gives us the ability to say yes to God's initiative. Remember, the Spirit is "the Lord and giver of life"[2] to bring us into this life-giving, reconciled relationship with God. The Holy One, through the Holy Three, has done it from beginning to end. And God, in Christ, through the Holy Spirit, continues to do it for our sake and the sake of the world.

---

2. Early Church Texts, "Nicene Creed," art. 3.

Because of our new status, God can and has entrusted to those who belong to Christ an ambassadorial task. We are to announce this message of reconciliation and call on others to be reconciled to God as well. God is making God's appeal to the world through daughters, sons, sisters and brothers of Christ, members of God's new creation, the new humanity of which the risen Jesus is the firstborn. Jesus' death, resurrection, and ascension are about more than forgiveness and about more than personal reconciliation with God. New life in Christ has a mission and purpose that has to do with the entire world, not simply those who believe it!

Believing in Jesus and what he did, being "saved," is about far more than going to heaven when we die. For God's new humanity in Christ, there is work to do. God is making God's appeal to an estranged world through a reconciled humanity called and empowered by God's Spirit to announce what God has done in Christ on behalf of all.

The war is over. God is not our enemy. God is not out to get or punish anyone. God simply wants to share God's steadfast love and mercy with all who will receive it. God wants all the world to be reconciled, not only to God but to one another. Think about how that would change this world!

Announcing this message is evangelism, sharing good news, and it casts a whole new meaning on "saving souls." God has done the saving in Christ. Now God relies on those who are members of God's new creation to get this word out as well as to live into it themselves.

Justification as Right Relationship with God

Paul rounds out his argument, saying, "For our sake [God] made him to be sin who knew no sin, so that in him we might become the righteousness of God" (2 Cor 5:2). Once again, it is an exchange metaphor, but now it is about *relationship* rather than sin. To be reconciled to God in Christ means to be put in a right relationship with God, to be "justified"—another image of relationship—to be aligned with God by God so that we are open vessels for God's Spirit.

Since the Reformation, justification has been read as a legal concept announcing a transferred verdict of not guilty to those who have faith in Christ. Among other things, that view has caused the image and dynamic of justification as relationship to become lost. If justification simply means we are no longer guilty, there is little else we need do but continue to believe it. If justification is about a new relationship, it creates a totally different understanding and dynamic to atonement as reconciliation.

Aligned with God in Christ, we receive and absorb the gift of God's love, grace, glory, and power, as God continues the work of restoring in us God's image. God is doing so, that we may be who God intended us to be when first creating us. God is turning us into those who live for God rather than ourselves, those who find life in serving God rather than serving ourselves.

Finally, there is one more thing a reconciled relationship with God in Christ demands—being reconciled to all for whom Christ died. Reconciliation is, unlike redemption, a word first and foremost about relationships. It is not simply about a relationship with God. It about righting relationships between all who are at enmity with one another. Here is where a believer's role in reconciliation must move beyond acceptance to initiative, utilizing Christ's victory over sin to reach out to those still estranged from God, from themselves, from family, friends, and neighbors, and from the world around them.

It is also true for those groups of Christians who find themselves estranged from one another. As I write, Orthodox Christians are killing one another over political issues in the Ukraine. Christians in the United States have allowed themselves to be divided over issues of sexuality, abortion, guns, and political party. Clearly, the powers of evil, sin, and death continue to exercise influence on us all. We need to hear what the Spirit is saying to us as we read Paul's words to the Corinthians about our relationships in Christ being more important than any others in life and do our best to foster them in a context that brings peace. And we need to remember Jesus' command that we love our enemies and pray for them as well as our friends (Matt 5:44–48; Luke 6:27–35).

In urging the Corinthians to be reconciled to God, Paul is not suggesting for a moment that there is something they can do to overcome the power of sin or tear down the divisions between God and themselves. But now that God has done that, Paul pleads with them to accept it,[3] believe it, and live into it, with all the ramifications that go with it. They must be reconciled with others for whom Christ died.[4] For if reconciliation is the

---

3. Hastings, "Reconciliation," 597.

4. In this case, Paul is also pleading for reconciliation between the Corinthians and himself. For though Paul was the ambassador who first brought the message of reconciliation to the Corinthians, the old Adam had raised its head among the Corinthians, creating divisions and hostilities among them, as well as between them and Paul.

defining act of God in all of this, love is the defining force. And if God's love is the defining force, then sharing in the glory of God in eternal communion with God is God's ultimate purpose for everyone (Rom 5:2). It is one of the litmus tests of being children of God and members of God's new creation.

This is what Paul seeks from the Corinthians and, by implication, from everyone in the church across the world. For though reconciliation is a past event rooted in Jesus' cross and resurrection, and though it has enabled our dying and rising with Christ, it is God at work in and through us in this world now that must continue until Christ's final return.

One's behavior and relationship with others is, as they say, "the proof of the pudding." It is not enough to simply believe Jesus died to save us. Believers must live into their salvation with all that such an imperative implies, depending upon the power of the risen Lord and his reign. If this message is to be credible in this broken and conflicted world, those reconciled to God in Christ must be more grateful and graceful! As someone has said, "If Christians are going to claim to be born again, they had best begin to look more like it."[5]

Jesus and the Second/New Adam

Another atonement theme that emerges out of this passage from 2 Cor 5 is Paul's development of the image of Jesus as the new or second Adam. Jesus was faithful where Adam was not. Through his actions throughout his life, Jesus was redoing life, revisiting those moments of Adam's failed test with obedience, faith, and faithfulness. Where the old Adam failed, Jesus remained faithful.

Theologians as early as Irenaeus have used another word to describe this—*recapitulation*. Things are being redone by God in Christ—restored. Though Paul does not use the phrase second Adam, he does employ a series of parallel contrasts between Jesus and Adam, to show how God was at work to undo the damage Adam's disobedience and sin had created. Adam was the "type of the one who was to come" (Rom 5:14). That "one who was to come" is, of course, Jesus Christ.

---

5. I think the quote is attributable to Søren Kierkegaard, but I have not been able to locate it.

Reflecting on the power of living in a just and reconciled relationship with God through Christ out of the grace of God, Paul writes to the Romans:

> For if while we were enemies, we were reconciled to God though the death of his Son, much more surely, having been reconciled, we will be saved by his life. . . . Therefore, just as sin came into the world through one man, and death came through sin, and so death spread to all because all have sinned . . . . Yet death exercised dominion from Adam to Moses, even over those whose sins were not like the transgression of Adam who is a type of the one who was to come. But the free gift is not like the trespass. For if the many died through the one man's trespass, much more surely have the grace of God and the free gift in the grace of the one man Jesus Christ, abounded for the many. . . . Therefore just as one man's trespass led to condemnation for all, so one man's act of righteousness leads to justification and life for all. (Rom 5:10–12, 14–15, 18)

Paul begins this passage by stressing the solidarity of all humanity with Adam in his rebellion, sin, and faithlessness, and what those transgressions brought to all humankind—death. Sin came into the world through Adam. Whether that is an inherited blemish of sin at our origins, as Paul and Augustine would understand it, or a more contemporary understanding of original sin as an action that lies at the origin of each of us as "the old Adam and Eve" rise within us, either way, it is the same form of rebellion. We all seek to be like God. We strive to be our own masters and devote all our energy in pursuit of prideful sovereignty.

Who does not want the freedom to be one's own master? The desire within humanity is as old as the garden. Yet, just as in doing so Adam and Eve cut themselves off from the tree of life, so too our rebellions cut us off from the source of life. Separated from the "tree of life," we are unable to find our way back. No matter how hard we search to find our own way to life, rebellious, self-made humanity continues to live under the sentence of death.

Paul announces that God has done what we cannot do for ourselves. God sent the "last Adam," Christ, the man. Where Adam's obedience failed and led to death, Jesus Christ's righteous obedience proved faithful, putting all humanity in a justified relationship that leads to life for everyone.

In solidarity with Christ through baptism, his life emerges in us. When we have been incorporated into his body, his conquest over death becomes ours as well. In baptism, we put on Christ like we put on a garment, are clothed in him, and become part of the body of which he is the head (Gal 3:27; see also Rom 7:4; Col 3:10; and Eph 1:22; 4:15). "As in Adam all die, so also in Christ shall all be made alive" (1 Cor 15:22 RSV). But more, the Spirit enters us and begins its work of taking full possession of us.

God's original intention in creation was disrupted and derailed by Adam's rebellious transgressions—his trespasses. In Christ's obedience, all of that has been undone. God's initial intention for humanity is redone as we are clothed in his image. Here, the Christ hymn of Philippians lies in the background as Paul compares the preexistent Christ's self-emptying of what was his own by nature—divine equality with God—and Adam's attempt to grasp at that equality to be like God (Phil 2:1–11, esp. v. 6).

Though Adam is never mentioned in Philippians, the contrasting parallel is obvious. The restoration of the divine image in humanity can now come to fulfillment through the restoration that has been accomplished by Christ as he undoes or, more correctly still, does what Adam failed to do. Thus, Christ has restored the image in which God first created humanity, the one Adam marred, but which is now being restored in all who live "in Christ."

Raised to New Life

Some in Corinth were scoffing at the idea of resurrection. Paul begins by reminding them that if there is no resurrection, then Christ was not raised, and Paul's proclamation, as well as their faith, is in vain. Worse, they are even misrepresenting God! More still, not only is their faith futile, but they are also still in their sins, and those who have died in Christ have simply perished. Paul continues:

> If for this life only we have hoped in Christ, we are of all people most to be pitied. But in fact Christ has been raised from the dead, the first fruits of those who have died. For since death came through a human being, the resurrection of the dead has also come through a human being; for as all die in Adam, so all will be made alive in Christ. But each in [their] own order; Christ the first fruits, then at his coming those who belong to Christ. Then comes the end, when he hands over the kingdom

to God the Father, after he has destroyed every ruler and every authority and power. For he must reign until he has put all his enemies under his feet. For the last enemy to be destroyed is death. (1 Cor 15:12–26)

Here again is Paul's Adam/Christ typology, but this time Paul uses it in a way that is even more inclusive and comprehensive. Christ has been raised, the first fruits of those who have died. His resurrection assures the future resurrection for all who belong to Christ.

The parallel between "for as all die in Adam, so all will be made alive in Christ" has led to much speculation about what Paul means by "all"—just "all those who are in Christ" or the whole of creation? Answering that is beyond the scope of what we are doing here, but suffice it to say that for Paul, Christ's resurrection and ascension are as central to God's atoning work in Christ as was his incarnation, passion, and death. As one commentator has written:

> Christ's resurrection was not some unusual event sequestered into the byways of history for Paul; it was the transformative event that marked the turn of history and linked it directly to God's culminating but not yet finished purposes in all of Christ. Christ's having been raised by God has as its consequence that others will be raised from the dead, and therefore that death itself will ultimately be defeated—and all of this has credibility because every bit of it rests on God's power and purpose, neither of which can or will be qualified by human reticence, recalcitrance, or failure.[6]

As the rest of 1 Cor 15 unfolds, Paul turns to the resurrected body. What is it like? That is the question that lay behind the Corinthians' denial of the resurrection. They were Greeks who believed in an immortal soul that could be raised to heaven. But as disciples of Plato, they could not conceive of a human body—the corrupt shadow of reality that housed the soul—being raised to immortality with the soul.

To counter that, Paul describes the resurrection as the perishable body being raised as an *imperishable* one. What was sown in dishonor was raised in glory. What was sown in weakness will be raised in power as the physical body is raised a spiritual body. Paul falls into the science of his day as he seeks to illustrate his point (1 Cor 15:37–43).

---

6. Sampley, "First Letter to Corinthians," 981.

The best vision of the spiritual body is the one given to us in Jesus' resurrection appearances. There is a real connection with the physical, but it has been transformed by God's power—glorified—into a body fit for an entirely new reality, life in God's eternal and "nearer" presence and reign, the realm we trivialize with our talk about "heaven." As one prominent New Testament scholar has said, "Things are *more real* in heaven; it is a non-corruptible corporality"—life animated by the Spirit, not composed of it.[7] Paul writes:

> If there is a physical body, there is also a spiritual body. Thus it is written, 'The first man, Adam, became a living being'; the last Adam became a life-giving spirit. But it is not the spiritual that is first, but the physical, and then the spiritual. The first man was from the earth, a man of dust; the second man is from heaven. As was the man of dust, so are those who are of dust; and as is the man of heaven, so are those who are of heaven. Just as we have borne the image of the man of dust, we will also bear the image of the man of heaven. What I am saying, brothers and sisters, is this: flesh and blood cannot inherit the kingdom of God, nor does the perishable inherit the imperishable. (1 Cor 15:44–50)

Life in Christ

Few phrases have been used more by Paul than "in Christ." It is almost a slogan for Paul. And though Paul did not originate it, he makes abundant use of it. It appears some nineteen times in Romans, twenty in the two Letters to Corinth, eight in Galatians, eleven in Philippians, five in 1 Thessalonians, and three in Philemon, and that is simply to name the letters that scholars unequivocally attribute to Paul.

"In Christ" is more than the baptismal union with Christ that Paul spoke of to the Galatians, where believers die to sin and death, and put him on. This is a *post-baptismal relationship* that sustains believers as they are drawn more deeply into new life as members of God's new creation. "In Christ" is about living in a relationship with Christ that gives us the resources to live new lives out of Christ's risen life and power. In that relationship, the Spirit that he promised to send enters our lives, as the

---

7. My lecture notes from Wright, "Get the Story Right."

Word entered Jesus at conception, and accompanies us through the rest of our lives continuing to make us more like him.

This new reality is where all of God's work in Christ has been aiming from the very beginning. It draws believers into lives where *everything* is new. It is a fulfillment of God's promise to Abraham that in and through him all the peoples of the earth would be blest.

Five Forms of Union in and with Christ

Paul's first use of "in Christ" is what one might call *auditory*. It is a union that comes from listening to Christ speak in and through his word as it is read, proclaimed, and meditated upon. It is more than simply "hearing something" in the background. There is a vivid conviction that in this word Christ is speaking directly to you and me. Ask anyone who has ever had a powerful call to do something in Christ's name. We almost always end up talking about "hearing" Christ's call, and it is unmistakable.

Paul's second use of "in Christ" is what we might call *mystical*. It is a bonding or merging with Christ and his risen power to form a sphere of influence on the believer. This is what happened to Paul on the road to Damascus after he heard Christ speak to him. Read the book of Acts carefully and see how many times this continued to happen to Paul and how it sustained him as he lived out his ministry.

This is what has happened to those saints across the ages who have found themselves joined to Christ in meditation, contemplation, visions, or appearances. It is more than imagination or projection. There is a connection that takes place in those "visionary" moments that brings about transformation in those lives and continues to do so throughout their lives.

Paul's third means of union with Christ is *sacramental*. It first comes about through baptism, as earlier described, in which one is "joined to Christ" or "puts him on" like a garment (Gal 3:27). The second is the sacramental covenant meal of holy communion the church calls the Lord's Supper, Holy Communion, or the Eucharist. In that union, believers are fed on and by the risen Christ to nurture and strengthen them as they grow in maturity to become like him.

Paul's fourth form of union is *ecclesiastical*. Baptismal union to Christ is also a priestly union through him with the rest of his body in the world, the church. He vividly described it to the Corinthians using the images of the various parts of the body, all connected to one another through their relationship to the body itself (1 Cor 12:12–27).

Paul's fifth form of union with Christ is *forensic*. Believers who entrust themselves in faith to Christ and his faithfulness have had their status and destiny before God shaped and determined by what God did in Christ in his passion, death, resurrection, and ascension. They are now clothed in Christ, and when God looks upon them, God sees Christ and his work in them, setting them in a new relationship with God and God's righteousness.

In each of these five, the Spirit engages us, unites us to Christ, and brings forth all the benefits of being one in and with him. From this perspective, to be "in Christ" means to belong to him in all regards in both death and in life. For, "as in Adam all die, so in Christ shall all be made alive" (1 Cor 15:22]. As Christ is dead to sin and alive to God, so too are those who are "in him."[8]

The New Creation

Behind these five forms of union and their benefits lies the larger theological consideration we have only touched on thus far: Paul's understanding of Christ as the firstborn and head of the new age and realm, who incorporates within himself all who belong to this new age and realm as members of his new creation (2 Cor 5:17; Gal 6:5).

In one of his earliest letters, Paul writes to the church in Galatia, "As many of you as were baptized into Christ have clothed yourselves with Christ. There is no longer Jew or Greek, there is no longer slave or free, there is no longer male and female; for all of you are one in Christ Jesus. And if you belong to Christ, then you are Abraham's offspring, heirs according to the promise" (Gal 3:27–29). Herein lies the radical nature of what it means to be a new creation in Christ.

All the divisions of life are gone. All the hierarchies most spend their lives striving to attain or maintain become meaningless. All have been absorbed into Christ as the foundation of the new world, reign, and being of the realm he inaugurated on God's behalf and leads us into. There is neither Jew nor Greek, male nor female, Orthodox, Roman Catholic, Reformed, Lutheran, Episcopal, Methodist, Baptist, Pentecostal, nor Free Church Evangelical, but one new humanity in Christ. All belong to God

---

8. Beker, *Paul the Apostle*, 272. See also Moo, *Epistle to Romans*, 380–81, n150.

in Christ, as they always have, but now the false divisions humankind, living captive to sin, have tried to lay over creation are revealed as a lie and are gone.

There is no longer slave or free. That ancient division of exploitation upon which the economies of the world have depended, and in many places still depend, is erased. It is why Paul insisted that Philemon must accept back his runaway slave Onesimus, not as a forgiven slave but as his brother in Christ (Phlm 1:16). There is no room in God's realm for exploitation of anyone—not just for fellow Christians—but anyone. Christ died, not just for those who believe in him but for all.

As Jesus was among the "little ones" in life—the outcast, the overlooked, the diminished, the marginalized, the abused—so he can be found among them today. One cannot be "in Christ" and not be concerned for those this world disregards and exploits. These are the ones that we who are one in Christ must welcome, care for, and lift up. In doing so, we care for Christ himself (Matt 25:40–45).

So too there is neither male nor female in Christ. Rather, the two who came from one to take away the aloneness and to be the other's helpmate, in Christ's new age and restored humanity, now remain one in equality, value, and respect, not simply before God but before one another. All the ministries of Christ's body are fully shared, without regard to gender, orientation, or other forms of identity this dying world uses to discriminate against others.

It is a message those in power need to heed now as much as ever. The hierarchical models for managing households and societies—and yes, most especially the church!—are part of the old order of things that has been undone in Christ. It must continue to be undone by us, or we are not in Christ, but rather, again, living in and serving the old creation. This is the radical nature of what it means to be members of God's new creation.

It is no wonder that so many have worked so hard, for so long, to attempt to undo, rewrite, or recast the radical nature of the good news Jesus was announcing, and Paul caught sight of in his vision of what it means when Jesus Christ is Lord and Savior of one's life.[9] One of the tragedies

---

9. A primary example of that is what many biblical scholars today consider the textual insertion in 1 Cor 14:33b–36. It appears to be a parenthetical comment that not only breaks the flow of Paul's argument but contradicts Paul's own behavior and relationship with women as peers in apostleship and ministry (1 Cor 11:5; Rom 16:1–4; Phil 4:2–3). By the latter two or three decades of the first century, people writing in

God's New Creation

of trying to constrain Paul's gospel to the ways of the world is that it reduces the gospel to a belief in things about Jesus that ensure one is saved and rewarded with heaven at death but requires nothing more of us than "belief." Authentic belief is a life that makes him Lord in all things!

Reducing the Gospel to Heaven?

While drafting this book, I have made it a practice to seek out people from diverse backgrounds to ask them if they believe in God and, if so, what that belief means for them. It has been easier to do now that I am no longer encumbered by a clerical collar or the title "Reverend." In most cases, those I talked with either did not know I was a minister or were otherwise simply unhindered in their answers because of it.

There were those who described themselves as having been "very religious" from childhood. There were those who came to religion as adults after some form of conversion experience. They include those who had been religious in childhood but dropped out and have not returned. And finally, it includes those with no religious background whatsoever. They have run the gamut: educators, tradespeople, bankers, news reporters, lawyers, Wall Street investors, stock traders, and social activist atheists.

It is the latter that are often the most interesting to talk with, primarily because they are busy with their own works of atonement at one level or another, seeking to be effective in their worlds. Indeed, many of them are model citizens with their efforts on the side of the angels, reminding me of Jesus' words that "whoever is not against us is for us" (Mark 9:40).

From those with no religious background, I have heard a lot about trying to be a good person, the importance of ethics, and some admiration for Jesus as a great teacher, though most cannot tell me what he taught. Most of those who could remember some of the Sermon on the Mount often thought his ideals were wonderful but far too idealistic to be put into use "in the real world."

From the very religious, I have heard answers that are formulaic, depending upon where they lie on the spectrum from conservative to

---

Paul's name in Ephesians, Colossians, 1 and 2 Timothy, and Titus, and those writing in Peter's name, were trying to tame the radical nature of the new creation by importing the acceptable household codes of behavior of that time (Eph 5:22; Col 3:18; 1 Tim 2:11–14; Titus 2:5; and 1 Pet 3:1–6). And the practice continues today as churches—not just Rome or the Orthodox Church but many conservative Protestant groups—continue to deny women the ability to respond to God's call in their lives.

liberal—but formulaic nonetheless. Often, they are as hard put to describe Jesus' teaching as are the nonreligious, because for them, Jesus is not a great teacher; he is the Son of God who is their Savior. And that seems to be all they think it necessary to know.

I am reminded of a quotation that is attributed to William Faulkner. He is reported to have said of himself that "[he was] forever in search of truth, laying his hands on it, putting it in his back pocket and sitting on it."[10] In such cases the gospel is conceived as a life insurance policy with a fire rider. Sitting on the gospel that way has nothing to do with being new in Christ or "being saved."

That is what comes from constraining the gospel to the simplistic "Believe in Jesus, accept him as your personal Savior, he will forgive your sins, and when you die, you will go to heaven."[11] Notice that all of that is orthodox Christian theology, as far as it goes, but a theology tied to the old age. It simply does not go far enough. Not only does it leave out the part about Christ being one's Lord, but it also completely misses the power that comes from being "in Christ" now, as a member of his new creation. Being saved is revealed in the life we live now—one stamped with the mark of immortality—one worthy of being lived eternally.[12]

Life in Between

Let us return to Paul's use of the phrase "in Christ" and what else it means. For Paul, it points to having been transformed from the old age that died with Christ in his death—the death we are baptized into—and rising into the new age that has been brought into being through the resurrection of Jesus Christ.[13] The risen Jesus is not only the Christ of God, but he is also the firstborn of God's new creation (2 Cor 5:17; Gal 6:15). In him, life "according to the flesh" has been displaced by "life according to the Spirit."

It is an *interim* condition, a life lived between the times of the new age's inauguration and its ultimate consummation—Christ's final return. That return is what theologians call the *eschaton*, that time when Christ

---

10. Though my memory tells me it was Faulkner, I have not yet been able to find it for full attribution. I am still looking.

11. This statement appears frequently in the writings of N.T. Wright. I first encountered it in his book *Simply Christian*, HarperOne, 2005.

12. My thanks to my former seminarian, colleague, and friend, Rev. Dr. Richard Sheffield, for acquainting me with this wonderful phrase, which originated with him.

13. Beker, *Paul the Apostle*, 272.

returns to judge the world and make *all* things new (Rev 21:5). Life "in Christ" is a life that is the "first fruits" of what is coming—where God is taking creation. Being between the times means living in a world where sin is still a reality, where tests and temptations still lie at the door of our lives like a lion threatening to devour (1 Pet 5:8). But for those in Christ, the power of that sin has been broken.

Those steadfast in faith resist sin, even to the point of suffering to do so, knowing that the God of all grace who has called them to eternal glory in Christ will restore, support, strengthen, and establish them in this life, as well as the one to come (1 Pet 5:8–10). This is as much the meaning of the word salvation for those striving to live in Christ in the world today as the idea of "being saved" for a future in heaven.[14] And not accidentally, those who commit themselves to living that way in this world find a faith and power for living that makes concerns about heaven quite secondary.

Salvation is the power of Christ that emerges in one who is "in Christ." It is what gives one the capacity and desire to have influence in the world on God's behalf. It is what provides the endurance to resist sins' allures and corruptions, and what sustains one in whatever suffering that living as Christ's ambassador in this world might bring.

Jesus is the Savior, to be sure. It is his grace empowering human lives in their times of deepest stress and testing that is the salvation the Bible proclaims in his name. In fact, his name quite literally means "God saves." And for those in Christ who stumble, succumb to the reality of sin, and fail, there is the gracious gift of confession, repentance, forgiveness, and the grace to begin anew, knowing that nothing in this life, not even our failures, can separate us from the love of God that has been revealed to us in Jesus Christ our Lord (Rom 8:38–39).

Life "in Christ" is not the final reality of *redemption*, where we are freed from the ravages and trials of life in a world infected with sin. It is life, "in between" one's baptism and the consummation. The consummation is that final moment in the future of the cosmos, when God liberates all of creation from its bondage to sin, as those now "in Christ" find themselves liberated from its ultimate power. Then sin and death will be no more. They will have been eternally destroyed, and all will be infused with God's glory and part of God's new heaven and earth (Rom 8:4, 8, 21; 1 Thess 4:17).

---

14. The word is *soteria*, meaning "deliverance, preservation, safety, salvation," both in the present and the future.

Until that time, the members of this new creation, in whom the Spirit dwells, know themselves to be children of God, because the Spirit enables them to cry out in their heart, "Abba, Father" (Rom 8:15; Gal 4:6). We do so not out of a spirit of fear or slavery but out of a spirit of adoption, knowing ourselves to be heirs of God and joint heirs with Christ—children of God.

God's children in Christ suffer with him that they may be glorified with him. Paul tells us that it is for these children that the rest of creation waits with "eager longing" (Rom 8:19). God's drama of atonement and redemption is still ongoing, and these children are active members of the cast.

Being "saved" is living empowered by Christ and the Spirit[15] to make and keep us members of his new creation in this world, as we seek to make him Lord and Sovereign. For there are other powers still seeking to be lord of our lives, and other idols of contemporary life that vie for our devotion, allegiance, and worship.

Contemporary Idolatries That Vie for Our Worship and Devotion

Let us return to Athanasius of Alexandria (Egypt), the fourth-century Trinitarian theologian. This time, let us review his argument for how evil first appeared in God's good creation and how it came to reign in life, so that all the inclinations and imaginations of the human heart were continually only evil (Gen 6:5; 8:21; Eccl 11:9).

Christian theology universally asserts that God did not create evil. Nor did evil exist independently of God as though it was in the world as the creation of a demiurge.[16] When such dualism begins to slip into Christianity, it is leaving its biblical and theological foundations behind and becoming something altogether different from the gospel of Jesus Christ.

---

15. In the New Testament, "the Spirit" almost always means "the Spirit of God" (Rom 8:9–16). On two occasions, the phrase "Spirit of Christ" appears (Rom 8:9 and 1 Pet 1:11). The Spirit is the Holy Spirit, the connection between the "Father" and the "Son" and the connection for us to "the Father" through Christ. The Spirit has been called "the Go-Between God" (Taylor, *Go-Between God*).

16. In Platonic thought, a subordinate deity who fashioned the material world; in Gnosticism, the one responsible for creation's corruption. That notion began to slip into Judaism through the influence of Cyrus' dualistic Zoroastrianism during the exile.

Athanasius was Irenaeus' heir and solidly grounded in both Scripture and theology. He is best known for his treatise *De Incarnatione* (*On the Incarnation*), but he is also the author of *Contra Gentes*. They were originally two parts of the same work.[17] In the latter, he said that the souls of men and women *imagined evil* as they pursued corruptible things in their darkness. Not satisfied with the invention of evil, they regressed further still.

> For learning of the diverse forms of pleasure and girded with the forgetfulness of things divine, taking pleasure in the passions of the body and only in things of the moment, it paid regard to opinions about them and thought that nothing existed other than visible phenomena, and that only transitory and bodily things were good. So perverted and forgetting that it was made in the image of the good God, the soul no longer perceived through its own power God the Word, in whose form it had been created, but turning outside itself it regarded and pictured non-existent things.[18]

Out of that evil, they began to apply the word God to the visible things they desired, and soon they were worshipping them. Thus emerged the sin of idolatry, the prime cause of which is evil.[19]

Athanasius was responding to the rampant idolatry of the Greco-Roman world with its mysteries and superstitions, multiple temples, and a range of gods from wrathful to capricious. *Contra Gentes* was written utilizing those idolatries and gods as a means of demonstrating their falsehood and treachery.

Idolatry was, for Athanasius, not simply one form of sin but the single greatest pitfall the children of Israel faced after they entered the land of promise. They were forever giving to the gods of their neighbors around them what belonged solely to the Lord and doing so to the point that God would finally give that generation up to their evil desires (Pss 81:11–12; 106).

The book of Judges tells us they did it again and again, in an ever-descending spiral of decadence and violence that led them to turning on and destroying one another.[20] All of this in spite of the fact that the commandment that immediately follows "No other gods before me"—the

---

17. Robert W. Thomson, in *Athanasius*, xx.
18. Athanasius, *Contra Gentes*, 19–21.
19. Athanasius, *Contra Gentes*, 21.
20. Athanasius, *Contra Gentes*, 20–23.

first of the Ten Commandments—is no idols: "You shall not make for yourself an idol. . . . You shall not bow down to them or worship them" (Exod 20:4–5). Israel's idol worship led them astray in so many ways, just as the contemporary idols that vie for our worship and devotion lead us astray.

The Evils of Contemporary Idols in God's New Creation

One of the reasons for the prohibition of idols and their worship is to protect us from the evils that emerge from them when we give them our worship. Behind this observation is the truth that whenever we give what belongs solely to God to some good thing that is not God, we unlock within that thing its capacity for evil rather than good.

Keep God in Christ at the center, and all good things in life are appropriate and useful. When we allow things to displace God in our lives, when we give those good things our worship, devotion, and trust—in a word, *our faith*—we have made and begun to worship an idol. That begins to unleash into life an ever-flowing flood of that thing's capacity for evil—not only into our own life but the lives of those around us and, in some cases, the lives of those we will never know.

For Athanasius, idolatry and its desires led to transforming good things into the opposite of their created purposes, producing murder, disobedience, adultery, and blasphemy—things he called "sins of the soul." Today, our idolatries unleash a host of other evils. Drug addictions, accidental suicides, alcoholism, pornography, the sex trade—including cases involving children and other segments of vulnerable humanity—all of these emerge from our idolatries. Human trafficking with would-be immigrants, including undocumented workers, those fleeing other forms of violence and abuse, or people simply looking for a better life for themselves and their children—all have their roots in the classic idol: the love of money (1 Tim 6:19; Heb 13:5).

The love of money has led to unrestrained greed that is both personal and corporate, with all the evils that can unleash. We are now living in a world where it is reported that 1 percent of the world's population owns almost half of the world's wealth.[21] Some among those 1 percent are thoughtful, grateful, generous, and working hard to use their wealth in responsible, positive ways on behalf of humanity and the earth and its

---

21. Credit Suisse, *Global Wealth Report* (2018), 20.

other creatures. On the other hand, far too many are losing their lives in their love for more and seem not to know the truth that enough is best.

Jesus' parable of the rich man building bigger and better barns in Luke comes to mind: "those who store treasures for themselves but are not rich toward God" (Luke 12:13–21). It is reported that corporate CEOs are beginning to realize that they have responsibility to more than simply their shareholders. It is said that there is a new "bottom line" taking hold that includes care for other stakeholders: their employees, their customers, as well as the earth, and that is news to be welcomed, affirmed, and celebrated.[22] One can certainly hope and pray that it is so.

Yet, our newspaper headlines report almost daily on corporate fines and lawsuits where the primacy in corporate decision-making is the bottom line, justified because of responsibility to shareholders. This corporate behavior has led to polluted drinking water, foul air, the warming of the planet, and the depletion of the Earth's protective layer of ozone. There seems to be little sense of responsibility to anything but shareholders.

Corporations—note, individual decision-makers are rarely held accountable—generate false narratives about what is "recyclable." Waste management corporations cloak themselves in names like "environmental services," when, in fact, they are polluting water and air, burying organic garbage along with hard products made of plastics and metals, producing leachate laden with "permanent chemicals" that are poisoning communities' aquifers. But destructive avarice is about more than the environment.

How is it that the United States, with its military and industrial complexes joined at the hip, has become the arms dealer to the world, often supplying both sides of the conflict? I have heard a CEO of a major weapons developer rationalize their death-laden industry because of "the bad guys out there doing bad things." Behind that lies the myth of redemptive violence. Violence always begets violence and produces death. It is why Jesus absorbed it rather than respond to it in kind.

Reliance on guns for personal security has, in the United States, produced the horrors of gun violence. When guns are turned on a crowd at a country music concert in Las Vegas, a school full of children at Sandy Hook and other places—most recently Uvalde—a worshipping synagogue in Pittsburgh, a congregation in Colorado, Texas, or elsewhere, we ask how that can happen. The answer we tell ourselves is it is the result

---

22. Gelles and Yaffe-Bellany, "Shareholder Value."

of isolated mental illness, not the madness of our own idolatry and love affair with guns as a means of protection and security.

The perversion seems to be sustained, if not fed, in many conservative religious circles. One journalist writes, "For many American Christians, Jesus, guns and the Constitution are stitched together as durably as a Kevlar vest." "The good guy with a gun myth" is being linked not simply to self-defense as a "God-given right"; it is being promoted as a form of evangelism to protect oneself, one's family, and one's neighbor from evil, and is seen as a Christian virtue.[23]

The worship of other forms of power has led to the buying of influence in the halls of state and federal government, the encouragement of the corrupt use of political power in the highest offices of the land, and the threatening of court officers and has given us the best government money can buy—quite literally! Our worship of technology, information, and social media have led to a nationalism that is both xenophobic and racist, to cyberbullying, the invention of fake news, hacked elections, and the use of violence in the name of religion.

For the church, the idols remain the three that Jesus overcame in his wilderness temptations—success, power, and security—plus a fourth: money. The prosperity gospel is a mockery of all Jesus lived and died for. The scandalous alliance of religious leaders with political parties and politicians—both left and right—in pursuit of their agendas in the culture wars of this land shames not only those leaders but belittles and discredits the faith they so publicly wear. It does so especially among nonbelievers—inoculating them to the gospel! As Jesus said, better they should have a millstone tied to their necks and thrown into the sea than cause one of these to stumble (Luke 17:1–3).

How Christians live the redeemed life matters. The more power, security, wealth, and success is ours, the more we are at risk of succumbing to the temptations of idolatry and releasing the evils that emerge from them when worshipped. To the one who asked Jesus what he must do to have eternal life, Jesus responded, "If you wish to be perfect, go, sell your possessions, and give the money to the poor, and you will have treasure in heaven; then come, follow me" (Matt 19:16–21; Mark 10:21; Luke 18:22). To others, he said, "Take up your cross and follow me," and to others still, simply, "Follow me."

---

23. Manseau, "Myth of Good Guy."

Let me say it once again: it is not enough simply to believe in Jesus. As the Epistle of James reminds us, "Even the demons believe" (Jas 2:19)! Confessing Jesus as our Savior is one thing; making him Lord is quite another. It is the latter he seeks from us. Paul, writing to the Romans, put it this way:

> I appeal to you therefore, brothers and sisters, by the mercies of God, to present your bodies as a living sacrifice, holy and acceptable to God, which is your spiritual worship. Do not be conformed to this world, but be transformed by the renewing of your minds, so that you may discern what is the will of God—what is good and acceptable and perfect. (Rom 12:1–3)

How easily power, security, success, and wealth have the capacity to conform us to this world and its idolatries. Transformation by the renewal of our minds is taking a step in the right direction. But how do we live in such a way that our lives continue to be transformed and bear good fruit? As Jesus said,

> Beware of false prophets, who come to you in sheep's clothing but inwardly are ravenous wolves. You will know them by their fruits. Are grapes gathered from thorns, or figs from thistles? In the same way, every good tree bears good fruit, but the bad tree bears bad fruit. A good tree cannot bear bad fruit, nor can a bad tree bear good fruit. Every tree that does not bear good fruit is cut down and thrown into the fire. Thus you will know them by their fruits. Not everyone who says to me, "Lord, Lord," will enter the kingdom of heaven, but only the one who does the will of my Father in heaven. On that day many will say to me, "Lord, Lord, did we not prophesy in your name, and cast out demons in your name, and do many deeds of power in your name?" Then I will declare to them, "I never knew you; go away from me, you evildoers." (Matt 7:15–23)

What then are the resources available to us to enable us to put on Christ daily and follow him faithfully into today's world and bear good fruit in his name? To that we now turn.

Chapter 13

Growing in Christ—Putting Him On

What Is Jesus Doing Now?

WE COME TO QUESTIONS that most atonement theories completely overlook: what is Jesus Christ doing now as risen Lord, what does that mean for you and me, what does that mean for the world, and how does that take place?

Most would probably answer that Jesus is praying for us, standing at God's right hand pleading our case, and indeed that is true enough (1 John 2:1). The risen and ascended Jesus Christ is one with the Holy One he called Father, interceding and advocating on behalf of his body, the church. But there is more.

The risen Jesus is also one with the Holy One in the Holy Three we know as the Spirit. Through the Spirit Jesus Christ is reaching out, continuing to make atonement: enfolding, entering, nurturing, and sustaining those who are his in faith and baptism—sisters and brothers in God's new creation—drawing them ever more deeply into this holy atoning union and its benefits. He is becoming ever more incarnate in his own, and they through him at-one with the Triune God.

This incarnational atonement is not only about Christ being born in the faithful but also about Christ being *borne by the faithful* in this world! Jesus' work is larger than saving and preserving the church or the faithful. He is still at work to redeem the world. He is using the members of his body in union with him and the Spirit to be his ambassadors, God making God's appeal through them (2 Cor 5:20). As Jesus' followers remain faithful to this work in the world, God continues to be at work both through them and *in them*.

Those in Christ continue to grow and mature, from one degree of glory to another. Jesus said he would not leave us orphaned, abandoned, or comfortless.

> In a little while the world will no longer see me, but you will see me; because I live, you also will live. On that day you will know that I am in my Father, and you in me, and I in you. They who have my commandments and keep them are those who love me; and those who love me will be loved by my Father, and I will love them and reveal myself to them. Judas (not Iscariot) said to him, "Lord, how is it that you will reveal yourself to us, and not to the world?" Jesus answered him, "Those who love me will keep my word, and my Father will love them, and we will come to them and make our home with them. (John 14:19–23)

To paraphrase the words of Athanasius once again: God became one with us in Christ that we might become one with God in him.

As the conduit of the Spirit engages believers' lives in ministry, they begin to be changed, "transformed into the same image [of the Lord] from one degree of glory to another" (2 Cor 3:10). What this means for each one who claims Jesus as Lord is the subject of what follows—God's atonement realized and actualized sacramentally by God in and through the members of God's new creation, the faithful being the body of Christ in the world.

Sacraments as Means of At-one-ment

We return now to what we discussed in chapter 3. Historically, the church has spoken about various "means of grace" through which Christ is joined to and sustains his followers.[1] That, in and of itself, points to them as means of atonement—making them increasingly one with him. It is through God's sacramental gifts, via God's Spirit, that the faithful continue to be joined to Christ. Christ pours out the same Spirit by whom he was raised from death onto all those being made new in him. In doing so he gives them the life-renewing and sustaining power of the Spirit as well as the Spirit's other benefits.

1. I have intentionally placed the emphasis on Christ being "joined to believers" rather than "believers joined to Christ," to keep the emphasis on the divine initiative and freedom that always lie behind the sacraments.

We recalled that, traditionally, a broad range of things was recognized as these means by which God's grace in Christ is given and received. Over the years, they have been spoken of variously as sacraments, sacramentals, mysteries, or rites, depending upon the theological systems and language being used by a particular church tradition to speak of such things. Behind the word sacrament lies the Latin word *sacramentum*, meaning to bless, consecrate, or hallow.

Classically, *sacramentum* meant the oath of loyalty that an ancient Roman soldier took to his commander and ultimately to the emperor. In the church's appropriation of the word, *sacramentum* becomes a dual oath: an oath God makes to the faithful in the particular gift named a sacrament, and an oath believers make to God in their reception of the gift in faith.

Though God can be present to us in the world in many ways, it is in four unique ways that Jesus has promised to meet us—each an essential element of Christian worship. Through these God-given means, we hear of, experience, confess, accept, receive, and live out the saving grace and lordship of God in Christ.

First among these ways that Jesus meets us is the Word of God proclaimed, read, meditated upon, and shared.[2] When Christ's call through that Word is experienced, heard, received, and accepted, baptism with water in the threefold name of God, "Father, Son, and Holy Spirit," follows.[3]

Second is baptism, in which one dies with Christ in the baptismal waters, puts him on like a garment, and receives the seal of the Spirit in one's life (Gal 3:27; Col 2:12; Acts 19:2-7; Eph 1:13). Therein one becomes clothed in Christ and a temple of the Holy Spirit (1 Cor 6:19).

Third is the meal Jesus instituted on the night of his betrayal as the new covenant meal of redemption—Lord's Supper, Eucharist, Holy Communion—and it follows the reception of baptism. In the Orthodox churches, infants are communed at their baptism by the priest dipping

---

2. Notice it is an uppercase *w*, which theologically is used to mean not the Bible but "the living Word"—Jesus Christ, as Scripture bears witness to him.

3. Attempts to modify this baptismal formula in order to make it inclusive, such as "Creator, Redeemer, Sustainer," have yet to be found that are both theologically sound and acceptable in the larger church catholic and ecumenical. The practice of baptizing infants, for those churches that do, is dependent upon knowing that God is already at work in the life of the child and that these children will be reared and nurtured in Christian faith in such a way that they will always know and confess Jesus as their Lord.

his finger in consecrated wine (or using a tiny silver spoon) and then placing it in the sucking babe's mouth. Increasingly, in other churches, too, communion is being given to baptized children from infancy as part of their nurture in faith.

Finally, there is the life of prayer. This is not simply offering daily prayers of adoration, blessing, thanksgiving, confession, praise, supplications, and intercessions; it is also *enacting* such prayers in the life of daily discipleship, including acts of witness and solidarity with those suffering from injustice.

To baptism and Eucharist, the early church added penance, holy orders (ordination), marriage, anointing with oil, and confirmation. These seven came to be understood as means of blessing all the essential aspects of one's life, consecrating and hallowing them in the faithful.

To these seven, the church also began to recognize other "sacramental" actions through which God's grace was given. Sometimes called sacramentals, they are actions or objects that draw one more deeply into conscious contact with the risen Lord. These include fasting, meditation, good works, giving alms, witness, devotional crosses, making the sign of the cross, water, oil, ashes, icons, candles, stained glass, and so on. Originally, beyond the first four, this list was quite fluid. In fact, there was a time in the Western church when there were as many as 365 different things that could be spoken of as a sacrament or sacramental.

The fifth-century CE African bishop St. Augustine of Hippo spoke of sacraments as "an outward and visible sign of an inward and visible grace," instituted by Christ.[4] It was the "instituted by Christ" that began to formally reduce the number of officially recognized sacraments to seven, with the others becoming sacramentals—that is to say, sacraments in nature but without the "dominical command" and promise of Jesus.

At the great schism between the Eastern and Western churches in 1054 CE, the Eastern Orthodox tradition maintained the seven sacraments but spoke of them using their Greek name, *mysterion*, pointing to the mystery of the spiritual power of God at work in them for the faithful. In addition, Eastern Orthodoxy included the church itself as a sacrament, while other actions or things remained "sacramental," or aids to living a holy life.

It was the conflict in the Western church at the Reformation that caused further reduction in the number of sacraments from seven to

---

4. See Diocese of Westminster, "What Is a Sacrament?"

two. The Reformers believed better distinction was needed between sacraments and sacramentals and insisted on Christ's "dominical" institution to make the distinction. A sacrament must have a scriptural warrant identifying it as Jesus' command for all believers and be for the benefit of Christ's church to be considered a sacrament.

Since the Reformers could find such dominical warrant only for baptism and the Lord's Supper/Eucharist/Holy Communion, they reduced the number from seven to two. However, the remaining five were not abandoned or discarded. They continued as sacramentals or rites, though Luther continued to hold the preaching of the gospel as a sacrament, while Anabaptists held also to the washing of feet.

The irony in all this sixteenth-century debate is that the other Reformers finally left out not only preaching the gospel (which was a hallmark of the Reformation) but prayer in all but its eucharistic form. Foot washing,[5] forgiving one another, feeding the hungry, clothing the naked, housing the homeless, bearing one another's burdens, visiting the sick, the imprisoned—each of these things Jesus commanded his followers to do—generally fell out of focus as well![6]

The Roman Catholic Church responded in what has come to be called the Counter-Reformation—the Council of Trent[7]—and identified the classic seven as valid sacraments. Today, it, along with Anglo-Catholics[8] and the Orthodox, still identify seven sacraments: baptism, Eucharist, confession, confirmation, holy orders (ordination), marriage, and anointing with holy oil prior to death (extreme unction) or in case of serious illness.

Yet, within the broad "Protestant house" today, there is all but consensus on baptism and Eucharist as the sole two sacraments, with preaching, prayer, fasting, confirmation, works of mercy, anointing, foot washing, holy orders (ordination), marriage, crosses, icons, and other religious objects of service or devotion falling into the broader scope of sacramentals or holy rites.[9]

---

5. Save aforementioned Anabaptists.

6. The point, of course, is those had not been included among the major seven, were not subject to controversy, and so were not even considered. The exception to this is in those monastic communities that especially gave themselves to these ministries.

7. Held in Trent (Trento, in northern Italy) between 1545 and 1563.

8. More commonly known as Anglicans (in the United States, as Episcopalians), they emerged out of the reforming actions of King Henry the VIII of England.

9. Some churches in the Protestant house do not recognize sacraments as

Following the Second Vatican Ecumenical Council (Vatican II), which met in Rome from 1962 to 1965, virtually all the major churches of the West were caught up in an ecumenical liturgical renewal that Vatican II had initiated in the Roman Church. That renewal spilled over into much Protestant practice, as an outpouring of enthusiastic liturgical and sacramental dialogue began to take place ecumenically throughout the twentieth century and continues to make its fruit known today.

Also behind the Protestant renewal lay the Church Service Society (CSS), founded in Scotland in 1865, dedicated to the study of the liturgies of the Christian church, in service to a more faithful form of prayer for worship and the administration of the sacraments in the Church of Scotland. The society studied not only the work of its classic Reformers, Calvin and Knox, but also Eastern and Roman Catholic liturgies. Its work would become a strong influence in Protestant committees on worship by the mid-twentieth century, not only in Scotland but also in the United States, joining its energy with the renewal sparked by Vatican II.

Further, in 1982, there emerged out of the World Council of Churches' Faith and Order Commission a document reaching back some fifty years to the WCC's first Faith and Order Conference in Lausanne in 1927—a paper titled *Baptism, Eucharist and Ministry*. *BEM*, as it is often known, explored the growing agreement and remaining differences among Protestants and Catholics in the fundamental areas of the church's faith, life, and ministry.

BEM stimulated an even richer interest in the renewal of liturgical life across the church, especially in matters of sacraments. Consequently, there is today an all but ecumenical consensus and conviction that the sacraments are means by which the Spirit draws the faithful into deeper relationship with God in Christ and with one another. In them, the faithful receive grace to be sustained in their lives of faith, witness, and work. These means, or gifts of the Spirit, continue their work of transformation in those who receive them, nurturing them in their lives as members of God's new creation.[10]

---

something in which God is at work conferring grace but rather identify baptism and communion as holy rites in which worshipers express their faith and devotion.

10. The consensus is about the role of the sacraments and some of what God is doing in and through them, rather than universal agreement about *how* that is done, beyond being the work of the Holy Spirit. See World Council of Churches. *Baptism, Eucharist and Ministry*.

In summary, whatever the sacrament, its content is Christ. It is this ecumenical understanding of sacraments that the churches now commonly share that forms the foundation for what follows in the rest of this chapter.

The First Means of Grace—Hearing God's Word

> God so loved the world that God gave God's only Son, that whoever believes in him shall not perish but have everlasting life. God did not send the Son into the world to condemn the world, but in order that the world might be saved through him. (John 3:16)

As this word is proclaimed, the Spirit of God quickens those whom God is calling in Christ, and they hear Christ's voice calling them beloved, chosen, and his very own. As Martin Luther himself thought, the preaching of this word is every bit as sacramental as baptism and Eucharist. Christ is as present in hearing the word as he is present in the waters of baptism and eating the bread of life and drinking the cup of salvation. And he is as present through the Scriptures and psalms of Israel as he is through the Gospels and other writings of the New Testament. John Calvin was especially insistent on this latter point. One cannot fully understand the message of the New Testament without a foundation and familiarity with the Old Testament and its promises.

One of the great gifts of the most recent liturgical renewal movement has been the common lectionary and a virtual consensus, across traditions, for the lessons to be read in worship on each Lord's Day, within a three-year cycle. That means that on any given Sunday, anywhere in the world, Christians can be listening to many if not all the same lessons and hearing the gospel proclaimed through them.[11]

A second result of the common lectionary is that it gives a broad range of biblical readings that can acquaint a congregation with the fullness of the gospel, not just their preacher's favorite twenty-some texts.

---

11. Following Vatican II, in 1969, the Roman Catholic church developed a three-year calendar of four lessons—Old Testament, Psalm, Epistle, and Gospel—that was utilized by the Protestant Consultation of Church Union to produce its 1974 lectionary that subsequently emerged in 1983 as the Common Lectionary. As the ecumenical liturgical work continued, the North American Consultation on Common Texts and the International English Language Liturgical Consultation published the Revised Common Lectionary in 1994.

But most important, use of the lectionary draws preachers back into the texts and the task of proclaiming the word, rather than this or that word they may have encountered in the news, a film, a play, a book, a counseling session, or some other event that has given them something to speak about on Sunday morning.

For Lord's Day worship to be its fullest and most faithful, all four texts should be included and foundational in the service. In the more formal liturgical communions, the readings are prescribed by the lectionary. In less formal "free church" traditions, the choice of lessons is left to the pastor. Many pastors in such churches find use of the New Revised Lectionary liberating, as it provides both direction and challenge to preachers to continue to stay abreast of biblical study, do serious critical textual study, and listen for Christ to speak to them as they write.

This has been my own experience, as in forty-three years of active pastoral ministry, I used the lectionary weekly, save three times.[12] Never did I find it routine, boring, or constraining, but always fresh, as Christ used those texts to speak to and through me in sermon preparation. In addition, there is no need to attempt to include all the lessons in the sermon. The text(s) that need to be proclaimed have a way of speaking to the faithful in worship as much as to preachers as they prepare. The point is not to explain what each of the individual lessons means but to proclaim the word of Christ that emerges from and through them all. For those who use less than the four, the Gospel should always be one of them, whether it is the sermon text or not.

Unfortunately, as time has passed, as life has become more conflicted, and as the church has become more divided by the culture wars in America, too many preachers have somehow thought it their responsibility to be "prophetic" rather than faithful to the Scriptures whose message they are called to proclaim. Of course, classically, and historically, prophecy is part of preaching. Too often, however—in both conservative and liberal circles—prophetic has come to mean proclaiming a version of, or approach to, this or that social challenge as the meaning of the text and baptizing that as "prophetically" announcing what it means to faithfully follow and serve Jesus.

---

12. The Sunday of the Three Mile Island crisis in Harrisburg, Pennsylvania; the Sunday of an annual meeting to receive the resignation of an associate pastor who had been trying to divide the church; and the year I decided to preach *lectio continuo* through the Gospel of Luke.

In such sermons, Christ has dropped out of the center as Sovereign, Redeemer, and Savior and has become instead an ethicist, political commentator, or life coach—not unlike the editorial stances we encounter on the op-ed pages of our favorite newspaper. Preaching then becomes giving sanctified advice or issuing a series of "shoulds"—depending upon the preacher's political inclinations—deemed essential to being Christian. Rather than proclaim a gospel of grace, too many Christians then hear a religion based on good works to demonstrate one's righteousness or reinforce and pursue a political agenda.

On the other hand, preaching the word does not mean an escape from the world into an ethereal dimension of "spiritual," apolitical experience. Jesus' preaching certainly engaged the context and the life of people. He spoke first and foremost of what God was doing in those circumstance—how God was at work. He then challenged people to ways of living faithfully as God's people in the context of empire and its idolatries.[13]

The first means of grace is proclaiming the truth that Jesus is Lord, not this or that political position, perspective, ethical, or social agenda. When we allow those other things to displace Christ and his righteousness, we are back into the trap of serving and proclaiming the desires of the human heart rather than the gospel of God in Christ, and depriving people of the "bread of life" that gives new and abundant vitality in what often is a cold, stingy, and selfish world. When we put Christ at the center, and listen for his voice in the word proclaimed, those other issues fall into their proper place.[14]

Responding to God's Word

As Christ is proclaimed, the Spirit engages the hearers' hearts, prompting and providing the desire and courage to respond to Christ's call with the obedience that the church calls faith. Authentic faith, as we hear it

---

13. I am grateful to my colleague Dr. Russell Sullivan—himself an exceptional preacher who powerfully navigates the sholes of a church embattled by the culture wars in contemporary America—for this helpful reminder.

14. Keeping "Christ at the center" is a phrase I first heard from the Rev. Dr. M. Craig Barnes, president of Princeton Theological Seminary, as he uses it to lead, challenge, and support the trustees, faculty, administration, and students through the cultural wars conflicting the church and theological education during these years of his presidency.

described by Jesus, is less thinking something about him or even believing in him. Authentic faith is about responding to his call to follow him (Mat 12:50; Mark 3:5; Luke 8:21). As he said in the parable of the wedding feast, there would be many who called him Lord that he would not know (Matt 25:10–13).

Saving faith in Jesus as God's Christ, the Redeemer and Savior of the world, is nothing less than hearing that call and responding yes! Saving faith embraces God's invitation to new life in Jesus Christ by making a lifelong commitment to follow and serve him, wherever he leads. And for most of us, it happens far more than once! As we continue to hear and respond yes, our salvation continues to unfold.

One in and with Christ

I am indebted to Justo L. Gonzáles who likens Christian Baptism to the graft on a tree that continues to give life to the branch long after the graft is made.[15] If one has been baptized, whether as an infant or child, a faithful and frequent "Yes!" is a confirmation of what was given to them in those baptismal waters. God made a promise in their baptism. Whether they remember it or not, God does! God joined them to Christ in that sacrament, marked them as Christ's own forever. Christ, through the Spirit, has been at work in their life, and now God is bringing that remembered promise to their awareness again. Though I am tempted to say, "bringing it to fulfillment," it is better said, "God is fulfilling the promise." Its complete fulfillment will take a lifetime and more!

As believers continue in faith and obedience, they come to know the joys and sorrows, victories and challenges, assurances and doubts, trials, and triumphs that being joined to Christ includes in this world. It will include times of spiritual breakthrough and joy as well as seasons of dryness; it can lead to hardship as well as victory. This will continue until it comes to fulfillment in them through their death, resurrection, and eternal life in and with Christ. Nor is every breakthrough or spiritual renewal an occasion to be rebaptized. Once is enough—like birth, it lasts a lifetime![16] Christian baptism is first and foremost about God's promise to us; and that promise needs no renewal.

---

15. Gonzáles, *Christian Thought Revisited*, 44.
16. Gonzáles, *Christian Thought Revisited*, 44.

Our promises, however, need *constant renewal*. The faithful do that regularly—at least weekly—at Christ's table. We will talk more about that in a bit. For now, a person's recognition of their union in and with Christ emerges in experiences of faith renewal. Often, that means that one baptized as an infant will want to take some action to declare that reawakening and quickening to faithful action. But another baptism is not the appropriate response. Since the fourth century, when those who had abandoned the faith under persecution sought to return, the church said no to a second baptism. As the Nicene Creed proclaims, there is "one baptism for the remission of sins."[17]

However, what has always been appropriate at such times is confirmation by a pastor or bishop, with a public affirmation of the baptismal vows taken for the confirmand as an infant, followed by the sacramental actions of anointing with oil and laying on of hands, with prayers of thanksgiving and consecration. In such a rite, it is also quite fitting for the person whose faith has been renewed to place their hands in baptismal water and bless themselves with the sign of the cross—even placing the water on their own head. It is a sacramental means of remembering their baptism and remembering that God *is* keeping the promise, bringing it to fullness day by day as they live into their new life in Christ.

The Second Means of Grace—Baptism as Union with Christ

In the waters of baptism God unites believers not only to Jesus but to his death and resurrection. Believers have been crucified with Christ and died to sin and its power—death (Rom 6:8; Gal 2:19). Sin's residue in their life has been washed away. As Jesus was raised from death and the grave to new life, so too they are raised with him out of those entombing waters, beyond sin's ultimate power, to new life (Rom 6:10–11). Though they die, should Christ not return before then, they will never know the "second death" (Rom 6:3–14; 1 Cor 15:20–23; 1 Thess 4:1).

God gives the baptized Christ's Spirit to become what we might call living sacraments of Christ in this world. They become "little Christs"—that is what the word Christian means!—clothed in Christ and his risen power and glory. Often, the baptized are dressed in new clothing,

---

17. MIT, "Nicene-Constantinopolitan Creed."

symbolic of new life, and given a candle, lighted from the Christ candle, as a reminder that they are to be Christ's light in this world of darkness.

God, through the Spirit, is restoring the image of God within them in this union with Christ (Gal 3:12), making them members of the new creation of which Christ is the firstborn (2 Cor 5:17; Gal 6:15). But they are not simply one with Christ. They have been made one, through him, with the Father and the Spirit, and remain at-one with God in Christ as they continue to live at-one with and in the Holy Three who are the Holy One.

Baptism as an Adult

If one has not been baptized, hearing Christ's call and responding to it in faith begins by presenting oneself for the sacrament of Christian baptism. That may involve a period of instruction and preparation, especially if one has not been previously associated with a church. Membership in the church—the body of Christ—is about far more than simply saying "I accept Jesus as my Lord and Savior" or accepting God's forgiveness of sin in him and his name. It is also becoming part of his body in this world in the church.

Those churches that baptize simply on a "profession of faith" without any instruction or other preparation are seriously shortchanging those Christ calls to himself. They are failing them by ill preparing them for the challenges as well as the blessings of discipleship. There are some basics that need to be learned about confessing faith and trust in Jesus, as well as what his faithfulness as Christ, Lord, and Savior means for them now. The ancient church took as much as three years between and initial confession of faith and the person's baptism, to prepare those new to the faith to be welcomed fully into the church.

What is quite easy to join is also quite easy to leave behind. Convenience is not a useful tool for evangelism and the making of disciples. A disciplined approach to baptismal preparation, whether with parents presenting their children for the sacrament or for those coming to faith in adulthood, is essential if the church is to fulfill its call to be Christ in today's world.

Many a person who "got saved" in an evangelistic service and shortly thereafter, without any preparation, was baptized in a pool, river, or lake, often simply tucked the experience into their back pocket to sit on as "life insurance." It is not surprising that, "saved," they soon left behind the daily disciplines of faith: worship, prayer, Bible study, service, and work on behalf of Christ in the world.

There are many reasons why that ancient preparatory process changed. Much of it has to do with the dominance of "Christendom" after Constantine embraced the faith and persecution was left behind. Not long thereafter, the baptism of infants and children became the norm in the church. It has remained so, except for those churches in the Reformation that rejected infant baptism. And even those churches have found what is called the "age of discernment"[18] becoming increasingly younger.[19]

On the other hand, as the church in the Northern and Western hemispheres enters the twenty-first century and finds itself increasingly in a post-Constantine world, Christendom is increasingly a thing of the past.[20] Parents who today ask for baptism for their infant children are clearly giving expression to their own faith and discipleship as parents, acknowledging the need for Christ's presence in their children, as they themselves seek to live out their vocation as Christian parents.

Baptismal Discipline

In the last fifty years, the sacramental churches have begun to press for discipline among those who present themselves or their children for baptism, requiring that the parents be not only professing but practicing Christians, seriously involved members in the congregation. Baptism is not magic!

Baptizing children but not rearing them in the faith is a significant breach of spiritual discipline not simply for parents but for the church and its ministers.[21] Many a pastor has lamented "caving in" to the desires of grandparents to have their grandchild baptized because their parents

---

18. The age by which children are determined to be old enough to make faith decisions for themselves.

19. I was baptized at the age of ten in an American Baptist congregation but had been contemplating it for two years prior to that.

20. Gonzáles, *Christian Thought Revisited*, 127–29.

21. Though some denominations leave the decision about whether to baptize someone to the priest or minister, in some of the more "ordered" churches, that is a shared decision with a church council, board of deacons, or elders. Baptism is about more than responding to a person or parent's faith; it is also about becoming a member of the church under their stewardship.

left the church behind after confirmation or marriage. On the other hand, if those grandparents are, in effect, the child's spiritual parents, and they are prepared to take on the spiritual responsibilities of nurturing the child in the faith, there is no reason to withhold baptism.

To these ends, the Roman Catholic Church and many mainline Protestant churches are reestablishing periods of baptismal training the church historically called the catechumenate.[22] Those training programs then lead to the baptismal candidates presenting themselves to the church for baptism, often on Easter Eve at the vigil or on Easter Day, publicly confessing their faith, making promises of discipleship, and being washed in the name of the Holy One-Holy Three—"the Father, Son, and Holy Spirit"[23]—and welcomed to the table of the Lord.

Is There Only One Way to Baptize?

How one is washed is a matter of preference, for no one way is *the* way. Immersion in a pool or lake has again become popular, and Baptists seem to insist on it, whether indoors or outside. Whether Jesus was fully submerged in the Jordan River or simply knelt in the river as John poured ample water over his head is a scholars' argument without much documentation or proof either way. Having visited the Jordan and its so-called baptismal sites and having observed the quantity of water there has left me wondering.

In the early church in climates of warm weather, the baptismal candidates stood on the western side of a pool outside the church and, facing east, renounced the devil, evil, and its ways. They then stepped down into a baptismal pool and were either immersed or had ample water poured over them in God's threefold name. They then emerged up the eastern

---

22. United States Conference of Catholic Bishops, "Rite of Christian Initiation of Adults"; Sacraments Study Group, *Invitation to Christ*; General Board of Discipleship (UMC), "By Water and Spirit." Orthodox churches have no formal catechetical programs that is universal, as it is left to the person the bishop appoints as catechist—often the bishop himself—but the process lasts usually between six to twelve months, whereas in the ancient Orthodox church it could be as long as three years.

23. The baptismal formula "I baptize you in the name of the Father, and of the Son, and of the Holy Spirit" is the only formula accepted by the universal, ecumenical church. Attempts to remove gender or person, such as "Creator, Redeemer, Sustainer," have resulted in people's baptisms not being recognized. As useful as "Holy One-Holy Three" might be in liturgical language, it is not an acceptable substitute for the historic formula.

side of the pool, were dressed in a white robe—symbol of the new life they had just entered—and welcomed into the church for Eucharist.

In colder climes of Europe, outside baptismal pools began to disappear. Baptismal fonts were placed inside a structure, whether a separate baptistry adjacent to the sanctuary or in the sanctuary itself, near its entrance door. The renunciations and confessions were made, and water poured over the candidate's head.

What We Do in Baptism

The practice in the ancient church, where embracing Christ was a costly decision, included the baptismal candidate renouncing the devil and all his ways. It was a recognition that the candidate was leaving behind old ways and turning to Christ and his victory over evil, sin, and death. In the post-Enlightenment age in Protestantism, the renunciations fell out of usage. But in the last fifty years, beginning with the recommendation of the aforementioned *Baptism, Eucharist and Ministry* document, there has been a renewed emphasis on the important of such renunciation as essential in any comprehensive baptismal liturgy. Whether one believes in "the devil" or not, evil is still very much with us. We all need to be reminded of our call to renounce it and its insidious and deadly ways.

Baptism reminds us that, dying to the past, Christians still live in a present time and culture susceptive to the power of evil and sin. Those joined to Christ will find themselves frequently at odds with the way the world organizes itself, whose powers in this world enslave many but must be resisted through the superior power of Christ. Recognizing this, many churches call on baptismal candidates, or their parents, to make such renunciations as a part of their confession of faith. In it, they are called to affirm that they renounce evil and its power that defies God's righteousness and love or renounce the ways of sin that seek to separate one from the love of God.[24] Among these churches are the Orthodox, Roman Catholic, Anglican (Episcopal), Presbyterian, Lutheran, Methodist, United Church of Christ, Disciples of Christ, and others.

---

24. I have quoted those in the order of baptism from my own Presbyterian tradition, recognizing that similar acts are found in Methodist, Lutheran, Anglican, Catholic, and Orthodox liturgies. See Purkey, *Holy Baptism*, 28.

Immersion, Effusion, Sprinkling

The Orthodox churches fully immerse an infant who is naked, and do so three times, once for each of the three named within the Triune God. Adults change into a bathing suit and robe, and step into either a pool or large tub to have water poured over them three times in God's Triune name. Whether inside or outside of the church often depends upon the climate.

Roman Catholics and Anglicans use a scallop shell to pour water over the baptismal candidates' heads three times, speaking the threefold name of God. Presbyterians, Methodists, Congregationalists, and others typically use handfuls of water, applied on the head three times. Most recently, if the baptism is held in the church rather than a pool, lake, or river, the rubric calls for an abundance of water to be used. Consequently, in the last seventy-five years of liturgical renewal, "candy dish" fonts have given way to more substantial bowls on stands or more large, permanent liturgical fixtures. The point is this: the water is symbolic and should be abundant in accord with what is taking place through the abundance of God's grace.

In Baptist and other free church traditions, a baptismal pool is usually part of the sanctuary's permanent structure, sometimes behind the pulpit and choir loft, at others cut into a side portion of the platform that supports the pulpit. Though the baptismal formula remains the same, some require immersion only once in the threefold name, while others require immersion three times, once for each name. There, the imagery of dying to sin, washing it away, and being raised to new life is the most graphic. It is no surprise that immersion is reentering the practice of many churches today, both mainline and free. I suspect it will only increasingly be the case in this century.

At least five things are being symbolically portrayed in baptism. First, there is the renunciation of evil we have spoken of above, promising to attempt to leave behind sin and the ways that lead to death—a promise essential to taking up a new life in Christ. Second, there is the obvious sign of washing and purification, as the roots of baptism can be found in the ritual purification bathing of Judaism. Sin's impurity is being removed, symbolically washed away. The third is dying to sin. Here, the font symbolically becomes a tomb or grave where one is buried with Christ, dying to sin. The fourth is being joined to Christ, putting him on as one puts on a new garment. The fifth is rising with Christ, coming up from that death, turning the font into a divine womb from which one is born anew into the Christian life as a sister or brother of Christ and member of God's new creation. It is these last three that distinguish Christian baptism from the baptism of John.

Often, holy oil is used to mark the sign of the cross on the forehead of the newly baptized, marking them as Christ's anointed and sealing them as his forever. The form, however, is far less important than the act. For what is often lost in baptismal debates is that Christian baptism is far less about what we do than what God is doing—enacting at-one-ment—becoming one with us in Christ, as we are joined to Christ in baptism, and in that union joined to the fullness of Godself.

Another Dimension to At-one-ment

As the Spirit makes us one with Christ and one with God in Christ, the Spirit unites us with all who belong to God in Christ. All are one, so that women and men, young and old, Jew and gentile, slave and free, can live fully into their divine vocation as children of God, sisters and brothers of Christ, members of God's new creation in Christ (Rom 5:5; 8:2–27; Gal 3:26). Empowered by the Spirit, the baptized are to live for God and God's purposes and glory, just as Christ lived and died for God's purposes and glory.

Baptized to Ministry

Baptism is "ordination" to ministry in Christ's name. In it, the baptized are called and commissioned to seek to be at-one—reconciled—not only with others who claim Christ as Lord but with those in the world who do not yet do so but for whom Christ died. This is Christians' ambassadorial task, God making this appeal through them (2 Cor 5:20). The ministry is a call and commission to be Christ to both neighbors and enemies, loving them as Christ loves the world.

Baptism means bearing Christ faithfully through lives that seek justice, compassion, forgiveness, peace, and reconciliation for all, doing so not for ourselves but because we have become agents of God in Christ. Paul used the phrase "living sacrifices" (Rom 12:1), offering life first and foremost to God in the routines of daily life (Rom 8:17). Baptism is the sign and seal of all of this. Thus, a new humanity is born and set back on the course and purpose for which God created humankind in the first place (2 Cor 5:17; Gal 6:15).

The Third Means of Grace—Bread of Life and Cup of Salvation

The third means of grace is the new covenant meal of bread and wine the church calls Holy Communion, the Eucharist, or the Lord's Supper.[25] When Jesus instituted this meal at the end of a Passover Seder, he commanded that his followers do this whenever they come together in his name and do so as a means of remembrance of him in an enacted commemoration of what he did.

That commemoration means remembering not only what he did later that evening and next day but that he is now risen and continues to be present in and among his disciples as they "re-member" him, both at his table and in his world. In chapter 3 we first introduced the dynamics of this meal and the significance of it coming on Passover after the Seder had ended. The bread and wine, so central to the Seder as symbols of God's redemption of Israel from its slavery in Egypt, Jesus named his own body and blood. It was a means of revealing to his disciples the meaning of his life and ministry among them, and what that bread and wine would come to mean for them after his death and resurrection.

We have looked at the various synoptic reports of the meal, as well as Jesus' own words in the sixth chapter of John. In John's Gospel, after feeding the five thousand with five barley loaves and two fish, he identified himself as the "bread of life," the One who completely satisfies all hunger. He promised that the eucharistic bread would impart eternal life, and the cup of wine as his blood would expiate sin and seal the new covenant's forgiveness of it. Indeed, he said that unless they ate his body and drank his blood, they would have no life in them.[26]

---

25. Roman Catholics also use the term *Mass*, though, technically, the Eucharist is only a part of the larger Mass.

26. The prominent New Testament Scholar Raymond E. Brown has written, "If we consider that John does not report the Lord's words over the bread and the cup at the Last Supper, it is possible that we have preserved in vi 51 [John 6:51] the Johannine form of the words of institution. In particular, it resembles the Lucan form of institution: 'This is my body which is given for you.' However, there is really no Hebrew or Aramaic word for 'body,' as we understand the term; and many scholars maintain that at the Last Supper what Jesus actually said was the Aramaic equivalent of 'This is my flesh'" (R. Brown, *Gospel According to John I–XII*, 285).

Those words were literalized by many in the crowd listening to him, and the notion of chewing on his flesh and drinking his blood so scandalized them that most of them fell away. When Jesus then turned to the twelve and asked if they too wanted to go away, Peter responded, "Lord, to whom can we go? You have the words of eternal life" (John 6:68).

Here is the clue to what Jesus is up to in bread and wine. In this meal, believers receive the risen Lord afresh, eat and drink, through the gifts of bread and wine, his glorified body and blood, and ingest him as the bread of heaven and food for the life of faith. It is food that truly satisfies, for it imparts the reality of his risen presence and gift of eternal life each time they are received in faith.

"Remembrance" Revisited

When we looked at the earliest report of the meal as Paul conveyed it when writing to the Corinthians, we focused on the emphasis of the meaning of the word behind remembrance (*anamnesis*). We recalled that it has little to do with thinking about, memory, reminiscence, tribute, or commemoration. Each of those is a synonym for "remember" in English. Unfortunately, those English synonyms have brought distortions to what Jesus meant when he said, "Do this as my *anamnesis*" (1 Cor 11:24).[27] Jesus was saying much more than "when you do this, think about me and what I did."

Looking at it from a different perspective, consider what Paul meant when he said, "As often as you eat this bread and drink the cup you proclaim the Lord's death until he comes" (1 Cor 11:26). Paul here is not talking about proclaiming Jesus' suffering and dying, though many a Protestant communion service is still captive to the notion that the meal is a wake or funeral rather than resurrection meal or marriage feast of the lamb (Matt 22:2–14; 25:1–12; Luke 12:36; Rev 19:7). Paul is saying that in eating the bread and drinking the cup, we proclaim what Jesus' death did—what it accomplished. By his death, he defeated sin and death for all humankind and inaugurated the Christian Passover of liberation from their enslaving bonds in life (1 Cor 5:7).

In Jesus' day, Passover remembrance was a ritual act of entering into the foundational event of Israel's life: its liberation from slavery in Egypt. In much the same way today, when Jews celebrate Passover,

---

27. *Touto poieite eis ten emen anamnesin* (This do into the remembrance of me).

they are transported back into that saving event, or more, that event is brought into their present. Jesus is saying, "Do this to enter into what I am doing for you." Here is the significance of the word "in" that prefaces "remembrance of me." The Greek word is *eis*, which means "in" or "into." Grammarians distinguish it by saying its central meaning is "entrance into" something.[28]

Doing Jesus' *anamnesis* is *entering into the mystery* of what Jesus was promising in this meal that prefigured life in him after his death, resurrection, and ascension. More than recollection or commemoration, it is anticipatory celebration. One renowned biblical scholar has written:

> Just as the Passover meal was for Palestinian Jews a yearly *anamnesis*, so too Jesus now gives a directive to repeat such a meal with bread and wine as a mode of re-presenting to themselves their experience of him, especially at this Last Supper. . . . Thus Jesus gives himself, his "body" and his "blood," as a new mode of celebrating Israel's feast of deliverance. His own body and blood will replace the Passover Lamb as the sign of the way God's kingdom will be realized from now on, even though its fullness will not be achieved until the eschaton.[29]

Here is the means through which Jesus' disciples will both recall and make present to themselves the saving effects of Jesus' death. Here is how they can "enter into it" and, in doing so, also proclaim it. It is what Paul means when he says, "For as often as you eat this bread and drink the cup, you proclaim the Lord's death until he comes" (1 Cor 11:26).

Paul does not mean proclaiming an excruciating and agonizing death filled with suffering as punishment for your sins and mine, much less the sin of the world. He means this meal proclaims an act in which Jesus did for humanity what humanity remains unable to do for themselves—defeat sin and death and create a means of freedom from their power to enslave. That is why we celebrate and give thanks (*eucharisto*). We are giving thanks and celebrating the freedom his incarnation, life, death, resurrection, and ascension have brought to humanity, and the at-one-ment we know with him as we participate in the meal.

Another approach to understanding the meaning of *anamnesis* is to do to the English word remember what we did with the word atonement—hyphenate it. For again, *anamnesis* does not mean to call to mind,

---

28. First Corinthians 11:24, in Danker, *Concise Greek-English Lexicon*, 112.
29. Fitzmyer, *Gospel According to Luke*, 1391–92.

as in think about or remember. It means to "re-call" or "re-member," as in, experience and be a part of Christ being present again in the meal as the Spirit joins us to Christ. It is a momentary prelude to our eventually being in his glorified presence eternally.

Sacramental Mystery

It is no accident that the Orthodox churches speak of the sacraments as *mysterion* or mysteries. There is no need to get caught up in the arguments of the Reformation over the how of all of this. In fact, the Orthodox intentionally shun that question. Everyone within the sacramental churches acknowledge that Christ is somehow present in the meal. Incidentally, for most Christians at the Reformation, the argument was not over *if* Christ is present in in the meal but over *how* he is present.[30]

Today, an ecumenical consensus among sacramental theologians acknowledges that Jesus is present in the meal through the gifts of bread and wine, not so much because of the several ways the traditions have attempted to explain it metaphysically, philosophically, or theologically, but because he *promised* so to be. The word sacrament is, after all, a promise—Christ's promise. We do not need a scientific answer to confirm what we accept in faith and experience sacramentally at Christ's table.

In this meal, Jesus promises to be present to the faithful through the means of a loaf of bread and a cup of wine, consecrated in his name. Drinking the cup, the faithful receive the blood of the new covenant that consumes and wipes out sin.[31] As blood expiated sin's corruption for Israel in its sacrificial system, so drinking this cup wipes out sin and its power over believers. It assures them of forgiveness and empowers them with the gift of salvation. As blood sealed the covenant with Moses, this cup seals Jesus' new covenant of forgiveness with those who come to him.

As bread was and remains the "staff of life," the risen Lord is present through the bread of his body to feed, nurture, strengthen, and make those who belong to him more like him. Thus, as our risen High Priest, Jesus continues to make intercession for us, while giving himself to us to dine on as the bread of heaven—food and drink through which we abide in him and he in us, food that will enable us to live forever (John 6:56, 58).

---

30. Zwingli seems to be an exception to this.
31. The formal word is *expiation*, as it was used in Israel's sacrificial system.

To eat this bread and to drink this cup is to renew one's own baptismal promises. It is why some churches have a font of water in the pathway to the communion rail or at the place of the distribution of the bread and cup. Many Christians use that as an opportunity to mark themselves afresh with baptismal water in the sign of the cross (just as others do on first entering the church). It is a way to remember, reenter, and renew one's baptismal promises as one comes to receive the eucharistic gifts.

As we eat the bread of life and drink the cup of salvation, God's new covenant is sealed in our lives yet again. Sin is forgiven. Those who receive these sacramental gifts are purified, made holy, and encounter the Holy One to whom they belong. Atonement is made, realized, and actualized sacramentally. This is the reason the church has done this on each Lord's Day since that first Resurrection Day in Jerusalem, and why so many Protestant churches are now returning to the practice weekly.

He Died for All—Are All Welcome?

In his life, Jesus welcomed all who would come to him. Excluding no one, he welcomed the outcast, the marginalized, the poor, the sick, the suffering—all of whom the religious establishment had designated sinners. He bound them into community within himself, eating and drinking with them. Even Judas was at that first table. How, then, can anyone claiming to minister in Christ's name turn another away who comes in faith?

The sacraments are means of grace, not discipline. To use the sacraments as a means of discipline is to stand between a sinner and Christ—not a good place to be![32] It is not only a distortion of the sacrament, it is an abuse of the gift and extraordinary privilege of pastoral ministry. Being a steward of the mysteries of God—one of the ancient terms for those the church ordains to the ministry of word and sacrament—does not mean we have been set aside to defend the risen Lord from those who would try to abuse him. He is quite able to do that for himself if need be.

More likely, Christ is welcoming the abuser, forgiving, and beginning that person's transformation. Dare we stand in the way of that? We must remember that the Eucharist is not a reward for having lived saintly lives but medicine for our mortality—food to nurture us more deeply into faithfulness.

---

32. Remember what he said about causing one of his "little ones" to stumble (Luke 17:2).

Gifts of God for the People of God

In most Christian traditions, the prayer at the table, blessing and consecrating the set-forth bread and cup, include the words Jesus used to institute the meal and comes to conclusion with the faithful praying the Lord's Prayer. If cups have been prepared beforehand, words of Scripture are spoken to identify the bread and cup as Christ's body and blood.

In many Protestant traditions, after the Lord's Prayer, bread is broken and a chalice is filled while the presiding minister speaks the words of institution—the words Jesus used to first institute the meal (1 Cor 11:23–25). Thereafter, the celebrant says, "Gifts of God for the people of God," and the faithful respond, "Let us keep the feast." In the most sacramentally active churches, worshippers then come forward to receive the gifts of bread and wine. In others, the gifts of bread and wine (or juice)[33] are served to worshippers as they are seated in their pews.

Earlier, we recounted how in Luke, on that first day of resurrection, Jesus encountered grieving followers on the road, walked with them, opened the Scriptures to them, and when invited to a meal, took bread, blessed, and broke it, and they recognized him. Then he vanished (Luke 24:13–33). Later that night, Jesus broke in on them in the upper room looking for something to eat (Luke 24:36–43). He did it again a week later, because Thomas had not been present the first time (John 20:26–28).

In John's last chapter—often referred to as the epilogue—the disciples had gone back to fishing, not sure what else to do with their lives without him. But then they saw a man on the shore tending a brazier with fish and bread. Peter, hearing from the beloved disciple who it is, dives in, and swims to shore, leaving the others to follow him (John 21:1–14). There, Peter is reconciled to the One he had denied and fed by the One who died to free him from the power of sin. It is then that Jesus commission him to "feed my sheep."

This is what it means to gather to worship God sacramentally in Jesus' name—to discover him alive, present, and breaking into our midst. It means to dive in, headfirst, swim ashore, be reconciled to the One we all too often deny or abuse, be fed by him with the bread of life and the cup of salvation and made more fully one with him to continue our part in God's new creation ministry in this world.

---

33. Understood to be "unfermented wine." Historically, the substitute for wine in this meal is water.

About More than Forgiveness

Atonement is about the forgiveness of sins, to be sure, but it is also about so much more. The extensive emphasis in the past on forgiveness of personal sin has obscured what else is going on. In this meal, a moment of at-one-ment takes place, and Jesus' presence is realized—what theologians call "realized eschatology"—the promised end is present now, if but for a moment.

To eat the bread and drink the cup is to know—as in *realize*—what it is to be one with the Holy-Three-in-One. It is in the sacrament that Christ is fully present to those who welcome him in a *oneness* that is transforming. In this meal, he meets his own to make them more like him, to restore the image of God in which we were all created. To meet Christ this way is to know the actualization of his presence as he comes again, and again, and again, until his final coming in glory—always to make us new—as much now as then!

The sacraments are means of grace that both sustain and transform those who receive them in faith, until they finally become fully like him (1 John 3:2). It is summed up in the pastoral entreaty some use when serving the bread to a communicant, "Behold what you are; become what you receive. Receive who you are; become whom you receive."[34]

Whenever You Do This—Or Don't!

John Calvin insisted that for Christian worship to be authentic it must be both word and sacrament on each Lord's Day. He spent his life in Geneva trying to convince the city consistory that had supervision of the churches there to make the change. They had been accustomed to communing only once a year, and that enforced by the threat of excommunication if they did not. The meal had been anything but what we have been describing. Rather, the emphasis had been on what happened to those who communed in a manner "unworthy" and the judgment that would bring upon them (1 Cor 11:27). Consequently, most, save the clergy—Protestant or Catholic—dared commune only once a year, and that after a disciplined time of penitential preparation we know today as the season of Lent.

The move from once a year to weekly seemed to the members of the consistory too radical and more than they or the people could withstand.

---

34. Attributed to Augustine, developed from "Sermon 272."

They opted for an increase to four times a year, with the promise to revisit it once the people became more accustomed to the frequency. Unfortunately, it is a promise they did not keep. Rather, the four times a year formula became enshrined in Reformed practice.

Until the midpoint of the last century, most Protestants approached the meal as a funeral in which Jesus' passion, suffering, and death were being remembered and commemorated, rather than a meal celebrating victory over sin and death for all and his risen presence among them in the meal. "Why," I was once asked by a fellow pastor, "would anyone want to do that more than four times a year, much less weekly?"

Ironically, some Baptists and other free church traditions, for whom the meal is not the sacrament we have described here but simply a devotional rite, insist on it at least monthly. Recently, I have become aware of some Anabaptist traditions that are beginning to view the meal sacramentally and have begun to celebrate it weekly.

In most Reformed churches, the minimum became the standard and four times a year became the rule. That continued until the work of the nineteenth-century Church Service Society of Scotland, mentioned earlier, began to take root in American Reformed circles in the early twentieth century. At that time, a movement began to emerge pressing for more frequent celebration. Yet, for most, that meant monthly. By the end of that century, a renewed sacramental consciousness enabled those who wrote the "Directory for Worship" for the Presbyterian Church (U.S.A.) to include the word that it is appropriate to celebrate the supper as often as each Lord's Day.[35]

I entered ministry in a congregation that had been founded in the 1960s that was only fourteen years old when I became their second pastor. They had opted for celebrating monthly, and that remained the practice during my five and a half years with them. Thereafter, I served two congregations that moved from monthly to weekly celebration. No one in those latter congregations would tell you that weekly communion makes it "routine" or "less special" or is an infringement upon preaching—inevitably, the initial objections one hears when suggesting weekly celebration. When subsequent pastors or associates arrived, questioning the practice, wanting to change it back to monthly to give them a longer time to preach, their request was denied.

---

35. Office of the General Assembly, *Book of Order*, W–2.4009.

Sacramental Worship

Through the sacramental gifts of the word, baptism, bread, wine, and prayer, Christ becomes one with believers through the Spirit, so that in the Spirit, they become one with Christ and one with the Holy One he calls Father and receive all the benefits of that union—incarnational atonement received sacramentally.

This sacramental worship is essential if the church is to faithfully be Christ's body in the world. One can argue that the divisions and the hostilities across the church, in which Paul's rhetorical question about Christ being divided has been wrongly and tragically answered in the affirmative (1 Cor 1:13), find their roots in the lack of or abuse of such sacramental nurture. This is precisely Paul's word to the church in Corinth that had turned the supper into a meal that abused the poorer members of the community and was dividing it (1 Cor 11:18).

Someone recently asked me how Christians can officially profess love for others and be so mean to one another. I responded, somewhat sarcastically, "They are hungry, and we all get grouchy on empty stomachs." Yet, that is, indeed what Paul is saying to the Corinthians. Until the church shares a common table, there will be no unity.[36]

The argument that we cannot all come to Christ's table as one body until we are ecclesiastically, organically one has placed the cart before the horse and is a terrible theology of the nature of the church. We are not the source of unity. The more we have tried to make ourselves the source of it, the worse the situation has become. By now, that should be abundantly clear.

Without Christ as the head, and at the center and present in us, it will not come to be. Seeking such unity before instituting a common table is simply getting things backwards. It places responsibility for accord on people's ability to abandon the idols that have taken residence in our lives—especially our idols in the church and its governing structures—rather than taking Christ in and trusting him to cast out the false gods and other demons that seek to possess us. Such a church is receiving less than Christ is seeking to give and denying him the unity he still pleads for before the Father (John 17:11, 22).

---

36. This is also what was at issue in Antioch when Paul confronted Peter over withdrawing from the common table (Gal 2:11–16), and part of the issue that was supposed to be resolved at the Jerusalem council (Acts 15:4:1–29). Could Jewish and gentile Christians share the same table?

Many churches today are starving their parishioners, either through the lack of Christ-centered preaching, weekly communion, or denial of the supper—fencing the table—to enforce church discipline. If Jesus welcomed Judas at his table on the night Jesus instituted this meal, and did so knowing full well what Judas was up to, who are we to turn anyone away? This is not our table; it is Christ's table.

It is heartening to hear that announcement increasingly being included in invitations to the table. Those of us in need are not looking for advice, Bible stories, or texts explained and applied. We are looking for the proclamation of what God is doing in Christ in our often-confused lives and in this dreadfully distorted world right now, and the signs and seals that the gospel's promise of redemption is truly taking place in all of this and in us. God is overcoming evil, transforming it into good.

Becoming fully one in Christ enables Christ's body to identify who it is that makes it one rather than this or that issue that vies for our and the church's lordship daily. Being one in Christ opens the church to God's continuing work of atonement realized at least each Lord's Day until it is brought to its fullness in the last day. That last day may well be the personal moment when one is drawn into Christ's fuller and eternal glory and God's "nearer presence" through death—fully redeemed. Or it will be that final day the church continues to long for. Until then, we will continue to pray for that cosmic final day when all creation comes to its fulfillment, all is made new, and God is all in all (1 Cor 15:28).

At the End, It Is More Than Personal

Personal transformation is not enough. Becoming Christlike means being as he was in the world—for others. The more that is realized in us, the more we become sacraments of Christ in and to this world, whether "poured out" or simply "given" for it. The gospel calls Jesus' followers to be living sacrifices until God's continuing work of atonement is brought to its fullness in what theologians call the last day—the *eschaton*—the day of Jesus' final return.

The book of Revelation speaks of it symbolically as "the new heaven and the new earth" (Rev 21:1–7). It is that day when that promise comes into being for the entire cosmos, and God becomes all in all. In the marvelous words of Charles Wesley:

> Finish, then, Thy new creation; Pure and spotless let us be;

Let us see Thy great salvation, Perfectly restored in Thee;
Changed from glory into glory, Till in heaven we take our place,
Till we cast our crowns before Thee, Lost in wonder, love, and praise.[37]

That will be not only the omega point of God's creation but also the alpha of Christ's final reign.

Until that day, nurture in word and sacrament is essential on each Lord's Day. We encounter the risen Christ as he speaks to us. We say yes and accept his invitation to new and eternal life. We return Christ's invitation, embraced in baptism, and find the Spirit making us one with him. He feeds us on himself with the bread of life and the cup of salvation to sustain and make us new. We become who God created and calls us to be—members of God's new creation—strengthened and sustained for lives of faith and faithfulness as Christ's disciples in this broken world. From one degree of glory to another, the Spirit is transforming us into the fullness of Christ, restoring the image of God in us that we have seen revealed in him. Atonement is *realized* and *actualized* as we become one with Christ who became one with us, so that we could become one with God in him. And so, we continue to pray,

Come, Lord, come; come and make it so!
Amen!

---

37. Wesley, "Love Divine."

Bibliography

Anderson, Gary A. "Introduction to Israelite Religion." In *The New Interpreter's Bible*, edited by Leander E. Keck, 1:272–91. Nashville: Abingdon, 1994.

Anselm. *Cur Deus Homo: Why God Became Man*. Middletown, DE: Beloved, 2017.

Aquinas, Thomas. *The Summa Theologica*. Translated by Fathers of the English Dominican Province. Christian Classics Ethereal Library, 1947. https://www.ccel.org/a/aquinas/summa/FS.html.

Athanasius. *Contra Gentes* and *De Incarnatione*. Edited and translated by Robert W. Thomson. Oxford Early Christian Texts. Oxford, UK: Oxford University Press, 2004. First published 1971 by Oxford University Press (Oxford, UK).

Augustine. "Sermon 272." St. Anselm Institute, n.d. https://stanselminstitute.org/files/Augustine,%20Sermon%20272.pdf.

Aulén, Gustaf. *Christus Victor*. Translated by A. G. Herbert. Middletown, DE: Crossroad, 2017.

Baillie, Donald M. *God Was in Christ: An Essay on Incarnation and Atonement*. Reprint, Whitstable, UK: Whitstable Litho, 1977.

Balthasar, Hans Urs von. *Mysterium Paschale: The Mystery of Easter*. Translated by Aidan Nichols. San Francisco: Ignatius, 2000, 2005.

Barth, Karl. *The Doctrine of Reconciliation*. Edited by G. W. Bromiley and T. F. Torrance. Translated by John Newton Thomas and Thomas Wieser. *Church Dogmatics* IV/1. London: T&T Clark, 2010.

———. *The Humanity of God*. Atlanta: John Knox, 1978.

Bauer, Walter. *A Greek-English Lexicon of the New Testament and Other Early Christian Literature*. Edited by William F. Arndt and F. Wilber Gingric, revised and augmented by F. Wilber Gingrich and Frederick W. Danker. 2nd ed. Chicago: University of Chicago Press, 1979.

Beker, J. Christiaan. *Paul the Apostle: The Triumph of God in Life and Thought*. Philadelphia: Fortress, 1980.

Bible Hub. "3045. Yada." Bible Hub, n.d. https://biblehub.com/hebrew/3045.htm.

Boswell, James. "The Life of Samuel Johnson, LLD." eNotes, last updated Jan. 19, 2017. https://www.enotes.com/topics/life-samuel-johnson-ll-d/quotes/hell-paved-with-good-intentions.

Bradshaw, Paul, and Maxwell Johnson. *The Eucharistic Liturgies: Their Evolution and Interpretation*. Collegeville, MN: Liturgical, 1996.

Brown, Francis, ed. *The Didache with the Original Greek Text, Bilingual English-Greek*. Middletown, DE: Orkos, 2014.

Brown, Raymond E. *The Death of the Messiah*. 2 vols. New York: Doubleday, 1994.

———. *The Gospel According to John I–XII*. Anchor Bible 29. New York: Doubleday, 1966.

———. *The Gospel According to John XIII–XXI*. Anchor Bible 29a. New York: Doubleday, 1970.

———, et al. *New Jerome Biblical Commentary*. Englewood Cliffs, NJ: Prentice Hall, 1990.

Bushnell, Horace. *The Vicarious Sacrifice: Grounded in Principles Interpreted by Human Analogies*. 2 vols. Eugene, OR: Wipf & Stock, 2004.

Calvin, John. *Institutes of the Christian Religion*. Edited by John T. McNeill. 2 vols. Philadelphia: Westminster, 1960.

Campbell, J. McLeod. *The Nature of the Atonement*. Introduction by James B. Torrance. Eugene, OR: Wipf & Stock, 1999.

Chung, Hyun Kyung. *Struggle to Be the Sun Again: Introducing Asian Women's Theology*. Maryknoll, NY: Orbis, 1990.

Clifford, Cornelius. "St. Athanasius." From vol. 2 of *The Catholic Encyclopedia*, n.p. New York: Robert Appleton Company, 1907. http://www.newadvent.org/cathen/02035a.htm.

Collett, Don. "The Book of the Twelve." In *T&T Clark Companion to Atonement*, edited by Adam J. Johnson, Bloomsbury Companions, 411–15. London: Bloomsbury 2017.

"Compendium of the Catechism of the Catholic Church." Vatican, 2005. https://www.vatican.va/archive/compendium_ccc/documents/archive_2005_compendium-ccc_en.html.

Credit Suisse. *Global Wealth Report*. Zurich: Credit Suisse, 2018. https://www.credit-suisse.com/about-us/en/reports-research/global-wealth-report.html.

Daly, Robert J. *Sacrifice Unveiled: The True Meaning of Christian Sacrifice*. London: T&T Clark International, 2009.

Danker, Frederick William, with Kathryn Krug. *The Concise Greek-English Lexicon of the New Testament*. Chicago: University of Chicago Press, 2009.

Dewrell, Heath D. *Child Sacrifice in Ancient Israel: Explorations in Ancient Near Eastern Civilizations*. Winona Lake, IN: Eisenbrauns, 2017.

Diocese of Westminster. "What Is a Sacrament?" Diocese of Westminster, n.d. https://rcdow.org.uk/att/files/faith/catechesis/baptism/sacraments.pdf.

Donaldson, James, ed. *Constitutions of the Holy Apostles*. Christian Classics Ethereal Library, n.d. https://ccel.org/ccel/anonymous/constitutions/anf07.ix.ix.ii.html.

Early Church Texts. "The Nicene Creed—Agreed at the Council of Constantinople in 381." Early Church Texts, n.d. https://www.earlychurchtexts.com/public/nicene_creed.htm.

Eberhart, Christian A. *The Sacrifice of Jesus: Understanding Atonement Biblically*. Eugene, OR: Wipf & Stock, 2011.

Episcopal Church. *The Book of Common Prayer*. New York: Church Hymnal Corp. at the Seabury, 1977.

Fiddes, Paul S. *Past Event and Present Salvation*. Philadelphia: Westminster/John Knox, 1989.

Finlan, Stephen. *Problems with Atonement*. Collegeville, MN: Liturgical, 2005.

Fitzmyer, Joseph A. *The Gospel According to Luke X–XXIV*. Anchor Bible 28a. New York: Doubleday, 1982.

Fretheim, Terrence E. "Genesis." In *The New Interpreter's Bible*, edited by Leander E. Keck, 1:321–674. Nashville: Abingdon, 1994.

Friberg, Timothy, et al. *Analytical Lexicon of the Greek New Testament*. Baker's Greek New Testament Library. Grand Rapids: Baker, 2017.

Gaster, T. H. "Sacrifices." In *The Interpreter's Dictionary of the Bible*, edited by George Arthur Buttrick, 4:147–59. Nashville: Abingdon, 1962.

Gelles, David, and David Yaffe-Bellany. "Shareholder Value Is No Longer Everything, Top C.E.O.'s Say." *New York Times*, Aug. 19, 2019. https://www.nytimes.com/2019/08/19/business/business-roundtable-ceos-corporations.html.

General Board of Discipleship. "By Water and the Spirit: A United Methodist Understanding of Baptism." UMC Discipleship, 2008. https://www.umcdiscipleship.org/resources/by-water-and-the-spirit-full-text.

Gerrish, Brian A. *A Prince of the Church: Schleiermacher and the Beginnings of Modern Theology*. Eugene, OR: Wipf and Stock, 2001.

———. "Schleiermacher." In *The Oxford Companion to Christian Thought: Intellectual, Spiritual, and Moral Horizons of Christianity*, edited by Adrian Hastings et al., 644–46. Oxford, UK: Oxford University Press, 2000.

Grant, Jacquelyn. *White Women's Christ and Black Women's Jesus: Feminist Christology and Womanist Response*. Atlanta: Scholars, 1989.

Grotius, Hugo. *A Defense of the Catholic Faith Concerning the Satisfaction of Christ, against Faustus Socinus*. Translated by Frank Hugh Foster. Andover, MA: Draper, 1889. http://yoel.info/grotius.pdf.

Guyer, Paul. "The Crooked Timber of Mankind." https://www.cambridge.org/core/books/abs/kants-idea-for-a-universal-history-with-a-cosmopolitan-aim/crooked-timber-of-mankind/A3A16BCFC94272A01351387F8007C150.

Hagan, Kenneth. "Luther on Atonement." *Concordia Theological Quarterly* 61 (Oct. 1997) 251–76. http://www.ctsfw.net/media/pdfs/hagenklutheronatonement.pdf.

Hastings, Adrian. "Twentieth Century: An Overview." In *The Oxford Companion to Christian Thought: Intellectual, Spiritual, and Moral Horizons of Christianity*, edited by Adrian Hastings et al., 720–27. Oxford, UK: Oxford University Press, 2000.

———, et al., eds. "Reconciliation." In *The Oxford Companion to Christian Thought: Intellectual, Spiritual, and Moral Horizons of Christianity*, edited by Adrian Hastings et al., 597–98. Oxford, UK: Oxford University Press, 2000.

Hogan, Linda. "Feminist Theology." In *The Oxford Companion to Christian Thought: Intellectual, Spiritual, and Moral Horizons of Christianity*, edited by Adrian Hastings et al., 238–49. Oxford, UK: Oxford University Press, 2000.

Isasi-Diaz, Ada Maria. *En la Lucha/In the Struggle: Elaborting a Mujerista Theology*. 10th anniv. ed. Minneapolis: Augsburg, 2003.

Johnson, Luke Timothy. *Hebrews: A Commentary*. Louisville, KY: Westminster John Knox, 2006.

Jones, Lewis E. "Would You Be Free from the Burden of Sin?" Hymnary, 1899. https://hymnary.org/text/would_you_be_free_from_the_burden_jones.

Kaiser, Walter C., Jr. "The Book of Leviticus." In *The New Interpreter's Bible*, edited by Leander E. Keck, 1:985–1191. Nashville: Abingdon, 1994.

Kelly, J. N. D. *Early Christian Doctrines*. New York: HarperOne, 1978.

Lewis, Alan E. *Between Cross and Resurrection: A Theology of Holy Saturday*. Grand Rapids: Eerdmans, 2001.

Lewis, C. S. *The Lion, the Witch and the Wardrobe*. New York: Collier, 1950.

Luther, Martin. "Christ Lag in Todesbanden." Hymnary, 1524. https://hymnary.org/text/christ_lag_in_todesbanden.

———. *Small Catechism*. Book of Concord, n.d. http://bookofconcord.org/small-catechism/.

Manseau, Peter. "The Myth of the 'Good Guy with a Gun' Has Religious Roots." *New York Times*, June 23, 2022. https://www.nytimes.com/2022/06/23/opinion/uvalde-evangelicals-guns.html.

Martyr, Justin. "First Apology." Translated by Alexander Roberts and James Donaldson. Early Christian Writings, n.d. http://www.earlychristianwritings.com/text/justinmartyr-firstapology.html.

McCormack, Bruce L. *For Us and Our Salvation: Incarnation and Atonement in the Reformed Tradition*. Studies in Reformed Theology and History 1. Princeton, NJ: Princeton Seminary Press, 1993.

McDivitt, Heather. "Creation and the Spirit of God." Gifford Lectures, n.d. https://www.giffordlectures.org/lectures/creation-and-spirit-god.

Milgrom, Jacob. "Atonement in the Old Testament." In *Interpreter's Dictionary of the Bible, Supplementary Volume*, edited by Keith Crim, 78–82. Nashville: Abingdon, 1962.

———. *Leviticus: A Continental Commentary*. Minneapolis: Fortress, 2004.

———. "Sacrifices and Offerings, OT." In *Interpreter's Dictionary of the Bible, Supplementary Volume*, edited by Keith Crim, 763–71. Nashville: Abingdon, 1962.

MIT. "The Nicene-Constantinopolitan Creed." MIT, n.d. https://web.mit.edu/ocf/www/nicene_creed.html.

Moffitt, David M. "Hebrews." In *T&T Clark Companion to Atonement*, edited by Adam J. Johnson, Bloomsbury Companions, 533–36. London: Bloomsbury, 2017.

Monergism. "The Definition of the Council of Chalcedon (451 AD)." Monergism, n.d. https://www.monergism.com/definition-council-chalcedon-451-ad.

Moo, Douglas J. *The Epistle to the Romans*. Grand Rapids: Eerdmans, 1996.

Moltmann, Jürgen. *The Crucified God*. New York: Harper & Row, 1973.

Office of the General Assembly. *Book of Order 2019–2023: The Constitution of the Presbyterian Church (U.S.A.), Part II*. Louisville, KY: Presbyterian, 2019. https://www.pcusa.org/site_media/media/uploads/oga/pdf/2019-23-boo-elec_010621.pdf.

Pitre, Brant. *Jesus and the Last Supper*. Grand Rapids: Eerdmans, 2015.

Purkey, Donald R. *Holy Baptism and Services for the Renewal of Baptism*. Supplemental Liturgical Resources 2. Philadelphia: Westminster, 1985.

Raith, Charles, II. "Thomas Aquinas' Pauline Theology of the Atonement." In *T&T Clark Companion to Atonement*, edited by Adam J. Johnson, Bloomsbury Companions, 195–211. London: Bloomsbury T&T Clark, 2017.

Rauschenbusch, Walter. *Christianity and the Social Crisis*. New York: Macmillan, 1913.

Reuther, Rose Radford. *To Change the World: Christology and Cultural Criticism*. Chestnut Ridge, PA: Crossroad, 1981.

Richardson, Cyril C., ed. "An Exposition of the Faith: Selections from the Work *Against Heresies* by Irenaeus, Bishop of Lyons." In *Early Christian Fathers*, Library of Christian Classics 1, 343–97. Philadelphia: Westminster, 1953.

Roberts, Alexander, and James Donaldson, trans. "The Didache." Early Christian Writings, n.d. http://www.earlychristianwritings.com/text/didache-roberts.html.

Rutledge, Fleming. *The Crucifixion: Understanding the Death of Jesus Christ*. Grand Rapids: Eerdmans, 2015.

Sacraments Study Group. *Invitation to Christ: A Guide to Sacramental Practices*. Louisville, KY: Presbyterian Church (U.S.A.), 2006. https://www.presbyterianmission.org/wp-content/uploads/Invitation-to-Christ.pdf.

Sampley, J. Paul. "The First Letter to the Corinthians." In *The New Interpreter's Bible*, edited by Leander E. Keck, 10:771–1003. Nashville: Abingdon, 2002.

———. "The Second Letter to the Corinthians." In *The New Interpreter's Bible*, edited by Leander E. Keck, 11:3–180. Nashville: Abingdon, 2000.

Scandalon. "Aristotle: The Prime Mover." Scandalon, n.d. www.scandalon.co.uk/philosophy/aristotle_prime_mover.htm.

Schwarz, Hans. *Theology in a Global Context: The Last Two Hundred Years*. Grand Rapids: Eerdmans, 2005.

Schweitzer, Albert. *The Quest of the Historical Jesus: A Critical Study of Its Progress from Reimarus to Wrede*. Translated by W. Montgomery. Reprint with new formatting, Vancouver, Can.: Kshetra, 2016. First published 1910.

Sklar, Jay. *Leviticus*. Tyndale Old Testament Commentary 3. Downers Grove, IL: InterVarsity, 2014.

Sobrino, Jon. *Jesus the Liberator: A Historical-Theological Reading of Jesus of Nazareth*. Translated by Paul Burns and Francis McDonagh. Maryknoll, NY: Orbis, 1993.

Sölle, Dorothee. *Christ the Representative: An Essay in Theology after the "Death of God."* Translated by David Lewis. London: SCM, 1967.

Stratis, Justin. "Friedrick Schleiermacher." In *T&T Clark Companion to Atonement*, edited by Adam J. Johnson, Bloomsbury Companions, 739–42. London: T&T Clark, 2017.

Tanner, Kathryn. *Christ the Key*. Current Issues in Theology 7. Cambridge: Cambridge University Press, 2010.

Taylor, John V. *The Go-Between God: The Holy Spirit and the Christian Mission*. London: SCM, 1975.

Tietz, Christiane. *Karl Barth: A Life in Conflict*. Oxford, UK: Oxford University Press, 2021.

Torrance, Thomas F. *Atonement*. Edited by Robert T. Walker. Downers Grove, IL: IVP Academic, 2009.

———. *Incarnation*. Edited by Robert T. Walker. Downers Grove, IL: IVP Academic, 2008.

———. *The Trinitarian Faith: The Evangelical Theology of the Ancient Catholic Church*. 2nd ed. London: T&T Clark, 2016.

Trelstad, Marit A., ed. *Cross Examinations: Readings on the Meaning of the Cross Today*. Minneapolis: Augsburg Fortress, 2006

———. "The Cross in Context." In *Cross Examinations: Readings on the Meaning of the Cross Today*, edited by Marit Trelstad, 1–16. Minneapolis: Augsburg Fortress, 2006.

United States Conference of Catholic Bishops. "Christian Initiation of Adults." USCCB, n.d. http://www.usccb.org/beliefs-and-teachings/who-we-teach/rite-of-christian-initiation-of-adults.

Von Rad, Gerhard. *Genesis: A Commentary*. Philadelphia: Westminster, 1972.

Wesley, Charles. "Love Divine, All Loves Excelling." In *The Presbyterian Hymnal: Hymns, Psalms, and Spiritual Songs*, edited by LindaJo H. McKim, #376. Louisville, KY: Westminster/John Knox, 1990.

Westermann, Claus. *Genesis 1–11: Creation, Sin, and the Nature of God*. Minneapolis: Augsburg, 1987.

Williams, Deloris S. "Black Women's Surrogacy Experience and the Christian Notion of Redemption." In *Cross Examinations: Readings on the Meaning of the Cross Today*, edited by Marit Trelstad, 19–32. Minneapolis: Augsburg Fortress, 2006.

———. *Sisters in the Wilderness: The Challenge of Womanist God-Talk*. Maryknoll, NY: Orbis, 2013.

Williams, Thomas. "Saint Anselm." Stanford Encylopedia of Philosophy, May 18, 2000; substantive revision Dec. 8, 2020. https://plato.stanford.edu/entries/anselm/.

World Council of Churches. *Baptism, Eucharist and Ministry*. Faith and Order 111. Geneva: World Council of Churches, 1982. https://www.oikoumene.org/en/resources/documents/commissions/faith-and-order/i-unity-the-church-and-its-mission/baptism-eucharist-and-ministry-faith-and-order-paper-no-111-the-lima-text.

Wright, N. T. "Get the Story Right and the Models Will Fit." Plenary lecture, St. Andrews Symposium for Biblical and Early Christian Studies, June 4–6, 2018, St. Mary's College, Aberdeen, Scot.

———. *Simply Christian*. San Francisco: HarperOne, 2005.

For Further Reading

Ackerman, Susan. "Isaiah." In *The New Interpreter's Study Bible (New Revised Standard Version)*, edited by Walter J. Harrelson, 989–1049. Nashville: Abingdon, 2003.
Alter, Robert. *The Hebrew Bible: A Translation with Commentary*. 3 vols. New York: Norton & Co., 2019.
Allison, Dale C., Jr. *Jesus and the Covenant: A Response to E. P. Sanders*. JSNT 29 (1987) 57–78. https://doi.org/10.1177/0142064X8700902903.
Anderson, Gary A. "Sacrifice and Sacrificial Offerings (OT)." In *The Anchor Bible Dictionary*, edited by David Noel Freedman, 5:870–86. New York: Doubleday, 1992.
Athanasius. "On the Incarnation of the Word." In *Christology of the Later Fathers*, edited by Edward Rochie Hankey, translated by Archibald Robertson, 3:46–110. Philadelphia: Westminster, 1954.
Barker, Margaret. *The Risen Lord: The Jesus of History as the Christ of Faith*. Edited by Alasdair Heron and Iain Torrance. Scottish Journal of Theology. Edinburgh: T&T Clark, 1996.
Barrett, Matthew. "The Geneva Bible and Its Influence on the King James Bible." Founders Ministries, Fall 2011. https://founders.org/2011/10/12/the-geneva-bible-and-its-influence-on-the-king-james-bible.
Bartlett, Anthony W. *Cross Purposes: The Violent Grammar of the Christian Atonement*. Harrisburg, PA: Trinity International, 2001.
Behr, John. "Irenaeus of Lyons." In *T&T Clark Companion to Atonement*, edited by Adam J. Johnson, Bloomsbury Companions, 569–75. London: Bloomsbury, 2017.
Blenkinsopp, Joseph. "Introduction to the Pentateuch." In *The New Interpreter's Bible*, edited by Leander E. Keck, 1:305–18. Nashville: Abingdon, 1994.
Boersma, Hans. *Violence, Hospitality, and the Cross*. Grand Rapids: Baker Academic, 2006.
Borg, Marcus J., and John Dominic Crossan. *The First Paul: Reclaiming the Radical Visionary behind the Church's Conservative Icon*. New York: Harper One, 2009.
Bornkamm, Günter. *Early Christian Experience*. New York: Harper and Row, 1969.
Braaten, Carl E. "Lutheranism." In *The Oxford Companion to Christian Thought: Intellectual, Spiritual, and Moral Horizons of Christianity*, edited by Adrian Hastings et al., 401–3. Oxford, UK: Oxford University Press, 2000.
Brock, Rita Nakashima. "The Cross of Resurrection and Communal Redemption." In *Cross Examinations*, edited by Marit Trelstad, 241–51. Minneapolis: Augsburg Fortress, 2006.

———, and Rebecca Anne Parker. *Proverbs of Ashes: Violence, Redemptive Suffering and the Search for What Saves Us*. Boston: Beacon, 2001.
Brown, Peter. *Power and Persuasion in Late Antiquity: Towards a Christian Empire*. Madison: University of Wisconsin Press, 1992.
Brueggemann, Walter. "Exodus." In *The New Interpreter's Bible*, edited by Leander E. Keck, 1:677–981. Nashville: Abingdon, 1994.
———. *Genesis*. Interpretation: A Bible Commentary for Teaching and Preaching. Atlanta: John Knox, 1982.
———. *Worship in Ancient Israel: An Essential Guide*. Nashville: Abingdon, 2005.
Byrne, Brendan, SJ. *Romans*. Edited by Daniel J. Harrington, SJ. Sacra Pagina 6. Collegeville, MN: Liturgical, 1996.
Cameron, Euan. "Luther, Martin." In *The Oxford Companion to Christian Thought: Intellectual, Spiritual, and Moral Horizons of Christianity*, edited by Adrian Hastings et al., 398–401. Oxford, UK: Oxford University Press, 2000.
Campbell, J. Y. "Son of Man." In *A Theological Word Book of the Bible*, edited by Alan Richardson, 230–23. New York: Macmillian, 1950.
Carbine, Rosemary P. "Contextualizing the Cross for the Sake of Subjectivity." In *Cross Examinations: Readings on the Meaning of the Cross Today*, edited by Marit Trelstad, 91–108. Minneapolis: Augsburg Fortress, 2006.
Carpenter, E. E. "Sacrifice, Human." In *The International Standard Bible Encyclopedia*, edited by Geoffrey W. Bromiley, 4:258–60. Grand Rapids: Eerdmans, 1988.
———. "Sacrifices and Offerings in the Old Testament." In *The International Standard Bible Encyclopedia*, edited by Geoffrey W. Bromiley, 4:260–73. Grand Rapids: Eerdmans, 1988.
Cavern, Toni, and Walter J. Harrelson. "The Psalms." In *The New Interpreter's Study Bible (New Revised Standard Version)*, edited by Walter J. Harrelson, 749–52. Nashville: Abingdon, 2003.
———. "Excursus: Death, Future Life, and Sheol." In *The New Interpreter's Study Bible (New Revised Standard Version)*, edited by Walter J. Harrelson, 835–36. Nashville: Abingdon, 2003.
Chapman, Steven B. "God's Reconciling Work: Atonement in the Old Testament." In *T&T Clark Companion to Atonement*, edited by Adam J. Johnson, Bloomsbury Companions, 95–113. London: Bloomsbury, 2017.
Charles, R. H. *The Apocrypha and Pseudepigrapha of the Old Testament*. Oxford, UK: Clarendon, 1913. Edited for Pseudepigrapha by Joshua Williams. http://www.pseudepigrapha.com/jubilees/index.htm.
Cone, James. *A Black Theology of Liberation*. New York: Orbis, 2020.
Conrad, Edgar W. "Satan." In *The New Interpreter's Dictionary of the Bible*, edited by Katharine Doob Sakenfeld, 5:112–16. Nashville: Abingdon, 2009.
Davies, Brian, OP. "Aquinas, Thomas." In *The Oxford Companion to Christian Thought: Intellectual, Spiritual, and Moral Horizons of Christianity*, edited by Adrian Hastings et al., 33–36. Oxford, UK: Oxford University Press, 2000.
———, and G. R. Evans, eds. *Anselm of Canterbury: The Major Works*. Oxford, UK: Oxford University Press, 2008.
Douglas, John Hall. "Theology of the Cross: Challenges and Opportunities for the Post-Christian Church." In *Cross Examinations; Readings on the Meaning of the Cross Today*, edited by Marit Trelstad, 252–58. Minneapolis: Augsburg Fortress, 2006.

Dozeman, Thomas B. "The Book of Numbers." In *The New Interpreter's Bible*, edited by Leander E. Keck, 2:3–268. Nashville: Abingdon, 1998.
Eberhart, Christian A. *What a Difference a Meal Makes: The Last Supper in the Bible and in the Christian Church*. Translated by Michael Putman. Houston: Lucid, 2016.
Fairweather, Eugene R., ed. *A Scholastic Miscellany: Anselm to Ockham*. Library of Christian Classics 10. Philadelphia: Westminster, 1956.
Finlan, Stephen. *Salvation Not Purchased: Overcoming the Ransom Idea to Rediscover the Original Gospel Teaching*. Eugene, OR: Cascade, 2020.
Florovsky, Georges. *The Byzantine Fathers of the Fifth Century*. Edited by Richard S. Haugh and Raymond Miller. Vol. 8 of *Collected Works of Georges Florovsky*. Belmont, MA: Büchervertriebsanstalt, 1987.
Fretheim, Terrence E. *The Suffering of God*. Fortress, 1984.
Gonzáles, Justo L. *Christian Thought Revisited*. New York: Orbis, 1999.
———. *The Story of Christianity*. 2 vols. Revised and updated ed. New York: HarperOne, 2010.
Gorman, Frank H. "Sacrifices and Offerings." In *The New Interpreter's Dictionary of the Bible*, edited by Katharine Doob Sakenfeld, 5:20–32. Nashville: Abingdon, 2009.
Green, Joel B., and Mark D. Baker. *Recovering the Scandal of the Cross*. Downers Grove, IL: InterVarsity, 2000.
Greenstein, Edward L. "Making *Non*-sense of the 10th Plague." *Masoret* (Winter 1994): 16–17.
Hall, Douglas John. *God and Human Suffering: An Exercise in the Theology of the Cross*. Minneapolis: Augsburg, 1989.
Hardy, Edward Rochie. *Christology of the Later Fathers*. Edited by Henry Chadwick. Library of Christian Classics 3. Philadelphia: Westminster, 1954.
Harrington, Daniel J., SJ. "Introduction to the Canon." In *The New Interpreter's Bible*, edited by Leander E. Keck, 1:7–21. Nashville: Abingdon, 1994.
Harrisville, Roy A. *Fracture: The Cross as Irreconcilable in the Language and Thought of the Biblical Writer*. Grand Rapids: Eerdmans, 2006.
Hayes, John H. "Leviticus." In *The New Interpreter's Study Bible (New Revised Standard Version)*, edited by Walter J. Harrelson, 145–88. Nashville: Abingdon, 2003.
Hedges, Christopher. *War Is a Force That Gives Us Meaning*. New York: Anchor, 2003.
Heim, Mark S. *Saved from Sacrifice: A Theology of the Cross*. Grand Rapids: Eerdmans, 2006.
———. "Saved by What Shouldn't Happen." In *Cross Examinations: Readings on the Meaning of the Cross Today*, edited by Marit Trelstad, 211–24. Minneapolis: Augsburg Fortress, 2006.
Hengel, Martin. *The Atonement: The Origins of the Doctrine in the New Testament*. Eugene, OR: Wipf & Stock, 1981.
Henze, Mathias. "Daniel." In *The New Interpreter's Study Bible (New Revised Standard Version)*, edited by Walter J. Harrelson, 1231–52. Nashville: Abingdon, 2003.
Herbert, A. G. "Atone, Atonement." In *A Theological Word Book of the Bible*, edited by Alan Richardson, 25–26. New York: Macmillian, 1950.
Hiebert, Theodore. "Genesis." In *The New Interpreter's Study Bible (New Revised Standard Version)*, edited by Walter J. Harrelson, 1–84. Nashville: Abingdon, 2003.
Holloway, Ben. "Tanner's Atonement." Holloway Quarterly, Aug. 25, 2021. http//hollowayquarterly.com/tanners-atonement/.

Jenson, Robert W. *The Triune God*. Vol. 1 of *Systematic Theology*. New York: Oxford University Press, 1997.
Jersak, Brad, and Michael Hardin, eds. *Stricken by God? Nonviolent Identification & the Victory of Christ*. Abbotsford, Can.: Fresh Wind, 2007.
Jewish Virtual Library. "Judaism: Akedah." From *Encyclopaedia Judaica* (N.p.: Gale, 2008). https://www.jewishvirtuallibrary.org/akedah.
Johnson, Adam J. "Atonement, the Shape and State of the Doctrine." In *T&T Clark Companion to Atonement*, edited by Adam J. Johnson, Bloomsbury Companions, 1–17. London: Bloomsbury, 2017.
———. "René Girard." In *T&T Clark Companion to Atonement*, edited by Adam J. Johnson, Bloomsbury Companions, 505–508. London: Bloomsbury T&T Clark, 2017.
Johnson, Luke Timothy. *The Real Jesus: The Misguided Quest of the Historical Jesus and the Truth of the Traditional Gospels*. New York: HarperCollins, 1996.
Jones, Paul Dafydd. "The Fury of Love: Calvin on the Atonement." In *T&T Clark Companion to Atonement*, edited by Adam J. Johnson, Bloomsbury Companions, 213–35. London: Bloomsbury, 2017.
Josephus, Flavius. *The Antiquities of the Jews: Complete and Unabridged*. Middletown, DE: Renaissance Classics, 2012.
———. *The Jewish Wars*. New York: Penguin Classics, 1984.
Kannengiesser, Charles. "Athanasius." In *The Oxford Companion to Christian Thought: Intellectual, Spiritual, and Moral Horizons of Christianity*, edited by Adrian Hastings et al., 47–49. Oxford, UK: Oxford University Press, 2000.
Kittle, Gerhard. "Hilistarion, Hilasmos, Lutron." In *A Theological Dictionary of the New Testament*, edited by Geoffrey Bromiley and Gerhard Kittle, translated by Geoffrey Bromiley, 3:300–16. Grand Rapids: Eerdmans, 1977.
Klauck, Hans-Josef. "Sacrifice and Sacrificial Offerings (NT)." In *The Anchor Bible Dictionary*, edited by David Noel Freedman, translated by Reginald H. Fuller, 5:886–91. New York: Doubleday, 1992.
Knight, Douglas A. "Joshua." In *The New Interpreter's Study Bible (New Revised Standard Version)*, edited by Walter J. Harrelson, 303–40. Nashville: Abingdon, 2003.
———. "Excursus: The Israelite Conquest of Canaan." In *The New Interpreter's Study Bible (New Revised Standard Version)*, edited by Walter J. Harrelson, 307–8. Nashville: Abingdon, 2003.
Kohler, Kaufmann, and Emil G. Hirsh. "Crucifixion." Jewish Encyclopedia, 1906. https://jewishencyclopedia.com/articles/4782-crucifixion.
Leech, Kenneth. *The Eye of the Storm: Spiritual Resources for the Pursuit of Jesus*. London: Darton, Longman, and Todd, 1992.
Levenson, Jon D. *The Death and Resurrection of the Beloved Son*. New Haven, CT: Yale University Press, 1993.
Levine, B. A. "Priests." In *The Interpreter's Dictionary of the Bible, Supplementary Volume*, edited by Keith Crim, 687–90. Nashville: Abingdon, 1962.
Litwa, M. David. "The Wondrous Exchange: Irenaeus and Easter Valentinians on the Soteriology of Interchange." *Journal of Early Christian Studies* 22 (Sept. 2014) 311–41.
Loewenich, Walther von. *Luther's Theology of the Cross*. Translated by Herbert J. A. Bouman. Belfast: Christian Journals, 1976.

Madden, Thomas, ed. *The Crusades: The Essential Readings*. Oxford, UK: Blackwell, 2002.
Mann, Alan. *Atonement for a Sinless Society*. 2nd ed. Eugene, OR: Cascade, 2015.
Mathews, Thomas R. *The Clash of the Gods: A Reinterpretation of Early Christian Art*. Princeton, NJ: Princeton University Press, 1993.
McDaniel, Jay B. "The Passion of Christ." In *Cross Examinations: Readings on the Meaning of the Cross Today*, edited by Marit Trelstad, 196–207. Minneapolis: Augsburg Fortress, 2006.
McGrath, Alister E. *Luther's Theology of the Cross*. Oxford, UK: Basil Blackwell, 1985.
McKnight, Scot. *A Community Called Atonement*. Living Theology. Nashville: Abingdon, 2007.
McLeish, Tom. "The 20 (+) Creation Stories in the Bible." Faith and Wisdom in Science, Nov. 3, 2014. https://tcbmcleish.wordpress.com/2014/11/03/the-20-creation-stories-in-the-bible.
Mettinger, Tryggve N. D. *The Riddle of Resurrection: "Dying and Rising Gods" in the Ancient Near East*. Stockholm: Almqvist & Wiksell, 2001.
Milgrom, Jacob. "Day of Atonement." In *Interpreter's Dictionary of the Bible, Supplementary Volume*, edited by Keith Crim, 82–83. Nashville: Abingdon, 1962.
Moltmann, Jürgen. "The Cross as Military Symbol for Sacrifice," *Cross Examinations: Readings on the Meaning of the Cross Today*, edited by Marit Trelstad, 259–63. Minneapolis: Augsburg Fortress, 2006.
———. "The Crucified God; Yesterday and Today: 1972–2002." In *Cross Examinations: Readings on the Meaning of the Cross Today*, edited by Marit Trelstad, 127–38. Minneapolis: Augsburg Fortress, 2006.
Nazianzus, Gregory of. "Oration 21." Translated by Charles Gordon Browne and James Edward Swallow. From *Nicene and Post-Nicene Fathers*, edited by Philip Schaff and Henry Wace, 2nd ser., 7. Buffalo, NY: Christian Literature, 1894. Revised and edited for New Advent by Kevin Knight. http://www.newadvent.org/fathers/310221.htm.
Newsom, Carol A. "The Book of Job." In *The New Interpreter's Bible*, edited by Leander E. Keck, 4:319–637. Nashville: Abingdon, 1969.
North, C. R. "Sacrifice." In *A Theological Word Book of the Bible*, edited by Alan Richardson, 206–14. New York: Macmillian, 1950.
Olson, Dennis L. "Emotion, Repentance and the Question of the 'Inner Life' of Biblical Israelites: A Case Study of Hosea 6:1–3." In *Mixed Feelings and Vexed Passions in Biblical Literature*, edited by E. Scott Spencer, 161–76. Atlanta: Society of Biblical Literature, 2017.
Oulton, John Ernest Leonard. *Alexandrian Christianity*. Edited by Henry Chadwick. Library of Christian Classics 2. Philadelphia: Westminster, 1954.
Patterson, Stephen J. *Beyond the Passion: Rethinking the Death and Life of Jesus*. Minneapolis: Fortress, 2004.
Paul, Robert S. *The Atonement and the Sacraments*. New York: Abingdon, 1960.
Perkins, Pheme. "The Gospel of Mark." In *The New Interpreter's Bible*, edited by Leander E. Keck, 8:509–733. Nashville: Abingdon, 1995.
Perrin, Norman. "Son of Man." In *The Interpreter's Dictionary of the Bible, Supplementary Volume*, edited by Keith Crim, 833–36. Nashville: Abingdon, 1962.

Pyper, Hugh S. "Adam." In *The Oxford Companion to Christian Thought: Intellectual, Spiritual, and Moral Horizons of Christianity*, edited by Adrian Hastings et al., 6. Oxford, UK: Oxford University Press, 2000.

———. "Melchizedek." In *The Oxford Companion to Christian Thought: Intellectual, Spiritual, and Moral Horizons of Christianity*, edited by Adrian Hastings et al., 420–21. Oxford, UK: Oxford University Press, 2000.

———. "Messiah." In *The Oxford Companion to Christian Thought: Intellectual, Spiritual, and Moral Horizons of Christianity*, edited by Adrian Hastings et al., 425. Oxford, UK: Oxford University Press, 2000.

Quinn, Philip L. "Atonement, Theories of." In *The Oxford Companion to Christian Thought: Intellectual, Spiritual, and Moral Horizons of Christianity*, edited by Adrian Hastings et al., 51–52. Oxford, UK: Oxford University Press, 2000.

Recht, Laerke. "Human Sacrifice in the Ancient Near East." Academia, 2010. https://www.academia.edu/1561457/Human_sacrifice_in_the_ancient_Near_East.

Richardson, Alan, ed. "Adam, Man." In *A Theological Word Book of the Bible*, edited by Alan Richardson, 15. New York: Macmillian, 1950.

Richardson, Cyril C. "Introduction." Introduction to "On the Incarnation of the Word," by Athanasius, in *Christology of the Later Fathers*, edited by Edward Rochie Hanky, 3:41–43. Philadelphia: Westminster, 1954.

Rivkin, Ellis. "Messiah." In *The Interpreter's Dictionary of the Bible, Supplementary Volume*, edited by Keith Crim, 588–91. Nashville: Abingdon, 1962.

———. "Pharisee." *The Interpreter's Dictionary of the Bible, Supplementary Volume*, edited by Keith Crim, 657–63. Nashville: Abingdon, 1962.

Ross, Ellen M. *The Grief of God: Images of the Suffering Jesus in Late Medieval England*. New York: Oxford University Press, 1997.

Schiller, Gertrude. *The Passion of Jesus Christ*. Vol. 2 of *Iconography of Christian Art*. Translated by Janet Seligman. London: Humphries, 1972.

Schnackenburg, Rudolf. *The Church in the New Testament*. New York: Herder and Herder, 1965.

Schreiner, T. R. "Sacrifices and Offerings in the NT." In *the International Standard Bible Encyclopedia*, edited by Geoffrey W. Bromiley, Gen. Ed., 4:273–77. Grand Rapids: Eerdmans, 1988.

Schwager, Raymund, SJ. *Banished from Eden: Original Sin and Evolutionary Theory in the Drama of Savlation*. Leominster, UK: Gracewing, 2006.

———. *Must There Be Scapegoats? Violence and Redemption in the Bible*. New York: Crossroad, 1987.

Smythe, Shannon Nicole. "Karl Barth." In *T&T Clark Companion to Atonement*, edited by Adam J. Johnson, Bloomsbury Companions, 237–55. London: Bloomsbury, 2017.

Snaith, N. H. "Righteous, Righteousness." In *A Theological Word Book of the Bible*, edited by Alan Richardson, 202–4. New York: Macmillian, 1950.

———. "Wrath, Anger, Indignation." In *A Theological Word Book of the Bible*, edited by Alan Richardson, 289–90. New York: Macmillian, 1950.

Solbert, Mary. *Compelling Knowledge: A Feminist Proposal for an Epistemology of the Cross*. Albany: State University of New York, 1997.

———. "All That Matters." In *Cross Examinations: Readings on the Meaning of the Cross Today*, edited by Marit Trelstad, 139–53. Minneapolis: Augsburg Fortress, 2006.

Spensley, Barbara. "Hebrews, Epistle to the." In *The Oxford Companion to Christian Thought: Intellectual, Spiritual, and Moral Horizons of Christianity*, edited by Adrian Hastings et al., 288–89. Oxford, UK: Oxford University Press, 2000.

Stevenson, Peter K. "John McLeod Campbell." In *T&T Clark Companion to Atonement*, edited by Adam J. Johnson, Bloomsbury Companions, 421–26. London: T&T Clark, 2017.

Streufert, Mary J. "Maternal Sacrifice as a Hermeneutic of the Cross." In *Cross Examinations: Readings on the Meaning of the Cross Today*, edited by Marit Trelstad, 63–73. Minneapolis: Augsburg Fortress, 2006.

Tatlock, Jason T. "Sacrifice, Human." In *The New Interpreter's Dictionary of the Bible*, edited by Katharine Doob Sakenfeld, 5:18–20. Nashville: Abingdon, 2009.

———. "The Place of Human Sacrifice in the Israelite Cult." In *Ritual and Metaphor: Sacrifice in the Bible*, edited by Christian Eberhart, 33–48. Atlanta: Society of Biblical Literature, 2011.

Taylor, F. J. "Savior." In *A Theological Word Book of the Bible*, edited by Alan Richardson, 220. New York: Macmillian, 1950.

Taylor, Laim. Review of *Jesus, Humanity and the Trinity*, by Kathryn Tanner. *Themelios* 28 (Sept 2002) n.p. https://www.thegospelcoalition.org/themelios/review/jesus-humanity-and-the-trinity/.

Tenney, Merrill C., ed. "Psalms of Solomon." Bible Gateway, n.d. Orig. from *Zondervan Pictorial Encyclopedia of the Bible* (Grand Rapids: Zondervan, 1975), 5 vols. https://www.biblegateway.com/resources/encyclopedia-of-the-bible/Psalms-Solomon.

Terrell, JoAnne Marie. "Our Mother's Gardens: Rethinking Sacrifice." In *Cross Examinations: Readings on the Meaning of the Cross Today*, edited by Marit Trelstad, 33–49. Minneapolis: Augsburg Fortress, 2006.

Tertullian. *On Repentance (De Paetintia)*. Translated by S. Thelwall. Tertullian, Dec. 14, 2001; last modified Feb. 3, 1998. http://www.tertullian.org/anf/anf03/anf03-47.htm#P11376_3226496.

Thompson, Deanna A. "Becoming a Feminist Theologian of the Cross." In *Cross Examinations: Readings on the Meaning of the Cross Today*, edited by Marit Trelstad, 76–90. Minneapolis: Augsburg Fortress, 2006.

Tilden, Elwyn E., and Bruce Metzger. "The Gospel According to Mark." In *The New Oxford Annotated Bible*, 47. New York: Oxford University Press, 1991.

Tolbert, Mary Ann. "The Gospel According to Mark." In *The New Interpreter's Study Bible (New Revised Standard Version)*, edited by Walter J. Harrelson, 1801–45. Nashville: Abingdon, 2003.

Torrance, Thomas F. *Theology in Reconciliation: Essays Towards Evangelical and Catholic Unity in East and West*. London: Geoffrey Chapman, 1975.

Toy, Crawford Howell. "The Psalms of Solomon." Jewish Encyclopedia, 1906. https://www.jewishencyclopedia.com/articles/12411-psalms-of-solomon-the.

Trelstad, Marit A. "Lavish Love." In *Cross Examinations: Readings on the Meaning of the Cross Today*, edited by Marit Trelstad, 109–24. Minneapolis: Augsburg Fortress, 2006.

VanderKam, James. "Culture and Religion among the Ancient Israelites." In *The New Interpreter's Study Bible (New Revised Standard Version)*, edited by Walter J. Harrelson, 2274–79. Nashville: Abingdon, 2003.

Van der Woude, Adam Simon. "Melchizedek." *The Interpreter's Dictionary of the Bible, Supplementary Volume*, edited by Keith Crim, 585–86. Nashville: Abingdon, 1962.

Walker, Bill. "Anthropology and Soteriology in Walter Kasper and Kathryn Tanner (with a little bit of Pannenberg)." William A. Walker III, Oct. 22, 2010. http://wawalker.com/anthropology-and-soteriology-in-walter-kasper-and-kathryn-tanner-with-a-little-bit-of-pannenberg.
Watson, Duane E. "Evil/Evil One." In *The Anchor Bible Dictionary*, edited by David Noel Freedman, 2:678–79. New York: Doubleday, 1992.
Weaver, J. Denny. *The Nonviolent Atonement*. 2nd ed. Grand Rapids: Eerdmans, 2011.
———. "Violence in Christian Theology." In *Cross Examinations: Readings on the Meaning of the Cross Today*, edited by Marit Trelstad, 225–39. Minneapolis: Augsburg Fortress, 2006.
Weinandy, Thomas G. "Athanasius' Incarnational Soteriology." In *T&T Clark Companion to Atonement*, edited by Adam J. Johnson, Bloomsbury Companions, 135–54. London: T&T Clark, 2017.
Weingart, Richard E. *The Logic of Divine Love: A Critical Analysis of the Soteriology of Peter Abelard*. Oxford, UK: Clarendon, 1970.
Wenham, Gordon J. *The Book of Leviticus*. Grand Rapids: Eerdmans, 1979.
Williams, George Huntston. *Anselm: Communion and Atonement*. Saint Louis: Concordia, 1968.
Williams, Rowan. *Resurrection: Interpreting the Easter Gospel*. Cleveland: Pilgrim, 2003.
Wink, Walter. *Naming the Powers: The Language of Power in the New Testament*. Philadelphia: Fortress, 1984.
Wright, N. T. *Jesus and the Victory of God*. Minneapolis: Fortress, 1997.
———. *Evil and the Justice of God*. Downers Grove, IL: InterVarsity, 2006.
———. *How God Became King*. San Francisco: HarperOne, 2012.
———. *Paul: A Biography*. San Francisco: HarperOne, 2018.
———. *The Day the Revolution Began*. San Francisco: Harper One, 2016.
———. *The New Testament and the People of God*. Minneapolis: Fortress, 1992.
———, et al. *What Did the Cross Accomplish: A Conversation About the Atonement*. Louisville, KY: Westminster John Knox, 2021.
Yee, Gale A. "The Book of Hosea." In *The New Interpreter's Bible*, edited by Leander E. Keck, 7:288–93. Nashville: Abingdon, 1969.

Subject Index

Aaron, sons of, 88
abad (Hebrew), 87, 91
abandonment, 219
  during Jesus' death, 188
Abel, 80, 84, 86
Abelard, Peter, 141–145, 154, 156, 160, 165, 170
  influence on Bushnell, 162
Abraham, 84, 103, 211, 213, 224
  God's promise to, 3, 22, 208
  offspring, 241
Abram, 83–85, 86
abuse of women, 195
acceptance theory, 141n13
actions, 25, 34
  on behalf of marginalized, 193
Adam, 70–72, 213, 237
  deception of, 135
  disobedience of, 136
  second, 214
adam, word meaning, 70
Adam/Christ typology, 238
affusion, 47, 48
age of discernment, 264
age of reason, 153
agnostics, 6
agorazo (Greek), 127
akedah (Hebrew), 84, 102
Alexander the Great, 8, 212
alienation, 181–182
altars, 88
  contamination of, 97
alteration, 56
American German Baptist church, 163

American Protestantism
  fundamentalist-modernist divide in, 167
  liberalism in, 160–163
American society, social evils of, 164
Amos, 89
Anabaptist tradition, 34
  and frequency of communion, 276
Anabaptists, 47n9, 48, 256
Anak, 89
analogy, in Bible, 162
anamnesis (Greek), 27, 270–271
anaphero (Greek), 118
ancient texts, investigation of, 167
Anderson, Fred R., autobiography of, 12–20
angel of death, 21–22
Anglican church, 34, 61, 152, 267
  and creed, 44
animal, in sacrifice, 93
annulment, 118
anointing, 33, 256
anointing with oil, 255
Anselm (saint), 6, 139, 140, 148
  Aulén and, 170
  influence on Luther, 145–146
  theory of atonement, 143–145
anti-liberal antagonism, 167
Antiochus Epiphanes IV, 212, 213, 124–125
anti-Trinitarian, 152
apartheid, theology addressing, 194
Apollos, 130
apology, 40
apostasy, 102, 106, 210, 212

Apostles' Creed, 44–45
Apostolic Constitutions, 56
apotropaic ritual, 104
apotropaic sign, 22
appearances, 62, 240
Aquila, 130
Aramaic, 8
arche (Greek), 67
Ark of the Covenant, 38, 39, 87, 90, 100, 112
Arminianism, 150
Armines, Jacob, 150–152
Arrupe, Pedro, 194
asam (Hebrew), 95–96, 107
ascension, 31, 233, 238
assurance of faith, 158
Assyria, 209, 210
Athanasius, 55–56, 60, 66, 77, 138, 172, 180, 246–248, 253
   atonement theology of, 137
   influence on Campbell, 158
   influence on Tanner, 197
athetesis (Greek), 118
atonement, 34–38, 113, 225, 268, 271, 273
   for all, 158
   Aquinas' writing on, 143–145
   Aulén on, 170
   Bible and theologians on, 1
   biblical narrative shift from, 208
   broadness of, 3–4
   Bushnell on, 161, 162
   as center of Christian theology, 197
   as change, 163
   contemporary theological thought on, 196
   as cruel doctrine, 197
   and death of Jesus, 223
   definition of, 3
   development of concept, 148
   different meanings of, 40
   embraced sacramentally, 184–185
   forgiveness of sins, 275
   God's work of salvation, 182
   and God's wrath or love, 176
   for Israel, 182
   Jesus suffering and, 144, 145, 177
   magical view of, 156
   means of, 253
   need for, 67–85
   as overcoming sin, 178
   place of, 112–116
   propitiatory view of, 152
   Protestant Christian thought on, 165
   and psychology, 156
   Rauschenbusch's doctrine of, 164
   realization of, 279
   recapitulation model of, 138
   relationship with sacraments, 34
   as result of God's love, 147
   sacrifice and, 102, 114, 117
   and sociology, 156
   theories of, 2
   Trinitarian doctrine of, 186
   in twentieth century theologies, 174–191
   works by atheist social activists, 243
atonement theology, 63, 80
   Aulén and, 172
   Ballie and, 174
   in English, 37
   feminist objections to, 195
   image of Jesus as new Adam, 235
   and philosophy, 6
atonement theories, 252
   based on incarnation, 200
   Campbell work to change, 159
   in Catholic church, 145
   critique of, 205
   historical transitions, 208
   in Protestant church, 145
   of satisfaction, 142, 153, 170, 172
   of substitution, 110–111, 153
auditory union, 240
Augustine of Hippo (saint), 33, 56, 81, 135, 223, 255
   theology of, 139
Augustus, 133–134
Aulén, Gustav, 170
Azazel (Hebrew), 101, 110–112

Babylon, 209, 210, 211
Bahá'í, 194
Baillie, Donald M., 174
Ballie, John, 179

Subject Index

Balthasar, Hans Urs von, 227
baptism, 5, 32–34, 46–53, 128,
    184–185, 223, 228, 232, 237, 245,
    254, 255–256, 261
  as adult, 263
  in ancient church, 47–52
  of children, 264
  church's difference in doctrine, 63
  effusion, 267
  in history vs. today, 41–66
  immersion, 267
  of infants, 264
  of Jesus, 216, 221
  of John, 50
  and link to Christ, 203
  methods of, 265–266
  preparation for, 263
  and reconciliation with God, 36
  for remission of sins, 262
  renewal of promises, 273
  as rite of initiation, 48
  sprinkling, 267
  symbolism in, 267
  training, 265
  as union with Christ, 262–263
  vows, 262
  water, 262, 273
  what happens in, 266
Baptism, Eucharist and Ministry
  (BEM), 63, 257, 266
baptismal candidates, 265–266
baptismal confession, Apostles' Creed
  and, 45
baptismal discipline, 264
baptismal fonts, 266
baptismal pools, 48
baptismal union, 239, 240–241
Baptists, 267
Barnes, Craig, 260n14
Barth, Karl, 174–180, 197
  dialectical method, 186
  influence on Moltmann, 185
Bathsheba, 106
Baxter, Richard, 152
Bediako, Kwame, 194
being "like God," 77
belief, 30
Benedict XVI (pope), 193n3

Berengar of Tours, 57–58
bereshit (Hebrew), 67
Bethany, 226
Bethel, 84–85, 86
Beza, Theodore, 158n11
Bible, 8
  prehistoric portion of, 67
  study, 264
  translations, 9–10
biblical exegesis, 121
biblical sacrifice, vs. pagan sacrifice,
  131
biblical storyteller, 71
biblical theologian, 136
Big Bang, God as source of, 69
Black Theology and Black Power
  (Cone), 194
A Black Theology of Liberation, 194
blame, 75
blasphemous sins, 98
blessing, 24
blood, 26, 39
  function of, 116
  holiness of, 97
  of Jesus, 28, 30, 115, 269
  in Jesus' death, 222–223
  life in, 105, 115
  manipulation, 105, 111
  power of, 131
  propitiation by, 114
  to purge, 38
  in sacrifice, 92–93, 100
  sprinkling of, 113
blood sacrifice, 119, 157
body of Jesus, 25, 28, 269, 272
Boesak, Allan, 194
Boff, Leonardo, 193
bondage, 145
Bonino, José Miguez, 193
Børresen, Kari, 193n2
bread, 28, 270, 272
  breaking of, 52–53
  in Eucharist, 57
  figurative vs. literal, 54–55
  as Jesus' body, 218
"bread of life," 30, 260, 269, 274
Brown, Raymond E., 31, 269
Buddhism, 194

burning bush, 70
burnt offering altar, 93
burnt offerings, 91–92, 95, 117
Bushnell, Horace, 160–163, 165
Byungmu, Ahn, 193n2
Byzantine church, schism with Roman Catholic church, 45–46, 58, 139, 255
Byzantium Empire, 46

Cain, 80, 82, 84, 86
Caleb, 89
Calvin, John, 34, 59–60, 64, 145, 176, 180, 257–258, 275
    and God's love, 149
    as successor of Luther, 146–147
Calvinism, 61, 151
    theology, 158
Calvinist churches, 81
Campbell, John McLeod, 157–159, 165
    heresy of, 158
Canaan, 89, 102
    people of, 90
candlesticks, 97
Canons of Dort, 149, 151
Canterbury, archbishop of, 139
capitalism, 164
caretakers, of creation, 68–69
Catechism of the Catholic Church, 62
catechumenate, 265
Catholic (universal), 46
Catholic clergy, 275
Catholicism, 61
CEOs, 249
cereal sacrifice, 93
Chalcedon, 166, 199
chaos, 69
Charlemagne, 45
cherubim, 81
child abuse, 195
children
    receiving communion, 255
    religious training, 243, 264
children of God, 246
Christ. *see* Jesus Christ
Christ the Key (Tanner), 196
Christ-centered preaching, lack of, 278
Christendom, 264
Christian assurance, 157
Christian dogmatics, 179
Christian faith, 3
Christian faith, in Denmark, 159
Christian life, 139
Christian thought, relating to contemporary issues, 197
Christian worship, 254
    sacraments in, 47
Christianity, and Marxist political philosophy, 193
Christians, meeting Sunday morning, 53
Christology, 175–176, 195, 197
Christ's blood, 54–56
Christ's body, 54–56
Christ's call, 254
Christ's presence, 60
    in Eucharist, 61
Christ's spiritual blood, 57
Christ's spiritual body, 57
Christ's victory, 171–172
Christus Victor, 135, 143, 170–172
Chrysostom, John, 56
Chung, Hyun Kyung, 194
church
    division in, 51
    patriarchy in, 193
Church Dogmatics (Barth), 180
Church history, debated issues, 41
The Church in the Power of the Spirit (Moltmann), 186
church management, 130
Church of England, 60, 150
Church of Scotland, 150, 157
    General Assembly, 158
Church Service Society (CSS), 257
Church Service Society of Scotland, 276
civil order, 151
civil rights movements, 194
class, and relationship to theology, 194
classic theory, Aulén and, 170, 172
cleansing, 109

Subject Index

in baptism, 33
from sin, 48
clergy, 275
coercion, 78
commemoration, 269, 270
Commentaries (Calvin), 180
commitment to God, 34, 103, 227
common lectionary, 258
communication, between God and humanity, 160
communion, 46–53, 65, 218, 254, 275–276
  to baptized children, 255
  with Jesus, 201
  as means of reconciliation with God, 36
communion prayer, 56
communion rail, 273
community, 94
compassion, 109, 164
Compendium of the Catechism of the Catholic Church, 62
compulsion of desire, 77, 78
conception of Jesus, 29, 221, 240
Concerning Christ's Body and Blood (Radbertus), 57
conditional grace, 157
Cone, James H., 194
confession, 112, 231
confession of faith, 266
confession-absolution, 34
confirmation, 33, 255, 256, 262, 265
congregation, 258
Congregational Church, 161, 163
Congregationalists, 267
consecration, 56, 58
conservative circles, 166, 259
conservative German counter movement, 168
Conservative Protestant denominations, 165
conservative religious circles, and guns, 250
Constantine, 41, 55, 264
Constantinople, 43, 46
constructive theology, 197
consubstantiation, 59
consummation, 244, 245
containment for sin, 98–99
contamination
  blood to purge, 38
  within Israel communities, 94
  purging of, 39, 97
  by sin, 38, 94
  from violations of law, 97
contemplation, 240
Contra Gentes (Athanasius), 247
convenience, 263
conversion, 243
  and baptism, 48
  Bushnell on, 161
corban (Hebrew), 121
Corinth, 25
  church in, 3
corporations, 249
corruption by sin, 199
Council of Trent, 145, 149, 256
counseling practices, 78
Counter-Reformation, 145, 256
courtyard of temple, contamination of, 97
covenant, 4, 22, 26, 84, 209, 221
  with Abraham, 103
  with Abraham, Jacob, and Noah, 227
  acceptance, 86
  with Israel, 27
  new, 25
  restoration of, 178
covenant fellowship with God, 40
covenant people, faithlessness of, 208
Coverdale, Miles, 36
covering, and atonement, 182
cpr (Hebrew), 182
craftiness, 78
Cranmer's Thirty-Nine Articles of Faith, 61
creation, 245
  biblical story of, 68–72
  God's intention in, 237
  myths, 69–70
  not a cosmic accident, 69
  renewal of, 227
  story in ancient Israel, 70
creeds, 41–46, 56
  rejection of, 45

Subject Index

cross, 3, 5, 7, 196, 202, 219–221
   as center of Christian theology, 190
   as Jesus' self-offering, 53–54
   and suffering, 54
The Crucified God (Moltmann), 186
crucifixion, 5, 188, 208
   as Trinitarian event, 189
cult, 231
cultic action, 25, 104
   sacrifice as, 108
cultic imagery of sacrifice, 116
cup of salvation, 269, 274
Cur Deus Homo (Why God Became Man) (Anselm), 6, 140
curiosity, 74
Cyprian, 54
Cyril of Alexandria, 56
Cyrus (king of Persia), 90, 211
Czech Bible translation, 9

Daly, Mary, 193n2
Damascus, Paul on road to, 227, 240
Daniel, 209, 212–213
Danish church, 159
d'Aosta, Anselmo (Anselm), 139
David, 3–4, 23, 70, 80, 87–88, 106, 209, 214
Day of Atonement, 40, 91, 99–102, 110, 112–113, 115, 118, 123
   liturgy, 67
Day of Pentecost, 52
day of purgation, 99
De Clementia, 146–147
De Incarnatione (Athanasius), 247
Dead Sea Scrolls, 168n28
death, 72, 76, 80, 110, 225, 271
   believers escaping, 191
   and containment laws, 99
   God experiencing, 224
   of Jesus, 28, 177–178, 228. *see also* Jesus' death
   life after, 228
   made holy, 206
death penalty, 61
debt
   owed to God, 141
   of sin, 145

Defensio fidei catholicae de satisfaction Christi (Grotius), 152
defilement, 96
Deism, 153
déjà vu (French), 27
deliverance, 182
demiurge, 246
Denmark, Christian faith in, 159
depravity, 81, 150
desire, 77
devil, 73–74, 79, 212, 266
   claiming Jesus, 135
   defeat of, 135–136
   Luther on, 172
   ransom to, 135
devotional meal, 59
devotional memory, baptism as, 34
devotional rite, 276
diakonon (Greek), 130
Dialectical theology, 186n28
Didache, 47, 54
didomi (Greek), 187
disciples
   of faith, 264
   growth of, 253
   on road to Emmaus, 226
discipleship, 48
   blessings of, 263
   challenges of, 263
discipline, 273
disobedience, 76
disposition, 158
divine agency, 221
divine atonement with humanity, 205
divine forgiveness, 156
divine gifts, 68–69, 197
divine goodness, 224
divine grace, 150
divine image
   within humanity, 199
   restoration of, 237
divine incarnation, 158
divine justice
   balance of, 142
   debt to, 140
   satisfaction for, 156
divine nature, 199–200
divine order, 69

divine protection, 22
divine providence, 75
divine surgery, 71
divine vocation, 117–118
divine vs. human, 175
divinity of Jesus, 135
divisions, 241–242
  in church, 46
"do this," 25
Docetists, 55
double cup communion, 24
double-predestination, 158
dreams, 213
drink the cup, 275
dualism, 246
duality of God, 180
Dutch Calvinists, 149

early church, 255, 265
  theologians, 53–54
earthen altar, 88
Eastern church
  exemplar model in, 139
  liturgies, 257
Eastern Orthodox, 64–65
  sacraments, 255
  schism with Roman Catholic
    Church, 139
eat the bread, 275
Eberhart, Christian, 115
ecclesiastical union, 240–241
economic conditions, and theology,
    194
ecumenical consensus, 257, 272
ecumenical patriarch, 46
ecumenical understanding of sacra-
    ments, 258
Eden, 70, 81–83
effusion, 267
Egypt, 21–22, 89, 104
  slavery in, 269–270
eis (Greek), 271
elect, 148, 158
Elizabeth I, 61
Emmaus, 52, 226
empiricism, 153
English language, Bible translations,
    9, 35, 36, 114

English Protestants, 36
English Reformation, 60
Enlightenment, 153–154
  theologians, 154
Ephesus, 130
Erasmus, 9
eschatological transformation, 191
eschatology, 190
eschaton, 244
eternal life, 30, 31, 32, 270
  not as reward, 191
  promise of, 2
ethics, 243
Ethiopian eunuch, 47
ethnicity, and theology, 194
Eucharist, 4, 24, 33–34, 44, 48, 52–53,
    184–185, 203–204, 223, 240,
    254–255, 269. *see also* Lord's
    Supper
  and baptism, 54
  church's difference in doctrine, 63
  community in twenty-first century,
    65–66
  in early church, 53–54
  in Eastern Orthodox church, 64–65
  prayer, 62
eucharistic form, 256
eucharistic material, 31
eucharisto (Greek), 271
evangelical liberal, 163
evangelism, 233, 263
evangelistic service, 263
Eve
  deception of, 135
  disobedience of, 136
  as partner, 71
evil, 4, 73–74, 79, 266
  creation of, 246
  invention of, 247
  reversal of, 225
  source of, 79–80
excommunication, 57
  nullification of, 46
  during schism, 46
exemplar theory, 139, 141, 173
exile, 209, 212, 214
  from Judea, 210
  sacrifice during, 90–91

existentialism, 160
exodus, 22, 88, 213
experiential theology, 163
expiation, 95, 114
    Bushnell on the misapplication of, 162
    of sin, 182
expulsion laws, 99
Ezekiel, 85, 90, 209, 210, 214

faith, 261
    assurance of, 158
    as gift of Spirit, 232
    as Harnack's focus, 166
    profession of, 263
    renewal, 262
    seeking understanding, 139, 145
faithfulness, 228, 273
    of Jesus, 221–222
faithlessness
    of covenant people, 208
    judgment for, 209
the fall, 78–79
false prophets, 251
fasting, 47–48, 256
Faulkner, William, 244
fear, 76
    of the Lord, 75
feast days, 65
Feast of Unleavened Bread, 126
Feast of Weeks, 91
Federal Calvinism, 167
feelings, and unseen world, 154
fellowship with God, 181
female theologians
    and atonement theory, 195–196
    atonement theory critique, 195, 196
    from Latin America, 193–194
feminist movement, 192–207
    atonement critique, 195–196
    critique of, 194
    liberation theology and, 193–195
    theologians in, 192–193
feudal law, 140, 147
filioque clause, 45–46
Finlan, Stephen, 125, 129n30
"first fruits," 245
First Great Awakening, 152

firstborn
    Christ as, 230, 241
    plague on, 104
Five Articles of Remonstrance, 150–151
flesh of Jesus, 30, 56
flood, 82, 84
followers of Jesus, 29
font of water, 273
foot washing, 256
foreign gods, Israel worship of, 208
forensic death, 202
forensic satisfaction, 147–149, 154
forensic union, 241
forgiveness, 27, 32–33, 116, 228, 233, 275
    fear of not finding, 160
    God's way with humanity, 228
    in Israel, 182–183
    resistance to accepting God's, 160
    of sins, 26
formal liturgical communions, 259
France, 136
    religious conflict in, 147
Free Church Evangelical Protestantism, 64
"free church" traditions, 259, 267
free will, 151, 161, 162
freedom, 77–78, 236
    to choose, 71
    gift of, 78–80
French Bible translation, 9
frontier evangelists, 161
fruit of the tree of knowledge of good and evil, 72
"fruit of the vine," 26
fulfillment, 155
fundamentalist-modernist divide, in American Protestantism, 167
The Fundamentals, 167

Gamaliel, 120
Gebara, Ivone, 193
gender, 10–12
    and language, 192
    and relationship to theology, 194
    roles, 130
Geneva, 275

Geneva Bible, 9, 36, 37
gentile Christians, 26
　Paul writing to, 122
German Bible translation, 9
German liberal theology, 166
German Lutheran Church, rejection of Harnack, 167
German Pietism, 163
German Reform, 185
German theologians, 166
Gethsemane, 218
gifts, 207
　sacrifices as, 118
Girard, René, 111n1
g'l (Hebrew), 183
Glasgow, 158
glossolalia, 64
Gnosticism, 55–56
goats, 39, 111
God
　abundant mercy, 144
　as child of humanity, 213
　covenant of, 22, 24, 25–27, 31, 83–85, 106
　as creator, 73, 197–198
　curse of, 80
　forgiving love of, 94
　as gift-giver, 197–198
　gifts of, 274
　honor of, 142
　in human flesh, 41
　vs. humanity, 160
　as humanity's enemy, 148
　language for, 8, 11
　malleability of image, 198
　meaning of *YHWH*, 213n6
　presence of, 72
　promise to people, 22
　relationship with, 1, 116, 232
　righteousness of, 115
　salvation plan, 136
　saving acts, 7
　silence of, 219–220
　sin as violation of honor, 140
　as Trinity, 1, 196
　unknowable, 153
　wrath of, 128
God-consciousness, 155

God's love, 176–177, 187, 228
　as defining force, 235
　Jesus' death as example of, 142
　proof of, 149
　and sacrifice, 106
God's word, 258
　responding to, 260–261
God's wrath, 149, 181–182, 184
Godself, 12
go'el (Hebrew), 182–183
Gonzáles, Justo L., 261
good, 79–80
good and evil, 76
　clash between, 212
gospels, 25–26, 256
　sacrifice in, 109–110
Gössmann, Elisabeth, 193n2
grace, 150, 228, 253–255, 257–258, 260, 262–263, 269
　sacraments and, 273
Grant, Jacquelyn, 194
Great Commission, 47
Great War, 165
greed, as idolatry, 248–249
Greek, 8, 9, 41
Greek biblical manuscripts, 9
　New Testament, 9
Greek Christians, 55
Greek philosophy, 125
Greek rulers, 212
Greek Seleucid subjugation, 212
Gregory Nazianzun, 197
Gregory of Nyssa, 56, 135
　influence on Tanner, 197
Grotius, Hugo, 151–152
　theological writings of, 152
guilt, realization of, 97
guilt offerings, 96
gun violence, 249
guns, as idolatry, 250
Gutiérrez, Gustavo, 193

hallel cup of thanks and praise, 24
Harnack, Adolf, 166–172
　critics of, 167
hattat (Hebrew), 38, 95–96, 107, 113, 118
hattat offerings, 115

hattat purification, 123
hattat sacrifice, 100, 110
healer, Jesus as, 217
hearts of stone, 228
Hebrew Scriptures, 8, 9
   atonement in, 36
   original meaning of sacrifice in, 205
   translation into Greek, 67, 113
Heidelberg Catechism, 149
Hellenistic culture, 131
Hellenistic literature, 114
Hellenistic philosophy, 124
helpmate, 71
Henry VIII (king of England), 36, 60
heresy, 46
   of Campbell, 158
hierarchical models, 241
   for managing households and societies, 242
high places, 90
High Priest, 99, 111, 215, 272
   and death of Jesus, 218
high-handed sins, 98
hilaskesthai (Greek), 117
hilaskomai (Greek), 113
hilasmos (Greek), 116
hilasterion (Greek), 115–116
   history in translation, 113–114
Hinduism, 194
historical context of words, 162
historical Jesus, 168n23, 174
Hodge, Charles, 156, 161
holiness, 38, 93–94
   of God's love, 177
   maintenance of, 96
Holy Communion, 4, 24, 34, 52–53, 240, 269. *see also* Lord's Supper
holy of holies, 38–39, 97, 100-101, 118
holy oil, 268
Holy Spirit. *see* Spirit
Holy Three, 252
honor, 140
   violation of, 147
hope, 186
hubris, 83
human nature, 155, 199–200
   Aquinas and, 143
   perfectibility of, 163

human perfection, 156
human sacrifice, 102
human trafficking, 248
human vs. divine, 175
humanity, 271
   vs. God, 148, 160
   God identifying with, 184
   as God's representatives, 68
   of Jesus, 181, 203, 206
   Jesus identifying with, 184
   made in God's likeness, 68
   malleability of, 198
   maturity of, 137
   participation in Jesus Christ, 202–204
   salvation of, 206
hymnody, 6
hyper panton (Greek), 231
hypostatic union, 199–200

"I am," 29
icons, 256
idealism, 165
idolatry, 260
   contemporary, 246–251
   against God, 215
   temptations of, 250
idols, 77, 210, 277
   evils of contemporary, 248–251
Ignatius of Antioch, 54
image of God, 201, 263
   Jesus as, 199–200
image of Jesus' blood, 127
imago Dei, 68
immersion, 48–49, 265, 267
immortality, 213, 238
imperishable body, vs. perishable, 238
impure body, 94
impurity, 38, 94
   vs. iniquities, 112
imputation, post-biblical, 164
"in Christ," 239–240, 244–245
incarnation, 8, 137, 142–143, 174–191, 195, 197, 199, 205, 221
   Ballie and, 175
   as mechanism of atonement, 200–202
   Paul's theology of, 136

providing basis for atonement
    theories, 200
  as restoration, 138
incarnation paradox, 160
incarnational atonement, 184, 252
incense altar, 97
inclusive language, 10–11
individualism, 164
infant baptism, 34, 264
  theological controversy over, 49–50
information, worship of, 250
iniquities, vs. impurities, 112
injustice, 157
inner shrine, contamination of, 97
innocence, fall from, 78
Institutes of the Christian Religion
    (Calvin), 147
intentional sins, 98
intercession, 120, 252
intervention in human affairs, 204
invitations to Christ's table, 278
Irenaeus, 66, 136–138, 142, 143, 172,
    235, 247
  influence on Campbell, 158
  influence on Tanner, 197
Isaac, 224
  binding of, 102
  as sacrifice, 84–85
  sacrifice of, 102–103
Isaiah, 209
Isasi-Diaz, Ada Maria, 194
Islam, 194
Israel, 3, 21, 27, 85, 94, 99, 111, 209,
    210–211, 269
  creation story of, 70
  God's promise to, 22
  sacrifice in, 86–107, 112–114,
    182–183
Israelites, 94, 97, 102, 104
  miasma's effect on community, 112
  progeny, 208
  redemption, 104
  redemption from slavery, 104–105
"It is finished," 221

Jacob's progeny, 208
jealousy, 74
Jeptha, 85

Jeremiah, 27, 85, 89, 209
Jerome, 8
Jerusalem, 21–23, 87, 90, 91, 104, 108,
    209
  destruction of, 209
  Jesus in, 21, 217–218
  rebuilt, 211
  return to, 211–212
  temple in, 211
Jesus Christ, 235
  appearance of, 214
  ascension, 233
  assuming human flesh, 215
  baptism, 47
  becoming one in, 261, 278
  belief in, 5
  birth of, 29
  blood of, 26
  body of, 25, 28, 269, 272
  centering of, 260
  conception, 199
  connecting humanity with God,
    201
  contemporary impact, 252–253
  divinity of, 135
  divinity vs. humanity, 55
  as eternal High Priest, 118
  as *exemplar*, 139
  of faith vs. of history, 175
  final coming of, 5
  God becoming human in, 136
  God's incarnation in, 140
  high priestly prayer, 28–29
  as historical figure, 169
  human attachment to, 201
  as humanity faithful to God, 181
  identity of, 133–134
  as image of God, 199–200
  incarnation, 55. *see also* incarnation
  as intermediary, 119
  in Jerusalem, 21
  as liberator, 195
  life of, 1
  love for humanity, 188
  meaning of life, 108
  mission, 5
  name of, 213n6
  obedience of, 137

(Jesus Christ continued)
  on Palm Sunday, 23
  participation in, 202–204
  as place of atonement, 116
  plan, 5
  post-resurrection appearances, 2
  as preexistent Christ, 117
  as rebel, 188
  resurrection of, 5, 108, 228, 232, 233
  sacrifice, 6
  as sacrifice, 116, 117
  and sacrifice in New Testament, 108–132
  as scapegoat, 110
  Schleirmacher's views on, 155
  self-offering, 110
  soul as ransom, 137
  Spirit incarnate in, 215
  suffering, 144
  suffering as substitute for punishment, 152
  as teacher, 243
  teaching on obedience, 109
  triumph over the devil, 135
  walking on water, 29
  in wilderness, 216
Jesus' death, 7, 221–222, 230, 232, 233
  in context of sacrificial cult, 117
  meaning of, 2, 107, 108
  not necessary to remove sin, 154
  not as payment for sin, 108
  purpose of, 4
  as ransom, 134, 140
  reason for, 67
  subjective theory of, 139
Jesus now, 252–253
Jesus of history, 175
Jesus Seminar, 168n23
Jewish Christians, 26–28, 55, 116
Jewish sacrificial cult, 116
Job, 80
John, 110, 136, 269
  on Lord's Supper, 28–29
  vs. other gospels, 220–221
  perspective of Jesus' death on cross, 220–221
  and sacramental imagery, 29–32

John of Damascus, 56
John the Baptist, 23, 51, 215
  baptism by, 48, 50
John XXIII (pope), 46
Johnson, Elizabeth, 193n2
Johnson, Samuel, 81
Jonathan, 88
Jordan River, 265
Joshua, 89
joy, obstacle to, 160
Judah, 209
  return from exile, 211–213
Judaism, 84, 116, 194, 267
  of Paul, 121
  of the Second Temple, 217
Judas, 26, 253
judgment, 209, 212
Junia, 130–131
justice, 144, 157, 164
  debt to God due to violation of, 147
  of God, 147
justice system, 157
justification, 127–128, 233–235

kaphar (Hebrew), 37, 39
  cultic usage of, 38
kapporet (Hebrew), 39, 100, 112–113, 115, 117
katallasso (Greek), 35–37
katallege (Greek), 35–37
katharismos (Greek), 118
Kierkegaard, Søren, 159–160, 165, 175
  Bushnell and, 163
King James Bible, 9, 37, 114
kipper (Hebrew), 182
kippur (Hebrew), 37
  cultic usage of, 38
Knox, John, 257

LaCugna, Catherine Mowry, 193n2
Lamb of God, 23, 110, 117, 215, 222
  Jesus as, 125–126
lamb's blood, 21, 104
lamb's slaughter, 126
Landes, George, 71n3
language

about God, 192
  limitations of, 12
  use of, 10–11
Lateran Council of 1215 (4th), 58,
  61–62
Latin, 8–9, 41, 254
Latin America
  church, 46
  female reform theology emerging
    from, 193–194
Latin manuscripts, 9
Latin New Testament, 9
Latin-speaking churches, 45
Lazarus, 225
leaven, 92
lectionary, 258–259
legal metaphors, 127
Leibniz, Gottfried Wilhelm, 224n21
Leo IX (pope), 46
lepers, 109
  restore healed, 39
Lessing, G.E., 168n23
Levi, sons of, 88
Levites, 89, 96
libation, 124
liberal circles, 259
Liberal Protestant churches, 165
  and Ballie, 175
  theology, 174
  thought, 166
liberal view, Schweitzer's criticism of,
  168
liberation, 124, 135, 195
liberation theology, 192–207
liberationists, 196
liberator, Jesus as, 195
life, renewal of, 227
life in Christ, 239–240
literalism, 162
liturgical renewal, 62, 258
living sacrifice, 124, 268
  from God, 207
living water, 47, 223
Logos, 136, 137, 215, 220
Lord, 133
  vs. Savior, 251
Lord's prayer, 274

Lord's Supper, 4, 24, 33–34, 52–53, 61,
  218, 240, 254–256, 269
  frequency of, 275–276
  in history vs. today, 41–66
  Mark on, 25–26
  Matthew on, 26–28
  Paul on, 25
love, 164, 177, 188
  of Christ, 230
  cost of, 187–188
  of enemies, 234
  of God, 144, 145
  paradox of God's, 188–189
Luke, 52
  on Lord's Supper, 24
Luther, Martin, 9, 145–146, 172, 224,
  256, 258
  atonement doctrine, 146
  challenging transubstantiation,
    58–59
Lutheran church, 34, 81

Maccabees, 124–125
Mackintosh, H.R., 180
marriage, 33, 255, 256, 265
Martyr, Justin, 54
martyrdom, 125, 131
  of Jesus, 142
martyr's blood, as purifying, 125
Marxist political philosophy, and
  Christianity, 193
Mary, 199, 216
Mary Magdalene, 226
meal of liberation, vs. sacrificial
  meals, 105
medieval church, 139
medieval thought, ransom theory in,
  139–142
meditation, 240
Melchizedek, 117, 214
mental illness, 250
meod tob (Hebrew), 69
mercy, 109
mercy seat, 39, 100, 112–113
merit through suffering, 144n15, 164
messiah, 4, 168, 174, 196, 213
messiah-king, people's expectations
  for, 214

messianic symbolism, 23
metaphors, 108
   in Bible, 162
   of Paul, 121–131
metaphysics, 56
Methodists, 34, 162, 267
miasma, 112
   of pollution by sin, 119
Micah, 85, 105
middle ages, 56–58, 153, 172
Middle English, 9
Milgrom, Jacob, 101, 111–112
militarism, 164
minha (Hebrew), 93
ministry, baptized for, 268
minjung, 194
   miracles, 166
   of loaves and fishes, 29, 269
modalism, 44n6
Moffitt, David, 118
Moltmann, Jürgen, 185–191
money
   love of, 248
   worship of, 250
money changers, 109
monthly communion, 276
moral example, 141–142
moral exemplar, 143
moral government theory, 151
moral influence theory, 139, 141, 154, 162, 163, 165
moral transformation, 139
Moriah (Mount), 84–85, 103
Mosaic covenant, 88
Moses, 3, 22, 27, 70, 86, 104–105, 109, 133, 208, 212, 213, 218, 272
   and promised land, 89
   New Moses, 22–23, 211
mujerista (Hispanic), 194
   and atonement theory, 196
mysteries, 254
mysterion (Greek), 32–33, 255, 272
mystic, 120
mystical, 57, 129, 159, 240
mystical union, 65, 170, 240
mythological stories, 67, 75

nakedness, 72, 75

nationalism, 164, 250
nature, 137, 154, 155, 199
The Nature of the Atonement (Campbell), 158
Near Eastern creation stories, 69–70
Nebuchadnezzar, 209, 210
neo-orthodox Protestant theology, 174, 175
Neopaganism, 194
nephesh (Hebrew), 94, 97
new Adam, 235–238
new covenant, 25–27, 51, 209
   for forgiveness of sins, 218, 272
   with Israel, 27
new creation, 241–243
New England Congregationalists, 152
New English Translation (NET), 114
new life, 33, 51, 115, 116, 126, 184, 222, 233, 236, 237–239, 261, 262, 263
new passover, 23–32, 218–219, 228
New Testament
   and application of sacrifice to Jesus, 108–132
   and baptism, 47
   Greek language in, 8
   meaning of sacrifice in, 205
   message of, 258
   translation, 36
Nicene Creed, 41–45, 55, 166, 262
   controversies, 138
Nicene Orthodoxy, influence on Torrance, 180
nineteenth century, atonement theories in, 154–164
Noah, 82, 84, 86, 227
non-sacramental churches, 34, 59
Northern Kingdom of Israel, 210
   God's judgment on, 209

oath, 254
obedience, 103, 261
   to God, 49, 51
   of Jesus, 188, 234–236
   of Jesus to death, 222
objective theory, 171
offering, 111
   mutual, 116

Subject Index

to God, 145
of thanksgiving, 96, 97, 109
Olah (Hebrew), 91–94
Old English, 9
Old Nicene Creed (354 CE), 42
Old School Princeton theology, 157
oneness with Christ, 275
Onesimus, 242
ontological argument for existence of God, 139
ontological atonement, 183
ontological change, 185
oppression of women, 195
order, 69
ordinances, 34, 64
ordination, 33, 255, 256
Origen, 55, 118, 135, 172
original sin, 4, 78, 144, 147, 152
orthodox Christian theology, 244
Orthodox church, 34, 48, 63n33, 64–65, 234, 243n9, 254–255, 265n22, 267, 272
　and creed, 44
　immersion baptism in, 48
　position on transubstantiation, 58
　vs. Roman Catholic church, 46
orthodox faith, 44
Orthodox Lutheran, 172
Orthodox theology, 139
orthodoxy, 42
outcasts, and Jesus, 217, 242

padah (Hebrew), 182
pagan, 182
　practice of offering sacrifice, 105
　understanding of atonement, 85
pagan gods, 102
pagan sacrifice, 38, 124
　vs. biblical sacrifice, 131
paganism, baptism as rejection of, 47
Palm Sunday, 23
parable of the wedding feast, 261
paradidomia (Greek), 187
paradise, 71, 72, 81
parousia, 227
Particular Baptists, 34
partnership, 72
paschal lamb, 214

not as sacrifice, 126
passion of Christ, 220, 228
Passion Sunday, 23
Passover, 21–32, 91, 126, 223, 228–229, 270
　first, 104–105
　Jesus at, 217
　new, 23–32, 218–219, 228
Passover Lamb, 104, 110
Passover sacrifice, 22
Passover Seder, 22, 24, 27, 218, 269
Pastoral Epistles, 129, 130, 131
patriarchy, 193
Paul, 3, 4, 24, 25, 26, 34, 47, 50–52, 113, 115–116, 120–129, 213
　and baptism, 51
　challenges to reading, 121–122
　contradictions of, 130–131
　criticism of church's acceptance of sinful behavior, 127
　education of, 121
　images of atonement, 124–125
　on Lord's Supper, 25
　on sacrifice, 121–124
　Schweitzer on, 169
Paul VI (pope), 46
Pauline terms, 127
Pauline writings, 121
　modifications of, 131
　resistance to, 129
Pax Romana, 212
pdh (Hebrew), 182
peace, 234
penal substitutionary atonement, 114, 149, 154, 156–157, 165
　criticisms of, 157
　rejection of, 162
penance, 33, 144, 255
Pentecost, 47
Pentecostals, 64, 152
people of God, 274
perfection of humanity
　need for, 155
　possibility of, 155
　progress toward, 165
perishable body, vs. imperishable, 238
perseverance of saints, 151
Persian Empire, 211, 212

persona (Latin), 43n2
personal punishment, 147–149
personal transformation, 278
personality, 164
pestilence, 89
Peter, 31, 52, 122n23, 270, 274
    denial of Jesus, 218–219
    Jesus' reconciliation with, 226
Pharisaical system of biblical exegesis, 121
Pharisees, 120
    Paul as, 121
Pharoah, 22
Philemon, 242
philosophy
    and atonement theology, 6
    of history, 167
    of religion, 167
    task of, 155
Phoebe, 130
physical body, vs. spiritual, 238–239
pilgrimage, 21
Placards Affair, 147
place of atonement, 100, 112, 115, 116
    Jesus as, 117
pleasure, 77
poetic biblical texts, in Hebrew, 37
Polish Bible translation, 9
political power, corrupt use of, 250
pollution, 97, 112
    in sanctuary, 99
Polycarp, 136
pope, 46
post-Apostolic Church, atonement theories in, 133–152
post-baptismal relationship, 239
power, worship of, 250
prayer, 255–256, 264
    of Jesus, 28–29
preacher, Jesus as, 217
preaching, 256, 260
    as prophetic, 259
    as sacramental, 258
predestination, 148n23, 150, 162
Presbyterians, 267
pride, 198
priesthood, 212
priestly code, 98

priests, 88–93, 95–96, 99–101, 217
    sustaining of, 92
primordial history, 83–84
Princeton Theological Seminary, 156
printing, 9
Priscilla, 130
Problems with Atonement (Finlan), 129n30
profession of faith, 48
prohibitions, 72–76
promised land, 89
    sacrifice in, 90
promises, 51
    constant renewal of, 262
pronouns for God, 10–11
prophesy, 50, 64, 259
prophets
    announcing Jesus' coming, 211
    Jesus perceived as, 29
    vision, 109
propitiation, 114, 183
    Bushnell on, 162
prosopon (Greek), 43n2
prosperity gospel, 250
prosphora (Greek), 108
prostitutes, 217
protection, 22, 75
Protestant churches, 33–34, 256, 265
    and Apostles' Creed, 44
    atonement theory in, 145, 148
    clergy, 275
    and communion frequency, 276
    communion service, 270
    division of thought, 165–166
    feminists in, 192
    renewal, 257
    traditions, 274
Protestant Reformation, 9
providence, 81–83
psychiatric care, 78
"The Psychiatric Study of Jesus," 170
psychology, 156
Ptolemy, 212
punishment, 81–83, 144, 155, 210
    in relation to Christ, 177–178
    of serpent, 79
purge, 37–38
purging sacrifice, 93, 95–97

purification, 37, 48, 113, 115, 267
  of blood, 98–99
  of inner sanctums of the temple, 111
  offering, 100
  sacrifice, 92, 95–97, 118
  of sanctuary during Yom Kippur, 102
purity, restoration to, 96
purity laws, 99

qodesh (Hebrew), 99
qorban (Hebrew), 87, 105
quarantine, 96
The Quest of the Historical Jesus (Geschichte der Leben-Jesu-Forschung), 168

ra (Hebrew), 71, 82
race, and theology, 194
Radbertus, Paschasius, 57
ransom, 109–110, 182
  to devil, 172
  Jesus as, 134–135, 137, 139, 140
ransom theory, 170
  Rauschenbusch's rejection of, 164
  St. Anselm on, 140
Ratramnus, 57
Rauschenbusch, Walter, 163–165, 208
Read, David H.C., 219n10
"realized eschatology," 275
reason, 154
  rejection of Christianity, 153
  religion of, 153
rebaptism, 34
rebel, Jesus as, 188
rebellion, 89
  against God, 215
rebirth, and baptism, 51
recapitulation, 124, 128, 136–138, 139, 143, 235
  Iranaeus and, 172
reconciliation, 35–37, 109, 113–114, 124, 127, 146, 165, 171, 175, 176–178, 230, 231, 232–234
  call to share message of, 233

  between Eastern and Western churches, 46
  as goal of atonement, 177
  between God and humanity, 228
reconciling sacrifice, 146
reconsecration, 123
redemption, 124, 128, 136, 145, 164, 178, 182, 185, 195, 212, 234, 245
  mission of, 219
  out of bondage, 183
  and sacrifice, 131
  through Christ's blood, 131
redemptive violence, myth of, 249
Reformation, 6, 9, 47, 48, 58–61, 62, 81, 145–149, 165, 233, 256, 272
  atonement theories in, 133–152
  conflict during, 255
  ransom theory in, 139–142
  rejection of infant baptism, 264
Reformation churches, and creed, 44
Reformed Baptists, 34
Reformed churches
  and frequency of communion, 276
  theologians, 157, 177
  theology, 34, 147, 167
  tradition, 176
Reformed orthodoxy, 156
Reformed Protestantism, 172
Reformers, 232
reign of God, 26
Reimarus, Samuel, 168n23
rejection of sacrifice, 105–106
relationship with God, 69, 234, 236
religions, male dominance, 193
Religionsgeschichtiche Schule, 167
religious doubt, 161
religious obligation, 109
religious officials, and death of Jesus, 218
religious practices of people in ancient Near East (ANE), 87
religious syncretism, 209
religious truth, 163
religious-political conspiracy, 220
remedy, Jesus as, 143
remembrance, 27, 52, 53, 270
Remonstrants, 150
renunciation of evil, 266, 267

(renunciation of evil continued)
   baptism and, 48
reparation, 96
repentance, 48, 106, 142, 154, 158, 218, 232
   baptism and, 50
resurrection, 2, 5, 7, 31–32, 108, 191, 213, 226, 227, 228, 232, 233, 237, 238–239, 274
   as God's answer about death, 202
   and hope, 186
   power of God in weakness, 225
   uniting Jesus with God, 190
Resurrection Day, 273
resuscitation, 225
retribution, 177
reversal of sin, 123
Revised Standard Version (RSV), 10
revivalism, 162
rich man, parable of the, 249
righteousness, 115, 233
risen Christ, 230
rites, 34, 254, 256
ritual act, 270
ritual actions, 32, 39
ritual bathing, 48
ritual meal, 27, 87
ritual repetition, 25
ritual sacrifices, 205
ritual washing, 96
Roman Catholic Church, 256, 265
   atonement theory in, 145
   Calvin's break with, 147
   and creed, 44
   criticism of Harnack, 167
   liturgies, 257
   vs. Orthodox church, 46
   schism with Byzantine church, 45–46, 58, 139, 255
Roman Catholics, 34, 267
Roman Church, 257
Roman Empire, 22, 46
   citizen of, 122
   occupation, 213
Roman law, 147
romanticism, 165
Rome, 23, 212, 214, 216
   origins of church in, 122n23

Rome's Counter-Reformation, 61–62
Rosh Hashanah, 91
Ruether, Rosemary Radford, 193n2
running water, 47
Rutledge, Fleming, 111n2

Sabbath, 69, 91
Sabbath of grief, 224
sacer facere (Latin), 87
Sacrament, 32–34, 272
sacramental actions, 255
sacramental Christians, 51
sacramental churches, 49, 51, 53, 264, 272
sacramental covenant meal, 240
sacramental mystery, 272–273
sacramental Protestantism, 62–64
sacramental theologians, 272
sacramental union, 59, 240
sacramental worship, 277
sacramentality, and theological controversy, 46–53
sacraments, 33, 46–53, 62, 64–65, 203, 223, 253–258, 275
   contemporary ways to speak of, 34
   as means of at-one-ment, 253–258
   relationship with atonement, 34
sacramentum (Latin), 32–33, 254
sacrificial feast, 88, 93
sacrifice, 4, 6, 22–23
   as act of redemption, 206–207
   as act of worship, 87
   in ancient Near East (ANE), 87–91
   basic actions, 91–94
   Bushnell on, 162
   change in definition, 134
   of Christ, 60
   of covenant-making, 92
   as cultic action, 108
   debate over, 86
   distortion of, 205
   during exile, 90–91
   feminist concerns about image of, 205
   five forms of, 121
   function in Israel, 207
   as gift to God, 87
   and God's presence, 93

Subject Index

in Hebrew Bible, 87
in Israel, 86–107, 112–114, 182–183
of Jesus, 6, 162
meaning in New Testament, 205
as means of purging, 38
as means of worshiping, 84–85
in New Testament, 120
original meaning in Hebrew Scriptures, 205
after Paul, 129–131
Paul's theology of, 123
in promised land, 90
to purify, 38–39
purpose of, 95
and redemption, 131
after Sinai covenant, 88
of thanksgiving, 92
in Torah, 95
of well-being, 92
as witness to God's forgiveness, 182
as worship, 106–107
Sacrifice of Jesus (Eberhart), 115n11
sacrificial actions, 92–93
sacrificial animal, 114, 117
   bull, 112
   consumption of, 96
sacrificial blood, 22, 27, 96–97
sacrificial codes, 37
sacrificial cult, 110, 112, 118, 182
   end of, 133
   imagery of, 123
   of Israel obsolete, 119
   language of, 128
   as means of worship, 121
sacrificial death, 2, 4, 152
sacrificial goat, blood of, 112
sacrificial imagery, 123
   Bushnell on the misapplication of, 162
sacrificial language, 131
   of Paul, 231
sacrificial meal, 22, 93
   foods, 91
sacrificial metaphor, 128
sacrificial nature, of Jesus' death, 123
sacrificial nourishment, 92
sacrificial practices, 123

sacrificial system, 94, 116
   abuse of, 109
   of Israel, 112–114
sacrificial worship, 84–85
sacrificing priest, 96
salvation, 2–5, 137, 148, 150, 158, 178, 235, 245
   and baptism, 50
   and Christ on cross, 202
   contemporary idea of, 171
   cross as precondition for, 202
   guaranteed for all believers, 158
   Paul's theology of, 115
   personal decision for, 161
   physical idea of, 171
Samuel, 209
sanctification, 66
sanctified advice, 260
sanctify, 34
sanctuary, 90, 94, 112
   contamination of, 97
   pollution in, 99
Sarah, 83–84, 102, 208
Satan, 4, 73, 212, 216
   defeat of, 228
satisfaction, 140, 148, 153, 165
   Anselm on, 143, 172
   of God's justice, 171
   for sin, 142, 143–144
   through penance, 144–145
"Satisfaction of Christ," 156
satisfaction theory, 139, 142, 170, 172
   Rauschenbusch's rejection of, 164
Saul, 88
saved, 264
saving faith, 132, 261
saving souls, 233
Savior vs. Lord, 251
scallop shell, 267
scapegoat, 100, 102, 112, 157
   Jesus as, 110
schism between East and West, 45–46, 58, 139, 255
Schleiermacher, Friedrich, 154–156, 163
scholastic Calvinism, 149–152
Schweitzer, Albert, 167–172, 175
   on existence of Jesus, 169

science, Torrance and, 179
scientific revolution, 153
Scottish Highlands, 158
Scottish theology, Campbell's influence on, 159
Scotus, Duns, 141n13
Scripture, patriarchy in, 193
Second Ecumenical Council, 43
second goat, 101–102
Second Great Awakening, 161
Second Temple, 91, 104, 108, 133
Second Temple Judaism, 125, 168, 213
Second Temple literature, 8
Second Vatican Council (1962–1966), 46, 62, 193, 257
Seder, 22, 24, 27, 218, 269
seed, 80
segagah, 98
Segundo, Juan Luis, 193
self-help industry, 78
self-offering, 118–119, 127, 142
self-sacrifice, in Greco-Roman culture, 124
Sennacherib, 209
separation
  of death, 188
  sin as, 78
Septuagint, 8, 67, 116
sermon, 259–260
serpent, 73–80
  as first theologian, 73
  punishment of, 79
service, 91, 164, 264
Seth, 80
seven sacraments, 34
shame, 75, 77
shrines, 90
shuph (Hebrew), 80
Sikhism, 194
silence of God, 219–220
Simon Peter. *see* Peter
sin, 4, 23, 32–33, 81–82, 94, 110, 166, 266, 267
  barrier of, 232
  biblical definition of, 78
  born by God, 184
  cleansing from objects, 39
  confession of, 101
  containment for, 98–99
  contamination of, 82, 115
  as disruption to God's creation, 178
  eradication by God, 222
  falling into, 198–199
  forgiveness of, 26
  God dealing with, 178
  God forgiving sin through time, 178
  God's judgment on, 181–182
  human nature and, 143
  humanity no longer enslaved to, 231
  of Israelites, 112
  Jesus' triumph over, 232
  origins of, 80
  pardoning of, 156
  penalty for, 157
  power destroyed by Jesus, 178
  propitiation for, 114
  punishment of, 141
  that harmed another, 95
  wages of, 157
  of the world, 117, 215, 271
sin offering, 38, 117
Sinai (Mount), 22, 27, 88
Sinai covenant, sacrifice after, 86
sinful body, 94
sinful self, crucified with Christ, 231
sinlessness, 216
slavery, 110
  in Egypt, 3, 21
snake, 78–80. *see also* serpent
social activist, 163
social challenge, 259
social media, worship of, 250
social progress, 165
Socinus, Faustus, 152
sociology, 156
solidarity, 164
  with Christ through baptism, 237
  Christ's death in, 231
  cross as God's act of, 202
  of humanity with Adam, 236
Sölle, Dorothee, 194
Solomon, 70, 90
  death of, 209
Solomon's Temple, 87, 90–91

Subject Index

Sophia (God's wisdom), 196
soul, 238
Southern Kingdom of Judah, 209
souvenir, 28
Spanish Bible translation, 9
speaking in tongues, 50, 64
special offerings, 91
species, 62
speculative theology, 162
Spirit, 64, 203, 232, 252, 262
    continuing work of, 204
    of Jesus, 221
spiritual body, vs. physical, 238–239
spiritual breakthrough, 261
spiritual capacity of humanity, 69
spiritual discipline, 264
"spiritual food and drink," 54
spiritual revival, 161
sprinkling, 267
"staff of life," 272
stone altars, 88
Student Christian Movement, 185
subjective theory of Jesus' death, 139, 171
subjugation of women, 195
substitution, 84–85, 153, 182
    God's gift of, 85
    as post-biblical, 164
substitutionary atonement, 110–111, 154
suffering
    of Jesus, 206
    as punishment for sins, 271
Sullivan, Russell, 260n13
Summa Theologica (Anselm), 143
supernatural event, rejection of, 168
symbolic presence, 59
symbolism of Eucharist, 57
symbols, 41, 44, 57, 162
Synod, 151
Synoptic Gospels, 109
systematic theology, 156, 197
    reconceptualization of, 197n13

tabernacle, 88, 89, 90, 97, 128
Tanner, Kathryn, 137, 196–207
The Teachings of the Lord to the Gentiles (or Nations) by the Twelve Apostles, 47, 54
technology, worship of, 250
telos (Greek), 155
temple, 23, 97, 109, 128
    building of, 90, 211
temple cult, 105
temptations, 73, 245
    of Jesus, 155, 216
tempter, 222
    and Satan, 80
    and the serpent, 80
Ten Commandments, 248
    violations of, 95
Tertullian, 33
thanksgiving, 53
    to God, 119
"the Doctrine of Grace in the Apostolic Fathers," 179
theodicy, 79, 224n21
theological controversy, 46–53
Theological Dictionary of the New Testament (Kittel), 113
theology
    and philosophy, 7
    relationship to, 194
Theology of Hope (Moltmann), 186
theosis, 66
Thomas (apostle), 226, 274
Thomas Aquinas, 81, 143, 148
    theology of, 62, 145
    writing on atonement, 143–145
thusia (Greek), 122, 123–124
thysia (Greek), 108
Tiberias, sea of, 226
tomb, 224, 225
tongues, speaking in, 50
Torah, 116
    abandonment of, 210, 212
    purging of violation, 97
    stipulations, 213
Torrance, T.F., 137, 179–185, 197
total depravity, 150–151
traditional Christian belief, 167
traditional theological themes, female experience inclusion in, 195
Trajan (emperor), 53

Subject Index

transformation, 56, 240, 251, 257, 273
   into God's image, 253
   personal, 278
   of the World, 191
transgressions, 210
   of Adam, 237
   confession of, 101
   pollution by, 99
translations of Bible, 8, 9–10, 112
transposing, 56
transubstantiation, 57, 61
   canonization of, 58
   and Roman Catholic church, 61
   in Western church, 58
tree of life, 71, 81
tree of the knowledge of good and evil, 71
Trent, 61–62
Trinitarian event, crucifixion as, 189
Trinitarian theology, 192
Triune God, 43–44, 48, 65–66, , 142, 172, 180, 199, 214, 221, 252
   Bushnell on, 161
   death of God the Son within, 189
   fellowship with, 180–181
   as God, 1
   love of, 186
Troeltsch, Ernst, 167
trust, 75
truth, 73, 76, 77, 244
tsela (Hebrew), 71
Tyndale, William, 9, 35–36, 110
Tyndale's scapegoat, 110–111
typology, 126

uncleanliness, 94
   of sanctuary, 102
unconditional election, rejection of, 150
union, 51
   with Christ, 240, 241
   with God, 51, 87, 227
Unitarians, 161
unity, 72, 277
universal atonement, 158
universal moral law, 157
unknown sins, 98
unlimited atonement, 150

unrepentant sin, 98, 101
upper room, 274
urban poverty, 163
Vatican Council (Second, 1962–1965), 46, 62, 193, 257
vendors, 109
vengeance, 177
versöhnen (German), 146
versöhnung (German), 146
via media, theology of, 61
vicarious satisfaction, 140–141, 147–149
vicarious suffering of Jesus, 164
"visionary" moments, 240
visions, 240
voluntary penance, 144
voluntary suffering of Jesus, 144, 145
Vulgate, 8–9

Warfield Lectures, 196
washing, 267
   of clothing during sacrifices, 101
   of feet, 28, 256
water
   of baptism, 262, 273
   in Jesus' death, 222–223
weakness, power of God in, 225
weekly communion, 276
   lack of, 278
well-being sacrifice, 93
Wesley, Charles, 278–279
Western church, 46, 105
   Apostles' Creed in, 45
   conflict in, 255
   debate in, 57
Westminster Confession of Faith, 149–150, 157–158
"What is Christianity?" 166
white garment, 48
whole burnt sacrifice, 93
wickedness of humanity, 82
William of Occam, 141n13
Williams, Delores, 194
wine
   in Eucharist, 57
   as Jesus' blood, 28, 218, 270
wisdom, 75–76
womanist concerns, 194

and atonement theory, 196
women
  of color, 194
  in leadership, 131
  origins in Bible, 72
  as peers in apostleship and ministry, 242n9
women theologians, 192
word, incarnation of, 200
Word of God, 5, 254
World Council of Churches (WCC), 62
  Faith and Order Commission, 62, 257
worldwide church, healing in, 46
worship, 53, 86, 259, 264
sacramentally, 274
and sacrifice, 95
wrath of God, 128, 177–178
wrath of love, 184
Wycliffe, John, 9

yeast, 125, 126
yirah (Hebrew), 76
Yom Kippur, 40, 99, 111

Zarathustra, 211n3
zealot, 22
zebach (Hebrew), 87
Zechariah, 80
Zwingli, Huldrych, 59–60, 64

Scripture Index

Old Testament

Genesis

	71n3, 83, 86, 86n2, 103
1	68–70
1–11	82
1:25–26	68
1:28b	68
2	70–72
2:4a LXX	67
2:4b–6	70
2:17	71
2:18	71
2:24	72
3	70, 73–75
3:1–5	74
3:6	75
3:13	78
3:22–24	81
4:3	85
4:7	82
6	82
6:1–7	82
6:5	82, 246
6:6	82
8	214
8:20	85
8:21	92, 214, 246
9	214
9:11	214
9:15	214
12	86
12:1–4	83
12:8	85
15	103
17:5	84n20
22:1–19	84
22:2	103
22:8	84, 84n21, 103
22:12–14	103
22:12b	84
22:14	84, 84n21, 103
23:2	89
32–3	74
50:20	74n9, 76

Exodus

	38n14, 88
3:13–15	70
12	104
12:1–14	105
12:27	22
15:1–31	89
20:3–6	77
20:4–5	248
24:5–8	92
24:8	27
25:8—27:19	88
25:12–14	71n3
25:17–18	39
27:1–8	88
28:43	88
29:18	92

(Exodus continued)

29:25	92
29:38–41	124n25
29:41	92
34:6	94, 228

Leviticus

	37, 38n14, 93, 93n12
1:4	37
1–7	95n14
1:9	92
1:13	92
1:17	92
2:1–3	93
3:14–17	92
4:2	98
4:22	98
4:27	98
5:15	98
5:18	98
11:44–45	93
14:1–8	39
16:1–34	37n12, 99
16:6–10	100
16:23–28	101
17:11	97
19:2	93
20:7	93
22:14	98
23:27–32	112
23:28	40
24:14	188
24:16	188
24:23	188

Numbers

	37, 37n12, 38n14, 93, 93n12
6:16	92
6:17	92
7:15	92
7:17	92
7:22	92
13:1—14:45	89
14:18	89, 228
15:8	92
15:27	98
15:28	40, 98
15:29	98
15:30	98
35:10–15	98
35:11	98
35:15	98

Deuteronomy

	98n15
4:42	98
19:4	98
23:14	93n12
32:37–38	92

Joshua

	98n15
15:13	89
20:1–9	98
20:3	98
20:9	98

Judges

	85, 247
11:30–39	85

1 Samuel

2:15	92
15:22	109
15:22–23	106
16	88
20:6	88
20:29	88

2 Samuel

12:15–23	106

1 Kings

6:15	71n3
8:11	90
16:34	85

2 Kings

16:3	85
17:17	85
21:6	85

1 Chronicles

	4
21:1	4, 80

2 Chronicles

	38n14, 85, 90n8
7:1–5	90
7:5	87
28:3	85
33:6	85
36:22–23	90

Ezra

	38n14, 91n9
6:3–5	90

Nehemiah

	91n9
9:17	228

Job

	4
1:6–12	4
1:9–12	80
2:1–7	4
2:4–6	80
26	67n1
28	67n1
38	67n1

Psalms

	38n14
8	67n1
19	67n1
19:1	69
22	220n11
22:1	188
22:21b–31	220n11
25:4–11	106
25:10	94
33	67n1
33:6	70
33:9	70
40:6–8	117
40:7	117
78:25	91
81:11–12	247
85:10	94
86:5, 15	228
86:15	94, 228
89	67n1
89:14	94
98:3	94
102	67n1
103	67n1
103:8	228
105:40	91
106	247
106:37–38	85
111:10	75
145:8	228

Proverbs

1:7	75
4:11	75
8	67n1
8:22–24	196
8:22–36	76n11
9:10	75
12:16	73n5
15:5	73n5
15:33	75

21:3	109

Ecclesiastes

11:9	246

Isaiah

	82n19, 210n2
1:11–14	106
11	67n1
28	67n1
40	67n1
40:1	210
42:1–4	82, 210
45	67n1
45:1–13	211
49:1–6	24, 82, 210
50:4–7	210
50:4–9	82
52:13—53:12	24, 82, 112, 210
53:3	220
53:4–6	157n8
53:10–11	157n8
61:1–2	211

Jeremiah

4	67n1
7:21–23	106
7:22	89
10	67n1
31:31	209
31:31–34	27

Ezekiel

	90
3:23	90
8:4	90
9:3	90
10:4	90
10:18	90
10:19	90
36:26	215

37:1–28	210
43:2	90
43:4–5	90
44:4	90

Daniel

1–6	212
7–12	212

Hosea

2	67n1
6:6	109

Joel

2:13	228

Amos

5:21–23	106
5:25	89

Jonah

4:2	228

Micah

6:6–9	106

Zechariah

3:1–2	4
3:1–3	80

Scripture Index

New Testament

Matthew

	26, 134, 220n11
1:1–16	213n7
1:21	213n6
3:2	169
3:11	50, 51
3:13–15	49
4:10	216
4:17	216
5:23–24	109
5:44–48	234
7:15–23	251
8:4	109
12:50	261
13:35	214
19:16–21	250
20:20–21	218
20:28	23, 109, 134, 182
21:11	213
21:12–13	109
21:46	23
22:2–14	270
23:19	45
25:1–12	270
25:10–13	261
25:34	214
25:40–45	242
26:2	187
26:26–29	26
26:28	223n17
26:34	219
26:53	221
27:46	219
27:63	217
28:18–20	34, 47

Mark

	25, 134, 168, 220n11
1:7–9	51
1:8	50
1:9	216
1:11	216
1:15	169
1:44	109
3:5	261
5:22–43	217n9
6:15	23
8:31	217
9:31	217
9:40	243
10:21	250
10:34	217
10:35–41	218
10:45	23, 109, 134, 182
11:15–19	109
14:22–25	25–26
14:30	219
15:34	219

Luke

	26, 259n12, 274
1:31	213n6
1:76	213
3:16	50, 51
3:22	216
3:23b–38	213n7
5:14	109
6:27–35	234
7:11–15	217n9
7:39	23
8:21	261
9:51	5
12:13–21	249
12:36	270
13:33	23
17:1–3	250
17:2	273n32
18:22	250
18:32	187
18:33	217
19:44	217
19:45–48	109
22:15	23
22:19	34
22:19–20	26
22:22	23
22:61	219

(Luke continued)

23:32–46	220
23:49	222n14
24:7	217
24:13–33	274
24:13–50	226
24:19	23
24:21	52
24:30–31	52
24:36–43	274

John

	28, 29, 139, 141, 173, 222n14, 223, 269
1	67n1
1:20	110
1:26	50
1:29	23, 215
1:33	50
1:36	23, 215
2:13–22	109
3:3–7	51n15
3:14	139
3:16	187, 224, 258
4:1–2	223n16
4:14	91, 223
4:19	23
6	29, 31, 269
6:14	23, 29, 213
6:16–21	29
6:26–27	30
6:29	30
6:30–32	30
6:35	30
6:36–44	30
6:38–53	223
6:48–51	30
6:51	31, 269n26
6:51–58	31
6:54–58	30
6:56, 58	272
6:58	272
6:60–62	31
6:63	31
6:67–69	31
6:68	270
7:37–38	223
7:38–39	223
7:40	213
8:28	139
9:17	23
10:17–18	221
10:18	221
11:1–44	217n9
12:31	222
12:34	139
13–16	29, 31
14:6	29
14:8	221
14:15–31	28
14:17	221
14:19–23	253
14:20	51
14:30	222
14:31	222
16:7	221
16:11	222
16:33	28
17	28
17:1–26	28
17:11	277
17:21–23	29
17:22	277
17:23	51
17:24	214
18:14	218
18:36	187
19:25–27	223n14
20:1–29	226
20:26–28	274
21:1–14	274
21:1–23	226
21:24	226n23

Acts

	130, 240
2:38	32
2:38–41	47
2:41–42	32, 52
8:36–39	47
11:14	49
15:1–29	277n36
16:15	49
16:31	49

16:34	49
18:8	49
18:24	130
18:24–25	50
19:1–6	50
19:2–7	254
20:28	206
22:3	120

Romans

	115, 116, 125, 130, 239
1:4	228
1:17	49, 123, 177
1:24	187
1:26	187
1:28	187
3:21	49
3:23–26	157n8
3:25	3, 113, 114, 115
3:25b–26a RSV	115
4:25	125
5:5	268
5:6	125
5:6–8	177, 231
5:8	125, 131
5:8–10	148–49
5:9	127, 128
5:10–12	236
5:11	37
5:14	235
5:14–15	236
5:15	231
5:18	128, 231, 236
6:3–4	34
6:3–8	231
6:3–11	51
6:3–14	262
6:8	262
6:10–11	262
7:4	237
8:1–2	51
8:2–27	268
8:3	123
8:4	245
8:8	245
8:9	246n15
8:9–16	246n15
8:15	246
8:17	268
8:19	246
8:21	245
8:31–32	187
8:38–39	245
12:1	124, 268
12:1–2	119, 129
12:1–3	251
12:5	51
16:1	130
16:1–4	242n9
16:7	131
21:1	207

1 Corinthians

	126n28, 239
1:2, 4, 30	51
1:13	277
1:14–16	47
1:16	49
1:17	115
3:16–17	128
5:7	123, 270
5:7–8	126
6:19	254
6:20	127
7:23	127
8:1–13	124
8:11	125
10:1–4	126n28
10:20–33	124
11:5	242n9
11:18	277
11:20	32, 52
11:23–25	274
11:23–26	25
11:24	270, 271n28
11:24–25	34
11:26	270, 271
11:27	275
12:12–27	241
12:13	34
14:33b–36	242n9
14:34–35	131
15	238
15:3	125, 131, 231

(1 Corinthians continued)

15:5–8	226
15:8	120
15:12–26	237–38
15:20–23	262
15:22	241
15:22 RSV	237
15:28	278
15:37–43	238
15:44–50	239

2 Corinthians

	36, 230, 239
1:21–22	51
3:10	253
3:13	66
3:18	51, 228
4:8–11	128–29
4:17	51
5	235
5:2	233
5:14–21	230
5:14b	231
5:15	231
5:17	51, 241, 244, 263, 269
5:18	37
5:18a	35
5:19	3, 37, 127, 146, 189
5:19 KJV	175
5:20	252, 268
5:21	123, 157n8
12:9	225

Galatians

	239
1:4	120, 125
2:11–16	277n36
2:19	232, 262
2:19–20	128
2:20	187
3:10	157n8
3:12	263
3:13	123, 157n8
3:26	130, 268
3:26–29	51
3:27	34, 237, 240, 254
3:27–29	241
4:4	213
4:6	246
6:5	241
6:12	115
6:15	244, 263, 269

Ephesians

	243n9
1:4	3, 115, 214, 221
1:7	131
1:9	32
1:10	213
1:13	254
1:22	237
2:16	37
4:5	51
4:15	237
5:2	122n24
5:22	243n9

Philippians

	237, 239
2:1–11	237
2:5–7	215
2:6	237
2:7	187n32
2:8	224
2:17	124
3:18	115
4:2–3	242n9
4:18	124

Colossians

	243n9
1:20	37
1:26	32
2:12	51, 254
3:10	237
3:18	243n9

1 Thessalonians

	239
4:1	262
4:17	245
5:9–10	231
5:10	125

1 Timothy

	129, 131, 134, 243n9
2:6	131, 134, 134n1
2:11–14	243n9
2:12	131
6:19	248

2 Timothy

	129, 243n9

Titus

	129, 243n9
2:5	243n9
2:14	206

Philemon

	129, 239
1:16	242

Hebrews

	116–20, 133, 134
1:3	117, 227
2:9	118
2:17 NRSV	117
3:31	203
4:10	216
4:15	155
4:16	119, 120
5:5–10	118
5:10	117
7:19	120
7:25	120
7:27	118
9:5	113
9:26	118
10	207
10:5–6	117
10:12	118
10:20	118, 119
10:22	120
10:26–27	120
11:6	120
13:5	248
13:8	120
13:15	119

James

	251
2:19	251

1 Peter

	131
1:18–19	132
1:20	214
2:9	206
2:24	157n8
3:1–6	243n9
3:18	157n8
3:19	225
5:8	245
5:8–10	245

2 Peter

1:11	246n15
3:16	129

1 John

2:1	252
2:2	113, 116
3:2	275
4:7–8	186n29
4:10	113, 116

Scripture Index

(1 John continued)

4:16–17	186n29	13:8	214
		17:8	214
		19:7	270
Revelation		21:1–7	278
		21:6	91
		22:1	91
2	91, 133	22:17	91
	67n1		

Deuterocanonical Books

4 Maccabees

		Sirach	
6:29	125	1:14	76
17:10	125		
17:21–22	125	**Wisdom of Solomon**	
		6:17	76

Early Christian Writings

Abelard, Peter	141–42, 143, 162, 165, 170	Apostles' Creed	45
		Apostolic Constitutions	56
Anselm of Canterbury	139–40, 142, 143, 144, 147, 157, 170, 171		
Cur Deus Homo (Why God Became Man)	6	Aquinas, Thomas	81, 143, 143n14, 144, 145, 147
		Summa Theologica	143

Athanasius
55, 60, 77, 138, 139, 143, 158, 172, 180, 197, 246, 248

Contra Gentes   247
9–13   77n12
19–21   247n18
20–23   247n20
21   247n19
De Incarnatione (On the Incarnation)   66n34, 247
165–66   138n6
269   138n7
Ep. fest. (Festal Letter)
4.19   56

Augustine
33, 56, 81, 135, 139, 143, 223, 255

"Sermon 272"   56n26, 275n34
56n26   56n26

Cyprian   54

Epistle 63
Section 13   55n19

Cyril of Alexandria   56

Didache

The Teachings of the Lord to the Gentiles (or Nations) by the Twelve Apolstles   47, 54
9:12   54n16

Duns Scotus   141n13

Gregory Nazianzum   197

Gregory of Nyssa   56, 135, 197

Ignatius of Antioch   54

Rom. (Epistle to the Romans)   54n17

Irenaeus   66, 136–38, 137n4, 139, 143, 158, 172, 197, 200n22, 235, 247

John Chrysostom   56

John of Damascus   56

Justin Martyr   54

"First Apology"
Section 66   54n18

Nicene Creed   41–42, 42n1, 45, 55, 262

Article 3   190n43, 232n2

Nicene–Constantinopolitan Creed   43–44, 44n3, 262n17

Origen   55, 135, 172

Contra Celsum
8.57   55n20

Polycarp   136

William of Occam (Ockham)   141n13

Greek and Roman Literature

Seneca

De Clementia   146

Tertullian   33